THE
FUTURE
OF
MOBILITY

THE
FUTURE
OF
MOBILITY

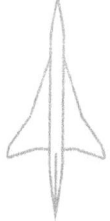  

STEVE GREENFIELD

Founder and CEO of *Automotive Ventures*

For information about this title contact the publisher:

Steve Greenfield/Automotive Ventures LLC
1922 Wildwood PL NE, Atlanta GA 30324
www.automotiveventures.com
steve@automotiveventures.com

ISBNs:
979-8-9864718-4-6 (hardcover)
979-8-9864718-3-9 (softcover)
979-8-9864718-5-3 (eBook)

Printed in the United States of America

Contents

Introduction

"Human ingenuity has made us much safer from natural calamities," Walter Russell Mead, professor of foreign affairs and humanities at Bard College, writes in the web publication *Tablet*. "We can treat many diseases, predict storms, build dams both to prevent floods and to save water against drought, and many other fine things. Many fewer of us starve than in former times, and billions of us today enjoy better living conditions than our forebears dreamed possible. Yet if we are safer from most natural catastrophes, we are more vulnerable than ever to human-caused ones."

In my first book, *The Future of Automotive Retail,* we focused on the challenges facing automotive dealers and automakers.

This book takes on a far greater task, attempting to connect how future advances in mobility (defined by the ways in which we move humans and cargo via land, water, air and space) might help alleviate some of the largest challenges facing humankind.

We will reflect on what human beings have done, and are doing, to the planet, specifically from the perspective of mobility, and propose how technology and innovations in mobility may ultimately be what's needed to help us to get out of the mess we've created.

Not that long ago, humans obtained most of the energy they needed from the animals and plants they ate and the wood they burned, often aided by domesticated animals. Windmills and waterwheels captured some extra energy, but there was little in reserve. All life operated within the fairly immediate flow of energy from the sun to the Earth.

The Industrial Revolution changed everything.

Beginning around 1750, an extra source of energy was discovered in fossil fuels—coal, oil and natural gas—which formed underground from the remains of plants and animals from much earlier geologic times. When these fuels are burned, they release energy that originated from the sun and has since been "stored" in fossils for hundreds of millions of years.

Then along came batteries, the biggest innovation in history for the nonorganic storage of energy.

The first true battery was invented by the Italian physicist Alessandro Volta in 1800. Volta stacked discs of copper and zinc separated by cloth soaked in salty water. Wires connected to either end of the stack produced a continuous stable current.

The lead-acid battery was invented in 1859 and is still the technology used to start most internal combustion engine cars today. It is the oldest and most enduring example of a rechargeable battery.

When modern capitalism emerged in the early nineteenth century in western Europe and in European offshoots in the Americas and Oceania, economists and political theorists Karl Marx and Friedrich Engels predicted in 1848 that capitalism would spread to the entire world.

By the end of the twentieth century, that prediction was confirmed: Capitalism had, indeed, become global, but only after a tortuous and violent course of institutional change.

Since the beginning of the Industrial Revolution, technology has seemed near miraculous, dramatically improving the quality of life, human productivity, and wealth. Billions of people around the world today enjoy the benefits of industrialization. Like a rising tide, it has brought innumerable individuals out of poverty.

"Much of this is due to fossil fuels," Mike Granoff, who heads Maniv Mobility, a venture capital fund with $160 million of assets under management, told me, intimating just how reliant we've become on this traditional energy source. "People lose sight of this fact. I'm not saying the foundation we built the industrial economy on over the last hundred years is the same one we should build going forward. We have to find better, cheaper, cleaner ways."

Rani Plaut, the CEO of "flying car" maker AIR EV, states it more simply: "Mobility is a need. It's about human interaction. People need to go places. Mobility will become the biggest sandbox we've ever seen."

Indeed, with energy being more accessible and cheaper than any time in history, most of us already do significantly less hard physical labor than earlier generations did. People today are able to feed more babies and bring them to adulthood. Many individuals vote and participate in modern states, which provide education, social security and health benefits. Large numbers of people enjoy levels of wealth, life expectancy and travel that could scarcely have been imagined before industrialization.

It's a truly great time to be alive. The Industrial Revolution, followed by health-care innovation, the introduction of the personal computer, the internet, the smartphone and cloud computing, has had the effect of increasing human productivity, driving economic growth, improving the world's average standard of living, and lifting generations out of poverty while reducing hunger.

The world population was around one billion in the year 1800. It is now over eight billion. Population growth, coupled with productivity gains, has meant billions emerging out of poverty, and massive growth of the middle class with more disposable income.

Since 1800, global life expectancy has increased from less than 30 to over 72 years of age. Every geography has benefited; in every region across the globe, people today can expect to live more than twice as long as their recent ancestors.

But along with progress often comes challenge; the Industrial Revolution, for all of its great benefits, has created colossal collateral damage.

+ Pollution has harmed the environment, perhaps irrevocably.

+ Access to cheap and easy foods has meant record-high rates of obesity and diabetes in the developed world.

+ Rapid population growth strains both access and equitable distribution of food.

+ Scientists have identified the birth of the Industrial Revolution as one of the tipping points for increased animal extinctions, as desirable species were hunted to the point of extermination and demand for lumber and expanding farmlands and factories meant leveling forest habitats. Pollution killed off even more animals.

+ Capitalism, the driver of the modern economy, is showing signs of fraying at the periphery; blindly pursuing individual self-interest has resulted in increasing inequality of income and wealth in some economic systems. While the standard of living is higher for all, many will be left behind as others become richer.

+ Demand for minerals has meant child labor and safety issues risking human lives continue unabated.

The rate of change is now so rapid that individuals and social systems struggle to keep up. Depersonalization in the age of mass production has led to increasing alienation among citizens of the West.

Despite capitalism's progress, great wealth disparities still exist. Millions of children go hungry each day. Children are still being exploited in both labor and the sex trade. And we still experience war, famine, and hunger, even if not at the same levels of the past.

More worrying: After a decade where world hunger declined, it's back on the rise, affecting nearly 10% of people globally. From 2019 to 2022, the number of undernourished people grew by as many as 150 million, a crisis driven largely by conflict, climate change, and the Covid-19 pandemic.

Ditto for global life expectancy.

After several centuries where it just continued to increase—life expectancy was only 30 years in 1800; today we'll live on average 72 years—and after 69 years of uninterrupted increase (from 1950 to 2019), longevity has dropped in the last 3 years.

Along with the increased complexity of the industrial system has come heightened fragility.

Industrialization depends on the interaction of many diverse components, any one of which could fail. We know that many of the essential components of the industrial system, and the natural resources it depends on, are being compromised. The soil, the oceans, the atmosphere, the underground water levels, plants, and animals all are at risk.

The main cause of many of the problems we're contending with today is because "we put people and things in the wrong places," says Michael Sena, who writes mobility-focused newsletter *The Dispatcher*. "When people live in places that can't support them, you have catastrophes, disasters, drought, fire."

Sena gives California as an example.

"If you're living on a fault line, you'll have people sitting under concrete when an earthquake occurs. If they live in a fire zone, they will lose their homes. In other places, like on the Gulf Coast, expensive homes are built on stilts because there are regular floods."

As for Miami, with its rising sea waters, "Why did they build there in the first place? It's a wonderful city located where it never should have been," Sena told me. Manhattan should do OK, as it's built pretty high on rock, but Sena is less sure about the coastlines of New Jersey, which he predicts could be "gone" if climate change continues unabated.

It's not just the physical world that's in danger.

As we've benefited from our daily lives becoming more and more digitized, we've made the conscious tradeoff to reveal increasing amounts of personal information to third parties. Our greatly expanded digital "surface area" renders us vulnerable to manipulation, hacking and cybercrime.

The global supply chain, while a technological marvel, has little to no margin for error—something that became apparent to anyone who tried to buy a car or computer during the Covid years—making it too susceptible to single points of failure. We'll explore the significance and legacy of "Just in Time" systems in chapter 10, "Supply Chain."

The challenges facing humanity can be organized into distinct categories:

1. Climate (and the impact on food insecurity, migration, refugees)
2. The Earth's condition (agriculture, soil health, monoculture)
3. Population growth (urban congestion and density)
4. Equitable distribution of food

5. Labor issues (child labor, safety, overwork, death)
6. Privacy and data (security, hacking, cyber)
7. Physical security (war, famine, terror)
8. Supply chain (and how Covid exposed global fragility)
9. Longevity of humans (medical advances, quality of life)
10. Financial security (wealth disparity, social safety nets, pensions, savings, world hunger)

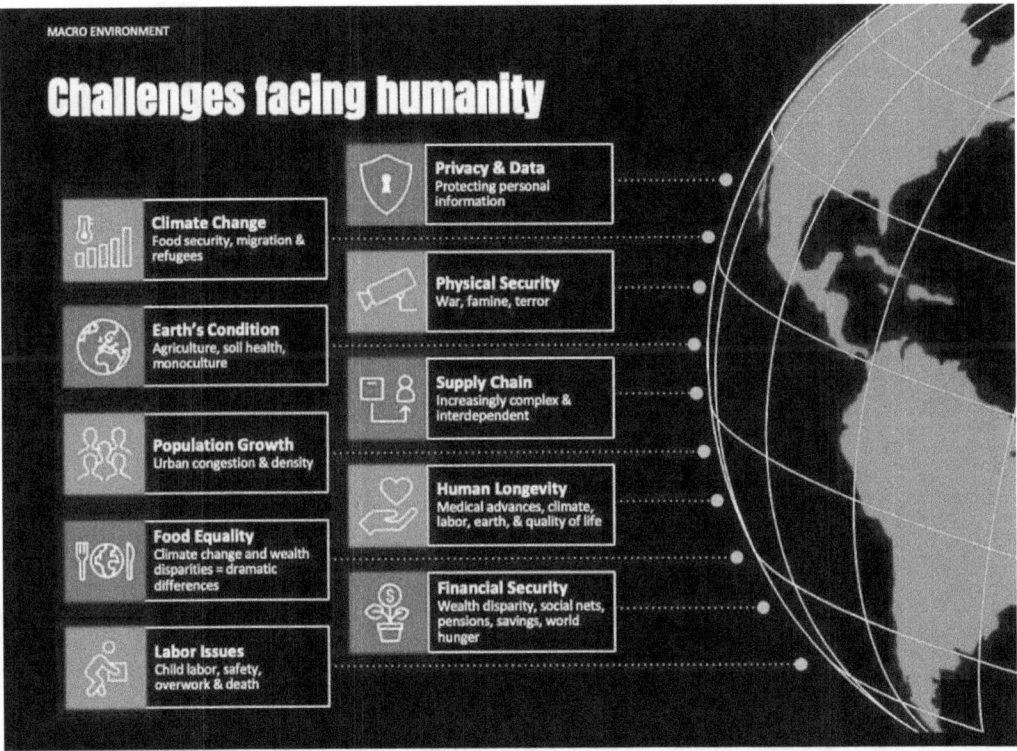

The largest challenges facing humanity. (credit: Automotive Ventures)

This book's central thesis is that mobility startups span a continuum of how to address some of the Earth's largest issues, driving efficiencies in transport of both humans and cargo across different modalities: land, water, air, and space.

To address these topics, *The Future of Mobility* is structured into eleven chapters, into which we will weave these main themes:

1. Ground transport (EVs, trucks, public transportation)
2. Micromobility (e-scooters, e-bikes, Neighborhood Electric Vehicles, shared assets, subscriptions, and the convenience economy)

3. Air and space (including eVTOLs, supersonic and space travel)
4. Marine (shipping, cruises, yachts, ferries, submarines, patrol boats)
5. Industrial tech (agriculture, construction, manufacturing, mining)
6. Battery technology and chemistry
7. R&D and new tech (including alternative fuels such as hydrogen, ammonia and SAF—Sustainable Aviation Fuel)
8. Autonomy (including robotics and artificial intelligence)
9. Data and connectivity
10. Supply chain issues
11. Warfare and security (including drones and policing)

We then wrap with an epilogue where I align all of this content with Automotive Ventures' investing thesis and present options to guide your own mobility investments.

I've written the book so that you can skip around. Each chapter can stand on its own. So, if one chapter appeals to you, start there. If you want to read the book cover-to-cover in order, I'm confident you'll get a lot out of it.

Will my predictions come true?

"Consumers are predictably irrational," Mike Granoff told me, quoting Duke University professor of psychology and behavioral economics Dan Ariely, "and none more so than the mobility consumer."

Caveats in hand, I truly hope that you enjoy the book as much as I did writing it!

The Role Of Climate Change

This book won't be straddling the climate change debate. As far as I'm concerned, there's no denying that human-fueled climate change is ravaging our planet, generating unbearably higher summer temperatures along with unrelenting and unpredictable winter storms.

A paper published in the journal *Earth System Science Data* reported the alarming statistic that the amount of explosive energy ensconced in our planet's climate ecosystem in just the last 50 years is the equivalent of 25 of the "Little Boy" nuclear bombs detonated in Hiroshima in 1945.

Between 1971 and 2020, around 380 zettajoules have been trapped by global warming. Of that, the oceans have absorbed around 89% of the energy, land has absorbed 6%, and around 4% has melted parts of the cryosphere, the part of the Earth's climate system that includes snow, sea ice, icebergs, glaciers, and more.

Just 1% of the energy is retained in the atmosphere.

That might sound like good news. But while the oceans have to a certain extent "protected" us from the worst ravages of temperature increase, that won't last forever, climate scientists Andrew King and Steven Sherwood told *The Conversation.* There's no choice but to continue looking for ways to decarbonize the planet.

Many companies are striving to come up with lifesaving technologies to mitigate the worst of climate change.

Yet, we may have already reached the tipping point.

GLOBAL GREENHOUSE GAS EMISSION PATHWAYS

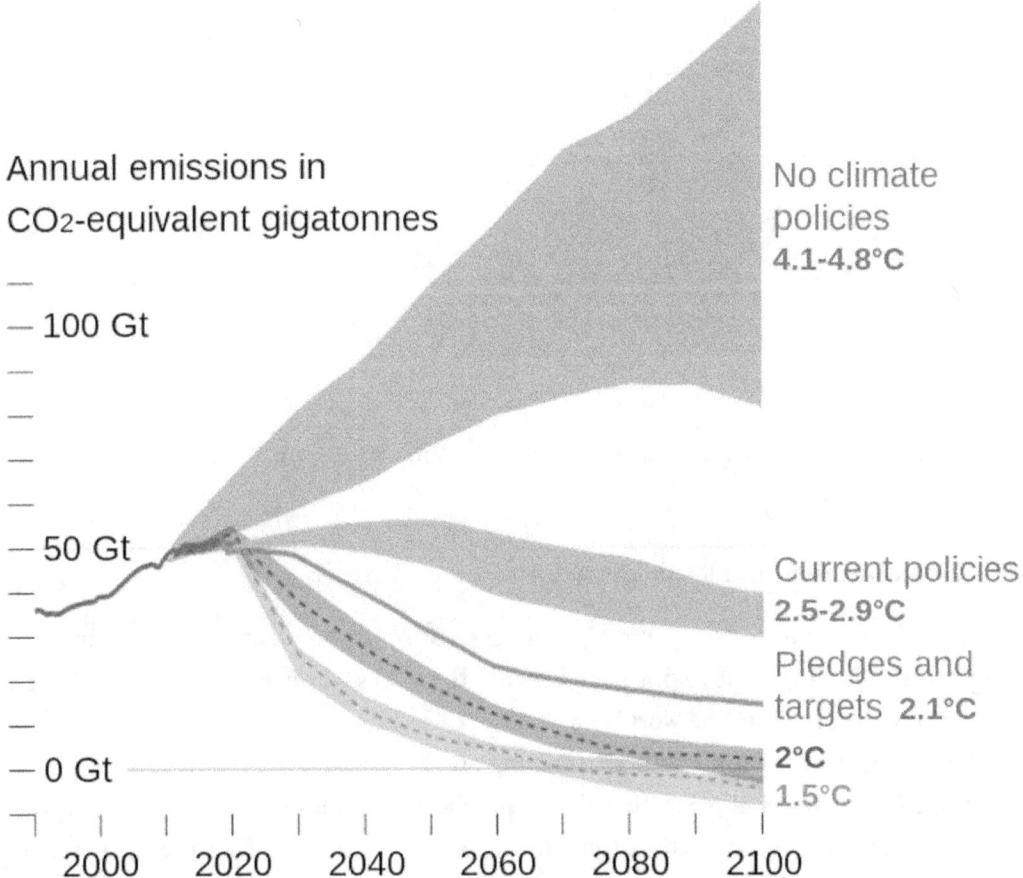

Source: Wikimedia Commons; Hannah Ritchie and Max Roser, adapted for svg and smartphone by Eric Fisk

The path to 1.5 degrees looks exceedingly unlikely. (credit: Wikimedia Commons)

It's no great mystery how we got here. Just look at this chart showing the relative energy densities of different types of fuels, which make it clear that batteries are a pale substitute to the ongoing dominance of fossil fuels for transportation.

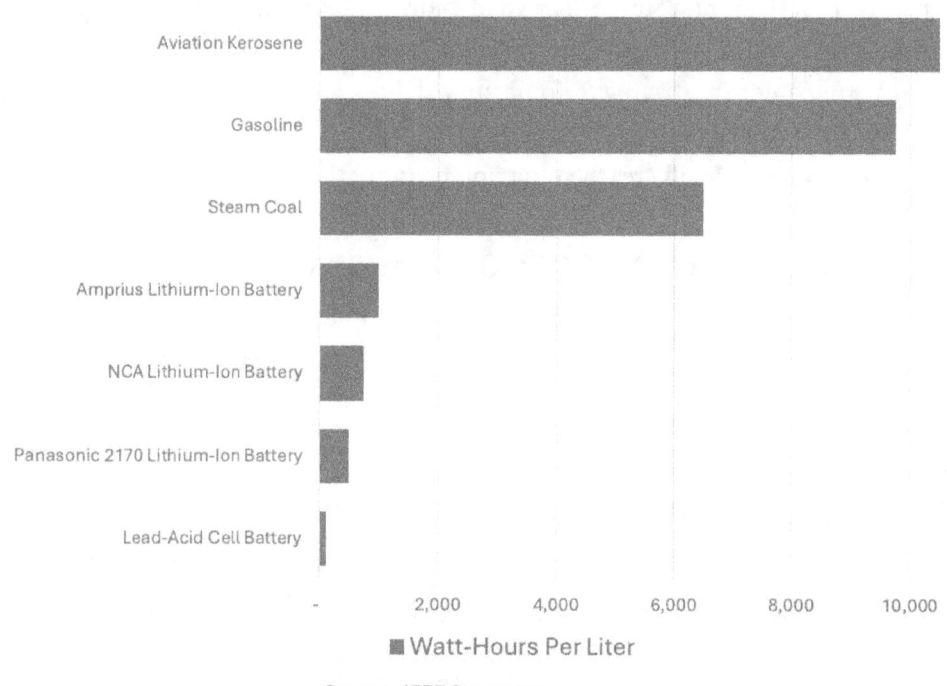

BATTERY ENERGY DENSITY
(compared to other energy sources)

Source: IEEE Spectrum

Petroleum has superior energy density compared to batteries. (credit: IEEE Spectrum)

This bleak future is impacting our youth

In a 2021 survey of young people in 10 countries, 75% of respondents said the future was "frightening," leading some to drastically change their lives—even to the point of deciding not to bring children into the world.

It's not just young people who are freaking out.

Tal Cohen, investor at Next Gear Ventures, who also heads up the Drive TLV innovation hub in Tel Aviv, doesn't believe that humanity has the wherewithal to address climate change without a game-changing technology and economical alignment.

"It will be less about a coordinated effort, since the world's ability to act together and address climate change is doubtful. Self-interest and geopolitics are negatively impacting coordinated progress, and so climate change is more likely to come through breakthrough technologies," he told me. "Even if we do innovate a solution, we might fight over it and have less than optimal results for the planet. We always think things get better. This time, that's not happening, and we're already witnessing it. I'm more pessimistic than I am optimistic.

It will require a lot of suffering to bring us together. Not only do we need to come up with an incredible timely innovation, we also need to be wise about how to let this innovation make the needed impact around the world."

Fear and disillusionment can serve as a potent agent for change.

"Fear is useful to wake us up and make us pay attention," Katharine Hayhoe, a climate scientist at Texas Tech University, told *The New York Times*. "But if we don't know what to do, it paralyzes us."

US CO$_2$ EMISSIONS ARE FALLING, BUT THEY'RE STILL THE HIGHEST PER CAPITA

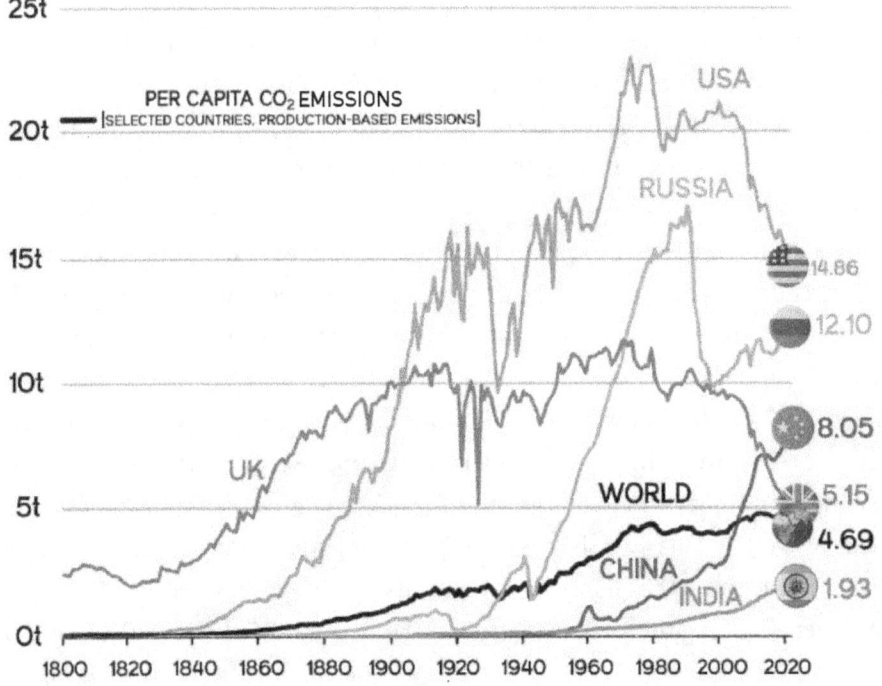

The developed world seems to be heading in the right direction, but that's not the case for China and India. (credit: Our World in Data)

Where to go from here?

"You can have the best technology in the world, but unless people accept it, it won't get to scale. We've seen that while technology may have half the solution, the community has the other half," writes John Doerr in *Speed & Scale: A Global Action Plan for Solving Our Climate Crisis Now*.

Doerr and others—including influential individuals such as Amazon CEO Jeff Bezos through his $10 billion "Bezos Earth Fund" or Bill Gates through the climate investment firm he established, Breakthrough Energy—are bringing their reputations, networks, and billions of dollars to bear to address the climate crisis.

What we can do is starting to come into focus.

First off, the transition to passenger vehicle electrification is gaining momentum, although there are still questions about exactly how much better for the planet the complete EV lifecycle is, when you include everything from manufacturing the batteries to their ultimate disposal in landfills or recycling.

"Climate may not be the driver for people signing up to buy EVs, but it pushes people over the top. It's a very positive thing, even if it's just one piece of the puzzle," says Elie Wurtman, CEO of Jerusalem-based venture capital firm PICO Partners. "In 10 years, we will be in an EV dominant environment."

To wit: China's CATL has pledged to make its battery production carbon neutral by 2035.

Economics also is playing a role: In much of the world, solar and wind power are now *cheaper* than coal and gas. And so, if before 2015, the world was expected to warm by about four degrees Celsius by 2100, today the planet is on track for "only" a three-degree increase.

If world leaders were able to put politics aside and meet their current commitments, the increase could be cut to a mere two degrees Celsius (although, ominously, that number is still more than the warning by climate scientists that anything over 1.5 degrees would be disastrous).

Indeed, 2023 was the hottest year in recorded human history, according to Europe's top climate agency. Data from the Copernicus Climate Change Service revealed that Earth's average temperature last year was 1.48 degrees Celsius (2.66 degrees Fahrenheit) hotter than the preindustrial average. Last year shattered the previous global temperature record by almost two-tenths of a degree—the largest jump scientists have ever observed. 2024 is expected to be even hotter, breaking the 1.5-degree Celsius barrier, *The Washington Post* reports.

"Two degrees is super hard, but it's doable, people are working on it," David Roberts, host of the *Volts* podcast and a former staff writer at *Vox*, told me. "A 1.5-degree target is *la la land*. We're kind of heading into something shitty. But we have acted enough already to avoid the truly sci-fi species extinction outcomes. That happened faster than we expected it to."

Every degree matters

Half a degree might not sound like much, but it could mean fewer wildfires, droughts, floods, and conflicts over dwindling resources.

In short, both the most extreme best and worst outcomes now appear to be outliers.

It's become popular for forward-thinking individuals to take on climate change by being strict with their plastic use, to compost and recycle, and to use shared micromobility services and public transportation wherever possible.

"Between 1900 and 2006, according to a Harvard University study, every political movement that gained the active and sustained participation of at least 3.5% of the population wound up succeeding," writes Doerr. "In the United States today, that's fewer than 12 million people!"

Sounds good. But individual action is no match for the systemic changes that only governments and large corporations can enact. When entire civilizations have built their economies around burning carbon for energy, the onus shifts from the common person to the politicians.

If those elected representatives dilly-dally, as they tend to do, "it can make the problem feel too big and individuals too small, feeding into despair," writes German Lopez in *The New York Times*.

That despair is not necessarily misplaced.

A 2023 report from the United Nations revealed that the U.S., Russia and Saudi Arabia will drill for more oil and gas in 2030 than at *any point in our history*. Moreover, almost all of the top 20 fossil fuel-producing countries plan to refine more oil, gas, and coal in 2030 than they do today.

"Governments are literally doubling down on fossil fuel production," United Nations Secretary General António Guterres said in a statement accompanying the report. "We cannot address climate catastrophe without tackling its root cause: fossil fuel dependence."

Even Norway, which has mostly phased out the use of fossil fuels for its own energy needs, remains a major exporter of oil and gas.

With consumption ticking ever upward, any gains made by renewable energy are being swallowed up.

We are "clawing into the positive digits when we need to be deeply pitched into the negative," writes Zoe Schlanger in *The Atlantic*. "In total, countries that hold the world's oil, gas, and coal deposits still plan to produce 69% more fossil fuels than is compatible with keeping warming under two degrees Celsius."

She concludes, "We are, in other words, simply not making a dent . . . and so we are now in climate purgatory."

Income matters too

Our collective climate crimes are not spread out evenly around the world.

"The wealthier we are, the more climate pollution we produce, because of how much electricity we consume, what we eat and how much we drive," writes Somini Sengupta in *The New York Times.* "But it's not just wealth. It matters a lot in which country we are wealthy."

A study from the International Energy Agency (IEA) and *The New York Times* puts the onus on the wealthiest people in the United States who have "an astonishingly large climate footprint, far larger than rich people in wealthy, industrialized Europe or in fast-rising China," Sengupta writes. "Not only that: Nearly everyone in the U.S., even those in the lowest income brackets, produces a lot of climate pollution relative to everyone else in the world. It's the way our economy is built. We take for granted long commutes and frequent flights. Our electricity comes from sources that are relatively carbon-intensive. The rest of the world is different."

Indeed, around 90% of the global population flies only once a year or not at all. Six percent fly more than twice a year and just 1% fly more than five times a year.

I bet you can guess where most of those frequent flyers live.

Here is some more alarming data per the IEA:

+ The richest 10% of Americans, or those who make an average of $233,600 a year, produce 56.5 tons of carbon dioxide emissions per person, per year on average. That's more than double the emissions of the richest 10% in Europe and nearly double that of the richest 10% of Chinese.

+ The lowest 10% of Americans, those making just $2,500 a year on average, still have a carbon footprint that's almost as big as every individual in India, excluding India's richest 10%.

+ The poorest 10% of Americans have a climate footprint larger in terms of per capita emissions than the poorest 30% of Chinese.

+ In China, the richest 10% have a footprint 33 times the size of the poorest 10%. In the U.S., the richest 10% pollute 16 times as much as the poorest 10%. In India, the climate pollution produced by the poorest 10% of the population is negligible as many still cook with charcoal or cow dung and may not have access to electricity around the clock. They are likely not to own a car; at best they may have a bicycle.

+ The richest 1% of the population are "super-polluters," notes *The New York Times.* Their emissions are 10 times as much as the whole world's richest 10%—combined!

+ The world's top 1% of emitters produce over 1,000 times more CO_2 than the bottom 1%.

✦ The top 10% of emitters are all over the world, although 85% live in advanced economies, including the U.S., Australia, Europe, Japan, New Zealand and the U.K. The bottom 10% of emitters live in developing economies in Asia and Africa.

The problem is acute with air travel and shipping

The next chart shows that domestic air travel is far ahead of any other medium, including cars, buses and motorcycles, when it comes to producing greenhouse gasses (GHG). Short and long-haul flights, when combined, also surpass emissions from cars.

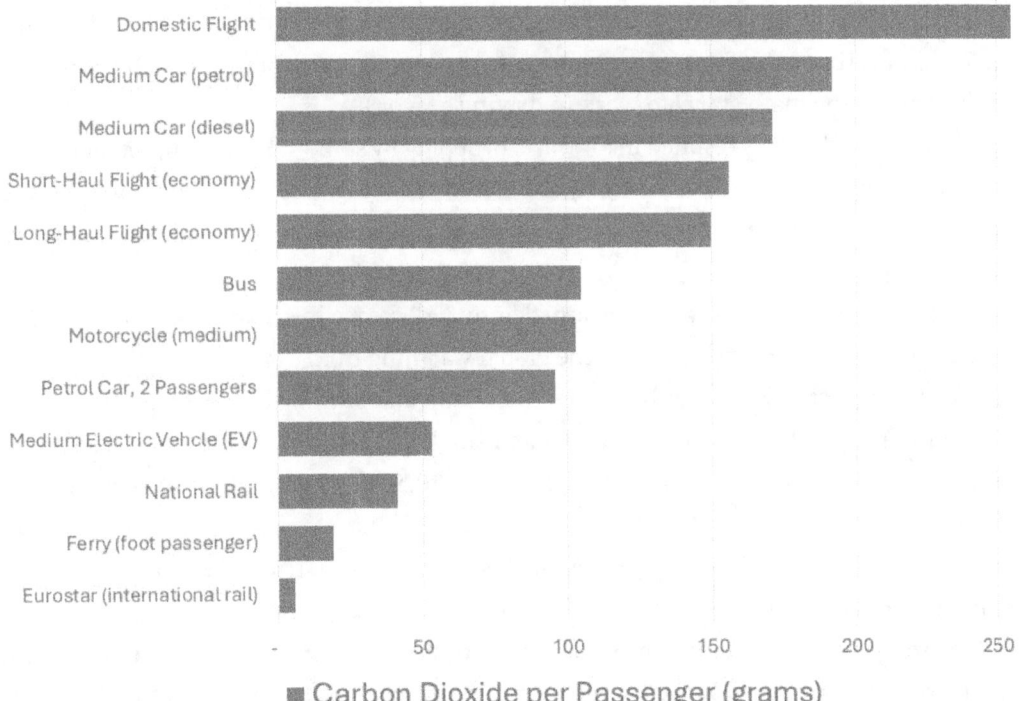

CARBON FOOTPRINT OF TRAVEL PER KM
(grams of CO_2 per passenger)

Flying and single-passenger cars are the biggest source of C02 emissions. (credit: UK Department of Business, Energy & Industrial Strategy)

And yet, ask people if they would be willing to curtail their plans to vacation overseas, and you'll hit resistance. It's one thing to care about the planet, but "does it have to impact my personal lifestyle?" many will ask before instinctively clicking the "purchase" button on Expedia or Kayak.

The environmental costs of air travel

A study published in *Environmental Research Letters* in 2021 found that 4% of human-induced climate change can be attributed to aviation. That's projected to result in a temperature rise of 0.1 degrees Celsius by 2050 if aviation continues growing at pre-pandemic rates.

Another data point from the report: 2.4% of global annual CO_2 emissions come from commercial air travel.

Four percent and 2.4% may not seem that high, but as Milan Klöwer, who led the study, points out, "That's more than most countries emit."

Indeed, if aviation were a country, it would be the world's sixth-largest offender, following China, the U.S., India, Russia, and Japan.

Driving is no better, by the way. While a cross-country airplane trip from New York to Los Angeles emits 0.62 tons of CO_2 per passenger, a car trip of the same duration emits 1.26 tons of carbon emissions. (That figure is for a single driver in a car. With three or four in the vehicle, the math starts to work in driving's favor.)

Covid-19 lockdowns resulted in air travel dropping by some 45% in 2020, which Klöwer estimates may have slowed warming by about five years. But CO_2 emissions persist in the atmosphere for hundreds of years, so a couple of good years do not obviate decades of past emissions.

Still, Klöwer estimates that a sustained annual decrease in air traffic of 2.5% by 2050 would halt aviation's contribution to the global warming mix.

A passenger traveling from New York to London and back will, on average, be responsible for emissions that are more than what a single person in Paraguay generates in an entire year. Four-and-a-half billion people flew in 2019; that's estimated to rise to 8.5 billion by 2025.

If the industry continues a "business-as-usual" approach, from 2021 to 2050, carbon emissions will total 21.2 gigatons.

Passenger air travel contributes over 80% of those emissions with freight making up the rest. The rate of CO_2 emissions from commercial flights increased by about 70% between 2005 and 2020—a reflection of the 60% rise in the number of flights worldwide. In 2017 alone, Airbus added 1,229 passenger planes to the market; Boeing contributed 1,031 new aircraft.

Every day, 100,000 commercial flights lift off, transporting some 10 million passengers. Estimates indicate that, by 2035, there will be twice as many flights as there are now with some 8 billion travelers passing through airports every year.

That's a hard trend to turn around.

Flying less—for business and pleasure—will help, but with work-from-home already under pressure by employers intent on getting their workers back in the office, I wouldn't count on us being able to curtail our desire to meet and tour exotic locations in person.

Maybe the next generation will be more willing to eschew air travel. In 2023, France passed a bill to ban short-haul flights where a train alternative of 2.5 hours or less exists.

Netta Ahituv writes in the Israeli publication *Haaretz* about "a senior manager in the aviation industry who likes to ask her colleagues, 'Who today constitutes the biggest obstacle to airline profits?' 'Elon Musk?' someone asks. 'The FAA?' 'No and no again,' the manager responds. 'It's Greta Thunberg who ignited a global environmental movement of youth and inspired young people to persuade their parents to fly less and opt for trains over planes."

Ahituv points out that, in Sweden, there's a term—*flygskam*—that means "flight shame" and refers to peer pressure to travel by train, not plane, for domestic trips.

You can't take a train across the ocean, of course. So, should we all switch from planes to ships? It might take longer getting from Boston to Barcelona, but could it help reduce emissions?

Hardly.

Shipping emits over one billion tons of carbon a year

Shipping is the only form of transportation today where emissions are *growing*. The International Maritime Organization (IMO) estimates that, by 2050, there will be three times as many products being shipped by sea than there are today, leading to a 50% growth in emissions.

Emissions from ships are among the worst in the world. *The Economist* reports that 15 of the biggest ships alone emit more NOx (nitrogen oxide) and SOx (sulfur oxide) than all the world's cars put together.

That's been exacerbated by a shift to liquified natural gas (LNG) as a fuel for deep-sea shipping. Methane leaks along the LNG supply chain resulted in a 150% growth in methane emissions from 2012 to 2018 since ships began using more LNG.

Methane is even worse for the environment than CO_2, trapping 86% more heat in the atmosphere than CO_2 over a 20-year period. It's still a smaller amount than CO_2 emissions, but more deadly.

The IMO is not sitting back and doing nothing.

In 2018, the IMO set a target for the international shipping sector to reduce greenhouse gas emissions by at least 50% by 2050, compared to a baseline of 2008 levels. To get there, the IMO says, the first zero-carbon ships must be commercialized by 2030.

Another regulation, this one from the European Union, is known as "Fit for 55." It aims to impose by 2030 a 55% reduction on CO_2 emissions from a climate baseline set in 1990. That's not just for ships—and not just for ships sailing within Europe.

So, for example, a shipping line couldn't run a heavily polluting ship for most of its journey, dock in the port of Alexandria in Egypt, and transfer its cargo to a "cleaner" ship to skirt the "Fit for 55" rules.

The same EU program is calling for a 90% reduction in CO_2 emissions by 2050.

The regulations aren't only hitting commercial shipping. Cruise lines are paying hefty fines to cover their carbon emissions. The cruise operator Carnival, for example, has paid more than $800 million in fines.

There's also pressure from consumers.

Amazon and IKEA have committed to running their cargo operations exclusively on zero-carbon shipping fuels by 2040 because consumers are increasingly demanding that.

"They're telling the shipping lines, if you want my business, you better get yourself a low-carbon ship because, if you don't, someone else will," Chris Cannon, chief sustainability officer at the Port of Los Angeles, told the shipping publication *FreightWaves*.

Joining Amazon and IKEA in their pledge are Unilever, Michelin, Brooks, Patagonia, Tchibo, Inditex and Frog Bikes.

Quality of Life meets climate change

The resistance to change comes in part because, as I noted at the start of this chapter, human beings today have a better quality of life than pretty much anyone who has ever lived on Earth historically. It may not seem like that, when miserable weather bears down on us, when disinformation fills our social-media streams and governments go rogue. But at the same time:

- Despite the declines of the last three years, people are living longer than at any time in history. Average life expectancy for men and women globally is now 73.2 years; some countries, like Hong Kong, top 85 years. (The U.S. didn't make the top 15.)

- GDP continues to grow in nearly every country (except Russia, which has seen a drop in its GDP of 2.5% following the invasion of Ukraine).

- The number of people who have died in wars has, since the end of World War II, consistently declined from as high as half a million per year to 100,000 today.

- While clearly not "solved," there is nevertheless less hunger than at most times in the past (although the Covid-19 pandemic contributed to an increase of 150 million people who are undernourished—that number is expected to drop as the global economy recovers).

NUMBER OF PEOPLE WHO ARE UNDERNOURISHED
(caloric intake insufficient to meet minimum energy requirements)

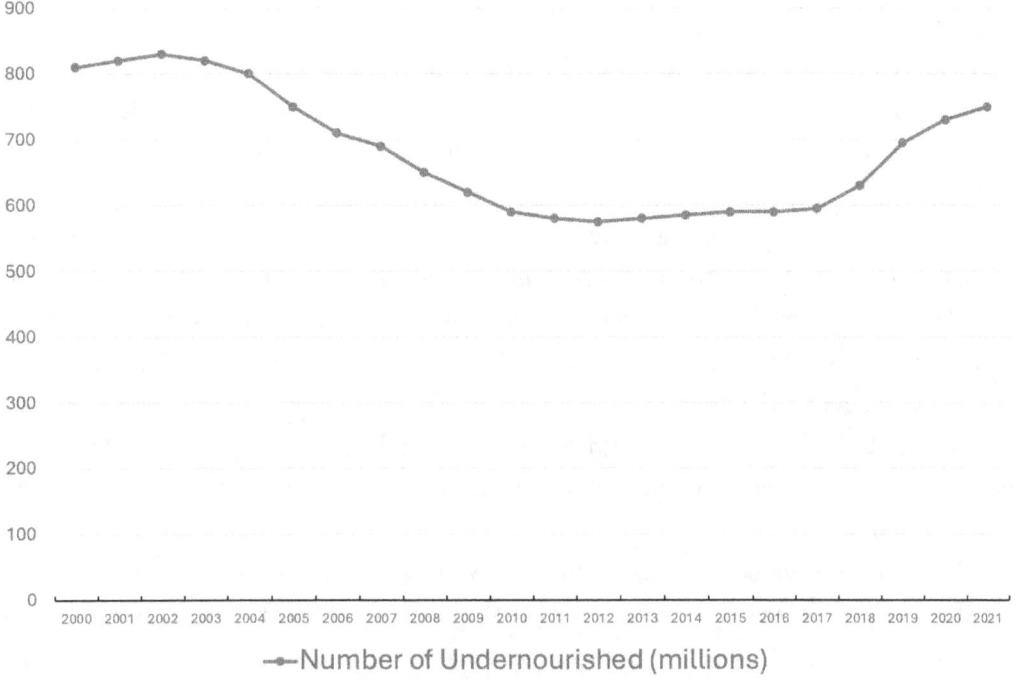

We were trending in the right direction. But this is not the case since 2017. (credit: Statista)

Food insecurity and political upheaval amid climate change

When we consider climate change, we tend to think about weather and the warming planet. But climate change also exacerbates two other areas: food insecurity and political upheaval.

One need only look at Syria to see the extent of the problem.

A 2015 study published in the *Proceedings of the National Academy of Sciences* says that drought in Syria, exacerbated to record levels by global warming, "pushed social unrest in that nation across a line into an open uprising in 2011."

How did that happen? *Scientific American* analyzed the data.

"Drying and drought in Syria from 2006 to 2011—the worst on record there—destroyed agriculture, causing many farm families to migrate to cities," writes Mark Fischetti. "The influx added to social stresses already created by refugees pouring in from the war in Iraq."

The resulting "desertification" devastated agricultural land in the eastern part of the country. Some 800,000 people lost their income and 85% of the country's livestock died.

With crop yields plummeting by up to two-thirds, the country had to start importing large quantities of grain. That led to a doubling of food prices.

"But the drought still continued, and people were hopeless," says Jamal Saghir, a professor at the Institute for the Study of International Development at McGill University.

That helps to explain why 1.5 million rural workers had no choice but to head to the cities for work, Saghir adds. "Those who stayed were mainly impoverished farmers who became easy targets for terrorist recruiters from groups like the so-called Islamic State."

"We're not saying the drought caused the war," Richard Seager, a Columbia University climate scientist and a coauthor of the *Scientific American* study, adds. "We're saying that added to all the other stressors, it helped kick things over the threshold into open conflict. And a drought of that severity was made much more likely by the ongoing human-driven drying of that region."

"Climate disruption was an amplifier and a multiplier of the political crisis that was building up in Syria," notes Staffan de Mistura, former UN Special Envoy for Syria between 2014 and 2018.

The crisis was further aggravated by the government's decisions to reduce fuel, water and food subsidies over the years, fueling tensions between Kurds, Arabs, Alawites and Sunnis.

"A toxic cocktail started to turn into an explosive mixture with the ingredients of the Arab Spring, the anger of losing jobs, migration to cities, as well as the purchasing power decline and the anger against the very tough and very cruel reactions by the government," de Mistura adds.

"The Syrian war has now taken on a life of its own," Seager notes. "However, a drought made worse by climate change was one important factor that initiated the social unraveling."

According to Amnesty International, 6.6 million people have been displaced within Syria and more than five million people have escaped since 2011.

It's not just Syria.

As *Scientific American* reports, "A 2009 study found that, over the past 30 years in sub-Saharan Africa, temperature rise correlated with an increase in the likelihood of civil war. A 2011 study implicated climate change in pushing up food prices in Egypt, fueling the Arab Spring there."

Food production is not only impacted by climate change; it helps to *create* and *prolong* the latter.

Joseph Poore and Thomas Nemecek published a report in *Science* that found making food for a hungry planet is responsible for approximately 26% of global greenhouse gas emissions.

That can be broken down as follows:

GLOBAL GREENHOUSE GAS EMISSIONS FROM FOOD PRODUCTION
(total: 52.3 billion tonnes of CO2 equivalents)

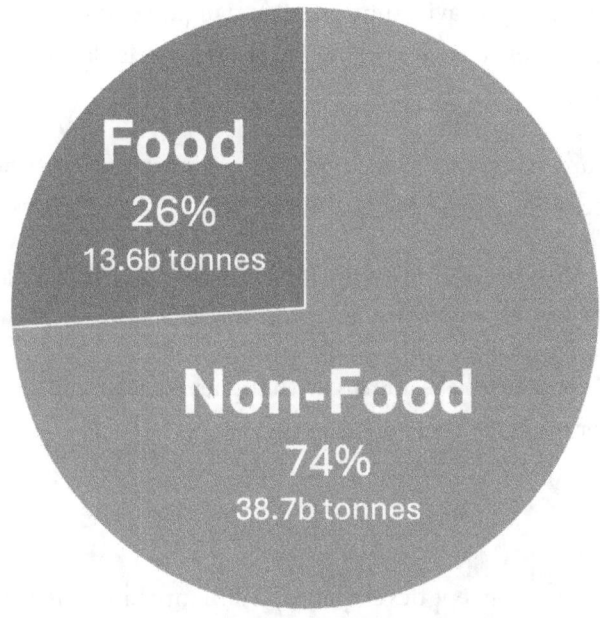

Food production is responsible for 26% of all greenhouse gas emissions. (credit: Joseph Poore & Thomas Nemecek, 2018))

✦ Livestock and fisheries account for 31% of food emissions. That includes methane-rich "cow burps," known by their more scientific term, "enteric fermentation."

✦ Crop production accounts for 27% of food emissions—21% from crops for direct human consumption and 6% from the production of animal feed.

✦ Land use accounts for 24% of food emissions. Land use for livestock results in twice as many emissions (16%) as crops for human consumption (8%).

✦ Supply chains account for 18% of food emissions. This includes transport, packaging and retail.

Can mobility help?

Can new mobility solutions address this aspect of our changing world? Absolutely, as we'll see later in the book. Here's a short summary:

+ Better technology including artificial intelligence (AI), drones, and cloud computing can help farmers in Syria and beyond do more with less water and resources.

+ Autonomous farm equipment can reduce costs (after the initial purchase price, which will need to be heavily subsidized) and improve productivity. Autonomy could also make it less expensive to bring fruits and vegetables from the farm to urban supermarkets.

+ New fuel sources for ag-tech machinery—from solar and electrification to ammonia and hydrogen—can bring prices down.

+ Smarter tractors can minimize the impact heavy machinery can have on the soil, allowing the ground to remain fertile for longer.

+ More work opportunities—ideally with higher wages—will reduce the propensity to join terror organizations like Islamic State.

Jevons Paradox

The Jevons Paradox is a concept developed by William Stanley Jevons 160 years ago to explain why productivity improvements compel people to find new ways to consume a given product, increasing demand and ultimately consumption, rather than lowering it.

You can find the Jevons Paradox in action all over the modern world.

As refrigeration has grown cheaper, for instance, we've added more refrigeration space in homes, shops and grocers. That's expanded the total energy required to keep stuff cold.

The Jevons Paradox also explains why highway expansions consistently fail to deliver the predicted benefits to reducing congestion. Why does this happen? A widened highway simply leads more people to travel on it during peak hours until it's just as gridlocked as before.

The same is true with the price of fuel.

"Any productivity gains would cause the price of coal to decline, compelling people and businesses to find new ways to use it. That increase in coal demand would lift its price—and ultimately lead to more coal production," writes David Zipper, visiting fellow at the Harvard Kennedy School's Taubman Center for State and Local Government, in *Fast Company*.

This has important implications for self-driving cars.

By making driving easier, Zipper notes, autonomy will bring more vehicles onto the highways, which he calls "a disaster for the environment" and a "nightmare for climate change" until autonomous vehicles, which will necessarily be battery powered, can be powered by a grid entirely based on renewables.

You don't have to wait for fully autonomous vehicles to see how the Jevons Paradox works in the real world.

A recent study by Scott Harman at the University of California, Davis's Institute of Transportation Studies, found that Tesla owners with Autopilot enabled drove nearly 5,000 miles a year more than their non-ADAS counterparts.

Some 36% of the 628 people who responded to Harman's research reported more long-distance travel. It's not all bad news: Most of those trips were weekend getaways that might otherwise have involved plane travel, a far more climate-unfriendly mode of transport.

In another study, a researcher at the University of California, Berkeley gave 13 people a "chauffeur" who would drive them anywhere they wanted for a week. The idea was to mimic how a self-driving car would operate. The researcher, Mustapha Harb, expected maybe a 20% or 30% bump in miles traveled. He was, therefore, shocked when, during the test week, subjects drove 83% more miles than the week before when they only had their own chauffeur-less cars to use.

One participant's experience was particularly telling.

He had his chauffeur drive him to work downtown, then return the car to his driveway until it was time for pickup, essentially doubling the number of miles the car traveled.

The reason for the switchback? To avoid paying for parking, "a worst-case scenario of an unregulated AV future," as Aaron Gordon writes in *Jalopnik*.

Moreover, the more comfortable an autonomous vehicle is, the less onerous a once lengthy commute will seem. That could lead to even more suburban sprawl, another concern of climate-change warriors.

Zipcar cofounder Robin Chase proposed in a 2021 White Paper, "Shared Mobility Principles for Livable Cities," that autonomous vehicle makers must commit to offering only shared trips within urban areas.

Autonomous vehicles will either bring the "heaven" of shared trips or the "hell" of private ones, Chase writes.

But won't most self-driving cars be for shared rides?

Not according to a study published on the *Transport Findings* website, co-sponsored by the University of Sydney and McGill University in Montreal, which found that the vast majority of trips will be taken privately, not with strangers, Zipper writes.

"When you share a ride with someone, it's a very intimate setting," Natalia Barbour, a professor of transport at Delft University of Technology, told *Bloomberg*. "If someone makes you uncomfortable, you can't change where you sit, while on public transit you can adjust your seat or move to another train car."

The past few years haven't changed commuters' attitudes.

"People's dislike of sharing rides with strangers has not changed compared with before the pandemic," the *Transport Findings* study found.

The unfortunate conclusion: AVs will lead to more driving which, unless the grid is 100% powered by renewables, means continued climate destruction.

A shared robo-taxi could even be dangerous, particularly for women, where the lack of a driver might mean less protection against inappropriate behavior or sexual predators.

One more note about the Jevons Paradox. The oil-producing companies that the autonomous and electric vehicle revolutions are bucking are not likely to go gentle into the post-fossil fuels night.

Could a push for less oil paradoxically lead to an increase in the use of oil?

Just look at Saudi Arabia, where the cost of extraction of petroleum from the ground is about $5 to $6 a barrel. Compare that with the U.S., where it costs at least $40 to produce a barrel of shale oil; the price can go as high as $90 a barrel.

The Gulf countries may talk a good talk—"We're going electric!" "We're switching to renewables!"—but when push comes to shove, anything that reduces Saudi revenue from oil is going to be perceived as a threat by the Kingdom.

After all, if the marginal cost of an oil barrel is, say, $8.98, and drills, factories, and processing are all sunk costs, then as long as the global oil price is above $9, Saudi Arabia will still be profitable.

But it will want more.

Saudi Arabia might say it wants to diversify, but what is to be done with its existing oil infrastructure—turn it into an amusement park? Might Saudi Arabia try to "convince" other countries *not* to go electric by keeping the price of oil artificially low? If the retail price of gas at the pump decreases from, say, its current level of $4 a gallon to something like 50 cents a gallon, how would this impact the demand for electric vehicles?

On top of that, consider that Saudi Arabia's foreign currency reserves are about $900 billion—one-fifth larger than its GDP—which means, according to Chas W. Freeman Jr., former U.S. ambassador to Saudi Arabia, in a talk he gave to the Middle East Policy Council in Washington, DC: "Saudi Arabia can afford to take a revenue hit for a few years—long enough for [competitors] to be wrung out of the market."

Are EVs actually better for the environment?

EV opponents play the "pollution card," arguing that EVs are not better for the environment than gasoline-powered cars.

The logic is that, while EVs don't emit noxious fumes like an internal combustion engine (ICE) vehicle, the manufacturing process—from body to battery—is just as bad, if not worse, in terms of its carbon impact. Add in the need to mine minerals such as lithium and cobalt in ways that may be dangerous for the planet—and certainly for the people who must work in the mines—along with the current reality that many batteries are ending up in landfills, and it's hard to dismiss the anti-EV claims out of hand.

However, pollution from nitrogen dioxide (NO_2) is dropping as more EVs are sold and stricter regulations for the remaining gas guzzlers come into place.

In London, for example, where congestion fees limit the number of vehicles entering the city, the number of residents living in areas exceeding the legal limit for NO_2 in the air dropped from two million in 2016 to just 119,000 in 2019, according to the World Health Organization. That's a reduction of 94%.

There's also electricity generation.

As long as EVs grab their power from the electric grid, how that power is generated makes a difference to the future of the planet.

For example, in China, electric production relies heavily on coal and oil. In 2022, China's electric power production pumped 530 grams of CO_2/KwH into the atmosphere, compared with just 368 grams of CO_2 per kilowatt-hour in the U.S.

Some 22% of the U.S.'s energy comes from renewable sources, according to the U.S. Energy Information Administration. Sixty percent of electricity produced in the U.S. comes from fossil fuels. Another 18% comes from nuclear power plants. But coal has dominated over the years to devastating effect: A 2023 paper in *Science* found that emissions from coal plants have killed nearly half a million people in the U.S. over the past two decades.

Despite China's reliance on coal and oil, EVs are still better for the environment there. Data from the IEA published in October 2022 revealed that, even when using the dirtiest battery materials, EVs still produced less than half the CO_2 emissions of combustion engines over their lifetimes.

Conflicting values

Efforts to address climate change have long been stymied by conflicting values: cleaning up the planet vs. hurting the global economy. It's a concept called "The Tragedy of the Commons," which the website *Investopedia* defines as "a social and political problem in which each individual is incentivized to act in a way that will ultimately be harmful to all individuals." (We go into more detail in chapter 3, "Air Travel.")

Mining nickel in Indonesia is a good example.

Indonesia is the world's top producer of nickel, according to the U.S. Geological Survey. As demand for nickel—a key part of current battery technology—soars, countries like Indonesia are in a quandary. Should they mine the nickel responsibly but more slowly or get it out of the ground as fast as possible?

Indonesia is betting on the latter.

Nickel mining company executives and Indonesia government leaders are now looking into a refining technology that has long been considered risky and potentially environmentally perilous. The process, called high-pressure acid leaching (HPAL) combines intense heat and pressure with sulfuric acid to remove nickel from raw ore.

Generating the required heat produces about 20 tons of CO_2 per ton of nickel—that's about double what "regular" nickel mining produces.

A bigger problem is the waste.

HPAL produces millions of tons per mine per year of corrosive "chemical tailings" which are particularly challenging to neutralize, store and contain. The waste can contain heavy metals that have been linked to respiratory illnesses and an increased risk of cancer.

Where does the waste from HPAL go? There are three options:

1. Bury it.
2. Dry it out and stack it on a vacant lot.
3. Pump it into the ocean.

A nickel processing plant on Indonesia's Obira Island, the main land mass in the Obi Islands, had planned to dump its waste in the ocean until public pressure forced the companies behind the plant to backtrack. They're now going for Door No. 2—drying the waste on land before dumping it back into the mining pit, then treating the residue water for reuse.

That's run into yet another problem: earthquakes.

Indonesia is a notoriously active seismic zone. In 2019, a 7.2 magnitude earthquake struck just 50 miles from Obira.

"It's a massive heap of waste. And if it's not stored properly, you can have landslides," a foreign mining consultant told *The Washington Post*.

That's unlikely to stop an industry desperate for more nickel.

Nickel production in Indonesia hit a record high of one million metric tons in 2021. By 2028, the country is expected to produce at least 2.5 million metric tons a year. China's

CATL and South Korea's LG are both opening HPAL plants in Indonesia, as is Ford. Tesla has a deal to buy $5 billion of nickel from Indonesia.

Indonesia's HPAL facilities "might not be how you want your nickel," Brian Menell, founder of TechMet, an investment firm that focuses on minerals required for a green-energy transition, told *The Washington Post*. "But right now, you've got no choice."

Could "anti-mobility" save our cities?

While not an overarching solution to the climate crisis, there are stopgap measures that cities can implement to reduce urban temperatures, some of which involve mobility—or in this case, "anti-mobility."

In cities across the world, highways are being dismantled and replaced with greenery: parks, rivers, and shade.

- Amsterdam has turned 10,000 square meters of roofs in public buildings into green areas filled with vegetation, rainwater storage units, and solar panels.

- In South Korea, the Cheonggye Expressway blighted adjacent neighborhoods for 35 years. It was ripped out two decades ago and now a $380 million project aims to bring back the stream that once flowed there, creating an urban park. The ground temperature in the park was 3.6 degrees Celsius lower than an area just 400 meters away.

- A highway running through the Dutch town of Utrecht was restored to its former glory: a historic canal.

- A 15-mile-long aqueduct in Athens, originally built by the Roman Emperor Hadrian in the year AD 140, is being repurposed to widen the city's green footprint and add more shade. Athens has also started repairing dozens of ailing fountains. The work couldn't come soon enough: the temperature difference between central Athens and its suburbs can reach 10 degrees Celsius during the hottest of days.

- Paris has a 50-mile network of underground pipes that pump water from the Seine to cool down buildings, including the Louvre. The city plans to expand that network to more than 250 kilometers, which is expected to save Paris a full degree of warming compared with using air conditioners for the same purpose.

- In the Colombian city of Medellín, dozens of green corridors with plentiful vegetation have been created. The project, which allows pedestrians to cross the city in constant shade, lowered Medellín's overall temperature by two degrees.

SOUTH KOREA'S CHEONG GYE CHEON
(before and after)

South Korea demonstrates how dramatically a city can clean up its act. (credit: Wikimedia Commons)

Making the urban environment more livable has always been important.

Now, it's urgent.

The United Nations' International Labor Organization notes that temperatures above 33 degrees Celsius can reduce one's work capacity by half.

There are today 350 major cities where people are struggling with temperatures above 35 degrees Celsius, says Elena Myrivili, the global "chief heat officer" for the United Nations.

"By 2050, it will be 1,000 cities and 1.6 billion city dwellers facing extreme heat for three consecutive months or more per year," she says.

Noting the heat emitted by cooling devices, she adds, "We can't just air condition everything. It's ridiculous. It's going to throw our planet into a total climate crisis immediately."

And that could further impact the social fabric of urban life in potentially devastating ways.

If we don't act, Myrivili says, "more and more we'll see vibrant cities like Athens empty out because nobody will want to be outside. We love sitting in cafés and eating and having

UTRECHT CITY CENTER MOTORWAY (NETHERLANDS)
(before and after)

The Dutch have some of the most pedestrian (and bike) friendly cities in the world. (credit: bicycledutch.com)

drinks at night outdoors; we love walking around and going to stores or just getting together and sitting in a park. All this will have to be withdrawn inside."

Myrivili believes that actions she and others are taking can turn things around—if not for the planet, then for our mental health.

"If I weren't doing all these things, I would become depressed, totally depressed," Myrivili told the Israeli newspaper *Haaretz*. "Climate change makes a lot of us feel disempowered, because we think that not enough is being done . . . it's important to find a role, or even to create a role, that will alleviate the feeling of helplessness and let you feel that you can bring about change."

That can be tough, says Scott Case, CEO of Recurrent, which generates battery reports for EVs ("What's your EV's 'real range?'" Case asks). Full disclosure: Automotive Ventures is an investor in Recurrent.

The problem is that the pollution we put into the atmosphere 30 years ago will still be there tomorrow and the day after, too, Case explains.

"Even if we didn't add another drop of CO_2," he says, "the outcome from 30 years ago is now preordained. Our children will be at the primes of their lives when the worst of the climate models are hitting."

That said, Case is optimistic that EVs can help. Pushing EVs, he suggests, doesn't need to come as the result of regulations and bans.

"EVs are just so much better than ICE vehicles," he told me, "that the uptake is going to be much faster than people think. Combustion engines had a great 100-year run. But they're done. It's inferior technology at this point!"

I want to leave the last word on climate change to David Roberts. Moving to 100% renewables is going to happen, he told me, not because companies are feeling especially altruistic. Rather, it's pure economics.

"It will be because renewables will become so cheap. I don't expect coal to have a resurgence. In addition, we will make batteries from new materials that aren't as expensive."

From Roberts's mouth to policymakers' ears.

A technology "Hail Mary"

In the dystopian sci-fi film *Snowpiercer,* scientists attempting to reverse climate change inject a substance into the atmosphere. It's intended to blunt the sun's rays, reducing temperatures and wild weather events on Earth.

But the tech backfires and the Earth quickly freezes over. Eventually, everyone on the planet dies, except for those on the eponymous "Snowpiercer," a futuristic train that circles the globe, never stopping.

The *Snowpiercer* effect is similar to the now infamous line from the Steven Spielberg-directed *Jurassic Park* movies: "Your scientists were so preoccupied with whether or not they *could* do something, they didn't stop to think if they *should*."

The tech in *Snowpiercer* is what's known as "geo-engineering" and it's a last resort—the ultimate Hail Mary play—when it comes to stopping the ravages of climate change.

Fortunately, the planet hasn't quite reached that point.

Many climate-change naysayers nevertheless believe that only technological advances will help us find our way out of the predicament we're in.

I'm very much a technological optimist, and I believe we are likely to yet discover incredible breakthroughs that will help us capture carbon at a greater scale and move humans and cargo much more efficiently, with dramatically less impact on our environment.

Some of those breakthroughs may be coming from Israel's high-tech sector. Among the companies that sound incredibly promising:

+ GroundworkBio AG's Rootella spray uses mycorrhizal fungi to draw down excess carbon into the soil.

✦ CarbonBlue, GigaBlue, and Rewind are all developing the technology for sequestering CO2 in ocean plants and sediment.

✦ Bomvento employs photocatalysis technology to convert nitrous oxide, a potent greenhouse gas, into ecofriendly nitrogen and oxygen.

✦ High Hopes is launching hot air balloons to capture CO2 at high altitudes.

✦ Rplace and Terra aim to revitalize wetlands as a means to capture carbon.

However, I think the best path is to work to dramatically reduce the amount of greenhouse gasses we're emitting into the atmosphere, while in parallel aggressively funding research to discover new technological advances that may create breakthroughs in reducing environmental damage, cleaning up much of the mess we've already created.

■ ■ ■

Chapter 1

Ground Transport

"We *call them 'Gen EV,' because, as these kids* are growing up, EVs are just a normal thing for them," says Doug Tran, founder of e-motorcycle startup Ryvid.

The development of electric vehicles by automakers—and their adoption by consumers—has tremendous momentum globally, with many automotive manufacturers pledging to cut gasoline-powered vehicles out of the mix within the next 10 years. That's ostensibly good news for the planet, as EVs don't pump toxic fumes into the built environment and, if they can be powered by renewable energy sources, contribute to a greener, cooler world.

This chapter discusses ground transport mostly from an EV perspective. However, there are other fuel alternatives—such as hydrogen—that we will explore in chapter 7.

There have been some hiccups in EV uptake.

Near the end of 2023, automakers saw EV sales grow but at a slower pace than expected. CNBC reports that in August 2023, "it took about twice as long to sell an EV in the U.S. as it did the previous January."

And while slightly more than half of consumers say that EVs are the future, less than a third of dealers hold the same view, according to *Kelly Blue Book* and *Cox Automotive*.

"Our commitment to an all-EV future is as strong as ever," Mary Barra, the chief executive of GM, told analysts on a conference call. But, she added, the market is turning out to be "a bit bumpy."

Passenger vehicle EVs are not the only vehicles that constitute mobility on land, of course. There are also buses, trucks, streetcars, agricultural equipment, scooters, bikes, and even the promise of underground transport on a future Hyperloop-type system.

Since some 90% of all mobility—including the movement of both humans and cargo—is not in the air, on the sea or through space, I wanted to start our exploration of the future of mobility and how it can help us address the key problems the planet faces with this most down-to-earth of mobility modalities.

Indeed, it's on land where the most immediate innovations can be seen, particularly technologies and startups bringing electrification and, ultimately, automation, to the forefront.

The share of electric cars of total sales has more than tripled in three years, from around 4% in 2020 to 14% in 2022, according to the International Energy Agency (IEA). In the first quarter of 2023, over 2.3 million electric cars were sold, about 25% more than in the same period in the previous year. There were 50% more charge spots in 2021 than in previous years.

Per the IEA:

> "We currently expect to see 14 million in sales by the end of 2023, representing a 35% year-on-year increase with new purchases accelerating in the second half of this year. As a result, electric cars could account for 18% of total car sales across the full calendar year."

U.S. ELECTRIC VEHICLE SALES BY POWERTRAIN
(millions of passenger EVs)

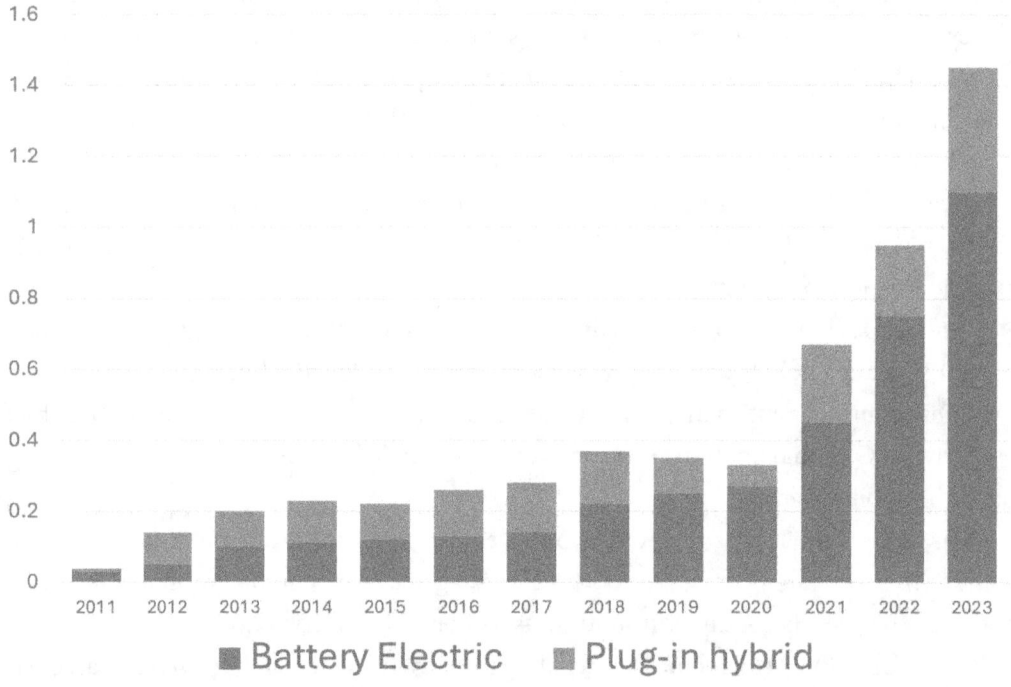

Battery Electric sales are increasing, but PHEVs are gaining fast. (credit: Nat Bullard)

Decarbonization expert Nat Bullard notes that in 2023, there was growth of 50.6% year-over-year (from 931,000 to 1.4 million) of EVs sold in the U.S. Of that total, 1.1 million were battery electric vehicles and 293,000 were plug-in hybrids.

Industry analysts predict EVs will make up a third or even half of all light vehicles sold annually in the U.S. as early as 2030.

This kind of EV uptake will reduce the world's need for oil by some five million barrels a day by 2030.

Mike Granoff of Maniv Mobility notes, anecdotally, that "everyone in my social group is saying their next car will be an EV—if they don't already have one. But it took a decade to get to this point. When the Nissan Leaf first came out, no one bought it, even though its cost of ownership was 20% less than an equivalent ICE car."

Granoff sees EV uptake as "inevitable, although inevitable is turning out to be longer-term than I had thought."

China accounts for 69% of EV sales, according to consulting firm Rystad Energy. Around 11.5 million new EVs are forecast to be sold in the country in 2024, accounting for 44% of all new car sales, and a 50% increase. In Europe, Rystad predicts sales of 3.3 million EVs in 2024. One in four of those European EVs will come from a Chinese manufacturer, according to analysis from the *Transportation & Environment* consulting firm.

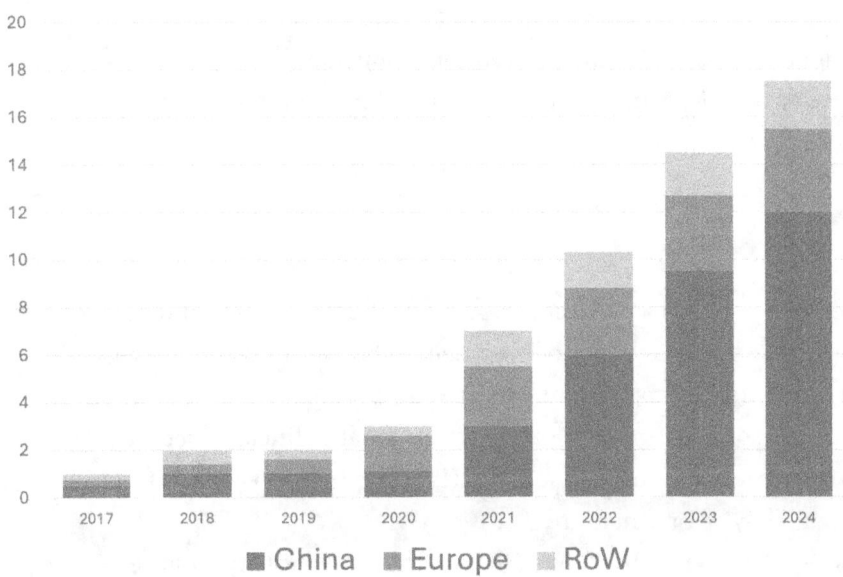

ELECTRIC VEHICLE SALES IN KEY REGIONS
(millions of units sold)

EV sales should get close to 18 million units globally in 2024. (credit: Rystad Energy's Energy Transition Solution, February 2024)

In the U.S., EV sales were up 60% in 2023 compared with 2022 figures, comprising 1.6 million in total.

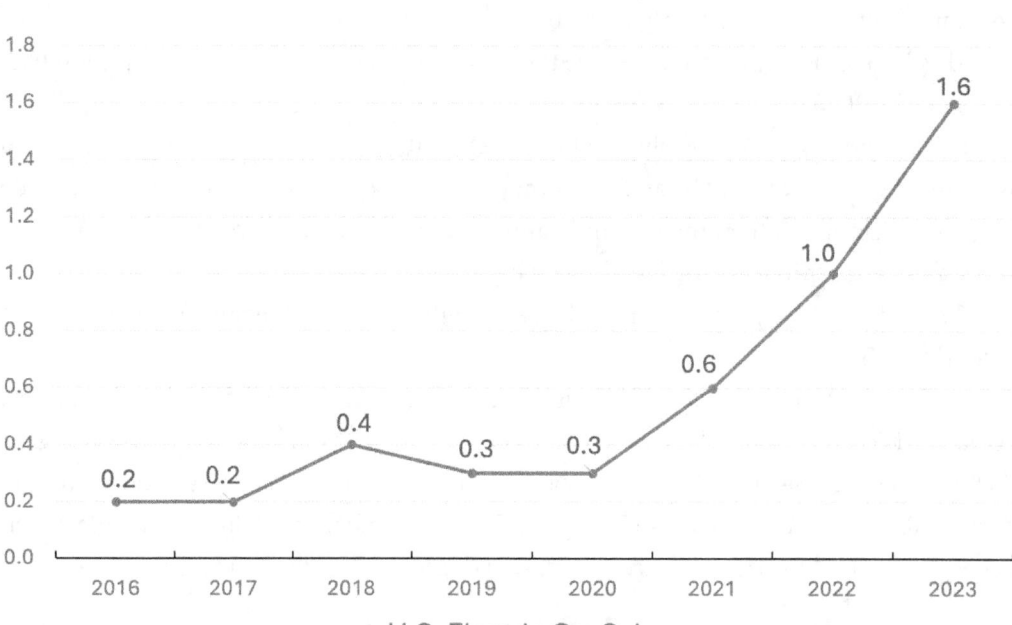

U.S. ELECTRIC CAR SALES

U.S. Electric car sales. (credit: Marketwatch; Data source: IEA.org)

It might seem as if EVs are a recent phenomenon but a quick peek into the history books reveals that electric cars have been with us longer than their ICE (internal combustion engine) equivalents.

A brief history of EVs

EVs have been heralded as the vehicle of the future for nearly 200 years.

What drove the initial sales of motorized vehicles—electric or otherwise?

The answer may surprise you: horse manure.

There was so much manure on city streets that politicians needed a solution to this stinky and nonreusable, um, "resource." (Farms refused to collect it to use as manure—there was already a horse manure glut!)

At one point, there were 200,000 horses in New York City alone, each one producing about 24 pounds of manure each day. It clogged the streets, was smelly and disgusting, and was fast becoming a public health hazard.

ELECTRIC LORRIES BEING CHARGED
(St. Pancras Goods Depot, London, July 11, 1917)

Early EVs (credit: Wikimedia Commons)

Electric Vehicle Co. Hansom Cab, ca. 1904. (credit: Wikimedia Commons)

In that respect, the advent of the car was initially seen to be environmentally friendly!

The very first electric vehicle was invented in 1828 by the Hungarian engineer and Benedictine priest Ányos Jedlik.

The first practical cars would become available in 1859, with the invention of the lead-acid battery by French physicist Gaston Plante.

Camille Faure improved on that early battery tech in 1881.

The first production electric car arrived initially in London in 1884 and was built by the English inventor Thomas Parker. A similar car in the United States was developed in 1890 by William Morrison of Des Moines, Iowa. The six-passenger wagon could zip along at the staggering speed of 14 miles per hour, with a maximum range of 40 miles.

Meanwhile, a small fleet of electric taxis took to the streets in both New York and London, where they were nicknamed "Hummingbirds" due to the whirring noise they made.

In New York City, in the spring of 1897, the Electric Carriage & Wagon Company (EC&WC) introduced a dozen electric taxicabs intended to compete with the existing horse-drawn taxi infrastructure.

The fleet expanded to over 100 electric vehicles, and the EC&WC was renamed the Electric Vehicle Company (EVC), which spread out to a half-dozen of the largest cities in the United States, with sales agents as far afield as Mexico City and Paris.

Regional operating companies were established, and EVC distributed some 2,000 electric vehicles to them. But by 1907, just 10 years after its launch, the company was beset by a myriad of managerial mishaps. Production delays and warehouse fires led to shareholder lawsuits and blistering public attacks.

The company eventually declared bankruptcy.

The real tipping point, though, was the gasoline-powered car, which could soon go further and required less time to refill than an electric vehicle did to recharge. Many would argue the same point today.

Still, in the early part of the 20th century, there was a point when electric cars looked like they might have a chance—at least on paper.

According to a 1912 survey, 38% of all American automobiles were powered by electricity, versus just 22% by gas. (The largest power system for mass-market cars at that point actually was steam, which was marketed to women, since such cars had fewer moving parts and didn't require a crank, something manufacturers felt would appeal to anyone in fancy attire.)

A total of 33,842 electric cars were registered in the United States, made by some 20 different manufacturers.

Electric cars had a number of key advantages: no vibration, no smell, no noise; no hand crank required to start the engine; and no gears. Steam cars were gear-free, too, but were eventually retired when their long start-up times—up to 45 minutes on cold mornings—made them a poor third choice.

EVs were so popular in the early days of the car that Henry Ford and Thomas Edison teamed up to make an early electric car. But battery range was no more than 80 miles—not unlike when EVs returned at the beginning of the 21st century—and charging took a long time.

"Edison comes up with a different battery technology—and it doesn't work," says Tom Standage, author of *A Brief History of Motion*, points out. "Here are two of the greatest minds in automotive technology history and they can't solve the problem. So, electric cars [gained] this reputation of being rubbish."

Still, it wasn't range or speed which ultimately doomed the electric car. It was the electric self-starter, invented by Charles Kettering in 1912. This eliminated the hand crank in internal combustion engine cars, making these newfangled vehicles more amenable to the less brawny.

When Ford introduced assembly-line production of the Model T in 1908, the price of his gasoline-powered cars plummeted. By 1912, one of Ford's gasoline cars sold for half the price of an electric car.

In those early, heady days of electric vehicles, no business model was too far out.

While failed auto-tech infrastructure startup Better Place and, later, startups such as NIO and Ample would come to popularize the concept of battery swapping in the modern age, it was first put into practice by the Hartford Electric Light Company in 1910, for electric trucks.

Owners would purchase their vehicle from General Electric's GVC subsidiary, but without a battery, which came from the Hartford Electric utility. GVC electric truck owners in 1910 paid a variable per-mile charge and a monthly service fee to Hartford Electric to cover maintenance and battery exchanges.

The service operated for 14 years. A similar service, with separate car and battery ownership, was opened in Chicago, in 1917.

The EV1

It took another 80 years before electric cars were back—albeit without a switchable battery—in the form of General Motors' EV1, which launched in 1996.

Originally given the inopportune name the "Impact" (that was quickly changed!), the EV1 was a sleek state-of-the-art car, with a range of 100 to 140 miles on an 8-hour recharge, full torque capacity without the need to shift gears, keyless entry and ignition, acceleration from zero to 50 miles per hour in just 6 seconds, a home recharger and strategically located public charging spots.

All told, GM spent close to $1 billion to design, produce and market the car.

The General Motors EV1. (credit: Wikimedia Commons)

The EV1 was adored by its owners, who included high-profile celebrities like Mel Gibson and Tom Hanks.

But just a few years after its launch, citing ostensible "lack of demand," GM moved aggressively to kill the project. During the car's three-year run, GM sold just 1,117 EV1s.

By 2002, GM had bought back or taken possession of every EV1 it had produced, and, beyond that, had crushed and demolished nearly all of them. The shocking latter process is captured on film in director Chris Paine's 2006 documentary, "Who Killed the Electric Car?"

Perhaps anticipating such a sour ending, drivers were allowed only to lease, not buy, the vehicles, making GM's total recall an easy operation.

Forty cars were saved for museums, but with their electric powertrains deactivated, and subject to an agreement that the cars were never to be driven on the road again. A single working EV1 was donated to the Smithsonian Institution.

One might think that GM's experience would have soured it on building more EVs. But the competition from Tesla was too much for GM's vice chairman of global product development Bob Lutz.

"That tore it for me," he explained in 2007. "If some Silicon Valley startup can solve this equation, no one is going to tell me anymore that [a car run on lithium-ion batteries] is unfeasible."

Alternate history

What would have happened if EVs had become the dominant car type 100 years ago? Would it have changed the climate-change game?

Probably not, says Standage.

"If you plugged in your electric car in 1902, that electricity was coming from a power station that was burning oil," Standage tells Steven Dubner on an episode of the *Freakonomics* podcast. "We're sort of conflating two things: the electrification of transport and the decarbonization of transport. You could have very easily had electric transport that was heavily carbon intensive."

You'd still have the same Middle East oil dependency and the resulting consequences of that politically, Standage warns. "It's only when we started to worry about carbon emissions and decarbonization that we said, 'Hang on a minute, we need to stop burning oil, and that includes in our cars.'"

I've heard the argument that EVs are not a panacea for carbon emissions, that the EV manufacturing process creates a substantial amount of CO_2. But, as can be seen in the

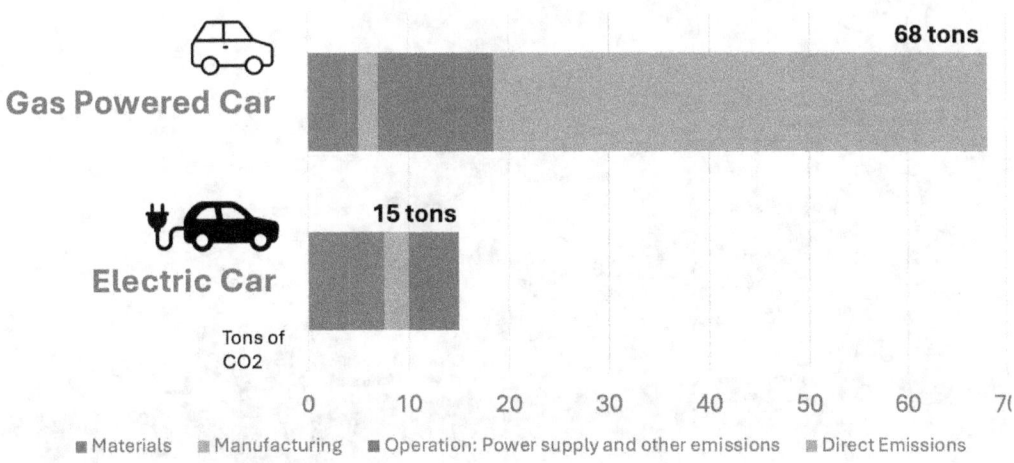

Lifecycle Carbon Emissions of ICE vs. EV
(tons of CO2)

Gas Powered Car — 68 tons

Electric Car — 15 tons

Tons of CO2

0   10   20   30   40   50   60   7(

■ Materials   ■ Manufacturing   ■ Operation: Power supply and other emissions   ■ Direct Emissions

EVs produce more CO2 during the manufacturing process, but far less over their lifetimes. (credit: IEA, Hokestra and Steinbuch, Quartz)

accompanying chart from the IEA, while the amount of CO2 produced when building an EV is actually greater than that of a gasoline-powered vehicle, once the cars hit the road, the level of direct emissions is essentially nil. Of course, the actual amount of CO2 produced over the lifetime of the EV depends on the source of electricity used to charge the vehicle. (Let's continue to lean into the shift from fossil fuels to renewables!)

The cost of an EV vs. a gasoline-powered vehicle

The Wall Street Journal reported in March 2023 that the cost of owning a gasoline-powered Toyota RAV4 for five years is now on par with owning a comparable electric Ford Mustang Mach-E.

A base model Mustang Mach-E sells for $46,000, if bought with cash in New Jersey, according to car pricing website Edmunds. The total cost of ownership over five years, including depreciation, insurance, fuel and maintenance costs, is, coincidentally, also $46,000.

A gas-powered RAV4 costs $34,000 to buy, says Edmunds, but its five-year total cost of ownership is $45,000. That makes the Mach-E only $200 more expensive per year than the RAV4. And if gas prices spike again, EV costs will look even better.

Here's another example:

The cheapest EV in the U.S. was for some time the Chevy Bolt, with a list price of $26,500. GM announced it would be discontinuing the Bolt by the end of 2023, but a few months later,

The Chevy Bolt (credit: Wikimedia Commons)

Chevy announced the Bolt will be back. And why not: it was *MotorTrend's* 2017 "Car of the Year." In the first half of 2023, about 80% of the 50,000 EVs GM built in North America were Bolts.

GM would only say the Bolt's re-release is on "an accelerated timeline." The new Bolt will use GM's Ultium battery technology.

If the Bolt keeps its $26,500 price tag, that's still some $2,500 more than a comparable gasoline-powered Hyundai Kona. However, if the Bolt is driven 15,000 miles a year and charged primarily at home, Edmunds estimates a Bolt owner can make up the difference in cost on fuel savings alone. And that's before any state or federal tax breaks, for which the made-in-the-USA Bolt would be eligible.

Dropping battery prices

The main reason for the decreasing cost gap between EVs and ICE vehicles is the declining price of batteries, still the single most expensive component in EVs.

Battery prices are dropping due to better economies of scale by battery manufacturers and via technological improvements—including using less nickel and cobalt, two of the more expensive minerals in modern batteries. That's sent the price per pound of cobalt plummeting—from $40 in 2022 to just $17 in 2023 as the mineral falls out of fashion.

The result has been dramatic: A 90% drop in the cost of a new battery from 2010 to 2020, according to Paul Augustine, director of sustainability at Lyft.

At Tesla, cheaper batteries didn't result in lower prices at first. Elon Musk resisted the trend, saying demand was robust and there was no need to drop prices. Indeed, in the first quarter of 2023, the Tesla Model Y surpassed Toyota's RAV4 and Corolla models to become the top-selling car model globally.

The Model Y starts at $47,490, which is a big bump up from a RAV4 ($27,575) and a Corolla ($21,550).

Still, by mid-2023, Musk and company threw in the towel and announced its next-generation car would cost between $25,000 and $30,000. (Musk has since walked back those comments and says Tesla is focusing now on building FSD robo-taxis.)

Lower priced Teslas are not entirely dead. In 2023, Tesla began cutting prices across all its vehicles by an average of 25%.

+ The base price of the Model 3 has come down 11% cumulatively since the start of 2023. It's roughly $44,000 now, down from $48,000.

+ The Model Y crossover has seen a 20% reduction in price—about $2,000 per vehicle.

+ The Model S had the biggest drop—from a high of $130,000 to $96,000 now.

The move appears to be working.

During its Q2 2023 earnings call, Tesla revealed it delivered a record 466,140 cars worldwide, nearly 20,000 vehicles more than analysts anticipated, and an 83% increase from the previous year. In 2023, the Tesla Model Y was the best-selling electric vehicle in the world. From May 2023 to May 2024, Tesla sold 618,000 cars in the U.S. alone, compared with 597,000 fully electric vehicles by other manufacturers, according to *Bloomberg*. But those other car companies are closing the gap—sales were up 56% at Hyundai/Kia and 86% at Ford in 2024, while Tesla sales dropped 13%. Tesla is still the largest EV maker in North America, but it may soon lose its "bragging rights" for selling more than all other EV makers combined.

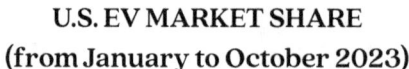

U.S. EV MARKET SHARE
(from January to October 2023)

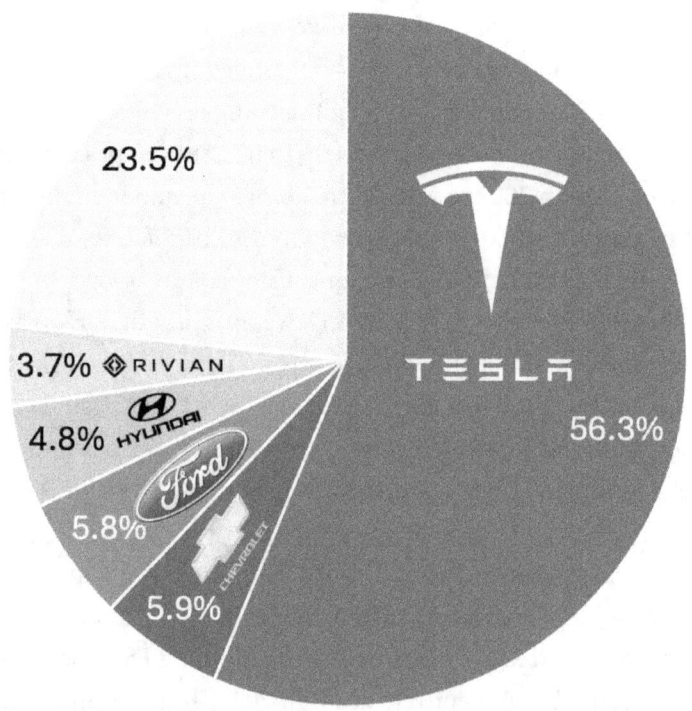

U.S. EV market share (credit: Automotive News)

Mike Granoff, of Maniv Mobility, told me that if Tesla were to begin selling a Model 3 with 150 miles of range for $25,000 or less, "It would satisfy 80% to 90% of consumers. Any household with two cars should have that car. But no one is doing it because range is still the sexier thing."

For Granoff, the question is financial.

"Would you pay a $10,000 increment for another 80 miles of range and then another $10,000 for more range? What is the optimal tradeoff that would address consumer psychology?"

Despite the positive bump in sales, Tesla CEO Elon Musk insists, "We're not 'starting a price war', we're just lowering prices to enable affordability at scale."

In a separate interview, Musk added. "I just can't emphasize again how important cost is. It's not an optional thing for most people . . . we have to make our cars more affordable so that people can buy them."

And yet, a price war is exactly what's happening, says Mark Schirmer, director of communications at Cox Automotive.

"There was nothing else he could do, in that he doesn't have anything really new to compete against these other companies," Schirmer told *Business Insider.*

The problem is that, once customers get used to paying $40,000 for a standard EV, they're not going back to $60,000.

Is Musk being his usual savvy if combative self—or acting out of desperation, as *Business Insider* suggests?

Sales at Tesla may be up, but the company's Q2 2023 earnings were "frightful across the board," writes Linette Lopez in *Business Insider.* "Tesla missed Wall Street's expectations on revenue, vehicle deliveries and free cash flow, which was down to $848 million from $3.4 billion a year before. Most importantly, the company reported that its gross margins—a measure of the company's profitability after costs—continued to shrink. This horrified investors who had just gotten used to Tesla making money."

That hasn't stopped competitors from taking a page out of Tesla's price-cut playbook.

Tesla's biggest Chinese rival, BYD, unveiled the Seagull in 2023, at just $11,000, the cheapest EV by far currently on the market.

The Seagull was released in China in 2023. It's selling overseas as well—rebranded as the "Dolphin Mini" in some markets—albeit at a substantially higher price. In four Latin American countries, for example, it lists a price of $21,000, nearly double what it costs at home. That reflects "transportation costs," write Tom Krishner and Ken Moritsugu for *The Associated Press,* "but also the higher profits possible in less cutthroat markets as China."

"We have a lot of respect for car companies in China," Musk says. "They are the most competitive in the world. They work the hardest and they work the smartest. I would guess there would probably be some company out of China [which] is most likely to be second to Tesla," he responded during a 2023 earnings call.

BYD's Seagull (credit: Wikimedia Commons)

Western car companies selling to China are not marketing the ones you'll see stateside—they're tiny and their range is not what U.S. consumers are seeking.

"We have this expectation in the U.S. that every weekend we're going to drive from L.A. to Vegas and this car has to be able to go there and back," notes Tyson Jominy, vice president of data and analytics for J.D. Power.

Jominy says that U.S. consumers want a car with 400 miles of range; in China, 200 miles is the typical max.

"China has a number of mega cities, so there is a much more urban environment which favors smaller vehicles with less required charge," Jominy explains. "If we had a better charging network in the U.S., consumers would see that they can drive from Boston to New York in an EV and not worry about running out, even with a smaller battery pack."

In other words, to get cheaper EVs with smaller batteries, a proper charging infrastructure needs to be built out.

A vehicle like the Wuling Hong Gang Mini EV from GM, for example, is available in a two-door convertible or three-door hatchback. It retails for just $5,800 and gets 170 miles on a full charge.

The Wuling Hong Gang Mini EV from GM (credit: Wikimedia Commons)

That's practically micromobility prices (although it's not the norm: The average EV in China retails for $25,000).

The Wuling Hong Guang Mini EV is one of China's best sellers, moving 58,000 units in the first quarter of 2023 alone. GM's joint venture SGMW has made three Mini EVs since 2020; together they've sold over a million units. The Wuling Bin Guo, a tiny four-door EV that's less than 13 feet long, sells for $10,000 and is also popular.

GM has had a tougher time selling its mainstream international brands in China. Chevrolet and Buick sales fell 35%; Cadillac sales were down 32% in 2023.

It's not just the size and price.

"The brand is also a trendsetter that prioritizes emotional value in young consumers, especially female users," GM China's communications team told the *Detroit Free Press*.

China may be going all-in on EVs, but other countries are embracing a hybrid approach. Not electric-gas hybrids, but a two-car family where one car is electric and the other is an ICE vehicle.

"It's important to think about miles driven and not just about vehicles," *BloombergNEF's* head of advanced transport Colin McKerracher told me. EVs are driven more than their ICE counterparts. "This could lead to an outsized environmental impact even if it's 'just' a second car."

EV leasing bypasses loopholes

BYD's super-low-priced Seagull is good news, according to Arnaud Deboeuf, chief manufacturing officer for Stellantis, who said in 2022 that if EVs in general don't get cheaper, "the market will collapse."

Stellantis, which makes Fiats, Rams, Jeeps and Peugeots, among other models and is planning to introduce more than 75 fully electric models this decade, is aiming to cut the cost of making electric vehicles by some 40% by 2030, Deboeuf adds.

Most new EVs still fit into the "luxury" category, where buyers "can bear the price," says Cox Automotive analyst Michelle Krebs. "We saw that with antilock brakes, we saw that with stability control systems, all the new safety features. Those things came first on luxury cars and then moved on down the line."

The same dynamic is now playing out with electric vehicles.

It wasn't always this way—at least not at first. The Nissan Leaf accounted for some 95% of U.S. EV sales in 2011. The price was a reasonable $33,600 at the time for a basic but not particularly sexy vehicle.

Tesla upended the Leaf's monopoly when it introduced the luxury Model S, in 2012, which started at $57,400 for the cheapest version.

The Model S handily displaced the Leaf as the best-selling electric vehicle in the U.S. And other high-priced luxury EV makers—from Rivian to Mercedes, BMW to Volkswagen—are crowding the space.

Financing can help

Perhaps the savviest and most cost-effective way to acquire an EV is to lease it. Indeed, leasing may become the main way that U.S. consumers pay for their EVs. It's based on a loophole in the Inflation Reduction Act (IRA).

The IRA gives U.S. consumers a $7,500 tax credit—but only for EVs made in the U.S. That covers fewer than a dozen EV models.

"They made it complex for a reason, but in the meantime, it's creating all kinds of chaos for consumers," says Chris Harto, senior policy analyst for *Consumer Reports*.

But in an under-the-radar loophole, the IRA classifies leased EVs as "commercial vehicles," for which the $7,500 tax credit *does* apply. Foreign automakers, fearful that they'd be shut out of the tax credits (which indeed they were) lobbied for this carve-out.

It's not just foreign automakers who are predicting a big future for EV leasing.

Marion Harris, CEO of Ford Motor Credit, the automaker's lending arm, expects 60% of EV drivers in the U.S. to lease in the short-term, rather than buy.

That's more than 3 times the 20% lease rate of ICE vehicles.

Hyundai has already seen the bump.

Only 5% of its U.S. sales in 2022 were leases. For the first quarter of 2023, it was up to 28%.

Edmunds' data shows that the total lease rate in the EV space in March 2023 was 34%, up from 7% in September 2022, after the credits law passed. It's now up to 60%.

Jessica Caldwell, executive director of Insights for Edmunds, calls leasing a "no-brainer [since it] allows you to have the credit applied immediately to your monthly payment, rather than waiting to get your money back next year when you file your taxes. Americans don't get quite as excited about waiting."

As a ballpark estimate, a consumer receiving the full $7,500 credit to lease could save around $225 a month over three years.

"We had no plans to lease a car," Gary Murphy of Castle Rock, Colorado, told *The New York Times*. "But when they confirmed you can get $7,500 on a lease, or nothing to buy, that's too big an incentive to pass up."

A survey by Cars.com found that around 80% of people shopping for an EV were swayed by the tax credits.

But leasing may not work for the lower-priced EVs that are expected to make the difference between niche and mass-market adoption. In 2021, 59% of leases were taken by consumers with a credit rating of prime+ and near prime. Individuals with subprime credit ratings, by contrast, comprised only 21% of total leases.

Range anxiety is real

No sooner had Tesla taken steps to reduce price anxiety among potential buyers, when it was hit by a scandal regarding the main gating factor for new EV buyers: range anxiety.

An investigation by *Reuters* found that Tesla has been inflating the miles per charge its EVs get—sometimes claiming double the range that a Tesla can get in inclement weather—while at the same time gaslighting consumers that there's no problem, nothing to look at over here.

Reuters reporter Steve Stecklow discovered that Tesla decided a decade ago to write algorithms for its range meter "that would show drivers 'rosy' projections for the distance it could travel on a full battery." When the battery falls below 50% of its maximum charge, the algorithm would then show drivers a more realistic projection for remaining driving range.

"Elon [Musk] wanted to show good range numbers when fully charged," a Tesla source told *Reuters*. "When you buy a car off the lot seeing 350-mile, 400-mile range, it makes you feel good."

To make matters worse, Tesla set up an internal "Diversion Team" to cancel as many range-related appointments at Tesla repair shops as possible. The cars didn't need repairs—they simply were range-hyped for marketing purposes.

Managers told Tesla employees they were saving the company around $1,000 per canceled appointment. But that left drivers stuck with their underperforming, nonfixable EVs.

Tesla has not been alone in inflating range to drive sales.

Gregory Pannone co-authored a study of 21 different brands of electric vehicles. The results, published in 2023 by the engineering organization SAE International, revealed that, on average, the cars fell short of their advertised ranges by 12.5% in highway driving.

Tesla was among the worst, Pannone told *Reuters,* falling short of advertised ranges by an average of 26%.

Pannone tried to give Tesla the benefit of the doubt. "What they're doing, at least minimally, is leveraging the current procedures more than the other manufacturers."

How much range do you really need?

Ed Niedermeyer, author of *Ludicrous: The Unvarnished Story of Tesla Motors*, points out in a *New York Times* article that the average American motorist drives just 40 miles per day and that 95% of U.S. car trips are 30 miles or shorter.

And yet, consumer demand in the U.S. for more and more range keeps rising.

In 2019, buyers said they wanted 300 miles of range. By 2021, according to findings from Cox Automotive, that was up to 341 miles.

Niedermeyer suggests consumers could buy two cheaper, 150-mile range EVs for the same price as a single EV with a 300-mile battery. Nor should we give up on plug-in hybrids so quickly, he says: Fifty miles of electric range for daily driving and a gas engine for the occasional road trip could be an ideal solution for the near term.

Mike Granoff says we have fallen into "an arms race towards the highest possible range vehicle. That's the wrong way to look at it. If the average consumer drives 30, 40, 50 miles a day, why would you put 10 to 15 times that number of miles in the car [with a huge battery]? You're placing the car out of the price range for most consumers. And it's less efficient because it's heavier. Ninety percent of the time, you're driving around with 'stranded assets' with this enormous battery that only gets used very occasionally."

Quin Garcia concurs.

Garcia, founder and managing director at Autotech Ventures, was an executive in the automotive alliance group at Israeli electric car infrastructure startup Better Place.

"Every increase in range is mainly there to satisfy psychological needs vs. daily consumption needs," he told me. "Most consumers aren't driving more than 30 or 40 miles a day."

Better Place's approach—which we'll discuss in greater detail later in the book—was to offer battery swap as an alternative to plugging in and needing a great big battery to go hundreds of miles.

"To put all the extra range in the infrastructure was, I thought, the right approach," adds Granoff, who was also an executive at Better Place before starting his Maniv Mobility VC firm.

Why is public transportation so poor in the U.S.?

In 1947, there were nine billion streetcar trips in the U.S. In 1972, that number had declined to just 200 million.

Annual per capita public transit trips in the U.S. plummeted from 115 in 1950 to 36 in 1970, where it's roughly remained ever since, even as the country's population has grown.

Chicago had arguably the most extensive and effective streetcar network in the country. Lines operated throughout the night, often with 8- to 10-minute intervals. But by 1957, there was not a single streetcar line left operating in the city.

What happened? Were cars simply more convenient?

Or was there a conspiracy where conglomerates like General Motors and tire maker Firestone, through their ownership stakes in bus operator National City Lines, surreptitiously acquired streetcar lines in order to convert them to gasoline-powered, rubber-tired vehicles?

Nicholas Dagen Bloom is a professor of urban policy and planning at Hunter College. In his 2023 book, *The Great American Transit Disaster*, Bloom argues that money, politics and race were the main culprits.

Buses were originally seen as a technological innovation that improved the transit experience compared with streetcars, Bloom explains. They weren't limited to fixed routes with tracks, they didn't require unsightly wires overhead, transit operators could easily add new lines to serve areas with lower density, and you only needed a single employee on a bus—the driver—rather than two (driver and fare collector) for streetcars.

This was, of course, long before we realized how much damage gasoline-powered vehicles were doing to the environment.

Streetcars and the transit systems that operated them were extremely profitable in the early 20th century. That was because the real money was aligned with real-estate investments, Bloom argues.

"Streetcar lines shortened the time it took for people to travel from city centers or industrial areas and residential areas. By shortening that time, you opened up an empire of land around cities."

In Los Angeles, the city's famous urban sprawl can be traced directly to the expansion of its "interurban" streetcar lines, as they were called, into the former hinterlands.

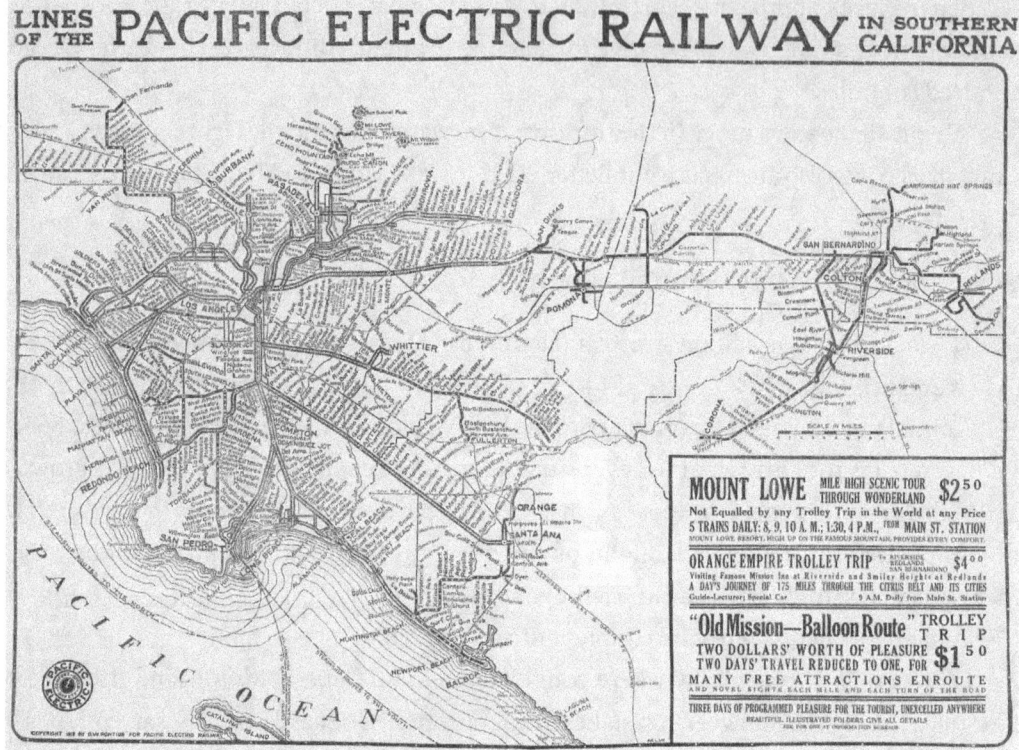

Los Angeles streetcar map (credit: Wikimedia Commons)

Yet, once the lines were built, "the transit companies had declining interest and they let the service deteriorate," Bloom explains. When the streetcars were eventually discontinued, people who had moved to the suburbs were left in the lurch . . . unless they had a car, of course.

Just look at Levittown, New York, infamously known as the "first suburb."

The Long Island Railroad should have made commuting to Manhattan a breeze, but the nearest train station was well outside of town; its service was limited, and the trains were old and dilapidated.

Commuters had no choice but to drive. For those outliers willing to brave the train, vast parking lots were constructed.

In the early days of mass transit, operators were essentially monopolies, which didn't endear them to the public. So, when the streetcar companies started struggling, consumers were unwilling to step up and help.

"You've profited at our expense for a long time," was the public attitude.

"It was hard to shift away from the popular view of the transit company as this evil empire," Bloom says.

Indeed, mass transit companies in the 1920s were as unpopular as cable companies and budget airlines are today!

Yet, suggests Bloom, maybe it's the city planners who should be excoriated here.

Not only did cities refuse to subsidize public transit for decades, but they actually taxed them.

In Atlanta, for example, in the 1960s, five cents out of every thirty-five-cent bus fare went to taxes. And these weren't publicly owned transit systems but private operators!

"Cities became so accustomed to transit being a contributor to municipal budgets that it was very hard to shift that approach until they essentially failed," Bloom says.

City planning didn't help.

As cities started to run highways through the center of urban neighborhoods, and as federal programs gave tax breaks on downtown parking, often making it free to incentivize the growth of city centers, is it any wonder public transportation in the U.S. got hit big time?

There was also the Great Depression, which crushed those companies that did not have New Deal-era federal government funding. That funding eventually shifted almost entirely to highways, where it covered nearly 90% of a new freeway's cost.

Frequency is the key metric

These days, streetcars—or light rail systems, as they're commonly known now—are making a comeback. But, argues Bloom, that won't shift drivers away from their private vehicles.

"The vehicle itself is far less important to riders than the frequency and reliability of whatever shows up," Bloom says.

Buses, streetcars, autonomous vans—consumers don't care as long as it comes often. Yet, frequency is a rare commodity.

Fifteen minutes seems to be the magic number where people can simply show up at a transit stop without consulting a schedule. But that is so far off from service levels in most American cities that even a 30-minute standard would be a stretch.

If a bus comes only once an hour, stops at 7 p.m. and doesn't run on Sundays—a service level typical in many U.S. cities—how many people will choose the bus over a private car?

In the following comparison, you can see how bad it really is. The red lines indicate routes where a bus comes at least every 30 minutes.

+ Columbus, Ohio, does not have a single route that meets the full-service standard of a bus every half an hour.

+ In Charlotte, North Carolina, the newly extended Lynx LRT is improving the situation a little.

Regular bus routes by city (credit: CityLab)

- Denver, Colorado, is adding new light and commuter rail.

- Portland, Oregon, often held up as an example of proactive planning with a large light rail network, doesn't have enough connecting lines.

- Washington, DC's Metro has the same issue as Portland.

- The best of the bunch: Toronto, which shows what a properly planned, high-level of transit service ought to look like in North America. Toronto has suburban sprawl like most other cities, but the frequency of service—which includes a postwar-built subway and a still-functioning streetcar system—means even Toronto's suburbanites are regular transit users.

Race has also played a role.

As wealthier, White residents fled the cities for the suburbs—often on those newly built streetcar lines—transit agencies were increasingly serving non-White inner-city dwellers. In a nation still rocked by racial inequality, it became increasingly harder to convince transit agencies to serve urban customers.

Trends for the future are not optimistic.

In 2020, voters in Austin, Texas, overwhelmingly approved a $7 billion public transit plan which would add two new light rail lines to augment the existing MetroRail service. A downtown subway tunnel would allow trains to bypass traffic-choked streets.

Then the projected costs started going up.

By 2022, the estimate was $10.3 billion. The Austin Transit Partnership (ATP) began trimming the scope of the new lines: Instead of 28 miles of new light rail, the city would get just 6 to 10 miles. The downtown tunnel was taken off the books, at least for the initial phase.

Austin is part of a rash of "resequenced" and downscaled public transit projects in the U.S.

- Philadelphia canceled a light rail extension after cost estimates increased by 50% in three years.

- Atlanta is pausing two planned light rail projects to focus on cheaper bus rapid transit, due to high costs. A proposal to extend the city's MARTA public transit system to suburban Gwinnett County was rejected by voters as recently as 2019.

- The Beverly Hills School District has spent nearly $16 million to fight against the city Metro's Purple Line subway extension, arguing that its construction would disrupt learning at the high school and threaten the health and safety of students.

✦ Another Purple Line, this one in Maryland, has been dogged by lawsuits that claim its construction, which involves dredging in streams and wetlands, is illegal under the Clean Water Act.

"These high costs prohibit us from doing all the good projects that are out there," says Eric Goldwyn, program director for the NYU Marron Institute and co-leader of the Transit Costs Project, which monitors how much it costs to build out public transportation around the world. "And then we don't even debate or discuss them because [the costs are] just so ridiculous."

In Austin, Peter Mullan, executive vice president for architecture and urban design at the ATP, says the original transit plan isn't dead, although "it's probably going to take a little longer than expected because of what we're seeing in terms of cost increases across the board."

What does Bloom suggest can be done to revitalize public transit, reverse the declines of the last half century, and clean up the planet to boot?

It's all about money.

"At the end of the day, someone's got to fund transit. Otherwise, we can end up with almost nothing," Bloom says.

Electric buses overtake diesel in Europe

In contrast to the U.S., in Europe the buses, subways and trolley cars are abundant, fast and relatively cheap.

Now, Europe has surpassed a new milestone. As of May 2023, the share of electric buses over eight tons (the majority) now exceeds the share of diesel-powered buses sold. When you include hybrid buses in the mix, the transition is even more impressive.

City buses make up about 60% of all heavy-duty passenger vehicle sales in Europe (the rest are coaches and interurban buses). The diesel version of these vehicles emits around three-and-a-half pounds of CO2 per mile (one kilogram of CO2 per kilometer). That's a lot more than cars—which emit less than 100 grams of CO2 per kilometer—about one-tenth that of public transport—although, of course, buses carry many more passengers than cars do.

The Netherlands and Denmark have committed to fully phasing out the purchase of diesel buses by 2025. Ireland has set a date of 2030 and Austria will do it by 2032. In total, half of Europe's capital cities plan for only zero-emission buses to roam their roads from 2040.

Natural gas can also play a role.

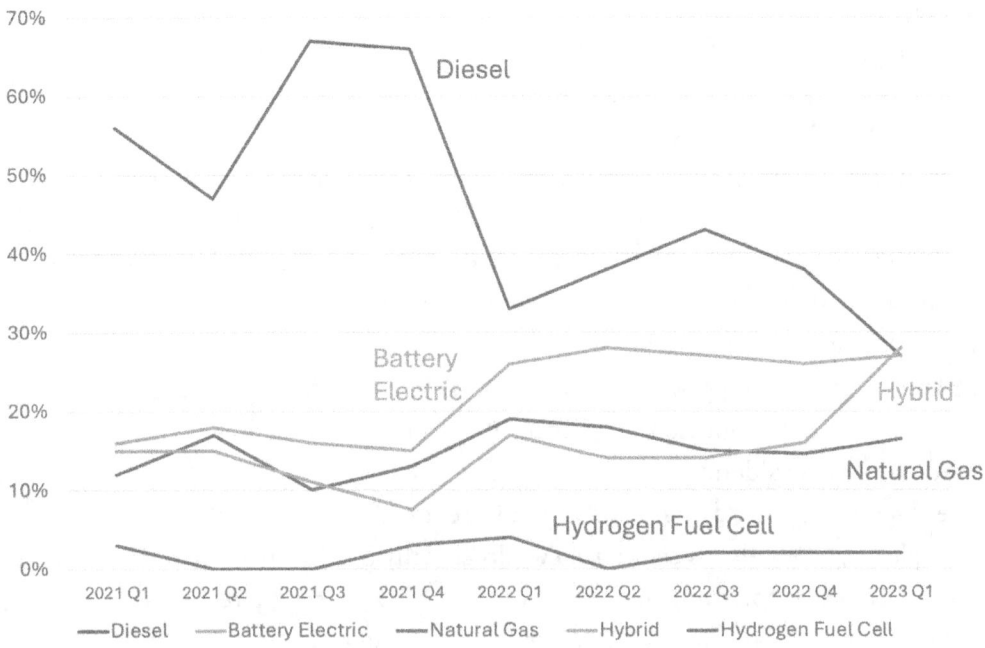

SALES SHARE OF CITY BUSES IN THE EU27 + UK

Share of city buses in the European Union (credit: Chatrou CME Solutions)

The International Council on Clean Transportation (ICCT) reports that buses running on natural gas reduce greenhouse gas emissions by 17% relative to their diesel counterparts. Running a battery electric bus off Europe's grid mix (which includes renewable sources) between 2021 and 2040 could bring a reduction of 75%.

When it comes to electrifying its buses, though, Europe is playing catch-up with China, where 91% of all buses sold in 2022 were zero-emission electric.

Hyperloop hype

Elon Musk's proposed Hyperloop is a form of public transportation. The tech, which promises to hurl passengers at more than six hundred miles an hour through tunnels in levitating autonomous electric pods—think of an air hockey table in a tube—could cut the trip from Los Angeles to San Francisco from six hours to just thirty-five minutes.

Hyperloop attracted lots of hype but, to date, there are no commercial Hyperloops in service. It's not even clear how interested Musk remains in Hyperloop and whether any new Hyperloop installations are going forward.

Bloomberg reported in 2022 that the Hyperloop test site in Hawthorne, California, "has been indefinitely shelved." Hyperloop's test track in California is now a parking lot for employees.

Bloomberg suggests that tunnels that were to be built by the Boring Company (another of Musk's companies) for Hyperloop are now being repurposed for Tesla owners to avoid surface-street-level traffic jams.

Paris Marx, author of *Road to Nowhere: What Silicon Valley Gets Wrong about the Future of Transportation*, and host of the podcast "Tech Won't Save Us," writes that Musk apparently admitted to his biographer that the main reason he'd been so bullish on backing Hyperloop was to stop the state of California from developing its own high-speed rail system.

Hardly an altruistic approach.

In December 2023, Hyperloop One, one of the longest-running hyperloop startups, once backed by Richard Branson, announced it would be shutting down.

Marx says good riddance.

The Hyperloop, he notes, has had "stagnating effects." Basically, anywhere Hyperloop goes, people say, "Well, this is coming, so we don't really need to invest in public transit."

So, was Hyperloop nothing more than a Trojan Horse to sell more Teslas?

If so, self-driving cars are having an even more chilling effect.

Groups funded by the conservative Koch brothers—which have big investments in the oil industry—have weaponized a future filled with autonomous vehicles as part of their argument to fight against new public transit projects.

"If self-driving cars are going to be here in a couple of years, why would you invest in this outdated infrastructure?" Marx asks, referring to public transit systems.

That hasn't stopped some cities and states from beefing up rail as an alternative.

The U.S. Federal Rail Authority in late 2023 finalized its environmental review for part of Brightline's project to run a bullet train between Los Angeles and Las Vegas. The Authority concluded "no significant impacts" for the planned forty-nine-mile line that would be located between Rancho Cucamonga and Victorville and run on the median of the I-15 freeway.

Another Brightline project, between Miami and West Palm Beach, opened in 2018. In September 2023, Brightline launched a second high-speed line in Florida, between Miami and Orlando. The three-and-a-half-hour train ride is thirty minutes shorter than driving by car.

Who moved my parking spot?

One of the biggest benefits to using public transportation, of course, is that you don't have to circle endlessly looking for parking when you arrive.

While on paper the United States, with its vast open spaces, doesn't have a parking problem ("There are three parking spots per car in the U.S.," notes Larry Burns, who served as GM's vice president of research and development until 2012), enter a city and you'll find yourself searching for an average of seventeen to twenty-one minutes to find street parking during the day.

It's not just an inconvenience: Some 30% of traffic in cities is generated by people on the prowl for parking.

It's a vicious circle: More cars circling equals more pollution.

Parking apps have stepped in to solve the issue, but "even if the technology enables you to know in real time where an open parking spot will be, it's impossible to save it for the next driver," explains Zohar Bali, CEO of sPARK, which developed the parking app Polly. "In a busy city, the spot will be gone in five to fifteen seconds."

There's nevertheless no shortage of apps helping harried drivers find their dream parking spot. In addition to sPARK, here are some of the other companies I'm watching:

✦ **Parko** uses GPS to sense a driver's speed. When the vehicle stops and the speed at which the phone was moving has slowed to a comfortable "walking pace," Parko assumes the user has parked. When Parko senses the driver is returning in the direction of the parked car, the app sends a message to other Parko subscribers that a spot may soon open up. Parko was acquired by EasyPark of Sweden in 2016.

✦ **Parknav** "takes data from many sources—cell-tower data, mobile-payment data, car-sharing data, data from sensors in the car and satellite imaging—and we combine it into predictions," explains Eyal Amir, the company's CEO. From that, Parknav calculates a percentage. "Green means you have at least an 80% chance of finding a spot on a particular street. Anything below 40% we color red."

✦ **Parkam** taps into existing cameras—speed cameras, security cameras—to assemble real-time data on open spaces. "If we need to add more cameras, we can place them on top of existing poles," says Asaf Naamani, CEO of Parkam.

✦ **SpotHero** (formerly Parking Panda) is a parking reservation service that works with different facilities to provide customers with parking in major U.S. cities. Customers can find, reserve, and pay for a parking spot in a lot or garage, often at a discounted rate. The parking pass is delivered via email or through the app. SpotHero has partnerships with sports venues including Dodger Stadium in Los Angeles and Yankee Stadium in New York.

✦ **Parkopedia** keeps tabs on more than 70 million parking spots in 89 countries. It will find the closest spot for your car, tell you in advance how much it will cost and how many spaces are available. The company calls itself the "parking partner" for automotive manufacturers including GM, Ford, Mazda, and Volvo.

Eyes on the ground and in the sky

Can a parking app ever know if there will be an *actual* spot available?

"No, it's a best guess," Amir, of Parknav, admits. "But it's a precise guess."

Polly's algorithm, for example, can tell you your chance of finding on-street parking at 10 a.m. in downtown Chicago is 22% if you circle for 11 minutes.

Taking away the guesswork from finding street parking is what Pumba Parking is all about. The company uses existing cameras in a city—and encourages citizens to buy one of Pumba's IoT cameras that can be connected to the company's parking servers.

The cameras take photographs of the street every 10 seconds, notifying the Pumba network of drivers when a space becomes available. If that open spot is subsequently taken, Pumba will suggest the closest nearby alternative.

The service is available as a subscription. If you host a sensor in your house or apartment, you can get it for free.

Pumba claims that it can reduce the time drivers search for parking by 60%, cut traffic congestion by 20%, and bring down CO_2 emissions by 15%.

Another parking startup, Wisesight, also uses captured image data to analyze traffic and parking patterns, guide motorists to vacant spots, categorize parking places (hourly, daily, subscription, exclusively for disabled drivers), monitor reserved spots and enhance security. Wisesight can be embedded into existing payment apps, from where it can send the vehicle owner a text message reminder, generate an invoice, or alert city parking inspectors if necessary.

One limitation of all parking apps is that they're not Google Maps or Waze. Alphabet's GPS navigation programs have far more functionality than most apps that have a single function: finding street parking. Parkam's Naamani suggests drivers continue using their favorite navigation app and then switch to a parking app "for the last mile."

Eventually, those apps will get better navigation—maybe through partnering with a Google or Apple—and more functionality that goes beyond parking.

"In 10 to 20 years, you'll be able to see if a Starbucks is open, if there is a table available with four seats outside and if they didn't run out of almond milk yet," Amir says.

How "parking explains the world"

Henry Grabar is the author of *Paved Paradise: How Parking Explains the World*. Parking drives us crazy, Grabar said on an episode of the *Freakonomics* podcast, because "in almost every place in this country, it is obligatory to have a car, and there is almost nothing you can do without a car."

The other issue making parking so miserable is that it is "not properly priced. We have acquiesced to the idea that parking on city streets has to be a total free-for-all."

What does Grabar think we need to do about pricing? Raise it.

"If you institute a parking fee, you'll find out exactly how many people are willing to pay to park there. If you keep raising prices until you always have spots available, you'll find out exactly how high it needs to be to create a few open spots on every block. It might seem like it only takes you a couple of minutes to find a spot for free, but the net effect is thousands of miles of driving every day across the United States."

Won't people who are used to parking on the street for free resent the imposition of new and higher fees?

"Yes," Grabar says, "but now, you won't have to stress anymore because you'll know there'll be a parking spot where you want it."

One might think, with all the problems this book has set out to address through improvements in mobility, that parking is the least of our issues.

Grabar disagrees.

"Time is money," he says, "and circling around the block and not knowing when you can find a spot or leaving 20 minutes early to find a spot to park, that's a cost as well."

Free street parking is a scourge: In New York City, some 97% of the curb spaces in the 5 boroughs are free. A 6-month study conducted by the consulting group *Transportation Alternatives* covering a 15-block area of the Upper West Side found that:

+ Motorists "cruise" a total of 366,000 miles a year as they search for metered parking in the 15-block survey area on Columbus Avenue. For comparison, that's farther than a one-way trip to the moon.

+ Drivers cruise on average 7 blocks (0.37 miles) to find a metered parking space. During peak periods, before lunch and from 6 to 8:00 p.m., motorists cruise an average of 14 blocks (0.7 miles) before finding a parking spot.

+ Drivers searching for curbside parking in the survey area generate 325 tons of CO_2 annually.

+ On metered blocks, curb parking is completely occupied up to half the time. Unmetered blocks are completely full up to 75% of the time.

+ The average vehicle parks for 93 minutes. Posted "One-Hour Parking" regulations are rarely observed or enforced. Each metered parking spot turns over 5.8 times per day. Each unmetered spot turns over 2.3 times per day.

✦ Between 28% and 45% of traffic on some streets in the survey area is generated by cruising for parking.

What's the right price for higher street parking fees?

In his 2005 book, *The High Cost of Free Parking*, Donald Shoup, an urban planning professor at UCLA, says the market should decide. Making the real-world costs of parking more transparent would benefit everyone, he contends. If cities simply charged for street spots according to market demand, drivers would likely relinquish them faster, freeing them up for use by others.

Grabar envisions cities with higher-priced, less available parking. He favors converting space currently reserved for parking to curbside dining for restaurants, planting new trees and gardens, and closing some streets—for example, outside of schools—so kids have a safe place to play.

"Those aren't even particularly expensive or ambitious ideas," Grabar stresses. "They just depend on 25 car owners saying, all right, we'll give up our rights to this little strip of land."

Transportation Alternatives proposes several changes:

✦ Raising curbside prices during peak periods and lowering them during off-peak to ensure the availability of one open space per block at all times.

✦ Running meters throughout the evening while restaurants and bars are still open in order to maintain parking turnover after 7 p.m.

✦ Replacing ineffective one-hour parking regulations with graduated metered rates that charge more for additional hours to encourage turnover. New York City has a "Commercial Congestion Parking Program" running in midtown. It charges $2 for the first hour, $5 for the second and $9 for the third.

✦ Installing parking meters that accept credit cards and enable more flexible pricing.

What would cities do with all the new revenue?

Use it to pay for public services, says Shoup. This includes repairing sidewalks and other improvements.

In an article in *Bloomberg,* Shoup notes that Boulder, Colorado, uses its downtown meter revenue to buy transit passes for all downtown workers. Drivers who park on the street essentially subsidize commuters who ride the bus.

The need for a similar arrangement in New York City is just as strong.

Charging for some or all of the Upper West Side's 12,300 currently free curb spaces would earn the city $237 million a year.

"Suppose the city spends this revenue to buy an MTA transit pass ($33 a week) for each of the Upper West Side's 110,000 households," Shoup continues. "The total cost would be $189 million a year. The remaining revenue could be used to clean and maintain the Upper West Side's 14 subway stations. Curb parkers would improve life for many more transit riders. Parking revenue would pay the transit fares, and the fare-free transit for residents would boost MTA ridership."

To use a medical metaphor, "streets resemble a city's blood vessels, and overcrowded free curb parking resembles plaque on the vessel walls, leading to a stroke. Market prices for curb parking prevent urban plaque," Shoup adds.

What we've learned

+ While passenger electric vehicles may very well have been around for over one hundred years, they've only just recently (re)gained the attention of consumers.

+ Only time will tell if the U.S. market will end up looking like Norway, where the vast majority of new passenger vehicle sales are EVs.

+ In the meantime, there are many great opportunities to invest in companies that will benefit from the trend toward alternative power sources and the infrastructure to support these new sources of power.

Are you wondering why we didn't delve deeper into micromobility in this chapter on ground transport? And why we didn't really touch on autonomy, alternative power sources or vehicle connectivity? Have no fear, we will cover these topics—and more!—in the chapters to come.

■　■　■

Chapter 2

Micromobility

Mike Granoff *would seem to be the ultimate EV owner* and advocate. A former executive at Israeli electric car startup Better Place, Granoff now runs Maniv Mobility, a venture capital firm focused exclusively on mobility investments.

But Granoff doesn't own an electric car himself. He doesn't really drive anywhere on his own, he told me.

Rather, if he needs to get to a meeting in Tel Aviv, he gets a lift to the train station. When he arrives, if his meeting is not near the train station, he either grabs a scooter, e-bike or, on occasion, order a taxi using Gett (Uber and Lyft are not available in Israel).

When he's in New York, he'll often grab a CitiBike, he tells me. Only if he needs to get out of town will he rent a vehicle.

Granoff says he ran the numbers and found that his non-car-owning strategy saves him thousands of dollars a year, not to mention the hassle of sitting in traffic and then trying to find a street parking space.

"I prefer anything than having to sit in traffic and not be productive and be frustrated and then having to park," he says.

Micromobility—encompassing e-scooters, e-bikes, and NEVs (Neighborhood Electric Vehicles)—has become an integral part of the mobility landscape in many urban environments.

It's been like that for many years in Asia.

"Growing up in Vietnam, a car was never a thing," Dong Tran, the founder of e-motorcycle startup Ryvid, says. Tran lived in Vietnam until he was 10 years old. "Cars were something I knew existed, but it was so beyond my comprehension—getting into a box that's covered!"

Changing rites of passage

Micromobility has the advantage that, in general, you don't need a driver's license to operate an e-bike or e-scooter.

Indeed, getting a driving license was once a nearly universal rite of passage into adulthood. No more.

Now it's something that a growing minority of young people either ignore—or actively oppose. The result is more support for big city anti-car policies.

It's a stunning turnaround from the U.S. Supreme Court's statement in 1977 that having a car was a "virtual necessity" for anyone living in America.

+ In 1997, 43% of the country's 16 year olds had driving licenses.

+ Fast forward to 2020 when that number had fallen to just 25%.

+ One in five Americans between the ages of 20 and 24 does not have a driver's license, compared with just 1 in 12 in 1983.

+ In the U.K., the percentage of teens able to drive almost halved, from 41% to 21% in the past 20 years.

Other indicators that the age of hulking car ownership may be coming to an end:

+ Between 1990 and 2017, the distance driven by teenage drivers in America declined by 35%. For those between the ages of 20 and 34, it dropped by 18%.

+ Car ownership for Gen Z is down too. A survey conducted by the Center for Automotive eMobility Innovation at Ca' Foscari University's Department of Management in Venice, Italy, found that one person in five (20%) in this demographic said they were not interested in owning a car.

+ Bankrate estimates that only about 80% of Gen Zers between the age of 20 to 25 had a driver's license in 2020—a 10% drop compared to Millennials when they were the same age.

What's behind this shift?

+ Online shopping has removed the need for the classic mall outing.

+ Streaming Netflix has hurt movie theater attendance.

✦ A rise in poorly paid or insecure jobs and a decline in home ownership among young people lowers demand.

✦ The rise of ride-sharing apps is also contributing.

This could all be considered part of the unbundling of transportation. We're seeing a decoupling of the type of trips that would have historically been done in a car.

Pollution drives changes

In 2006, I was spending a lot of time in China. Air pollution was horrendous back then (it still is). Most days, you never saw blue sky in Beijing or Shanghai unless there was a brisk wind blowing the pollution out of the cities.

Shanghai imposed restrictions for vehicle entry back in 1975. The rules were based on the last digit of your license plate. Even numbers could enter one day, odd numbers the next. Very affluent people might own two cars—one with an even-digit and one with an odd one—while those with less means tend to opt for micromobility.

The need to curtail pollution—now, not later—has become paramount. Scientists examined pollution data from air-monitoring stations in 6,475 cities and 117 countries, regions, and territories around the world to see how many places had average PM2.5 emissions levels in 2021 that fell below five micrograms per cubic meter (the air quality standard set that year by the World Health Organization). The scientists found that *not a single country* measured up to this standard. Just 222 cities—about 3.4%—made the grade.

A few key findings:

✦ Some 93 cities had average annual PM2.5 concentrations that were more than 10 times higher than the WHO standards.

✦ The five most polluted countries were Chad, Iraq, Pakistan, Bahrain, and Bangladesh.

✦ Central and South Asia had 46 of the world's 50 most polluted cities. Just two cities in these regions—Zhezqazghan and Chu in Kazakhstan—met WHO air quality standards.

✦ In Africa, only one of 65 cities examined met the WHO air quality standards. In Asia, just four of 1,887 cities in the analysis met WHO standards. It was only slightly better in Europe, where 55 of 1,588 cities achieved this.

✦ In the U.S., average PM2.5 levels in 2,408 cities climbed from 9.6 micrograms per cubic meter (mcg/m³) in 2020 to 10.3 mcg/m³ in 2021. Atlanta and Minneapolis saw significant increases in pollution. Los Angeles was the worst offender, although its average levels of PM2.5 actually decreased 6% from 2020 to 2021.

2022 AVERAGE PM2.5 CONCENTRATION
(micrograms per cubic meter)

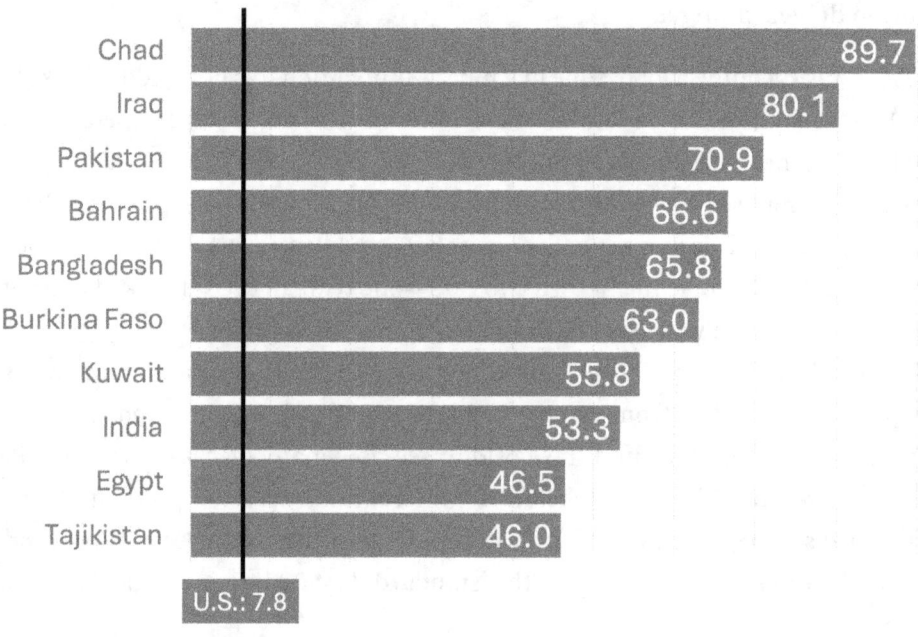

Chad	89.7
Iraq	80.1
Pakistan	70.9
Bahrain	66.6
Bangladesh	65.8
Burkina Faso	63.0
Kuwait	55.8
India	53.3
Egypt	46.5
Tajikistan	46.0
U.S.: 7.8	

Particulate emissions in the worst offending cities (credit: IQAir)

Congestion fees are catching on

A key tool for cities desperate for cleaner air is the legislation of "congestion fees" for entering downtown areas with a private vehicle during peak hours.

✦ New York City was due to put such a policy into effect in the second quarter of 2024.

✦ London, Milan, and Stockholm previously enacted such policies.

✦ Los Angeles is considering adding congestion pricing as well.

It's not a surprising trend: Congestion is expensive.

According to a 2019 study by Texas A&M's Transportation Institute: "Urban congestion causes Americans to travel an additional 8.8 billion hours while burning an extra 3.3 billion gallons of fuel, costing the economy an estimated $179 billion."

The average American's income is just over $26/hour. If that average person spends about 48 minutes driving each day, "That means the value of driving is just over $20 or about $7,600 a year per person," writes Olaf Sakkers, founder of RedBlue Capital, which invests in mobility startups. "That's more than $1 trillion worth of labor invested into driving when multiplied across the American workforce."

Here's how some major cities are adopting congestion pricing.

+ When Singapore added entry restrictions in 1975, traffic was reduced by 20% within mere months.

+ More recently, Brussels put into place its "Good Move Plan" limiting vehicular movement in the center of town; within the first year, car traffic had dropped by 25%, noise was reduced, and bicycle use was up 16% (36% if we go back to 2021).

+ Lisbon ran a three-month trial in 2023 barring cars from driving through (but not from driving to) the heart of Lisbon's downtown. The ban covered most vehicles over 3.5 metric tons—including tourist buses but excluding public transit—between 8 a.m. and 8 p.m.

How much will it cost?

Montreal has taken a different approach. A 2019 paper from the Communaute Metropolitane de Montreal proposed congestion fees there that would be based on the weight of a vehicle. The city previously based permit prices on engine size.

A permit for a vehicle weighing 1,249 kilograms (2,748 pounds) or less, applicable for gas-powered or non-plug-in hybrid vehicles, would, according to the proposal, cost $115. Over 1,600 kilograms (3,520 pounds), the price jumps to $205.

At those rates, the only way to get the lower price would be to drive a tiny Toyota Yaris.

For owners of electric or plug-in hybrids, the weight limit goes up: $115 for up to 1,550 kilograms (3,410 pounds) and $205 for a vehicle weighing more than 1,850 kilograms (4,070 pounds).

Per the proposal, it will cost $385 to obtain a sticker for a second vehicle, regardless of weight.

The city of Lyon, France, is taking a similar approach, enforcing increased parking charges based on a car's weight as of 2024. Low-income families and those with more than three children (who constitute some 60% of the population of Lyon) will benefit from a reduced parking tariff.

In New York City, weight doesn't seem to be a consideration.

The city proposed charging motorists as much as $23 to drive south of 60th Street during peak hours and $17 off-peak. The fee was to be daily and would apply to both passenger cars owned by individuals and for-hire vehicles like Uber and Lyft. EZPass drivers earning less than $50,000 a year would receive a 25% discount starting on their 11th trip within a calendar month—the Metropolitan Transit Authority (MTA) estimates that about 16,000 drivers would qualify.

Vehicles carrying people with disabilities and authorized emergency vehicles would be exempt from the new fees. In addition, people whose primary residence is inside the district and who have an annual income of less than $60,000 would be eligible for a state tax credit equal to the amount of the new tolls.

However, in June 2024, New York Governor Kathy Hochul paused the plan "indefinitely" citing the potential adverse economic impact on commuters, NYC residents and businesses recovering from the Covid lockdowns. "A $15 charge may not mean a lot to someone who has the means, but it can break the budget of a working- or middle-class household. It puts the squeeze on the very people who make this city go: the teachers, first responders, small business workers, bodega owners."

In neighboring New Jersey, Governor Phil Murphy has taken a similar approach, saying his state's residents shouldn't have to pay for the MTA's revenue troubles. Murphy has vowed to stop any fees across the Hudson River.

The revenue generated by the congestion fee—like Henry Grabar's proposed increased curb parking costs—was intended to improve the MTA's subway and bus infrastructure which has been suffering from reduced ridership as a result of the pandemic.

Congestion fees could raise as much as $1 billion annually in New York City.

Taxi drivers weren't thrilled either. If they aren't exempted from the fees, warns Bhairavi Desai, head of the New York Taxi Workers Alliance, it would be "an absolute slap on the face clearly meant to vanish this industry."

Any congestion fee for New York City would come on top of a 2019 congestion surcharge that added $2.50 for all trips south of 96th Street in Manhattan. For-hire vehicles pay $2.75. All fees go to the MTA.

Congestion fees supercharge EV trips in London

In London, drivers of diesel and gasoline-powered cars pay as much as $30.72 to enter the center of London. That's not only reduced congestion but has supercharged the city's

EV transition, as electric cars and taxis are not subject to the same fees. Uber now does a greater share of trips with EVs in London than in any other major city. It's brought London's pollution index on par with comparably-sized cities such as Madrid.

For London Mayor Sadiq Khan, the issue is personal.

Khan was diagnosed with adult-onset asthma after completing the London Marathon in 2014. He blames it on the city's pollution.

"I knew nothing about this hidden killer," he told *The New York Times*. "You can't see things like particulate matter. But me, running along the roads, I'd actually been breathing in poison."

Greater London now has more than 10,000 EV charge points.

London first instituted a £5 fee on combustion vehicles entering the city center in 2003. In 2019, that was upped to £12.50 for older, higher-emission vehicles. Greater London's "Ultra Low Emission Zone" covers 3.8 million residents.

"I'd like to wave my green flag and say 'Yeah, I'm an eco-warrior,' but my switch to electric was initially about money," Charlie Holding, an Uber driver, told *The New York Times*.

Starting in 2025, even electric vehicles will need to pay a congestion charge to enter London's center.

Congestion in China

Cities like Beijing are so congested, consultant Glenn Mercer told me, that (unless you already own a car) you can't buy a new one without getting a license plate first—and the government regulates the number of plates issued annually. For years now, there has been a lottery-type system for acquiring new plates in China's capital. And the state adjusts that lottery to promote electric-vehicle sales. Thus, in both 2022 and 2023, when Beijing released 100,000 additional license plate slots, 70,000 were set aside for electric vehicles, and only 30,000 for ICE cars. "You can see how this would boost battery electric vehicle demand in that city," Mercer notes.

Will some cities take an even more radical move by limiting or banning private cars (and/or just ICE vehicles) from entering the city center entirely?

The 15-Minute City

Several major metropolises, including Paris and Brussels, are taking the congestion fee concept to another level. These cities are examining ways to update infrastructure and amenities to make it possible for residents to access food, shopping, schools, sports and medical facilities without having to travel more than 15 minutes, preferably on foot. It's not as radical as an outright ban, and I believe that gives it a greater chance for success.

The initiative has been dubbed the "15-Minute City," and nowhere has the change been more dramatic than in Paris.

Paris Mayor Anne Hidalgo removed parking spots, narrowed streets and turned a motorway that used to run along one bank of the Seine into a park. In 2021, she announced plans to redevelop the Champs-Elysées to reduce the space allotted to cars by 50%, emphasizing pedestrians and urban greenery instead.

Hidalgo won a second term in part on her jumping wholeheartedly into the 15-Minute City concept.

The resulting boost in livability can be seen in the U.S., too, in New York City, where vehicles have been banned in Central Park below 72nd Street since 2018.

Price can be a strong motivating factor.

In the U.S., the AAA estimates that the average cost of owning a vehicle and driving 15,000 miles in it rose by 13% between 2022 and 2023 to just over $12,000.

Walking is a free and healthy alternative. But it's not always feasible.

"People walk less in the United States because it's more dangerous to walk here and walking conditions are worse compared to other countries," explains Ralph Buehler, professor of urban affairs and planning at Virginia Tech. "So, we're caught in a bit of a spiral that discourages walking and encourages driving."

Buehler published an article in the journal *Sustainability* revealing that, overall, Americans walk less than individuals in many other countries while also having a higher fatality rate per mile walked.

Americans make fewer than half the walking trips per day compared to Britons yet are about six times more likely to be killed while walking per mile traversed.

That said, Americans still saw a 26% decline in pedestrian fatalities per capita from 1990 to 2020. That sounds good until you compare it with the U.K., where the drop in fatalities was 78%.

"You don't know where to look anymore as a driver or as a pedestrian," says Elie Wurtman, of the Jerusalem-based venture capital firm PICO Partners.

His frustration is not reserved for cars.

"There are two-wheelers coming at you from every direction. So, just like cars require roads, two-wheelers will require more than the lanes currently being built for bikes."

Clearly marked, well-lit sidewalks and crosswalks along with safety islands built into intersection corners and medians could help. But do American city planners have the will?

"What interests me most is making environments safe for pedestrians. It's the Halloween candy test," says Reilly Brennan of Trucks VC. "Would you want your kids to trick-or-treat in that neighborhood? Are the cars safe and not going too fast, so that you're not worried about your children's safety? It's a nice rubric for thinking about street design: If you live on one of those blocks, you can tell there are a lot of great benefits."

Another way to promote micromobility: tax breaks and subsidies.

You get nothing today for buying an e-bike," RedBlue Capital's Olaf Sakkers, told me, "even though the efficiency is way higher and the draw on the electric grid is a minuscule fraction of what electric cars require. E-bikes also don't damage the road, make noise and mutilate people when they crash. Cars do. It's totally upside down"

Walking may be dangerous in America, but micromobility faces challenges of its own—even in mobility-friendly Europe.

A cautionary tale on two wheels

Paris is promoting the 15-Minute City concept while, at the same time, trying to ban the very micromobility vehicles that would make that city more livable.

In April 2023, 89% of Parisians who took part in a referendum on rental e-scooters in the city voted to ban the vehicles from the streets of the French capital. Very few Parisians turned out for the vote—only about 100,000, less than 7.5% of those eligible—but Mayor Hidalgo said she would respect the nonbinding vote and allow all existing micromobility rental contracts to expire as of September 1, 2023.

That shouldn't be altogether shocking: Despite her backing of the 15-Minute City, Hidalgo helped lead the campaign against e-scooters, describing them as a "nuisance."

Before the ban, Paris had about 15,000 shared micromobility vehicles zipping around town.

"Why weren't more people in favor of e-scooters not motivated enough to take part in the vote?" wonders Roger Woodman, an assistant professor of human factors at the University of Warwick.

"Scooter operators and supporters were [apparently] not able to motivate the many thousands of scooter users to vote in this case, which is a bit of a sad thing," adds McKinsey micromobility expert Kersten Heineken.

Did micromobility hit Paris and other cities too early?

When the first Bird electric scooters descended on Santa Monica in late 2017, the city was entirely unprepared. Reckless riders without helmets were running roughshod over sidewalks and pedestrians, causing accidents, and leaving their discharged Birds strewn over pedestrian walkways and streets. It was a mess.

Brennan doesn't get it.

"We were a one-car family for a decade," he told me. "Now we have two e-bikes. My vision is that, in the same way wealthy people provide funds for museum wings, I'd like to see people donating to build protected bike lanes. These should then show up on Google Maps with the donor's name."

The "Steve Greenfield Bike Parkway" perhaps?

"We need to get designers to make streets that are usable for people," Brennan adds. "The U.S. is too car-centric. Walkability is a good first step."

Ownership of scooters

Paris left one loophole in its micromobility backlash: Privately owned scooters are still permitted.

McKinsey looked at whether consumers prefer to own their own e-scooters or rent them via shared services like Lime or Bird. Some 64% said they preferred private ownership. Another 23% preferred either operational leasing or subscription. Only 13% of respondents were interested in some kind of shared service.

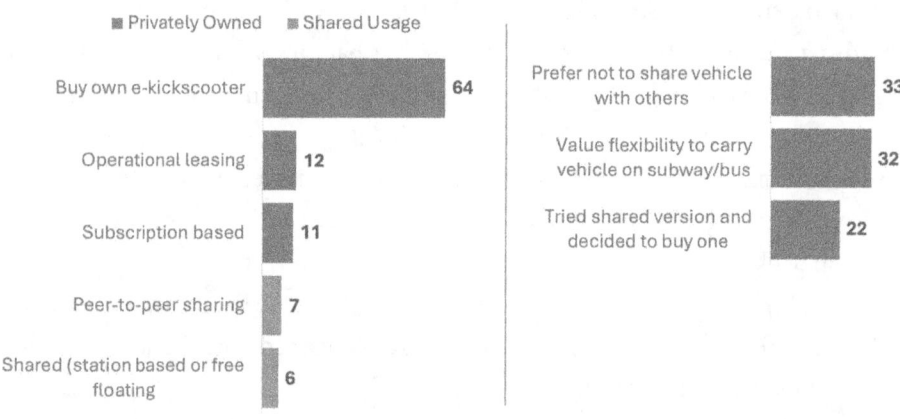

The vast majority of people would rather own their e-kickscooter. (credit: McKinsey & Company)

What's behind the preference for ownership? Respondents cited several reasons:

✦ 33% stated that they did not want to share a scooter with others.

✦ 32% wanted the flexibility to carry their scooter onto a subway or bus.

✦ 22% of respondents stated that they decided to purchase a private e-scooter after trying one out in a sharing service.

While scooters will undoubtedly still maintain a mix of private ownership and shared use, sharing a car is an open question.

I spoke with Andrea Amico, CEO of Privacy4Cars, which has developed software allowing customers to delete their personal data from their connected vehicles. Automotive Ventures is an investor in the company.

"Cars today are giant laptops," he told me. "Can you imagine that the future of the office is shared laptops, where you come into the office and pick up your computer for the day? No IT person is going to find this acceptable. The same will be true with car-sharing."

And e-scooters likewise, apparently.

While scooters make sense financially, no one has figured out a business model yet that allows them to be profitable. Many of the early players have gone bankrupt, and the remaining players have explored pretty aggressive pricing increases.

Cities may very well cap both the number of scooter vendors permitted, as well as limit the total number of scooters overall.

Reversal of bans

Paris is not alone in its scooter backlash.

Copenhagen and Montreal banned them in 2020, although the Danish capital allowed them to return in June 2021—albeit under strict conditions.

Among the new Scandinavian rules that brought 3,200 scooters back into the city:

✦ Scooters cannot be rented from locations within the city center.

✦ They can only be parked in one of 240 designated areas, not dumped anywhere the rider sees fit.

✦ Inappropriately parked scooters will be picked up, with the cost—about $60 per unit—billed to the provider.

Several U.S. cities that previously banned e-scooters and e-bikes have since reversed those restrictions.

✦ Dallas and St. Louis banned micromobility operators in 2020. In May 2023, they let them back in.

- ✦ In Santa Monica, scooters can no longer be ridden on sidewalks anywhere in the city, nor can scooters be piloted on the city's scenic beach path or on the tourist-friendly pedestrian Third Street Promenade.

- ✦ Atlanta, Cleveland, Cincinnati, Colorado Springs, Nashville and Richmond, Virginia, have all reversed curfews that had prohibited riding after dark.

When the bans were lifted, some upsetting reasons were revealed. It seems that conservative leaders, confronting a new and confusing technology, simply opted to shut it down entirely rather than take action to improve safety. Drunk riding tests, stricter age restrictions and dedicated parking for scooters can make the experience more pleasant for all involved—riders, pedestrians, and cars. So, why not explore them?

Regulating scooter use

Four archetypes for regulating e-scooters have emerged:

- ✦ Thirty-five cities, with a cumulative 290 million people, ban scooters. This archetype is mostly driven by China, where 75% of the population lives in cities that don't allow e-scooter use at all!

- ✦ "Tender regulated" refers to cities that allow e-scooter use but only under specific limitations, including the age of the driver, maximum speed and a defined riding area. Washington, DC and Los Angeles are in this group.

- ✦ "Open but regulated environment" cities don't limit which or how many companies can operate but do impose other regulations, similar to the tender-regulated archetype.

- ✦ Twenty-nine out of the 100 cities McKinsey looked at have no regulations for e-scooters at all. Nine of these cities are in India.

Micromobility manufacturers have responded by unveiling 10 recommendations for scooter best practices. Lime, Void, Dots, TIER Mobility and Superpedestrian collaborated to create a framework—a rare moment of working together in this highly competitive industry. Together, these 5 companies operate 750,000 vehicles across 37 countries.

Here's what they recommend:

1. Limiting the number of operators in a city to avoid oversaturation. In markets with 1,000 to 2,000 scooters, 2 operators should be the maximum. In markets with more than 2,000 scooters, 3 operators can be licensed.

2. There should be no more than 80 to 120 vehicles per square kilometer (207 to 310 vehicles per square mile) in order to balance reliability with tidiness.

3. Contracts with a city should last for a minimum of two years for trial runs and three to four years for permanent programs. Anything less won't give the operators time to evaluate if the service is working, nor will it allow space for sufficient consumer adoption.

4. Fees should be consistent across operators. That makes it easier for consumers to choose and ensures that operators don't withdraw from a market due to unsustainable fees they may have set themselves in an effort to win the bid. Fees should be similar to those for bike-sharing.

5. Data must be uniform and easily shared through the Mobile Data Specification (MDS) and General Bikeshare Feed Specification (GBFS) protocols which facilitate consistent submission of information to cities while keeping user identification private.

6. Tenders are the best way to select micromobility operators. Financial contributions (such as city fees or user pricing) should never be used, as they tend to create unsustainable market conditions where operators overpromise and ultimately abandon a market.

7. The operating area should maximize access to destinations throughout the city. If that's not possible, then operating areas should at least be contiguous and connect people in the neighborhoods with the cultural, business and recreational hubs of the city.

8. Don't forget parking: There must be plenty of it close to where riders start and end their trips. The consortium recommends 25 parking bays per square kilometer (64 per square mile) and a minimum of 3 parking spots for each scooter. (That means 1,000 scooters require 3,000 parking spots.)

9. Limit speeds to 25 kilometers/hour (15 miles/hour—consistent with other vehicles such as e-bikes). But don't make the speed limit too slow: Capping speeds below 20 kilometers/hour (12 miles/hour) actually *increases* the safety risks for riders of micromobility vehicles and incentivizes users to ride on the sidewalk alongside pedestrians.

10. Helmets should be encouraged but not made mandatory. Helmet requirements discourage the uptake of micromobility and may exacerbate social inequalities. Covid-19 also led riders to shun shared helmets.

The final point about helmets is the only one on the list I disagree with: Too many riders have been injured by not wearing helmets. It may reduce usage but fewer live riders is better than a greater number of dead ones.

The case for micromobility

The case for micromobility can be seen in this one key statistic: "More than 50% of commute miles globally are undertaken on two-wheelers," says David Roberts, host of the mobility podcast *Volts*.

"Scooters are huge in developing countries," Roberts told me, "but they're horrifically polluting at the moment. They're worse than cars. Technology may be able to solve this problem."

Analysis from *ReportLinker* predicts that, by 2030, there will be 76.8 million scooters, motorcycles, and mopeds in operation. While the U.S. only had an estimated 430,000 units in 2022 according to *ReportLinker*, China is projected to reach a market size of 12.4 million units by 2030.

"It's tempting to look at EVs like the Ford F-150 Lightning as game changers," writes Brian Kahn in *Protocol*. "But two-wheelers are already driving the EV transition. The inherent efficiency and affordability of small, two-wheeled EVs mean they could play a vital role in speeding it along [and in] reducing carbon emissions more effectively than fleets of Teslas ever could."

That said, "we have to stop fighting the car," says Michael Sena, publisher of the automotive newsletter *The Dispatcher*.

Sena points to Boston, which has built a "series of intermodal transit systems with large parking facilities. You can use your car to get to where you need to go quickly, just not to the center of town. It's logical, not rocket science."

Micromobility is also where battery swap continues to thrive—manual battery switches from vending machines keep scooters, e-bikes, and rickshaws running consistently. We'll delve into the history of battery swap for cars in more detail in the chapter on battery technologies.

The 15-minute conspiracy theory

Micromobility makes cities more livable. So how did the 15-Minute City turn into a conspiracy theory? So much so that Nick Fletcher, a Conservative MP in South Yorkshire in the U.K., chose to label 15-Minute Cities "an international socialist concept."

15-Minute Cities would create a "surveillance culture that would make Pyongyang envious," added Mark Dolan on the U.K. TV program *GB News*, prompting X (formerly Twitter) user Dave Vetter to wonder whether "traffic lights are a Maoist plot, pavements the Red Brigade scheming, and seat belts chains invited by the Reptilian Lord Snqruaarrgle to enslave us all."

Truly, QAnon couldn't have said it better.

Oliver Wainright, writing in *The Guardian,* noted that the feigned outrage is like "suggesting that public parks are part of a sinister plant-worshipping plot to demolish our homes and replace them with grass. Or that public transport is the work of a satanic bus cult."

And yet some online forums have claimed that 15-Minute Cities represent the first step "towards an inevitable Hunger Games society, in which residents will not be allowed to leave their prescribed area," Wainright continues. "They see it not as a route to a low-traffic, low-carbon future, but as the beginning of a slippery slope to living in an open-air prison."

Brexit proponent and former MP Nigel Farage described the 15-Minute City like this: "The climate change lockdowns are coming."

When a 15-Minute City plan was proposed for the town of Oxford, one group claimed that the plan would be to "lock residents into one of six zones to 'save the planet' from global warming."

Canadian culture warrior Jordan Peterson has weighed in too.

In a tweet that's received close to 7.5 million views, he wrote, "The idea that idiot tyrannical bureaucrats can decide by heart where you're 'allowed' to drive is perhaps the worst imaginable perversion of that idea. And make no mistake, it's part of a well-documented plan."

A plan pushed vigorously by Carlos Moreno.

Moreno, a Colombian-born professor at the Pantheon-Sorbonne in Paris, coined the term "15-Minute City" but has become a lightning rod for conspiracy theorists, perhaps because in his youth, he was a member of a left-wing guerrilla group.

Moreno laments that, for the first time in his career, he's started receiving threats to his life.

"I wasn't a researcher anymore. I was Pol Pot, Stalin, Hitler," Moreno recalls. "I have become Public Enemy No. 1. It is totally unbelievable that we could receive a death threat just for working as scientists!"

Tokyo: the anti-car paradise

The world's biggest city is also a pedestrian paradise. Tokyo has remarkably few cars on its streets. Street parking is rare, honking nonexistent.

Among the planet's richest cities, Tokyo has the lowest car use in the world. According to Deloitte, just 12% of journeys in Tokyo were undertaken by car. Cycling accounts for 17% of all journeys.

Tokyo's public transit is the most-used system in the world, with 30 million people commuting by train each day.

Car ownership in Japan is about 590 vehicles per 1,000 people In the U.S., it's 800 cars per 1,000. If the world average is 1.06 cars per household, Tokyo is an outlier, with just 0.32 cars per household.

Life expectancy in Tokyo is high at 84 years old. Did the fact that air pollution in Tokyo is considerably lower than most other cities, given the lack of cars, contribute to its citizens' good health? Typical commutes are still long—at 40 minutes each way—but at least they're not in smoggy car traffic.

How did Tokyo get this way?

One surprising reason: World War II.

The city was almost entirely flattened by American bombers. That gave city planners the opportunity to rebuild a kinder, more human-centric city, where cars were not prioritized over pedestrians.

It's a vastly different approach to most other developing world cities where planners find it impossible to resist constructing more and more roads on the assumption that most people will simply drive rather than use public transportation or micromobility.

"Our dysfunctional housing and land policies are screwing everything up," Roberts told me. "Our goal now is twofold. Half is finding carbon-free fuels, but the other half is reducing demand for that kind of transportation. Even if we switched all our ICE vehicles for EVs, it still would not be sustainable. The current system of sprawling cities, more highways and longer and longer commutes can't go on forever."

Roberts stresses the need to "leapfrog, not replicate the dumb things we in the U.S. did. There's still time."

Japan seems to have figured that out.

Japanese streets are much narrower than those in the U.S.—sometimes resembling medieval alleyways in Europe—and its homes are much smaller. That doesn't leave a lot of room for garages and curbside parking.

According to Andre Sorensen, a professor of urban planning at the University of Toronto, 86% of Japanese streets are not wide enough for a car to stop without blocking the traffic behind it!

But the biggest reason for Tokyo's livability is that Japan doesn't subsidize car ownership the way other countries do. Annual registration fees for cars older than 10 years are high, prompting Japanese vehicle owners to sell (and export) their cars before they're too old.

There is also an annual automobile tax of up to 50,000 yen, and a 5% purchase tax on the vehicle itself. Gas is taxed too—it costs around $6 a gallon, less than in Europe but more than an amount most Americans would accept.

Even if you can pay all the taxes, there's another hurdle: You must prove to the local police that you have somewhere to park the car. That's got to be a garage because overnight street parking of any sort has been illegal in Tokyo since 1957. The fine (after retrieving your car from wherever it was towed) is around $1,700 per incident.

More than 95% of Japanese streets have no street parking, even during the day. Only 42% of condominium buildings have parking for residents. Garages typically cost around $8.50 an hour.

One more disincentive to car ownership: There are few expressways in Japan that are not toll roads, and the tolls are the most expensive in the world—around three times higher than on similar roads in France.

It's not surprising, then, that trains, not cars, are a huge point of national pride; the Shinkansen, or Bullet Train, first reached speeds of 210 kilometers an hour (130 miles an hour) in 1964.

Don't expect this exemplary Asian model to be replicated in the West, though. There are just too many cars already on the roads to impose the sort of curbs on ownership Tokyo has implemented.

Moreover, because people in the West are so invested in their cars, they feel free to live in places where public transportation is poor (I'm looking at you, Levittown).

Sadly, the Tokyo system is simply not realistic outside of Japan.

Micromobility in India

Perhaps nowhere in the world is micromobility as popular as in Southeast Asia, where it's warm enough to ride year-round (other than during the summer monsoons) and scooters are a highly cost-effective alternative, compared with pricey passenger cars and trucks.

Now, micromobility is going electric thanks to battery swap.

Charging up an e-scooter or e-bike by plugging in would take too long for most drivers. Battery swap, on the other hand, takes less than two minutes per exchange. That's because we're not talking about a robotic system that automatically reaches a mechanical arm into the vehicle, removes the spent battery and replaces it with a freshly-charged one.

Rather, battery swap for micromobility is entirely manual.

I spoke with Pulkit Khurana, CEO and cofounder of Battery Smart, India's largest battery-swapping network for electric two- and three-wheelers. Launched in 2020, Battery Swap has built 485 Android-powered swap stations (they operate across 15 cities, most in the Delhi area) and has 16,000 customers in India. The company estimates it has powered 150 million electric kilometers (93 million miles) to date. Battery Smart aims to build a network where every customer will have one of its vending machine-like swap stations within one kilometer.

The battery swap market for micromobility vehicles is estimated to reach $17 billion by 2025. Battery Smart has raised $65 million in several rounds.

Go-go Gogoro

Battery Smart may be a leader in India, but Taiwan-based Gogoro has taken Southeast Asia by storm.

Like Battery Smart, Gogoro has taken a vending machine approach to battery swap. When your battery is running low, you simply pull over to a Gogoro battery swap station, remove your spent battery by hand, and slide a new one in.

In Taipei, where Gogoro is based, and where two-wheel vehicles outnumber cars two to one, nearly a quarter of all new scooters sold are electric. Nationally, 97% of e-scooters sold in Taiwan in 2021 were either manufactured by Gogoro or powered by Gogoro's batteries and charging infrastructure. Gogoro scooters can travel at a speed of up to 56 miles per hour.

Taiwan aims to be zero-emissions by 2040, and the government is putting some $5.8 billion toward subsidies and other incentives to see the share of new electric scooters hit 35% by 2030 and 70% by 2035.

Gogoro has more than half a million subscribers—20 times more than Battery Smart—and 11,000 swapping/charging stations in Taiwan, handling some 265,000 swaps a day, also a 20-fold multiple. There are 14 million scooters on the roads in Taiwan, with Gogoro-branded e-scooters the country's most popular, having nine times more subscriptions than its closest competitors. Gogoro batteries are compatible with 47 types of vehicles. Customers ride, on average, between 300 and 700 miles a month.

Gogoro expanded to China in 2021, operating under the brand Huan Huan. In late 2022, the first Gogoro scooters could be spotted in Israel, where 10 stations are spread across the center of the country. More than 150 stations are planned to be completed within four years.

In India, Gogoro will launch its first swapping stations through a partnership with Hero MotoCorp, which also makes its own Hero-branded electric two-wheelers based on Gogoro's technology. HeroMoto serves 40 countries and Gogoro hopes that India will just be the start of a fruitful partnership.

Gogoro scooters can get 106 miles of range at slow speeds, 62 miles with more spirited riding.

In Gogoro's business model, consumers buy their own scooters, but Gogoro owns the batteries. By subscribing to the service, scooter owners know they'll always have a charged battery available.

A Gogoro swap machine (credit: Gogoro)

"In India, China, and Indonesia alone, there are more than 500 million two-wheelers roaming around every day, taking people to school, to work, to the market. They are the absolute utility dependency vehicle that people look for when they're moving around town," says Gogoro CEO Horace Luke.

How much will it cost?

Around 30 U.S. cents per swap, paid as a flat fee, in India. In Gogoro's Israel operation, the cost is $37 per month for 620 miles worth of battery swapping (the first six months are unlimited). Riders can pay a prorated amount for additional distance.

The e-scooters are high-tech marvels, a far cry from the basic mopeds of yesteryear. Among the wizardry built in: Bosch anti-braking system (ABS); keyless start with near-field communication (NFC); higher-security unlocking options including face ID, fingerprint ID or Siri voice command; a reverse gear for parking assistance; and more.

Battery swap for rickshaws

Battery Smart has identified another micromobility niche: auto rickshaws (tuk-tuks) that can seat three to four people vs. a single-person scooter. Across India, more than three million tuk-tuks operate, ferrying passengers an average of five to 10 kilometers (three to six miles).

India introduced electric-powered auto rickshaws in 2010. According to government specifications, all rickshaws have the ability to swap the battery out. That means that multiple rickshaw models are compatible with Battery Smart's technology.

Some 35% of all 3-wheelers in India are now electric.

Another difference between Battery Smart and Gogoro: While Gogoro owns its own battery swap vending machines which can be freestanding on a street corner, Battery Smart works specifically with mom-and-pop partners—"entrepreneurs," as Khurana describes them.

"We have an Airbnb model," Khurana explains.

The mom-and-pops go through continuous training and audits. They are then responsible for maintaining the swap stations on their property (another advantage: Battery Smart doesn't have to pay for extra real estate).

Whether run by Gogoro or Battery Smart, battery swap schemes for micromobility have one thing in common: "They help solve the downtime problem," Khurana told me. That is, if it takes 12 hours to fully charge a rickshaw battery at home (there are virtually no fast chargers in India), well, if a driver runs out of juice midway through the day, that's the end of that vehicle's revenue.

"Our key value proposition is the 'two-minute battery swap,'" Khurana emphasizes. "We have a station every 400 to 500 meters in the big cities. Our mobile app directs drivers to the nearest station."

Battery Smart's app also nudges drivers when it's time to charge their vehicle. "We want to see a smooth demand curve across locations," Khurana says.

In 2022, Audi announced that it would send batteries from its e-tron electric SUVs to India for use in electric rickshaws when they had passed their Western prime. Audi's energy and sustainability manager, Alexander Kupfer, told *Automotive News* that Audi is running the project with Nunam, a German-Indian environmental nonprofit.

While these batteries "may not be ideal for car use anymore," they are still strong enough to power lightweight vehicles like rickshaws, Prodip Chatterjee, cofounder of Nunam, told *The India Times*.

The old e-tron batteries, which are lithium-ion, are a step up from the lead-acid batteries that are used in most electric tuk-tuks in the country.

Battery swap for micromobility sounds like an idea whose time has come, but it will remain in Southeast Asia for the foreseeable future. "India will keep us plenty busy for the next few years," says Khurana.

Issues with e-scooters

Mobility investor Quin Garcia, who heads the VC firm Autotech Ventures, and who was a key executive at battery-swap pioneer Better Place, believes micromobility is a logical modality for battery swap.

Swapping for scooters, he told me, is a "great use-case, as there are convenience stores on every corner" in places like Taiwan. "In China, consumers simply take their batteries with them to their homes and offices and charge them there. The same will be true in Africa."

Ensuring that scooters of the future are electric may be a tougher sell.

"Unfortunately, because of the economics of it, the chance of scooters being clean is not very high," Gogoro's Luke says. "When compared to a gasoline vehicle in, say, California, there are five times more pollutants coming out of the tailpipe per kilometer, easily. On top of that, you have people not using premium fuel and other carelessness that makes owning a two-wheel vehicle extremely polluting."

What about safety? Aren't micromobility vehicles inherently dangerous?

That's what shared e-scooter company Revel discovered when it had to revise its safety protocols after a rash of accidents that led the company to suspend operations in New York in 2020.

"We can't believe we have to say this, but no running red lights," Revel said in an email to its New York customers on July 16, 2020.

The number of collisions subsequently dropped by 50% but it's still not good enough.

Revel restarted its service, which includes enhanced safety training for drivers, increased accountability to weed out unruly operators, and a requirement for users to take a selfie of themselves wearing a helmet before unlocking the scooter. (The user's camera roll is locked so that an old photo can't be surreptitiously selected.)

Ultimately, it was not enough. By the end of 2023, Revel shut down its shared moped business in New York and San Francisco. Revel had already pulled out of Washington, DC and Miami in November 2022. It will still operate an EV ride-hail business.

Neighborhood Electric Vehicles

As the school day ends at a high school in Peachtree City, Georgia, the usual flood of teenagers heads to the parking lot, keys in hand. But they don't pile into cars. They get into golf carts. With about 9,300 golf carts registered among Peachtree City's 13,000 households, this town 31 miles southwest of Atlanta may be the most golf cart-friendly city in America, with 100 miles of car-free multi-use paths crisscrossing the town's 25 square miles.

Anyone over age 16 can drive one, even if they don't have a driver's license. A new golf cart retails for $13,000 for a four-seater and $16,000 for a six-seater.

The industry term for the next generation of golf carts—"Golf Carts 2.0," if you'd like—is "Neighborhood Electric Vehicle" (NEV). In some places, they're dubbed "microcars" or LSVs (for "Low-Speed Vehicle").

Not all of these NEVs resemble golf carts.

Quantum Motors in Bolivia is pushing a $7,500 NEV that can seat three people ("They can't be very fat," jokes Daniel Derenne, a 62-year-old retiree in the Andes town of Cochabamba) plus groceries in the trunk.

The Quantum NEV can go 60 miles on a charge. It takes six to seven hours to charge up overnight, but you can't beat the price: Quantum owners say they spend about $7 a month to charge their NEVs.

And of course, finding parking is way, way easier.

The Citroen Ami is designated as a "quadricycle" rather than a car. ("Quadricycle" is the preferred term for NEVs in Europe.) That allows the tiny 458-kg (1,008-pound), meter-and-a-half wide, two-and-a-half-meter long Ami to sidestep a whole host of regulations full-size cars must meet. Range is a paltry 45 miles, but that's par for the course for an NEV. And it costs only $10,000.

The BBC's *Top Gear* quipped about the Ami: "Think of it less as a car, and more as the world's most complicated umbrella—instead of biking across town or risking the vagaries of public transport, you just totter around in an Ami, keeping yourself personally secure and your hair dry."

That last point may seem trivial but it's a big reason for some people's reluctance to use micromobility solutions where there's no protection from the elements.

Like at Peachtree City, in the U.K., the Ami can be driven by anyone over the age of 16, even without a driver's license.

As the BBC memorably quips, "Yes, it's a rubbish 'car'... because it isn't one. But it is fun to use and an entirely lovable object."

Vice's Aaron Gordon notes that if the credits of $7,500 per electric vehicle were available not just for American-made full-size electric vehicles but NEVs like the Ami, the Quantum or the Kandi Kruiser 4P, a Chinese-made NEV that retails for between $11,000 and $12,000 depending on the battery size, the price would drop to $4,500.

"Many states offer EV incentives on top of the federal one, shaving anywhere from a few hundred to a few thousand dollars off," Gordon writes. "With only a little bit more federal or state assistance, NEVs could be pretty damn close to free."

Given that, according to the U.S. Department of Transportation, 60% of all vehicle trips are six miles or shorter, NEVs make a lot of sense.

The Citroen Ami (credit: Wikimedia Commons)

Just look at The Villages, the massive 55-and-over retirement community in Florida with 130,000 residents spread out over 32 square miles—an area larger than Manhattan. NEVs are a main way of getting around, so much so that the "two-car garages" in The Villages are actually for one car and one NEV.

About half of The Villages' residents own an NEV and a third of all trips in The Villages are taken in an NEV.

Other municipalities that have embraced NEVs instead of cars as the main way to get around include Sun City, Arizona, and Palm Desert, California.

One other NEV is worth mentioning: the City Transformer.

This NEV is like the latest version of the Samsung Galaxy—it folds. Four City Transformers can fit into a single standard parking space. The vehicle has better range than most NEVs—up to 110 miles per charge—and a top speed of 60 miles per hour. At $14,000, it's a bit pricier than competing NEVs, but not by much.

The voluntary emergency response organization United Hatzalah has signed on as a client, reportedly purchasing 1,000 CityTransformers in a deal worth $22 million. The vehicle is due to be commercialized for sale to the public in 2025.

A City Transformer (credit: Wikimedia Commons)

"More than four billion people currently live in urban areas, and that will only increase in the coming years," CityTransformer CEO Asaf Formoza says. "People need vehicles for city centers, for narrow streets, for tomorrow's world."

Powering NEVs with scooter batteries

At the 2023 Japan Mobility Show, Gogoro showed how its scooter batteries can be used to power an NEV called Project X, a concept built by the Foxconn-led Mobility in Harmony (MIH) consortium. This cute little EV is a three-seater; the spot in the backseat where you'd normally place a fourth person is taken up by two Gogoro battery pack slots.

MIH aims to sell 100,000 of its minicars per year in India, Thailand, and Japan starting in 2025. The company will initially target fleet operators and ride-hailing services rather than individual customers. The price isn't yet fixed but should top around $20,000. If the range for a Gogoro-powered e-scooter is around 105 miles, a Project X vehicle, with its larger size, will probably come in somewhat less.

For now, Gogoro's batteries for NEVs are fixed and not swappable, but that may change going forward, in turn creating a new revenue stream for the company and helping to open new international markets.

Project X powered by Gogoro (credit: MIH)

Micromobility can address accessibility

A final point about micromobility: Individuals with mobility limitations will find it a blessing. Two-wheel scooters may not do the trick, but three-wheeled Segways and Segway-like vehicles could provide the balance and stability needed.

I only need to look at my own family to know this is true.

My mother is 85. She isn't going to pick up a Bird or a Lime off the streets in Santa Monica. But she should be able to zip around in something.

Something like an e-wheelchair?

Electric wheelchairs are not a new idea; they've been around for nearly a century. The first e-chair was invented by George Klein and debuted in 1929. Klein wanted to assist veterans who had been injured during World War I.

The Everest & Jennings company began commercial manufacture of an electric wheelchair in 1956, shortly after their invention of the folding wheelchair. Wheelchairs—not electric, of course—have been used in China since AD 526.

Next up: the autonomous e-wheelchair.

Two such devices were showcased in 2018 at Tokyo's Haneda International Airport. They included state-of-the-art mapping technology and sensors to keep the chair from bumping into obstacles.

"Self-compensating drive control was one of the earliest smart chair systems, and it is so seamlessly integrated that most wheelers aren't even aware it is on their chair," writes Bob Vogel for *New Mobility*.

"It's basically the wheelchair equivalent of the lane-centering technology that is being rolled out on many high-end automobiles," Vogel continues. "Just like lane-centering technology keeps your car in the lane, self-compensating drive control autonomously corrects a chair's direction, keeping it going where the controller input intended by compensating for uneven or bumpy surfaces. [That] enables the driver to relax, talk and enjoy their surroundings."

There's still a lot of work to be done.

"We would love an autonomous power chair that could navigate any sidewalk, and/or chairs that can perform obstacle avoidance for people using 'sip-and-puff' or head array controls, but the technology isn't there yet," says Mark Smith, general manager of public relations for Pride Mobility/Quantum Rehab.

"It's easy for sensors to avoid vertical objects on a flat indoor surface, but outdoors is another story," he adds. "Current technology can't tell a puddle from a dark patch from a pothole. And current sensors aren't capable of distinguishing between curb angles, or if a curb is shaded by a tree."

But they'll get there in time. And that's good news for anyone with mobility issues, especially my mother!

What we've learned

+ Will more cities implement restrictions on internal combustion vehicles (or passenger vehicles in general), opting instead to invest in infrastructure to support environments that are much more friendly to passengers and cyclists?

+ With greater focus on environmental health, it's likely we'll find more progressive cities that embrace smaller modes of transport that don't belch tailpipe emissions, and that deliberately build out pedestrian-friendly areas.

+ Battery swap isn't dead; it's just migrated to two- and three-wheelers: scooters, auto-rickshaws and NEVs.

✦ What does this mean for the micromobility investor? We'll continue to see innovation in the space, be it across improved charging speed and range, battery-swapping infrastructure, and new technology to ensure the safety of both the rider and surrounding pedestrians.

■   ■   ■

Chapter 3

Air and Space

Commercial air travel has changed in numerous ways over the last half century. In the 1960s, tickets could easily run up to five times what they cost today. Passengers could smoke on the plane and consume as much free booze as they wanted.

Today? You can still get your drink on (but you'll most likely have to pay for it), and ultrabudget tickets, with tiny seats and added baggage fees, are ubiquitous.

There's one aspect to air travel that, strangely, hasn't changed: how fast the plane goes. We're still flying at essentially the same speeds we did in the years before humanity stepped foot on the moon.

And, given modern congestion that adds extra time for planes to get in and out of airports, it actually takes *longer* today than it did 50 years ago flying on the same routes.

Why hasn't speed increased? The answer, it seems, is economic.

The engines developed in the 1960s are still the most efficient engines today. They tend to top out at speeds of 400 to 620 miles per hour. Military aircraft can go much faster—they use turbojet engines rather than the turbofan engines that are standard on commercial planes, reaching speeds of more than 1,500 miles per hour in some cases, but the fuel requirements can be draconian, a nonstarter when airlines are trying to both reduce costs and minimize their carbon footprint.

The one plane that could fly at supersonic speeds—the Concorde, which reached 1,300 miles per hour at cruising altitude—used 46.86 pounds of fuel for every mile flown. The Boeing 787 Dreamliner, by contrast, uses only 18.7 pounds of fuel per mile when flying 650 miles per hour. The Concorde could also seat just 100 passengers vs. nearly 300 on the Dreamliner.

Airlines reasonably concluded the extra speed wasn't financially justified and the Concorde was retired in 2003.

Fast forward to the mid-2020s and air travel is poised to make some of its biggest changes in years: the return of speed as next-generation super and hypersonic craft are deployed; new fuels that are better for the environment (plane maker Boom says that using sustainable aviation fuel can reduce the amount of gas required by 80% compared with the Concorde); and the dawn of an entirely new class of craft: the eVTOL, short for "electric vertical take-off and landing," which is similar to a helicopter but smaller, quieter and lighter.

"Mobility is a constraint in every city. That's why we see a huge global market demand for AAM—advanced air mobility," Florian Reuter, CEO of eVTOL startup Volocopter, said in an interview with McKinsey. "I think urban air mobility—for example, air-taxi applications within cities—will start a profound transformation in the air-mobility sector overall. Specifically, the digitization and the electrification in urban applications will spread to other, longer-range missions until eventually we develop the means to fly, with 100% sustainability, from continent to continent. In 30 years, AAM will be as ubiquitous as any other transportation mode."

Reuter estimates the overall mobility market at $10 trillion in the next 10 to 15 years. "If AAM can get $300 billion of that, that is a gigantic market opportunity [and one that only] represents a very small fraction of the total market."

Dawn of the flying car

Over three seasons starting in 1962, TV viewers were transported to a push-button future with robots, "slidewalks" and flying cars.

The Jetsons set the tone for a future that is finally, after 60 years, starting to look less like animated sci-fi fodder and more like a good day for beleaguered husband and Spacely Space Sprockets button-junkie George Jetson.

Flying cars didn't enter the entrepreneurial imagination with *The Jetsons*.

In 1926, Henry Ford unveiled the Ford Flivver, "a flying car for the masses that was supposed to do for airplanes what the Model T had done for autos," writes Tony Reichardt in *Smithsonian*. "Within two years, though, Ford's dream of affordable aviation had ended, due to the fatal crash—on February 25, 1928—of the Flivver and its only test pilot, one 25-year-old Harry J. Brooks.

Fast-forward a century and everyone, it seems, is talking about flying cars again.

"One way to think about eVTOLs is democratizing access to helicopters for the masses— but safer, cheaper, more environmentally friendly and with less noise," says Mark Lore, an entrepreneur who sold his startup Jet.com (which despite its name did not make aircraft, it was an e-commerce site) to Walmart for $3 billion in 2016.

The Ford Flivver (credit: Wikimedia Commons)

"When you think about a vertical-lift aircraft like a helicopter, you hear that 'wop-wop.' You don't hear that with [an eVTOL] at all. That's one reason why consumer adoption will be dramatic," says Bonny Simi, head of air operations and people for Joby Aviation, a leading eVTOL maker.

The AIR ONE, an eVTOL being developed by the Israeli startup AIR EV, has collapsible wings for easy parking in a "vertiport" or at home in someone's garage. It can take off from or land on any flat surface.

Other eVTOLs have rotors ensconced in a safety enclosure, making them less dangerous when landing in a crowded urban environment or even a rooftop dock.

eVTOLs are mostly positioned as commuter vehicles—an "aerial ride-sharing service"—that, like an Uber or Lyft, can be ordered via an app.

There are eight main use-cases where we can expect to see eVTOLs in action:

1. Commuting to and from work
2. Errands (although probably *not* shopping for furniture and major appliances because the eVTOL has a maximum weight limit)

3. Business travel
4. Short-distance leisure travel—for example, a trip to the movies
5. Longer-distance leisure travel, such as visits to family members in nearby cities
6. Trips to and from the airport as part of a longer journey that will continue on a commercial jet
7. Delivery of food and medicine
8. Emergency medical services—rescuing people from areas where a plane or helicopter couldn't fit

Investors have been bullish on eVTOLs (although that sheen is starting to wear off a bit lately, with shares in publicly traded eVTOL startups down 50% in 2021 compared with the previous year). Still, Morgan Stanley estimates the market will be worth $1.5 trillion a year by 2040.

LEK Consulting estimates that AAM could account for 50% of all taxi or ride-share journeys greater than 15 kilometers (10 miles) by 2040.

"It's a question of when, not if," says Sergio Cecutta, a partner at SMG Consulting.

Vertiports, which typically have room for one take-off and landing at a time—along with larger "vertipads," "vertibases" and "vertihubs"—are key to the broader business proposition.

Unlike a helicopter pad that can serve one vehicle at a time, a vertiport will have 6 to 10 gates, all connected via a central taxiway, where passengers can board while the aircraft is charging. There will be all the typical airport amenities—a lounge, food, and beverage stands.

"We envision people flowing through this infrastructure quickly," notes Daniel Wiegand, CEO of Berlin-based eVTOL maker Lilium, "not spending a lot of time there like we do today in airports. It will take two or three minutes, not an hour or more, to get from a car into an airplane."

eVTOLs vs. helicopters

Joe Ben Bevert, the CEO of Joby Aviation, told *60 Minutes* that eVTOLs are "a combination of a helicopter and a plane. They take off like a helicopter but are efficient like a plane, with six propellers and four batteries in the wings." The vertical take-off and landing aspect means you don't need a huge runway. "Having wings lets the VTOL fly far and fast," Ben Bevert added.

Helicopters are essentially a subset of the overall VTOL category. Adding the "e" makes them electric, but why not simply call them helicopters? It's a well-known term and probably easier to remember than a four-letter acronym.

There are several reasons:

1. **Environmental impact**. The average small helicopter burns through 20 gallons of fuel an hour. That's bad for the environment and expensive. eVTOLs, because they run on electricity, typically emit zero fossil fuel emissions during operation.

2. **Quiet**. An eVTOL aircraft cruises with a noise level of 45 dB—that's quieter than a car or even a normal conversation level. Helicopters are notoriously noisy, generating 78 dB at a cruising altitude of 2,000 feet. Since sound is measured logarithmically, a helicopter is actually *1,000 times louder* than an eVTOL. "The perceived noise level of the eVTOL jet, when it's in its initial hover phase, is about the same as a dishwasher from 100 meters away," notes Wiegand. "And when it's cruising, you will barely hear it at all . . . low noise is crucial to community acceptance. Helicopters have been able to do vertical takeoff and landing for a very long time, but they are very noisy and costly." (For some other reference points, soft pleasant noises like rustling leaves are about 30 dB. A car traveling at 30 miles per hour generates 62 dB when 50 feet away. A subway car 200 feet away blasts out 95 dB. And a jet plane taking off: 140 dB.)

3. **Safety**. Helicopters have two rotors. One provides lift and the other provides stability. A helicopter's tail rotor provides a counteracting force to the main rotor; without the sideways thrust produced by the tail rotor, the torque generated by the main rotor would spin the helicopter's body in the opposite direction. If a helicopter's main rotor fails, the results can be catastrophic. An eVTOL, by contrast, has *multiple* rotors—the eVTOL from manufacturer Archer, for example, has six forward and six aft rotors, mounted on two wings. Half those motors would have to fail for the craft to crash.

Some services blur the line between helicopter and eVTOL.

Blade transports wealthy commuters from the city to the airport. That sounds like an eVTOL, but Blade uses helicopters. Its main innovation is its app, which makes booking a ride on a Blade as easy as calling an Uber. If it's $150 and five minutes on a Blade from Manhattan to La Guardia or JFK airports vs. $75 stuck in traffic for an hour on the Van Wyck Expressway in a yellow cab, which are you going to use?

Here's a thought: What if an automaker were to offer a certain number of Blade or eVTOL rides as part of a monthly subscription? You could pay, say, $700 for your Hyundai Ioniq 5 EV, or $1,200 and Hyundai will throw in 3 trips in a flying car every month.

A flying car in your garage?

Here are some of the leading firms that may get us to our destinations faster by skipping the highway off-ramp.

AIR EV

The AIR ONE is a two-seat electric personal air taxi that is expected to retail for around $200,000, CEO Rani Plaut told me, with the target market being individuals of high net worth, rather than taxi or aviation companies. That sounds like a lot to plunk down, but it's not that much more than the first Tesla Roadsters.

The AIR ONE (credit: AIR EV)

A single AIR ONE is the size of two cars parked side-by-side. When "folded," the AIR ONE is no larger than a Ford F-150.

Plaut's goals for AIR are at once ambitious and down-to-earth.

"There are approximately 1.5 billion cars in the world with about 80 million produced every year," notes Plaut. "If we can get 10,000 'cars' into the air, we can start making a dent" in the planet's worsening traffic congestion.

"We want to bring aviation to the masses," Plaut says.

Israel-based AIR's AIR ONE eVTOL is heading to Australia, where electric aircraft company FlyOnE aims to deliver 25 of the AIR's "flying cars" by 2025. Other customers include Espere AAM and AeroAuto.

An AIR ONE prototype was unveiled at the 2022 Kentucky Derby.

Urban Aeronautics

Another eVTOL from Israel, Urban Aeronautics' CityHawk, is one of the reasons I am somewhat reluctant to always append an "e" to VTOL—the CityHawk will be powered by long-range hydrogen fuel cells. (An hVTOL?)

Another feature unique to the CityHawk: Its "Fancraft" rotors are entirely internal, protected by the plane's skeleton. That, plus its relatively small footprint, makes it safer to land in crowded urban environments, say on a sidewalk near your home or office.

The CityHawk (credit: Urban Aeronautics)

The CityHawk is about the size of a large SUV. It will have five seats and a pilot and should be ready by the end of the decade. A prototype known as the Cormorant was unveiled in 2015. The CityHawk was previously known as the AirMule.

The company's first deal is with Hatzolah Air, a Brooklyn EMS organization staffed by volunteer paramedics, nurses, and doctors. In an EMS configuration, the CityHawk can carry one pilot, two caregivers, a patient, and 400 pounds of equipment.

Urban Aeronautics aims to address "the golden hour"—the period of time immediately after a traumatic injury during which there is the highest likelihood that prompt medical attention will prevent death—by getting to an incident site faster than the competition.

What's next? Tele-operated firetrucks? A swarm of firefighting drones armed with tiny hoses?

Pentaxi

There's no escaping the business model for this Israeli startup—it's baked into the name. Unlike AIR, Pentaxi is intended for ride-sharing, not ownership, and, after proving the technology is safe, will be pilot-less to boot—which may be why one of the first uses proposed for the craft is cargo.

The initial model will carry 120 pounds for 62 miles, although the aim is to be able to transport up to 800 pounds for 200 miles at a speed of up to 150 miles per hour. The team behind Pentaxi has been working on unmanned autonomous vehicles (UAVs) since 1974.

The Pentaxi (credit: Pentaxi)

The company's CEO, Yair Dubester, headed the UAV division of Israel Aerospace Industries for seven years prior to founding Pentaxi.

"When a potential customer comes to us, I say, 'I've crashed more UAVs than anyone in the world,'" Dubester told *ISRAEL21c*. "The point is: I have all the lessons learned from those years."

Dubester hopes the cargo version of Pentaxi will be ready for liftoff by 2025.

Lilium

Based in Munich, Lilium went public in 2021 and planned to begin commercial operations in 2024 with launch sites in Germany, Brazil, and the United States. The company is working on a 7-seater craft with 36 ducted fans (for noise reduction) on tilting banks.

Lilium is differentiating its business proposition from competing eVTOL makers by offering scheduled shuttle services from one city center to another, rather than positioning the company as another air-taxi service.

Lilium eVTOL (credit: Lilium)

The company's website describes a futuristic world where a trip from San Francisco to Lake Tahoe takes under an hour by eVTOL compared with 4 hours in the car. Zurich to St. Moritz—2.5 hours by car—would take just 29 minutes by air.

CEO Wiegand calls it "expanding the radius of life . . . we'll be able to live in the countryside and work in the city. An eVTOL is five times faster than a car."

The company is named after Otto Lilienthal, who is lauded as the inventor of aircraft in Germany.

"On the ground today, there's everything from sports cars to trucks to buses," Wiegand told McKinsey's Robin Riedel. "We will see something similar in the air: There will be eVTOL aircraft used on intercity shuttle routes, which is what Lilium is focused on right now. There will be sightseeing applications, taxi applications, cargo applications, and so on."

Lilium's expected starting price will be $2.25 per passenger mile. A ride in an Uber (ground-based for now) runs between $1 and $2 per mile, but that doesn't include Uber's many "extras"—booking fees (at a minimum of $1 and a maximum of $10), surge pricing, airport and wait-time fees, and sales tax depending on the location.

By contrast, the cost to own and operate a private car, including gas, maintenance and insurance, is $0.72 per mile, according to the AAA.

Volocopter

Another German firm, Volocopter, is working on three types of eVTOLs: a two-seater called VoloCity, the VoloConnect for traveling between cities and suburbs, and the VoloDrone for transporting cargo. VoloIO is the company's digital booking and infrastructure platform.

"As a consumer, I will be able to simply tap my smartphone and it will show me all the different options," says Volocopter CEO Florian Reuter. "And I can choose the one that best meets my specific needs at that time—whether my priority is the lowest price or the shortest trip or something else."

Volocopter hopes to launch electric air-taxi services in Singapore soon; a test flight was completed successfully in 2019. The Lion City is looking into offering eVTOL rides over Marina Bay as a tourist attraction. Cross-border flights are expected to follow. Volocopter says it will hire some 200 employees for the Singapore operation alone.

A Volocopter Veloport (credit: Wikimedia Commons)

The Volocopter (credit: Wikimedia Commons)

"The partnership with Volocopter will help build new capabilities for our mobility ecosystem," says Tan Kong Hwee, executive vice president of Singapore's Economic Development Board.

Volocopter has raised more than €322 million to date.

Joby

With six propellors and batteries in the wings, Joby Aviation's air taxi will carry four passengers plus a pilot for 150 miles at 200 miles per hour. Toyota has invested $400 million in Joby. The founder of Pinterest is now the company's chairman.

Joby intends to launch in three cities; fees will be $3 to $4 a mile, which CEO Ben Bevert says is a little more than an Uber.

"If we can take 80% of the miles from congested roads and move them to the air, that will have an impact," Bevert says.

Joby head of operations and people Bonny Simi is more effusive, predicting Joby will be "the world's largest airline."

That possibility got a boost in 2020, when Uber sold its flying taxi business, Elevate, to Joby, giving the latter invaluable access to Uber's data on where people drive daily.

Joby Aviation (credit: Wikimedia Commons)

Joby proposed terminal in Dubai (credit: Foster + Partners)

Joby was featured at the World Government Summit in Dubai in 2023. The city-state plans to build four vertiports near the Dubai International Airport; in downtown Dubai; at the manmade Palm Jumeirah archipelago; and along the Dubai Marina.

The price for the flying taxis will "be in the range of a limousine service in Dubai, maybe slightly higher," notes Ahmed Bahrozyan, an official in the Emirate's Roads and Transport Authority. Limos in Dubai cost around 30% more than taxis, which have a minimum fare of $3.25. With its 150-mile range, a Joby eVTOL could reach neighboring Abu Dhabi from Dubai.

With Dubai's futuristic skyline featuring the world's tallest building, adding eVTOLs would put the city clearly in "Blade Runner" territory.

There are 1.8 million registered vehicles in Dubai; the hope is that a quarter of the land-based vehicles in this Emirate will be driverless as early as 2030.

Wisk Aero

In 2019, Boeing and Kittyhawk formed a joint venture to bring a pilot-less electric two-person air taxi to the market. The new company was dubbed Wisk (orginally Zee Aero).

Boeing committed $450 million to Wisk, which has completed more than 1,600 test flights. Boeing is not only an investor but also a strategic partner, providing development, testing and certification support. Wisk hopes to launch in 20 cities in the next decade.

Like Pentaxi, Wisk may try to capture the cargo market first.

"There's a ton of folks that are trying to move things from Santa Monica out to Van Nuys and then back down to Long Beach and doing that all day long," says Dan Dalton, vice president of global partnerships at Wisk. "And in reality, at least from our perspective, that's something that could be very easily done by aircraft that don't necessarily need pilots."

Kittyhawk

In 2022, Kittyhawk, which was backed by Google cofounder Larry Page, announced it would be shutting down after eight years of development. "Kittyhawk's decision to cease operations does not change Boeing's commitment to Wisk," a Boeing spokesperson said at the time.

What sunk Kittyhawk?

While there's been no official explanation, in 2021, Kittyhawk CEO Sebastian Thrun stated cryptically, "No matter how hard we looked, we could not find a path to a viable business."

Doroni Aerospace

Named after its founder, Doron Merdinger, the Doroni H1 semiautonomous eVTOL is intended to be flown by mere mortals with just 20 hours of training and a standard driver's license. You'll also have to come up with the purchase price for an H1, estimated to be in the range of $200,000 to $250,000.

Merdinger, a former Israeli Air Force pilot who established Doroni Aerospace in Pompano, Florida, says it makes no sense to get stuck in land traffic when the skies are open.

Doroni Aerospace (credit: Doroni)

"We are still traveling in this two-dimensional world using a 4,000-year-old invention called the wheel," Merdinger told NBC's affiliate in South Florida. "To facilitate traveling in a two-dimensional world, you have to put down asphalt and concrete and take out the trees. Why do we need that if we already have the technology" to fly high?

What if newbie pilots run into trouble in the air? The H1 is designed to automatically descend if something goes wrong in flight. In extreme situations, there's a parachute on board too.

Another innovation: the two-seat H1 has wheels. Most eVTOLs land on pads but Merdinger wanted owners to be able to drive straight into their home garages to recharge overnight.

To speed adoption, Doroni is positioning the H1 to be certified as a "light sport aircraft" rather than a new category which would slow down the certification process. In mid-2023, the Doroni H1 had 200 units preordered. Merdinger hopes first deliveries will be by the end of 2024.

The H1 will have a range of 60 miles and a top speed of 140 miles per hour for a flight time of around 40 minutes. Batteries can be charged from 20% to 80% in about 20 minutes. The H1 can carry a maximum payload of 500 pounds.

Archer

San Jose, California-based Archer Aviation and United have announced plans to use flying cars to ferry passengers between Chicago's O'Hare International Airport, and a vertiport just minutes from downtown. Mayor Lori Lightfoot said that "Chicago residents will be the first in the nation to experience this innovative, convenient form of travel."

Chicago is as good a place as any to start.

In the third largest metropolitan area in the U.S., with 9.6 million residents, commutes can be brutal, a 15-mile drive can easily take an hour or longer during rush hour. The city is forecast to grow by another million residents in the next 25 years.

The Archer (credit: Shutterstock)

Archer will offer its "Midnight" eVTOL to the city of Chicago. ComEd, a local utility company, will work with United and Archer to establish the power infrastructure necessary to support the Midnight's operations.

These short battery-powered eVTOL flights make sense to Jennifer Holmgren, CEO of LanzaTech, which has developed a new "biologic" technology to create sustainable aviation fuel (SAF) for long-haul flights. (More on SAF in chapter 7)

"eVTOLs will revolutionize short-haul travel, providing efficient and convenient flights between small hubs that larger airlines often overlook," she told me. "This means more destinations will be easily accessible, reducing the need for long drives and making regional travel faster and more enjoyable."

This is not Archer's first rodeo with United.

In 2021, United placed a $1 billion order for Archer's flying cars. In 2022, the pair announced they intended to establish a flight route in New York City. That route is expected to cost $100 for the 10-minute ride. Chicago's should be about the same.

Archer's Midnight can carry a 1,000-pound payload for 100 miles. The craft itself weighs some 6,500 pounds. Its 12 propellors rotate depending on whether it is taking off or landing vertically or flying horizontally. The company, which employs 500 on staff, has raised close to $1 billion. On the winds of the United deal, Archer went public in 2021, at a valuation of $1.7 billion.

Archer is also working closely with the Los Angeles Department of Transportation. The city's vast inventory of parking lots and high-rise rooftops gives the region plenty of space for vertiports.

"You can imagine a route like LAX to Pasadena or downtown to Santa Monica," Archer CEO Goldstein points out. "Those will be routes where you can imagine invisible tubes in the air. These vehicles will be almost like a gondola or ski lift where vehicles will be trailing each other on routes that take people 60 to 90 minutes on the ground and that can be moved into the air and flown in a matter of 5 to 10 minutes."

"L.A. is kind of that perfect location," says Dalton, of Wisk, which is also planning eVTOL routes in Southern California. "It's got a huge amount of sprawl. It's got a huge amount of traffic and has people who are interested in getting out of the traffic but still enjoying sprawl."

Eve Air Mobility

It's not all Archer all the time for United.

In June 2023, United chose another eVTOL maker, Eve Air Mobility, to offer commuter flights in the San Francisco Bay Area. The flights are expected to start by 2026 and will operate between a downtown hub and SFO, the city's main airport. United made a $15 million order for 200 Eve eVTOLs, with an option to acquire another 200 craft.

Eve is partnered with Brazilian aircraft manufacturer Embraer to build the vehicles. A key part of that relationship is access to Embraer's global service centers, parts warehouses, and field service technicians, paving the way for a reliable operation for both Eve and United.

Eve's eVTOL has a range of just 60 miles, so the close proximity of the city center to the airport was a key reason for choosing San Francisco and not another city.

Eve and United say the first craft will be piloted but the growth path is toward "uncrewed operations" in the future.

Alef—the first flying car with wheels?

Of all the eVTOLs out there, Alef Aerospace's Model A looks the most like an actual flying car. Unlike other eVTOLs, the Model A has wheels and is meant to be as comfortable on the ground as in the air.

The first prototype, unveiled in 2022, has a 200-mile driving range and a 110-mile flying range. The company is also looking into building a hydrogen-powered version of its flying car, which could significantly increase the range.

The Model A can carry 1 or 2 passengers and is expected to cost $300,000. Interested buyers can put down a $1,500 deposit, giving them priority when the vehicle becomes available. (No delivery date for the Model A has been released, although *CNET* has suggested the year 2025 in its reporting.)

The Model A moniker harkens back to the days of Ford. But Detroit never made a Model Z (for "zero emissions"), which is what Alef CEO Jim Dukhovny says could be available by 2030. The Model Z would have longer driving and flying ranges, and sell for $35,000. Dukhovny told *Reuters* the Model Z would be "not more complicated than a Toyota Corolla" and should, therefore, have a similar price.

The Model A will take off vertically using eight propellers housed inside a body about the size of a large sedan. Once in the air, the craft transitions to horizontal fixed-wing flight by pivoting 90 degrees. When it pivots, one side of the car's body becomes the top wing, and the other side is transformed into a bottom wing.

Won't passengers then be flying on their sides too? No. In another design innovation, the "bubble," in which passengers sit, pivots. So, you're always facing forward and sitting upright.

Dukhovny told CNBC in 2022 that the Model A doesn't always need to transition to a fixed-wing orientation. The craft is mostly intended to stay on roads, only traveling through the air for short heights and distances to "hop over obstacles when needed."

Is a "hybrid" approach, like the one Alef is taking, a good idea?

In general, hybrids are not as efficient as purpose-built designs. So, a flying car will be worse at driving than an exclusively land-based vehicle and will be worse at flying than an eVTOL without wheels.

Nevertheless, in June 2023, Alef became the first company to receive from the FAA a "Special Airworthiness Certification" to legally fly the Model A in the United States in certain locations.

Alef Aeronautics (credit: Alef)

"The Alef is likely to be a fairly sucky car, but it will be good enough to get you to and from the places you take off and land," writes Brad Templeton in *Forbes*.

Being able to fit in a standard parking spot (since the Alef doesn't have enormous wings) will also help distinguish this eVTOL.

The Alef Model A is currently limited to a maximum speed of 25 miles per hour when driving on a highway (it's designated an LSV, or low-speed vehicle). That will increase as the technology is proven, but it seems to me a non-starter for most customers—certainly those willing to pay $300,000 a pop.

In the meantime, high-profile Silicon Valley investor Tim Draper put $3 million of seed money into the company in 2022.

"This is one small step for planes, one giant step for cars," Alef CEO Dukhovny quipped.

Safety in the air

While most flying cars/eVTOLs will have a pilot initially at least, it's really not necessary, other than for the psychological comfort. Flying has long been—and remains—far safer than driving a car.

Fatalities are much more frequent in vehicles than on planes. (credit: Ian Savage)

"Forget about the hole in the side of the plane, the iPhones dropping from the sky and the door plug falling in some guy's backyard," writes *The Wall Street Journal's* Ben

Cohen. "The skies have become so amazingly, unexpectedly safe that it now takes nearly catastrophic failures to remind us that air safety is a remarkable American success."

But that's not how most people perceive the experience.

"It's against human nature for a person to fly," Plaut, of AIR EV, told me.

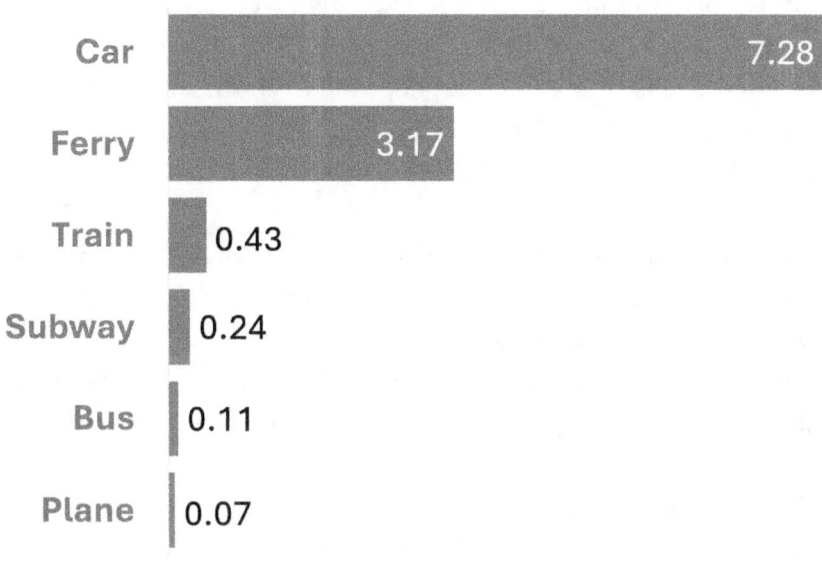

PASSENGER FATALITIES PER BILLION MILES

Car	7.28
Ferry	3.17
Train	0.43
Subway	0.24
Bus	0.11
Plane	0.07

Note: Data from 2000 to 2009

Petroleum has superior energy density compared to batteries. (credit: IEEE Spectrum)

Plaut is onto something.

After all, anyone who's ever been on a plane knows that flying can generate a lot of anxiety as you must give all your control and sense of freedom to people—the pilots, the flight attendants, the ground crews—whom you've most likely never met and don't know their backgrounds.

Plaut shared this understanding as we were talking about whether eVTOLs would ever go autonomous, a development that might be possible technically but would break the "social contract" we have with flying, where—since we're not able to make life-or-death decisions on our own—we can at least trust that the folks in charge have the proper training to keep us safe.

"People in general don't like to be governed by machines," Plaut says. "Even in most subways you have a driver. It's for a reason. You want to know that Joe is there. If you're close to the steering wheel yourself, you're going to want to grab it. And if you don't grab it, you want to have someone else there who can grab it for you."

Traveling in a two-ton metal box at 60 miles per hour "with six feet between you and the next two-ton metal box where the tiniest glitch will turn you into a pile of scrap metal—that seems safe while flying does not?" Plaut ponders. "It's all a matter of perception. We go into a metal tube to travel over the ocean but flying in a small vehicle with a parachute that goes just 100 miles is scary? That's very curious to me."

Indeed, in 2022, there was only a single fatal crash of a commercial airliner anywhere in the world—a China Eastern flight that killed all 132 passengers on board. The crash was thought to be caused by a suicidal pilot. Add in crashes on smaller airlines and the total number of fatalities in 2022 was 174. The same number of people die in car crashes every day-and-a-half in the U.S. Worldwide, 1.3 million people die every year on the roads.

That's in part because the stakes are higher when you're sailing through the skies.

"When you move fast and break things, safety is tossed aside," says Marc Ausman, CEO of Airflow.aero, another eVTOL maker.

Reuter, of Volocopter, adds that "many of the startup best practices—like A/B testing, 'fail fast' and all that—don't really apply to this industry . . . this is a marathon rather than a sprint."

Balkiz Sarihan, head of strategy for Urban Air Mobility at Airbus, which is working on an eVTOL dubbed the "CityAirBus NextGen," concurs.

"There is a lot of excitement and interest in the industry but at the end of it we are building an aerospace product that will carry passengers, so this is not a race from our perspective," he says.

This conservative outlook ensures that air travel just keeps getting safer.

In the 1970s, there was 1 death for every 350,000 passengers who took a commercial flight anywhere in the world. By the 1990s, that had dropped to 1 in every 1.3 million passengers. Today, it's 1 in every 1.8 million passengers.

That still doesn't mean self-piloting flying vehicles are on the horizon or that people will all of a sudden perceive flying as safer than driving.

"I love the idea of self-driving cars," pilot Adam Uhan told Stephen Dubner on the *Freakonomics* podcast. "But I also know, because I've seen it, where the machine does something that just doesn't make sense . . . something that was unexpected."

That's where a human operator—a driver or a pilot—can make all the difference.

"The other thing is your emotional response of getting on an airplane where there's no voice that comes from the front," Uhan continues. "I don't know how many people are ready for that. I know I'm not. I want somebody to be able to—if the machine goes wrong—at least shut the machine off and turn it back on again, to control-alt-delete it back into correction."

A pilot-less eVTOL, then, represents a serious psychological barrier, one that may be illogical in an objective sense—most planes today already essentially fly autonomously—but cannot be ignored.

"Our planes are operated largely by technology," Delta Airlines CEO Ed Bastian told Dubner for *Freakonomics*. Pilots are there mainly "to manage the technology and intervene as necessary."

Last-mile connectivity

Turning from passengers to cargo, could eVTOLs deliver items from Amazon and Walmart? Probably not—as noted above, weight limitations can't be escaped.

But drone delivery is definitely coming. Drones are less expensive than eVTOLs to manufacture and operate, and since they can be loaded up with items to deliver from a warehouse, rather than being used by an individual on an eVTOL-powered open-ended shopping spree, the drone's weight can be determined in advance.

There are still issues to be worked out.

+ How close can a drone come to houses without endangering residents' safety?

+ Does drone delivery work better in rural or urban areas?

+ If a drone lands in your front yard, is there the potential for theft (of the drone!) or deliberate damage by residents annoyed by the buzzing sound?

+ Would it be best for drones to drop off at a specific location—similar to a post office—where recipients would go to pick up their purchases? That's what Strix Drones is doing with its DroneDrop Delivery Mailbox, where residents get a key to their own "drone-postal box."

Drone delivery is sexy—on paper—but there are risks.

"The more delivery drones in the sky, the greater will be the chances of an accident," notes Plaut. "If an Airbus plane only fails one in a billion times, if you start doing deliveries at scale, with hundreds of millions of packages delivered a year, you will definitely have crashes. If you use the same statistic as for the Airbus plane, in New York City alone, at scale, you'll have 5 to 15 of these dropping out of the sky every year. It's a bad idea and will not be accepted."

Plaut may be taking an extreme position, but frankly, it's more likely that autonomous ground transport will corner the last-mile delivery market.

What about drone use in warfare and homeland security? We'll discuss that in detail in chapter 11, "War and Robots."

Strix Drones (credit: Strix)

Hydrogen vs. electric in the air

Whether a plane needs a pilot is certainly an interesting discussion to have at some point. But there's a much more pressing issue: What's the best way to power an aircraft—whether a small eVTOL or a full-size commercial jet?

As we noted in the introduction to this book, jets running on fossil-based fuels were in 2018 responsible for 4% of human-induced climate change and 2.4% of global annual CO_2 emissions. The International Energy Association (IEA) reports that the percentage dropped to just 2% during the pandemic but by 2022, emissions levels were up to 80% of their pre-Covid level.

The carbon footprint of air travel is also the worst among mobility modalities. Domestic flights contributed 255 grams of carbon dioxide equivalents (including CO_2 and other greenhouse gasses) per passenger kilometer. Short- and long-haul flights bumped that up by another 300 grams per passenger kilometer.

Electric batteries may be all the rage, but they're a nonstarter if the craft needs to travel more than a few hundred miles on a charge, as with commercial airliners.

That's clearly not a sustainable business model. After all, who would want to have to land at a dozen Podunk airports in order to get from San Francisco to New York? Fancy a stop in Bakersfield on the way to Los Angeles? I didn't think so.

That hasn't stopped Eviation.

The company's Alice electric passenger aircraft (not an eVTOL) took off in 2022 at the Grant County Airport in central Washington State. Alice reached an altitude of 3,280 feet and traveled at 155 miles per hour for a test flight lasting 8 minutes. Alice is powered by 21,500 small Tesla-style battery cells that weigh over 4 tons.

The Alice in action (credit: Eviation)

Following the test flight, Eviation took orders for 140 planes, 75 of them to Massachusetts-based regional airline Cape Air at a cost of $4 million per craft. DHL Express also purchased 12 planes intended for cargo. Alice can transport goods weighing 2,755 pounds. That translates into 9 people plus their luggage, a number that *BloombergNEF's* Colin McKerracher told me is the eVTOL sweet spot.

"You will never have a wide-body long-haul aircraft that is all electric," he says. "Only in the under-400-kilometer [250 mile] segment—small planes carrying no more than 50 people."

Eviation may be set on electric batteries but, for the rest of the industry, the answer to long-haul air travel may come from alternative types of fuel, in particular hydrogen and SAF—sustainable aviation fuel.

Long-distance air travel: The business case for hydrogen

We'll delve into the details of how hydrogen and SAF are made and how best to make them "green" in a later chapter. For now, let's just look at some data points pertaining specifically to hydrogen, the most promising and immediate of the up-and-coming technologies.

Hydrogen packs more energy density than batteries, can power a plane, ship or EV for a range equivalent to that of a gasoline or diesel engine, and can be produced entirely "green."

- ✦ McKinsey estimates that hydrogen could power up to 38% of all aircraft by 2050.

- ✦ Yet, by the same year, the amount of clean energy that would be required to generate all that hydrogen would be the equivalent of 10 to 25 of the world's largest wind farms—or a solar field the size of Belgium.

- ✦ About 89% to 96% of the energy would be used for long-distance aircraft. Only 4–11% would go to hydrogen-powered VTOLs. (should we call them "hVTOLs?")

Where would hydrogen be produced for planes? The most efficient solution would be at the airports.

"While airports have been touted as possible energy hubs, the scale of energy demand for alternative propulsion will make it extremely difficult to perform all energy production at airports," the McKinsey report states.

An airport that wanted to have its own hydrogen liquefaction (as well as a battery electricity generation network) on-site would require 5 to 10 times more electricity than London's Heathrow Airport currently consumes. Paris-Charles De Gaulle Airport would require approximately 5,800 hectares of solar panels to generate sufficient electricity to meet its demands. The entire airport today occupies just 3,300 hectares.

As a result, most energy production will be located off-site through partnerships with energy providers.

Even so, shifting to alternative propulsion will require a capital investment of between $700 billion and $1.7 trillion by 2050, with 90% of this for off-airport infrastructure.

McKinsey warns there's little time to debate the merits of hydrogen vs. batteries or where to place the infrastructure. "The investments needed to meet 2050 alternative propulsion-related infrastructure goals must start now!"

AIR CEO Rani Plaut is hitching his wagon to batteries, not hydrogen.

"Hydrogen is still a very new thing," he explained to me. "That raises a lot of questions about risk and efficiency. Compare that with batteries which are a bit risky but it's a known risk."

Plaut concedes that hydrogen has "five times the range" of batteries, but for AIR, he's concluded, "extra range is not an important feature for the early users. If we have two identical aircraft that sell for the same price, one based on batteries and the other based on hydrogen, even if the hydrogen-powered craft has three times the range, manufacturers aren't thinking about those issues in the short-term. They're thinking about certification, about how the eVTOL will be used in daily life, about whether air mobility is even feasible."

That said, Plaut is a realist.

"Batteries are marvelous but it's not enough in terms of density," he says. The future of winged travel will be some fusion of "hydrogen plus batteries."

That should help AIR with its relatively limited range—110 miles on a charge at speeds of up to 155 miles per hour with a flight time of 1 hour. That's good enough for a commute from Palo Alto to San Francisco, or from Hoboken to Brooklyn, but not for cross-continental air travel.

Still, Plaut says that preorders for the AIR ONE "are in the triple digits."

How about other eVTOL makers? We've already discussed Urban Aeronautics, which is launching as a hydrogen-powered craft. But even companies like Joby may eschew electric batteries eventually.

Flying toward the future

"A lot of people say the future of aviation is electric," says Joby's Simi. "I say, that's not the future—that's now. We're flying electric aircraft now. What comes next? We believe that hydrogen is next; perhaps first a hybrid of hydrogen and electric, and then ultimately pure hydrogen down the road. We believe that, in the aviation community broadly, hydrogen will be the standard by 2050."

Tech firm Universal Hydrogen has developed a conversion kit for regional carriers that replaces existing turboprop engines with a hydrogen fuel cell electric powertrain. The kit allows hydrogen fuel cells to be placed in the rear of plane.

To test its system, Universal Hydrogen outfitted a de Havilland Dash 8-300 turboprop plane (it was dubbed "Lightning McClean") with two engines—one running on standard fuel and one with an electric motor fed by a hydrogen fuel cell. According to Universal, the 2023 test flight constituted the largest aircraft to travel using, for the majority of its duration, hydrogen power.

The Universal Hydrogen test came after another startup, ZeroAvia, achieved a successful test flight of a small propeller aircraft (a 19-seat Dornier 228) partially powered by hydrogen fuel cells. It flew over Gloucestershire in southwest England.

Universal's business model is to deliver its hydrogen in modular capsules to be used by Boeing and Airbus single-aisle aircraft.

"The majority of aviation emissions are produced by the single aisle (also known as narrow body) fleet dominated by the Boeing 737 and the Airbus A320 families of aircraft," the Universal Hydrogen website explains. "Both Boeing and Airbus are likely to develop a replacement for these venerable models for entry into service in the mid-2030s. The only way aviation can meet Paris Agreement emissions targets is if the new single aisle airplanes are hydrogen powered . . . a hydrogen single aisle does not need to be a radical new design. Accommodating enough hydrogen for a transatlantic range without sacrificing passenger capacity would add nine meters to the length of a conventional A321 fuselage, still keeping it shorter than a 757-300."

Universal Hydrogen CEO Paul Eremenko hopes the first hydrogen retrofit of a regional airliner could come as early as 2025 or 2026. ZeroAvia hopes to take flight commercially around the same time.

ZeroAvia should not be confused with FlyZero, a proposed 279-seat plane that its backers—the U.K. government-backed research firm Aerospace Technology Institute—say will be able to fly from London to San Francisco without refueling. The FlyZero jet will store hydrogen in cryogenic fuel tanks at a temperature of minus 418 degrees Fahrenheit. There will be two tanks at the rear of the plane, with two smaller tanks placed near the plane's front to keep it balanced.

Hydrogen-powered drones

Nearly every drone in the air today is battery-powered. Not so with Israeli startup HevenDrones, which is developing hydrogen-powered, autonomous UAVs. In 2018, CEO and founder Bentzion Levinson had joined a volunteer initiative to help the Israeli army figure out how to fight the growing phenomenon of "fire kites" with small explosive payloads which would float over Israel's border with the Gaza Strip to burn Israeli fields, playgrounds, and homes.

The volunteers came up with the idea of building drones that could both determine where a fire had been ignited and then take action to put out the blaze. To do that, they'd need drones that could stay in the air potentially for hours (most battery-powered drones run out of juice within an hour) and they'd need to be able to carry much heavier payloads.

When the project was done, Levinson was smitten. He launched HevenDrones to address the military's needs—not only for firefighting but also for delivery of essential equipment, ammunition, and medicine to soldiers in the field. HevenDrones has been granted exclusivity through 2026 as the sole provider of hydrogen fuel-cell powered drones for the Israel Defense Forces.

HevenDrones' H2D200 can carry up to 10 pounds, fly for over 300 miles and stay in the air for 4 hours. The larger H2D250 ups the payload to 25 pounds, can last for more than 400 miles and stay aloft for up to 8 hours.

While HevenDrones is not focused exclusively on military applications for its drones, Levinson says the army was in some ways the "easiest" client to land, as it controls the airspace in times of conflict and is not subject to the same sort of regulatory demands that an Amazon delivery drone hovering over Teaneck might encounter. (I describe Amazon's delivery drone program more in chapter 10, "Supply Chain.")

Growing demand for advanced air mobility

For eVTOLs to be successful, they can't exist in a vacuum but rather must be embedded into "a bigger transportation network that covers an entire country," says Lilium's Wiegand. "That means being connected to ground transportation—taxis, car services, trains—all the way up to the big airlines, to which Lilium would act as feeder flights."

eVTOLs on their own "are just a minute addition," adds Plaut. "Air mobility only reduces congestion on the ground for the guy who bought the aircraft. In New York City, even if there are 500 eVTOLs moving through the air, that's nothing in the grand scheme of things. If electric aviation will account for 100,000 new air vehicles sold in a year, compare that with passenger cars, where 20 million are sold in the same time period. It has an impact, although in proportion to the big number it's still very small. But that doesn't make it nonviable."

Maybe if you had tens or hundreds of thousands of people coming by air into the city, it might move the needle. "In any case, those people will all still need to have ground transportation when they arrive at their destination," Plaut notes.

If the number of eVTOLs aren't enough to make a real difference, what's the point?

"Not everyone can be Elon Musk," Plaut quipped. "You have to do your tiny thing, in addition to other solutions like micromobility, and hope it will have an impact. The numbers may not be as large as many people think but I am sure it will be worthwhile!"

What's next?

"Autonomous aircraft," says Reuter. "Autonomy will free up an additional seat in the aircraft and it will make AAM much more affordable and scalable."

Won't that represent a threat to pilots who will worry about becoming unemployed in a few years?

"In phase one, we put a pilot in the aircraft to fulfill the traditional regulatory requirements," Reuter stresses. "We make it easy for the regulator to simply accept the VoloCity and VoloConnect as aircraft that resemble a helicopter, to a certain degree, and can integrate into existing air-traffic-management systems and can use existing heliport infrastructure. That's how we can get started tomorrow."

Eventually, there will be a "natural progression from being a pilot on board—which will become more boring because the vehicle will be much more automated—to being a pilot on the ground. I believe this offers a compelling career path for pilots; it gives them tremendous opportunity for growth in a tech environment."

Autonomous or not, Wiegand believes that, in the 2030 to 2045 timeframe, "using an eVTOL aircraft will be as normal as driving a car is today."

Richard Aboulafia takes a contrarian point of view in an article he penned for *Forbes*. Writing in early 2022, he takes to task Boeing's $450 million investment in Wisk.

"Boeing seems to be taking another step away from everything that made it great," he writes.

What's Aboulafia's concern?

The eVTOL market "can be euphemistically termed 'pre-revenue,'" he complains. "That is, there is no revenue at all."

The market for eVTOLs is no more than "a mirage," Aboulafia claims. "Multimillion-dollar rotorcrafts are too expensive for mass adoption, and yet their business plans depend on mass adoption to justify big upfront expenses. The result will likely be a flurry of bankruptcies."

Solving the contrail problem

Aviation contributes to climate change in one more way: Airliners can leave behind contrails—condensation trails—that form when the exhaust from jets mixes with water vapor at extremely high altitudes.

These minuscule ice crystals create artificial cirrus clouds. That might not sound so terrible, but the clouds trap heat in the Earth's atmosphere. So, reducing contrails contributes to slowing global warming.

The good news, according to researchers at Breakthrough Energy and Google: This is low-hanging fruit that may be easier to solve than other vexing climate change conundrums.

It's the "highest leverage climate opportunity we know of," says Breakthrough Energy's Marc Shapiro. Reducing contrails is "the equivalent of removing carbon from the atmosphere at a cost of $10 per ton or less."

In 2022, the Intergovernmental Panel on Climate Change estimated that contrails represent about 35% of the aviation industry's contribution to global warming. Contrails formed while flying at night have an even bigger warming effect, as trapped heat is not offset by reflection from incoming sunlight.

Studies have put the amount of warming caused by contrails at 1% of the total human causes of climate change.

Hydrogen won't necessarily help. While hydrogen does not produce CO_2 emissions, it still contributes to contrail formation.

There is one easy solution, however: If pilots can maneuver their aircraft to avoid humid "ice supersaturated regions of the atmosphere," this might reduce the formation of contrails. It's not that hard—it typically requires changes in altitude similar to those pilots already perform to avoid turbulence. Adjusting a plane's altitude by just a couple of thousand feet can reduce contrail formation by half.

"The airline industry knows how to avoid turbulence," notes Juliet Rothenberg, lead product manager for climate AI at Google. "It's a very straightforward extension to avoid contrails."

Breakthrough Energy was founded by Microsoft Chairman Bill Gates to pursue climate solutions. The organization began collaborating with Google's research division in 2022. Their approach uses data from weather satellites to train machine-learning software to recognize and then predict where contrail-conducive regions are likely to occur in the future.

American Airlines has joined the party too.

Google and Breakthrough Energy integrated their predictions into American's pilot flight-planning software. The result: Over the course of 70 flights between January and March 2023, the software reduced contrail creation by 54%.

The downside: All that maneuvering bumped up fuel usage by 2 percent.

The two groups hope to establish an independent organization that will collect contrail data and publish it in a publicly available clearinghouse that will provide verification that changes in flight paths are, in fact, making a difference.

"All airlines are going to have to do this eventually—[in] years, not decades," Jill Blickstein, American's VP of sustainability says, although she tempers that desire with economics.

"Burning more jet fuel is not inconsequential to American or any other airline. We wouldn't do this at any cost."

Researchers at Google and Breakthrough Energy believe the cost won't be that high: Only a small fraction of flights will need to change altitude to avoid contrails, meaning the additional fuel burned should only be 0.3% higher, not 2 percent.

"This is really unique among climate solutions in that it can scale in years, not decades," notes Rothenberg.

NASA's solid-state battery

A new solid-state sulfur selenium battery developed by NASA could revolutionize air travel by making it possible to power a plane with electricity.

For years now, NASA's Solid-State Architecture Batteries for Enhanced Rechargeability and Safety (SABERS) project has been developing a battery with the efficiency to run an aircraft long-distance. We'll go into more detail on battery technologies in chapter 6, but for now, what's important is that solid-state batteries such as NASA's new prototype have much greater range than lithium-ion electric batteries.

CleanTechnica reports that the NASA prototype has an energy density of 500 watt-hours per kilogram (about 227 watt-hours per pound)—double the energy density of conventional lithium-ion batteries.

Another benefit: NASA's sulfur selenium battery discharges energy ten times faster than competing solid-state batteries. This is important because an airplane needs to be able to discharge its energy quickly enough to achieve liftoff.

All that energy release causes temperatures to spike, but the researchers found the sulfur selenium battery could withstand temperatures twice as hot as those that lithium-ion batteries can tolerate. The NASA prototypes are also safer, maintaining their solid structure even when damaged, which significantly reduces the risk of fire.

The NASA team also made the batteries 40% lighter than before. Smaller batteries can mean more batteries, and, therefore, more fuel can fit on one plane.

It will, nevertheless, be a long time before we see these batteries on actual working planes. Solid-state batteries are costly to produce, and any new airplane component to be used on commercial flights must undergo rigorous testing before approval. Still, this advancement is an exciting development in energy storage that could revolutionize air travel in the future.

In the meantime . . .

While we're waiting for eVTOLs and commercial airplanes running on hydrogen, SAF or solid-state batteries, there are still a few things concerned travelers can do right now.

+ **Avoid short flights.** Drive (ideally with three to four other passengers) or take the train instead. Here's a comparison of carbon emissions for a 200-mile trip:

CARBON FOOTPRINT OF A 200 MILE TRIP
(pounds of CO2e emitted per passenger)

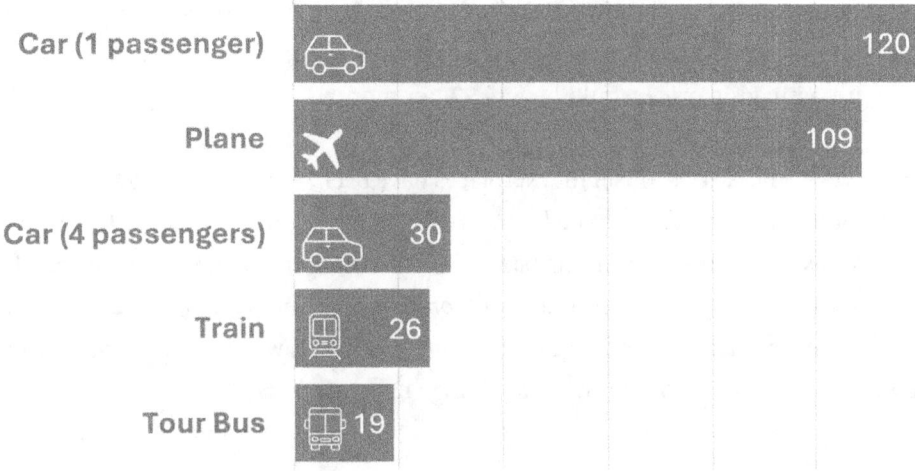

Single passenger car rides produce more pollution per passenger than air travel. (credit: Sustainable Travel International)

+ **Go non-stop**. Jets produce the greatest amount of carbon emissions during take-off and landing. Each stop or layover adds more CO2 to the atmosphere. If you can go direct, you help the planet.

+ **Take fewer but longer vacations.** That's better for the planet than multiple shorter ones.

+ **Fly economy**. If everyone flew business or first class, there would be fewer passengers on the plane, which would result in a higher CO2 burden per passenger. Packed planes may be uncomfortable but they're better for the environment.

+ **Limit your luggage**. The more weight a plane takes on, the more fuel it must burn. If you reduce your luggage weight by 15 pounds on a 10-hour flight, you can cut your emissions by roughly 80 pounds. If there are 150 people on your flight, that's 12,000 pounds of emissions cut if they all make this small change. Bring clothing you can re-wear and items that are easy to wash.

+ **When you arrive, use public transportation**. Don't rent a car, especially if you'll be mostly touring a city. Use the bus, train, streetcar, rickshaw or, if you're feeling particularly helpful, a (non-electric) bike!

✦ **Buy carbon offsets**. Companies like Terapass make it easy for individual travelers and corporations to purchase carbon offsets. Just enter the number of miles you'll be traveling on the website, pay the estimated fee, and you can feel less guilty about that flight with the family to Disney World. A monthly subscription to Terapass starts at $8.34. (I input in my own heavy travel schedule and Terapass told me my guilt-assuaging price would be $44.92 per month.)

However, some carbon-offset marketplaces have been, as the climate publication *Grist* puts it, "riddled with fraud" or, to be less extreme, exaggeration. For example, a bird sanctuary in Pennsylvania markets offsets based on its stewardship of 2,300 acres of oak forest. But the sanctuary's director admitted to *Bloomberg* that the trees have been untouched for nearly a century and face no real danger of being cut down. In other words, you'd be paying for an offset that does nothing to change net emissions.

Hypersonic travel

How much would you pay for a hypersonic flight that could get you from New York to Tokyo in just 2 to 3 hours, saving 13 hours of travel time in the air?

ARK Investment Management estimates that well-heeled business travelers would be willing to pay $100,000 to take that flight and that passengers on short-haul private flights would be willing to pay some $15,000 for every 2 hours saved.

While that might not be a convincing financial argument, it's the first data point I've seen that suggests the possibility of hypersonic flight as a viable alternative to today's long- and short-haul flights . . . at least for a certain demographic.

If and when the price comes down, the sky will literally be the limit.

Hypersonic jets scream through the air at speeds approaching Mach 5 before touching the edge of the atmosphere (52 kilometers or 170,000 feet). That's high enough that residents below won't complain of constant sonic booms.

There's an elephant in the room, though, and it's one that will have many trumpeting in collective outrage.

Hypersonic flights use an enormous amount of fuel.

According to the International Council on Clean Transportation, hypersonic travel burns up to nine times more fuel per passenger than subsonic flights. As we've discussed, electric batteries can only get you so far, making them a nonstarter. Four hundred to 500 miles of range might be acceptable for an EV on land, and maybe for short hauls in the air in an eVTOL. But running out of juice beyond the Earth's atmosphere . . . well, that's a fatal attraction.

ESTIMATED FLIGHT TIME FROM TOKYO TO LOS ANGELES
(one-way flight time in hours)

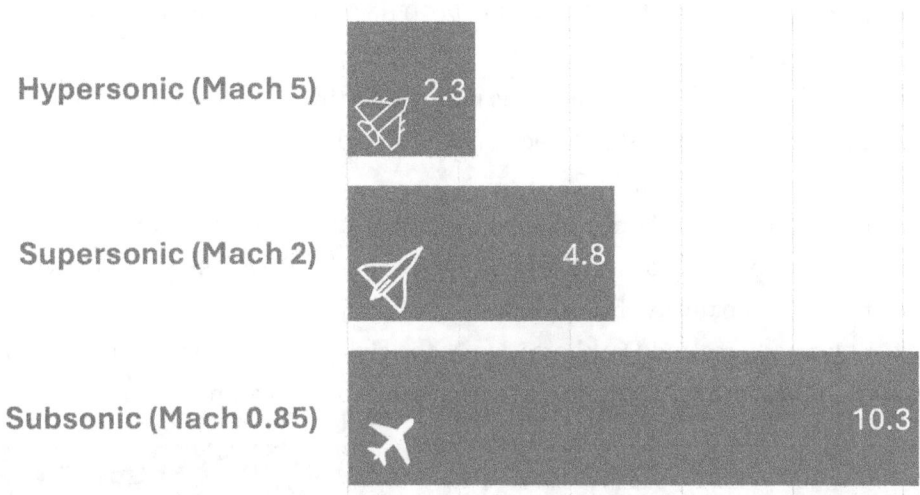

Imagine a trip from Tokyo to Los Angeles in 2.3 hours? (credit: Spaceworks)

Research into developing new hypersonic craft has become a focus of the defense industries. Deloitte reports that annual unclassified defense spending requests for hypersonic tech and weaponry reached more than $3 billion in 2020. That's a 25% compound annual growth rate since 2014.

In the meantime, there's a lot of room for innovation here. Think about it: It takes just as long to fly from India to New York as it did 50 years ago.

Maybe hypersonic travel is an example of trickle-down technology: Start with the rich and someday we'll all fly faster.

Still, if you're ready to zip across the Atlantic in just a few short hours, here are the companies that show the most promise:

Hermeus

Hermeus has set its sights on building a Mach 5 aircraft, which would fly at 5 times the speed of sound. The company has raised $100 million (including from OpenAI CEO Sam Altman and Peter Thiel's Founders Fund) to develop and test at its 110,000-square-foot Atlanta-based facility the company's first full-scale engine that will eventually power its debut aircraft.

"Hermeus is pursuing an ambitious vision that seems impossible at first glance, but they pair it with an engineering culture and business road map that can actually bring it into reality," Altman said in a statement.

The company's CEO, AJ Piplica, said in 2020 that it would take "around a decade of development" before Hermeus could produce commercial passenger aircraft.

The first, dubbed the Quarterhorse, is more for testing.

"It's effectively the smallest possible airframe to flight test our engine," Hermeus COO Skyler Shuford told CNBC in 2022.

A second model, Darkhorse, "will be capable of sustained hypersonic flight and be able to carry cargo or payloads." Darkhorse is earmarked "for defense and intelligence customers," the company's website notes.

After Quarterhorse and Darkhorse comes the Halcyon, which will be the company's hypersonic 20-passenger aircraft with a range of 4,600 miles. Estimated launch date: 2029.

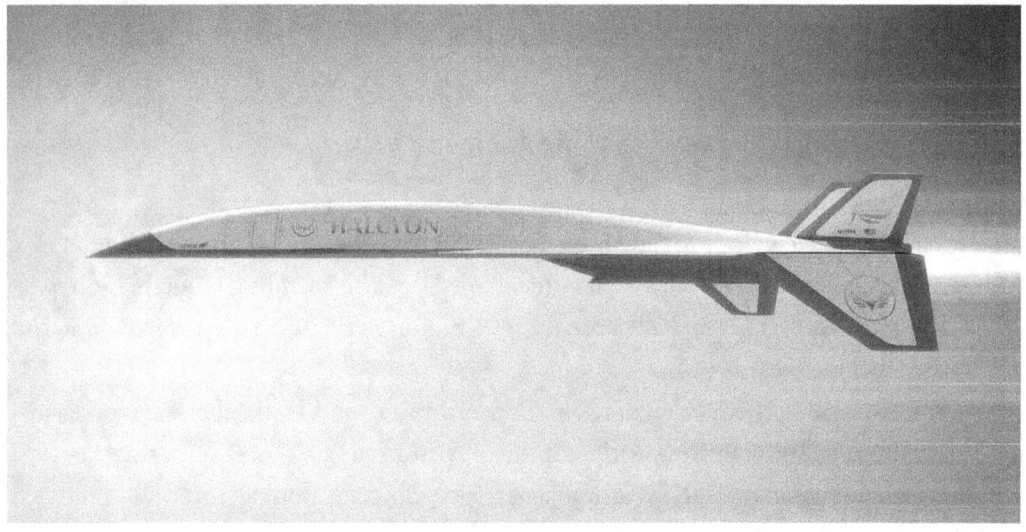

The Hermeus Halcyon (credit: Hermeus)

Hermeus says it has completed over 100 engine tests to date. In 2021, the company won a $60 million contract from the U.S. Air Force to flight test the Quarterhorse.

NASA's X-59

The main claim to fame of this joint venture between NASA and Lockheed is that it is supposed to be significantly less noisy. The X-59 will produce a sonic "thump" rather than a boom when it breaks the sound barrier.

The craft's unique design—it has a longer, pointy nose and sharper wings than traditional airplanes, giving it an appearance like a dart—will spread the sound waves more equally along the length of the aircraft. This sleeker airframe should prevent individual soundwaves from adding up, hence the muffled boom.

The X-59 (credit: Wikimedia Commons)

The X-59 is missing a transparent front windshield, replacing that with a screen for the pilots to see out of.

The X-59 will generate a 75 perceived level decibel (PldB). The first commercially viable supersonic plane, the Concorde, by contrast, generated 105 decibels when it boomed at a max speed of Mach 2. The X-59 will cruise at a speed of Mach 1.42.

"Our researchers are going to work with the public and we're going to fly over various cities and towns, and they're going to give us the feedback of that thump," says Nils Larson, the NASA test pilot whose job it will be to prove the X-59 can replace the boom with a thump. "Was that thump too loud? Did you even hear it at all?"

Iain Boyd, a professor of aerospace engineering at the University of Colorado in Boulder, stresses that the noise issue must be overcome if hypersonic travel is to take off.

"The inconvenience and discomfort of extra noisy aircraft just for a relatively small number of rich people, that doesn't sound good," he notes.

Could the X-59 finally help lift the FAA ban forbidding supersonic planes from flying over populated areas? We'll find out when the first planes take off—in 2035.

As I was writing *The Future of Mobility*, NASA announced it was canceling a separate "X" project—the X-57, what would have been NASA's first all-electric plane. NASA cited safety concerns it said were "insurmountable" with the time and budget they have for the project.

The X-57 (credit: Wikimedia Commons)

"Unfortunately, we recently discovered a potential failure mode in the propulsion system that we determined to pose an unacceptable risk to the pilot's safety, and the safety of personnel on the ground, during ground tests," Bradley Flick, the director of NASA's Armstrong Flight Research Center in California, says. "Mitigation of that failure would take the project well beyond its planned completion at the end of this fiscal year, so NASA has decided to end the project on time without taking the vehicle to flight."

Stargazer

This hypersonic plane, from Houston-based aerospace startup Venus Aerospace, is aiming to be the fastest of them all, traveling at nine times the speed of sound. At Mach 9, a trip from Tokyo to Los Angeles would take little more than an hour. You could pop over for lunch in Roppongi and be back on the West Coast before dinnertime.

"How much does the world change if you can get anywhere in an hour?" asks Venus CEO and cofounder Sassie Duggleby.

The Stargazer's speed is more than four times faster than the Concorde and triple that of the fastest aircraft ever built, the Lockheed SR-71 Blackbird, which could achieve Mach 3.2.

In 2022, Venus raised $33 million to build its plane, which will hold 12 passengers and travel at 11,000 kilometers per hour (6,800 miles per hour) at an altitude of 170,000 feet (51.8 kilometers). That's not quite outer space, which is still about 50 kilometers (30 miles) higher than Stargazer's maximum altitude. But passengers should still be able to see the curvature of the Earth.

The Stargazer, named after the Federation starship that Jean-Luc Picard captained before taking the helm of the Enterprise in *Star Trek: The Next Generation,* will use engines to take off—like a conventional airplane—then transition to rockets "once at an altitude and away from the city," Venus Aerospace CTO Andrew Duggleby told *Gizmodo* in 2021. The craft uses a "rotating detonation engine" where the wave of detonation travels in a circular channel spinning at 20,000 rotations per second, rather than generating the classic long exhaust plume of traditional rockets.

First commercial flights aren't expected until the end of the 2020s. Venus is aiming for a schedule of four flights a day once it gets up and running.

Duggleby hopes that tickets for Stargazer will be roughly the same price as first-class tickets on a commercial aircraft.

Destinus

This Swiss-based startup is also developing a hypersonic jet that can travel at Mach 5. The twist: Destinus's planes will be powered by hydrogen, not fossil-fuels. That gives them the range that batteries cannot provide and, if the hydrogen is produced in a green manner, a much-improved environmental profile compared with gasoline or even SAF.

Destinus says its hydrogen-powered hypersonic jets can transport passengers or cargo from the U.S. to Shanghai in just 3.5 hours. An unmanned prototype deploying hydrogen "after burners"—an additional combustion component used on a turbojet engine for generating more thrust by injecting additional fuel, in this case hydrogen, into the turbine exhaust stream—was launched in May 2023 and reached speeds of 250 miles per hour. A faster prototype is in the works.

The Destinus (credit: Destinus)

Boom

Boom Supersonic's Overture is not a hypersonic craft, although with a top speed of Mach 2.2, it's nearly three times as fast as a 747.

Boom is building a massive factory in North Carolina for the 80-seat Overture. Boom hopes the first planes will be ready for test flights in 2026, although you won't be able to board one as a paying passenger until at least 2029.

The Boom Overture is about the same size as a 757 and, as a relatively svelte craft, has a two-two seating configuration with no middle section. The plane will be run entirely on SAF, which Boom says could result in an 80% reduction in the amount of fuel required compared with the Concorde.

In 2021, Boom ditched Rolls-Royce as its third-party engine maker and began developing its own Symphony engine, which Boom says will help the Overture "operate at net-zero carbon."

The Overture also uses a carbon-fiber technology that is lighter and more fuel-efficient than past supersonic jets.

Boom has clients in the U.S. (United ordered 15 of its jets in 2021; American put in an order for 20 planes) and Japan (Japan Airlines was the first to make an order from

Boom—20 jets in 2017). Boom is focusing on transoceanic routes that will benefit from its speed.

"It changes where we can vacation, changes where we can do business, changes who you can fall in love with or who you can be close to," says Boom CEO Blake Scholl.

Another advantage: "Instead of paying in business class for a flying bed, you get the best bed in the world, which is the one at your home the night before you have to leave," Scholl notes.

To make such sweeping changes to our culture, the price of a flight can't be $12,000, as was the fee to ride on a Concorde in the 1990s.

Scholl says not to worry.

Twelve-thousand dollars is "not travel," Scholl says. "That's a thing you might hope to do once in a lifetime versus what we want to get to, which is anywhere in the world in 4 hours for $100."

He adds, somewhat sheepishly, "it's going to take us time to get there" and that initial fares will still be around the cost of a business-class ticket.

But, Scholl recalls, "electric cars, when they first came out, were pretty expensive. But we kept working on them. The price came down. And they got better and better. We're going to do the same thing. We're going to keep innovating."

Hypersonic travel is definitely for the 1%, an edge case of an edge case for hedge fund managers and the hyperaffluent. If the fuel and cost issues can be addressed, though, I am down for hopping on a hypersonic jet and meeting readers for croissants and coffee in Paris.

Eulogy for the Concorde

Fast travel between continents had a poster child in the Concorde, the now-retired, super-fast aircraft that jetted passengers across the Atlantic in a fraction of the typical time. It took just three hours to fly from New York to London on a Concorde.

The Concorde failed for a number of reasons, not the least of which was the deadly crash in 2000 that killed all 109 people on board when it burst into flames after smashing into a hotel shortly following takeoff from Paris's Charles de Gaulle Airport.

But the Concorde was also too expensive, too polluting (it generated five times the pollution of a subsonic plane) and less comfortable than a business-class seat on a conventional airline.

Britain and France agreed to develop the Concorde in 1962. They spent some $2.4 billion on the project (an amount equivalent to more than $15 billion today). The first commercial flight, replete with champagne, caviar, lobster, and a bevy of celebrities, athletes and business moguls, was in 1976; it last took off in 2003.

The Concorde (credit: Wikimedia Commons)

In its heyday, the Concorde flew at close to Mach 2 speeds, that is, twice the speed of sound. The sonic booms that resulted were highly upsetting to people living on the ground. When the U.S. Air Force ran a test of a supersonic plane in the 1960s, residents of Oklahoma City reported hundreds of broken windows. The Federal Aviation Administration subsequently deemed U.S. territory a supersonic no-fly zone.

None of this was what grounded the Concorde, though. Rather, it was unfavorable economics.

After the plane resumed flying in 2001, after a year-and-a-half investigation following the deadly crash in Paris, the terrorist attacks on the World Trade Center and Washington, DC, cut demand for plane travel, at least temporarily. Wealthy travelers favored private business jets that could fly directly to and from their airports of choice, avoiding the zealousness and annoyance of local TSA inspectors.

The Concorde's controlling partners, British Airways and Air France, realized they could no longer afford the fuel and operating costs.

Only 14 Concorde jets ever entered commercial service and flew on just 2 approved routes.

Hypersonic ups the ante by cutting travel times in half again—just 90 minutes from New York to London—as the fastest planes travel at 5 times the speed of sound.

Will that be enough to get passengers back on the super/hypersonic bandwagon?

Blake Scholl, of Boom, is not giving up.

"Remember, the Concorde was designed 60 years ago, with slide rules and draft paper and wind tunnels—and no computer. Everything's changed."

Space: The final frontier

The most sky-high application of advanced mobility will be in space—truly the final frontier.

Maybe someday there will be a Ritz Carlton (or a Motel 5) on the moon—or if Elon Musk has any say in the matter, on Mars—where you can post a selfie with Kim Kardashian or one of her kids. Maybe the next season of Big Brother will be on the International Space Station. But I'm not ready to take bets on when, where or how.

Nor am I sure what the balance should be between government-sponsored missions (NASA) and wealthy entrepreneurs (SpaceX, Blue Origin, Virgin Galactic).

Elon Musk, via SpaceX, now effectively controls most space launches from the U.S. The company's rockets powered 66% of flights from American launch sites in 2022 and handled 88% in the first six months of 2023. The result: huge valuations for SpaceX.

The SpaceX starship (credit: Shutterstock)

The Russian Soyuz rocket has been off-limits for many buyers since Russia's invasion of Ukraine.

Are we effectively privatizing space exploration? Maybe that's not so bad.

Governments tend to get pretty bloated. On the other hand, 100% privatization would seem to me a risk too far; it's dangerous when you have billionaires with little accountability running their own playbooks.

In the meantime, though, there is plenty of space-tech to consider, just not involving manned flight yet.

Pharma in space

Scientists developing new antibiotics are forever playing catch-up. Virulent bacteria evolve slowly, sometimes taking years before becoming dangerous enough to trigger a full-fledged outbreak.

In zero gravity, the trajectory of that same bacteria's destructive power can be charted sometimes in a matter of days. Proteins crystalize differently and molecules take on different shapes when there's less atmospheric "noise" in the way.

On Earth, for example, "a petri dish allows you to grow a culture in two dimensions," explains Yossi Yamin, CEO of Swiss-Israeli startup SpacePharma. "But with low gravity in orbit, you get a third dimension. The culture grows more like in the body itself, not smashed to the surface of the dish."

As a result, pharmaceutical companies increasingly are looking to conduct experiments in space. Merck, Procter & Gamble and Eli Lilly have all run experiments on the International Space Station over the past decade.

Can space travel bring us medical advances?

For just $230,000—a tiny fraction of the development budget for a new drug—clients can rent one of SpacePharma's orbiting "mini-labs" for up to six months.

SpacePharma preloads the tiny labs—no larger than a milk carton—with all the components required for a variety of tests and hitches a ride on a rocket.

"When there are no G-forces, everything grows and reacts much more clearly than on Earth," Yamin notes.

SpacePharma has two mini-labs already in operation. One went up with the help of India's national space agency in February 2017. The other is integrated into the International Space Station and was launched from Virginia's Wallops Flight Facility later that year.

Tests done in outer space don't always have to be returned to Earth in full; sometimes all that's needed is the data.

Sometimes there can be bizarre reactions.

A scientist working for NASA once sent flatworms to space to test their regenerative properties. Some of the worms grew two heads.

Even crazier, when they reproduced in space, their offspring also had two heads.

Bringing space junk down to earth

Space is getting crowded.

In addition to the tens of thousands of satellites already orbiting the Earth, the space-tech industry anticipates that about 14,000 new satellites will be launched by the end of the decade.

That's on top of the 25,000 pieces of debris larger than a softball—and the truly astounding 100 million pieces of space debris larger than a millimeter—already up there.

There is currently about 9,000 tons of space debris orbiting the Earth, everything from rocket thrusters, derelict satellites, and tiny fragments of debris from collisions and explosions.

It's gotten so bad that the U.S. issued new regulations in 2022 that won't allow the launch of a satellite unless it has a convincing capability to move out of the way after five years from the end of the mission.

That's a fivefold reduction from the previous regulation mandating removal of space junk only after 25 years.

One space mobility firm that might be able to help is Space Plasmatics, which has developed teeny-tiny plasma thrusters that can fly a nanosatellite (also known as a "CubeSat") out of the location of heavy space debris using ionized gas in an electric field, rather than the traditional propulsion method of chemical reactions. The thrusters get their power from solar cells mounted on the satellites themselves.

Space Plasmatics is just one of a dozen startups addressing our interstellar traffic jams. Here are four other promising firms I'm watching:

+ Japan-headquartered **Astroscale** has raised over $200 million since it was founded in 2013. The company makes a robotic arm which connects to the docking plates preinstalled on satellites, in order to bring a decommissioned satellite low enough into Earth's atmosphere that it burns up upon reentry.

+ **ClearSpace** received a $100 million contract from the European Space Agency (ESA) in 2020 to "de-orbit" debris from a Vega rocket, jointly developed by the Italian Space Agency and the ESA. ClearSpace's mission: to capture a "secondary payload adapter that was left after the Vega launched in 2013. Like Astroscale, ClearSpace's technology forces old satellites and space junk into the Earth's atmosphere where it will burn up. The company also intends to provide "on-orbit servicing facilities" that can fix satellites in space instead of discarding them.

+ **Share My Space** doesn't remove space junk but it allows its customers to know where it is, thus avoiding potentially mission-challenging or fatal collisions. The company's collision-warning system is based on astronomical observations and deep learning algorithms that predict the risk related to in-orbit smash-ups.

+ **Obruta** takes its cue from commercial fishing. The company has developed a tethered, autonomous "space net" to scoop space debris out of the way. It can be used for inspection, orbital refueling, satellite life extension and end-of-life debris removal.

Won't satellites eventually fall out of orbit and burn up on their return to Earth naturally? Yes, but it's hard to predict when or how quickly that will happen. It could be days—or 1,000 years, depending on how high up the satellite is. Natural decay also means loss of control—will the debris fall on a populated area?

Space mining

The AppleTV+ show *For All Mankind* depicts an alternative history where a U.S. startup called Helios (not to be confused with the actual space-tech startup of the same name) has set up a massive—and lucrative—mining operation on the moon. Its main goal is to bring down helium-3, an element critical for nuclear fusion but which is scarce on Earth.

There's nothing science fiction about mining the moon for minerals that are hard to source on Earth, though. In addition to helium-3, the moon also has deposits of scandium, yttrium, platinum, palladium, rhodium, and water. (Didn't Tom Lehrer write a song about that?)

The movie *Moon* starred Sam Rockwell as an astronaut stationed there to mine minerals.

In the real world, if the fusion process could be perfected, Gerald Kulcinski, a nuclear engineer and director of the Fusion Technology Institute at the University of Wisconsin–Madison, estimates that just 40 tons of helium-3 could power the entire U.S. for a year. Kulcinski believes there are a million metric tons of helium-3 embedded in the outermost layer of the moon's crust.

NASA aimed to send a test drill rig to the moon in 2023, and to build and operate a pilot processing plant by 2023. The first customers are expected to be commercial rocket companies that could use the moon's resources for fuel or oxygen.

Ferrying vast amounts of lunar soil to Earth for processing would quickly prove impractical. So, any such mining must be done on-site in space.

That requires infrastructure.

3D printers will become an important part of the mix, as will autonomous robotic mining equipment, the kind I describe in more detail in the chapter on ag-tech. A lunar base will need to be built to house the off-world technicians managing the mining operations.

Wouldn't massive mining potentially destabilize the moon, much as strip mining has decimated swaths of rural America?

The website *911 Metallurgist* predicts that, even if one metric ton of minerals were removed entirely from the moon each day, it would still take 220 million years to deplete just 1% of the moon's mass.

Yeah, I'm not too worried.

Solar power from space

It sounds far-fetched, but satellites orbiting well above the Earth's atmosphere could collect solar energy, convert it to current and then beam it back home via microwaves. The microwaves would, in turn, be captured by photovoltaic cells or antennas and converted into electricity.

Why go to all that trouble when the sun shines just fine on Earth?

The problem is that the sun doesn't shine at night, and clouds also hamper solar energy collection.

The ESA announced in 2022 that it is seriously considering such an approach to reduce greenhouse gas emissions. Dubbed SOLARIS, ESA has given the program initial funding with the aim to start beaming solar power home by 2025.

Europe presently consumes just under 3,000 terawatt-hours of electricity on an annual basis. Massive facilities in a geostationary orbit could meet between one-quarter and one-third of that demand.

The biggest downside: Development and deployment of these kinds of systems would cost hundreds of billions of euros. The price is particularly high because the satellites would need to be very large—each with a mass 10 times larger than the International Space Station. SOLARIS would require dozens of satellites and launching all their component parts into space would require thousands of launches. (The satellites would be assembled in low Earth orbit.)

The concept also has run into stinging criticism from Elon Musk.

"It's the stupidest thing ever," Musk told *Popular Mechanics*. "If anyone should like space solar power, it should be me. I've got a rocket company and a solar company. I should be really on it. But it's super obviously not going to work."

Why is Musk so down on solar power from space?

"With a solar panel in orbit, you get twice the solar energy, but you've got to do a double conversion: Photon to electron to photon back to electron," Musk explains. "What's your conversion efficiency? All in, you're going to have a real hard time even getting to 50%. So just put that solar cell on Earth."

Physicist Casey Handmer also has his doubts.

Even if there were "100% transmission efficiency, low orbital launch costs, complete development and procurement cost parity, and a crippling land shortage on Earth, even then, space-based solar power won't be able to compete."

Space-based solar power, Handmer estimates, would be at least "three orders of magnitude" more expensive than terrestrial-based energy sources.

"In some distant future, the Earth will probably get its power from space," writes Eric Berger for *Ars Technica*. "But will that be this century or 200 years from now?"

Don't blast off. Fling it.

One of the oddest technologies in space-tech I've seen involves a company called SpinLaunch which has built a device that can literally "fling" objects into space.

The SpinLaunch launcher (credit: SpinLaunch)

Instead of using a conventional rocket to vertically propel things into orbit, SpinLaunch's unit taps into centrifugal force and kinetic energy.

A launch vehicle is attached to a rotating arm in a large vacuum chamber. The arm spins faster and faster until it's ready to "fling" the craft into space at around 5,000 miles per hour.

About a minute into flight, when the rocket reaches 200,000 feet, a two-stage fuel-powered rocket kicks in and takes advantage of the thinner atmosphere and shorter distance to propel the satellite the final bit of the journey into space. This process, the company claims, means it is able to launch a rocket into space at 20 times less than the cost of a conventional rocket.

SpinLaunch has already fired a payload at 1,000 miles per hour to a height of nearly 30,000 feet and has a contract with NASA to further explore the potential to reduce fuel requirements using the SpinLaunch system. SpinLaunch has completed nine flight tests to date, all successful, the company's CEO Jonathan Yang says. It aims to start flinging satellites into orbit in 2026.

The idea sounds far-fetched, but the company has raised $150 million from top VCs including Kleiner Perkins, ATW Partners, ATMA Capital and Lauder Partners.

A mag-lev rocket to orbit

Winnie Lau, who served as a vice president for SpinLaunch, is now the founder of Auriga Space, a new space-tech company that raised $5 million in 2023 for its electromagnetic launch system.

Auriga is building a ground-based electromagnetic track that uses electricity to create a powerful magnetic field. The energy from the magnets accelerates a projectile down the track at super-fast speeds—it's a technology similar to a high-speed maglev train.

By aiming the accelerator upward, Auriga can use kinetic energy from the launch to propel a vehicle into high altitude. The electromagnetic launch system essentially replaces the first-stage rocket. The vehicle only fires its own engines for the final, less intensive last leg to orbit.

Automotive Ventures is an investor in Auriga.

Space law

In 2020, then-U.S. President Donald Trump signed an executive order stating that any American citizen or company can extract and use resources in space.

That order covers any planet, satellite (like the moon) or even asteroids, as all may be a solid source of minerals in space.

While this seems like exactly the sort of decision that prompted the space race in *For All Mankind*, it turns out to be completely legal. That's because the United Nations Outer Space Treaty allows each signatory government to determine what rights its own citizens have in space.

That's in contrast to what the treaty says about *settling* outer space—it explicitly prohibits the appropriation of any region of space. Space, according to the treaty, is a "global commons."

"Nonappropriation" essentially means that "no nation can sell a piece of property [in space] to its citizens," notes Kim Ellis-Hayes, an international space lawyer. One of the rights we see in terrestrial real estate is that when you buy a property, you exclude others from that property.

But wouldn't extracting resources from an asteroid or the moon by definition exclude others coveting the same resources?

The UN's Outer Space Treaty is not the only one to set laws for space. The 1979 Moon Treaty bars the use of the moon for nonscientific purposes.

NASA's Artemis Accords also hope to "establish a common suite of principles to govern the civil exploration and use of outer space."

But the U.S., Russia, and China have all refused to sign the Moon Treaty, and Russia and China won't sign on to the Artemis Accords.

With Russia and China planning a joint moon mission, analysts fear that the same international disputes we see on Earth could be mirrored in space.

The current treaties have a built-in problem: They are "only between space-faring nations and not commercial businesses" like Elon Musk's SpaceX or Richard Branson's Virgin Galactic, says Neta Palkovitz, founder of the space law, regulation, and policy consulting group, NewSpace Firm.

States can take their space squabbles to the International Court of Justice, but commercial entities don't have standing there, Palkovitz notes. "So, right now, if there is a dispute regarding space activities, there is no specific place to go to solve things without involving states."

That said, Palkowitz doesn't feel that space is a complete Wild West situation.

"There are five space treaties," she notes. "But having said that, there are areas which need to be further regulated."

Palkowitz says that her biggest challenge "as a space law practitioner and academic researcher is to offer a decent dispute-resolution mechanism for commercial space activities."

What worries Palkowitz the most?

In space there are no "rules of the road," she says. "If there' s a collision, it is extremely difficult to know who is at fault." There are no traffic lights, no stop signs. "And what happens if only one driver can actually control its 'vehicle'? Space debris and small satellites without propulsion cannot move out of the way even if the owners wanted them to!"

Who will pay for cleaning up all that space junk is another issue that concerns Palkowitz.

"It is still a long way to go but it will have to be solved," she says. If not, then "launches would still be possible, but they'd be much more expensive for satellite owners. In many jurisdictions, a satellite operator would have to obtain a license from the state. The state, in return, would ask for third-party liability insurance and, when collisions become part of daily reality, it would mean the premium prices would just be too expensive for operators to pay."

There's one more space law question to be solved, and it's also mired in morality: Do we have any rights to what's on the moon at all?

Michelle Maloney, cofounder of the Earth Laws Alliance, says no.

"Every living organism on planet Earth has seen that moon," Maloney says. "The moon is an entity to itself; we don't own it."

That may turn into wishful thinking because of a phenomenon known as "The Tragedy of the Commons."

Tragedy of the Commons

The concept of the Tragedy of the Commons is that, even when certain countries or well-placed global players try their hardest to do the right thing, if other countries cannot—or refuse to—take a similar approach, it zeroes out the overall benefits.

The website *Investopedia* defines the Tragedy of the Commons as "a social and political problem in which each individual is incentivized to act in a way that will ultimately be harmful to all individuals."

We see this with climate, which is both local and global, and in space too.

In a Tragedy of the Commons scenario, individuals consume resources at the expense of others—and there's no way to exclude anyone from consuming.

Imagine if every shepherd in a community acted only in their own self-interest and allowed their flock to graze on the community's common field? (That's, in fact, where "Tragedy of the Commons" gets its name.) If everyone acts in their apparent own best interest, it results in harmful overconsumption—(i.e., all the grass is eaten)—to the detriment of everyone.

For a Tragedy of the Commons to occur, a resource must be scarce, rivalrous in consumption and nonexcludable.

The knock-on effect of the Tragedy of the Commons is under-investment. After all, who's going to pay to plant a new seed if everyone is looking out only for themselves and you can't prevent another person from consuming the product for themselves? The goods ultimately become scarcer until they're entirely depleted.

Is there anything that can be done to remedy the Tragedy of the Commons?

Top-down government regulation or direct control of common-pool resources is one option. This can include regulating how many cattle can be grazed on government lands or implementing fish-catch quotas.

A further way of mitigating the Tragedy of the Commons—and perhaps the most effective—is the most obvious and also the hardest: cooperation. That's where individuals bond together to come up with their own best practices, such as crop rotation and seasonal grazing. If everyone is on the same page, pushback to top-down rules can be mitigated or the regulation themselves can be minimized.

That may not be as easy in space, where surveillance is tougher than on Earth and where the rules are still being written.

But cross-country cooperation is essential if we want to avoid wars in space or have any hope in cleaning up the growing problem of space junk.

What we've learned

+ Aviation and space will be among the most exciting areas of innovation over the next 10 years. Questions to be addressed include:
  - Will a wide segment of consumers have access to eVTOLs for short trips that avoid ground transport traffic jams altogether?
  - Will supersonic air travel ever be attainable for the average business traveler?
  - Will air travel move away from burning fossil fuels to more sustainable and environment-friendly power?
  - Will we be able to beam solar power down to the planet cost-effectively?
  - Will we be able to launch payloads into orbit without using rockets?
  - Will we set up mining operations on the moon?
  - When will the first human land on Mars? Will we see the planet's colonization within our lifetime?

+ There may be more questions than answers at this point, but it's certain there will be multiple billion-dollar companies created pursuing many of the areas above.

■   ■   ■

Chapter 4

Marine

The pirates were confused.

The ship they were trying to commandeer turned out to be autonomous and was thus bereft of a crew. There were a few security personnel on board, but no captain or first mate to hold hostage. The cargo was worth something, for sure, but far harder to fence on the black market than a straight-up prisoner situation.

While the scenario I've just presented is speculative, the question raised is real—or will be soon enough: Will a future of autonomous marine travel finally put an end to piracy on the open seas?

Or will pirates opt to sign up for coding workshops so they can add hacking skills to their swashbuckling repertoire?

Autonomous shipping may not go mainstream in the near term (more on that later in this chapter), but other big changes are coming to the maritime industry.

The most immediate: electrification.

The maritime industry transports more than 90% of the world's goods and energy on massive container ships, accounting for $14 trillion in world trade. In addition, close to 40% of all global shipping is devoted to moving fossil fuels around.

In addition, 60,000 ships are what *Forbes* contributor Nishan Degnarain describes as "essentially large oil-fired power stations in the middle of the ocean, attached to a transportation device."

As noted earlier, shipping is among the most polluting mobility modalities and one of the most difficult to make green. Researchers at IDTechEx have calculated that a single large ship emits as much CO_2 as 70,000 cars, as much nitrogen oxide as two million cars, and as much fine dust and carcinogenic particles as 2.5 million cars. Out of total global air emissions, shipping accounts for 18% to 30% of the world's nitrogen oxide.

Virtually all ships today run on diesel. When they burn the 370 million tons of fuel they consume a year, it releases 20 million tons of sulfur oxide into the atmosphere.

Can going electric positively impact marine-based climate change? Yes, but where would a battery-powered container ship plug in to recharge in the midst of the Pacific? Is that simply an environmental pipe dream?

Electrifying marine transport

"We won't see electric ships anytime soon," Zvi Schreiber, the CEO of Freightos, which has built a kind of "Expedia for cargo," allowing manufacturers to find the best and cheapest shipping arrangement with a few clicks online, told me. There are a few electric battery-powered ferries and smaller coast vessels, mostly in China, Germany, Sweden, and Norway, but nothing bigger, he noted.

The Angel Island Ferry in the San Francisco Bay Area makes for a good case study. It will be going electric in 2024 for its short, 30-minute ride. The electrification will be undertaken in cooperation with Pacific Gas and Electric, the region's utility, and Green Yachts, a California firm that sells and services electric-powered boats.

The Angel Island ferry boats are 59-feet long and can carry 400 passengers for their regularly scheduled service. There are also sunset cruises and charter events.

The project demonstrates just how difficult it is to move marine vessels away from oil.

"An electric semi truck requires 2 kWh to go one mile, and the Angel Island Ferry requires 30 kWh to go one mile," notes Graham Balch, managing broker of Green Yachts.

Smaller marine vehicles such as yachts could have a more immediate electric future. Technology could create a whole new ecosystem of "yacht sharing" (the marine version of ride-sharing?), where yacht owners could make their crafts available to others via an app, suggests Trucks VC head Reilly Brennan.

"Pleasure boats have very low utilization," Brennan notes. "They're usually used less than 50 days per year. People have been begging for ideas on how to make its utilization higher."

A sophisticated app could limit the yacht's speed or offer one-time on-demand insurance. "These ancillary efforts, particularly for boats, are incredible," Brennan says.

Would Brennan like to see autonomous yachts in the future?

"No," he exclaims. "Driving a boat is pretty fun!"

What other sea vessels have already or will soon be going electric?

✦ In 2017, China's Guangzhou Shipyard launched the world's first electric container ship, putting it in commercial use a year later. It's 70-meters long and contains more than 1,000 lithium-ion batteries and supercapacitors, giving the vessel a range of 80 kilometers. Its initial voyages were along the Pearl River in the southern province of Guangdong.

✦ An electric-battery-powered container ship built for China's COSCO Shipping Heavy Industry, was floated at the shipyard in Yangzhou in July 2023. It will be one of two river EV containerships developed by COSCO. The vessel, notably, will have the largest installed battery capacity yet placed aboard a ship—36 replaceable 20-foot containers will serve as its power source, each with a capacity of 50,000 kWh.

✦ A hybrid-electric powered cruise ship, the MS Roald Amundsen, from Norwegian shipping company Hurtigruten, was introduced in 2019. Lithium-ion batteries enable the ship to sail for at least 30 minutes with electric power. While that doesn't sound like much, it means the passengers can glide in complete silence along Norway's fjords.

✦ Also in Norway, ElFly is pitching all-electric seaplanes that can take off from and land in a city center but mostly fly over water. "With more than 1,000 fjords and 450,000 lakes, most of the Norwegian population lives close to a potential 'momentary runway,'" the company's website explains. Seaplanes are also a quick way of transporting people over Norway's many mountains and can turn hours spent in a car between small cities into just minutes.

✦ The Stena Jutlandica, from ferry operator Stena line, is planning to add a battery system to its ferry between Gothenburg, Sweden, and Frederikshavn, Denmark. The battery will have to be massive: 20,000 kWh in order to enable the ferry to travel the distance between the two cities.

✦ A ferry called "Ellen," also operating in Denmark, is part of the Horizon 2020's "E-Ferry" project. It cost some €21.3m to build the Ellen, which has a 4,300-kWh battery system.

✦ German cruise line AIDA is installing a 10,000-kWh battery, making it "the first regular cruise vessel with a battery on board," notes Corvus Energy CEO Geir Bjørkeli.

✦ "Project e5" hails from Japanese marine transportation company Asahi Tanker. The new electric tanker is being built as a joint venture between Asahi and Mitsubishi. The 5 "e"s in the name: electrification, environment, evolution, economy and efficiency.

Hybrid ships

The analysts at IDTechEx predict that worldwide sales of fully electric and hybrid ships could reach $20 billion by 2027.

Hybrid ships will play an important role in the near term. The batteries on board can be charged while an internal combustion engine is operating. Solar panels would add to their capacity.

In 2012, the *Tûranor PlanetSolar* became the first solar-powered boat to sail around the world, a journey that took 585 days. A fully electric ferry in Germany has 15 solar modules that store energy in two battery blocks that enable the ferry to sail for 6.5 hours.

Since 2014, four solar-powered ferries, the *FährBär 1 to 4*, have been sailing on the Spree River, which reaches Berlin.

Solar power could allow a ship to sail using nothing but electricity for a considerable amount of time.

An all-electric or hybrid-powered cruise ship would also reduce pollution when docked. Cruise ships need power when they're docked to run their hotel operations. As a result, they tend to operate their motors and auxiliary power units.

That's led some cities, Amsterdam among the most prominent, to ban cruise ships from the city and close its shipping terminal. Ilana Rooderkerk, chairperson for the D66 political party in the Netherlands, emphasized in the statement that "polluting cruise ships do not fit with the sustainable ambitions" of Amsterdam.

It would be much more environmentally friendly to locals in the area of the port if the ships could "plug in" to the electricity on shore, especially if that electricity can be generated by renewables (hydroelectric makes sense since we're already on the water).

Such shore-side electricity facilities are rare, however. Will that change?

Battery swap at sea?

Smaller inland vessels and ferries might be better candidates for battery swap than plugging in (although that will be part of the mix, too, of course, as I noted above, when a ship is docked overnight).

A startup called FleetZero wants to capitalize on the fact that transoceanic shipping doesn't necessarily go "straight" across the ocean. From East Asia to U.S. West Coast ports, it's almost as direct to follow the coast much of the way, the company explains. It looks longer due to the curvature of the Earth, but it's not.

By staying close to land, battery swap is possible.

Ideally, this will allow swapping stations to be placed fairly close together. The more stops there are, the more opportunities to swap and the less battery capacity is required on board to move the same amount of cargo, says Steven Henderson, FleetZero's CEO.

By contrast, a direct shot across the ocean on a 10,000-container mega ship would require a battery stack a couple of miles tall that could weigh up to 1.6 billion pounds. The same size ship running on diesel would require a relatively much smaller amount—just 33 million pounds of fuel.

A swarm of smaller sea vessels with lighter loads and less power requirements could conceivably work on a technological level, but the logistics of battery swap and charging would be daunting.

The sweet spot is a 4,000-container unit ship. That's small enough for the ships to access smaller ports and it gives logistics companies more flexibility in the supply chain than they have today.

They could, for example, send goods to a smaller port like Portland where there's less congestion. The goods would be closer to customers and transporting them by ship would "effectively take thousands of trucks off the road," says Henderson.

Stopping at smaller ports fits with FleetZero's battery-swap model.

Plug-in is a nonstarter, according to FleetZero, because the ships would have to carry too heavy a load of batteries. Nor does dockside fast charging currently exist.

FleetZero's onboard batteries would be stored in shipping containers which can be easily removed and replaced.

"You unload and load them just like any other cargo," Henderson says. The batteries are then taken "to a warehouse or local utility" where they can be charged overnight using off-peak electricity, ideally from renewables.

FleetZero is not alone in promoting battery swap for ships.

The Dutch company Port-Liner also stores its batteries in containers to be exchanged at the port. Port-Liner aims to produce 15 electric ships for the Netherlands and Belgium in the coming years, with each vessel having the capacity of 1,600 automobile batteries.

Where will the space come from to store these batteries on board?

Removing the diesel engines, fuel, and ballast tanks opens up a huge amount of space—for batteries and more cargo.

The alternative—electrifying docks—"is expensive. All these ports are 50, 100 years old," Henderson says. With battery swap, "you don't have to build a substation at every dock."

Problem solved? Not quite.

"We needed a battery that didn't self-oxidize," says Henderson, as would happen with typical lithium-ion batteries, especially at sea. FleetZero is using lithium iron phosphate batteries instead—more stable but less powerful.

FleetZero has raised $3.5 million, and Henderson says the company will be ready to scale within three years.

Technology to improve shipping

There are a number of tech companies I'm keeping my eye on that can help improve shipping efficiency, reduce emissions, and address some of the issues I'll discuss later concerning the Great Supply Chain crisis.

Here are my top three picks:

Freightos

When Israeli shipping startup Freightos went public in early 2023, it injected much-needed capital into the company's mission of being the "Expedia for shipping companies."

CEO Zvi Schreiber explained to me how the Freightos system works.

"Look at how much passenger travel changed at the end of the 1990s and the beginning of the 2000s," Schreiber told me. "Everything went online, traditional travel agents got replaced by Booking.com and Kayak, passenger flights became cheaper and fuller and the whole market became more efficient."

Freight never went through that revolution, Schreiber says. "So that's become our job."

Freightos enables manufacturers to find a wide variety of shipping options, choose the one that is the fastest and least expensive, and book it with just a few clicks.

While travel agents were able to connect electronically via American Airlines and its SABRE technology to book passenger flights as far back as 1963, the first electronic connection for cargo at American, says Schreiber, didn't happen until 2022. Lufthansa beat American by a few years, launching electronic booking for cargo in 2018. British Airlines followed in 2019.

Today, Schreiber says Freightos, which got going in 2018, is doing over $1 billion of bookings a year, with thousands of bookings per day. *Bloomberg* reports the company had 2022 revenue of $19 million.

Freightos can also provide insight into the shipping industry's impact on climate change.

"We estimate the carbon footprint for every shipment we do," Schreiber explains. "So, we know that flying a ton of goods from Shanghai to New York emits four tons of CO_2."

That's not made much of an impact with shippers so far: Customers don't pick one route because it's slightly greener; they want the fastest and cheapest choice.

The only thing that might move shippers on the pollution needle is "a carbon tax, like in Sweden. People don't change voluntarily," Schreiber says.

Covid was tough for the shipping industry because "American spending on goods jumped by 15%," Schreiber points out. "That may not sound like a lot, but no one had 15% spare ships and 15% spare cranes."

The ongoing ripples from Covid and the supply chain crisis forced Freightos, in 2023, to lay off 13% of its staff—about 50 positions—due to what the company describes as a "prolonged downturn in freight markets."

"Given the persistently weak market conditions, we are refining our priorities to deliver on our plan to reach profitability with the capital already raised," Schreiber said in a statement.

ShipIn Systems

ShipIn places AI-powered cameras on ships to proactively alert shipowners and managers to any onboard anomalies around bridge activities, safety and security, cargo operations, and maintenance. Through real-time notifications and remote audits, ShipIn promises a reduction of 40% in incidents while bumping up cargo operations efficiency by 8%.

In 2023, ShipIn received an investment from Munich Re Ventures, one of the leading providers of reinsurance. The company has raised $24 million to date.

"As ships are getting bigger, crews are getting smaller," says ShipIn CEO Osher Perry. "ShipIn's mission is to give seafarers the advanced digital tools required to do their jobs better."

"I can foresee a future where having ShipIn on board may reduce the cost of insurance for ship owners and will benefit the insurance industry as well," adds Kirsi Tikka, a ShipIn advisor and former executive with the American Bureau of Shipping.

Mythos AI

Mythos AI uses artificial intelligence to map marine highways for use by self-driving "in-shore vessels" (seafaring craft that stay close to the shore). The company is running a pilot with the Port of Monroe—a strategic waterway that connects the Great Lakes in Michigan to the Atlantic Ocean—in which Mythos will create a "digital twin" of the region in order to train its machine learning on waterway-specific conditions.

Automated marine highways, the company claims in a press release, "are the key to increasing port efficiency, lowering maritime carbon emissions and creating supply chain resilience. Disaggregated marine shipping will use smaller boats, rivers, and in-land waterways to move goods more efficiently and resolve bottlenecks."

Because Mythos AI runs its processing in the cloud, it supports real-time survey monitoring and editing maps from anywhere.

The company describes its "Archie" (short for "Archimedes") boats as "the world's first autonomous survey vessels." Archie calculates water depth in shipping channels using onboard sonar, so no permanent equipment need be installed in the waterway itself, reducing time, complexity and expense.

Airplane wings on a ship

Nayam Wings is a startup founded by three ex-naval officers in Haifa, Israel. Amnon Asscher, the company's CTO and cofounder, is an aeronautical engineer by training and an experienced sailor.

"A few years ago, I started to think about how to add the technology of aircraft, which has a much higher lift force, to maritime vessels," Asscher told *Israel21c*.

What's lift? NASA describes it like this:

Airplane wings are shaped to make air move faster over the top of the wing. When air moves faster, the pressure of the air decreases. So, the pressure on the top of the wing is less than the pressure on the bottom of the wing. The difference in pressure creates a force on the wing that lifts the wing up into the air.

That's exactly what Asscher wanted to do with ships. But rather than lift the ship *up*, the wings needed to be positioned vertically so the wind could provide *forward* motion.

What makes them effective for wind propulsion? There are three main factors.

First, computer algorithms and machine learning sense which way the wind is blowing and pivot the wings to take advantage of the best angle.

"The wing is autonomously adjusted in three dimensions, so that in every second you have the optimum forward propulsion," Asscher explains.

Second, the wings are asymmetrical. That makes it possible for the wind to move faster at the broad top of the wing and slower at the bottom (or the sides, in a vertical orientation), creating lift.

Competing "sail" systems, from companies like Norsepower, Anemoi, Yara-Bar, OceanBird, EconoWind and NewoLine all use symmetrical wings. Some are shaped more like a cylinder, in what's known as a "Flettner rotor," to capture wind power.

That's better than a regular sail, but only provides about double the effectiveness, not 3.5 times as Nayam Wings claims for its design.

Finally, Nayam Wings's wings are not made of cloth or nylon but are solid and rigid, constructed from carbon fiber. Soft sails flap around, creating turbulence which lowers forward propulsion. Nayam Wings claims its wings "are three-and-a-half times stronger per square meter" than simple sails. That gives Nayam a wing up, so to speak.

Nayam Wings has only installed two proof-of-concept wings on ships so far, but the company estimates that a Nayam Wings system retrofitted onto an existing ship can bring down emissions by around 15%.

If Nayam Wings' tech is included on a brand-new ship, the reduction could be up to 35%.

A ship with Anemoi cylindrical "wings" (credit: Anemoi)

Shipping corridors

In 2022, the Maritime and Port Authority of Singapore (MPA) and the ports of Los Angeles and Long Beach agreed to establish a "green and digital shipping corridor" between the locations. It follows a similar partnership between Shanghai and Los Angeles, the world's busiest trans-Pacific shipping lane.

In 2020, ocean vessels moved 31.2 million twenty-foot equivalent units across the Pacific Ocean, making up some 21% of the world's total container movement, according to the United Nations Conference on Trade and Development.

In order to operate in one of these two new corridors—kind of like an HOV lane in the water—ships will need to be zero-carbon container ships; these are expected to be ready by 2030.

It's a brave move but I'm not sure if the industry will be ready. It takes 3 years to design and complete construction of a typical commercial ship. Moreover, cargo ships can easily operate for 30 years, inland vessels for 45 years and passenger ships for even longer. It will take time to replace all those ships.

But the real issue is fuel. What will constitute net-zero fuel in just a few years? Will there be enough to fuel ships, even a limited number on a specific route?

Chris Cannon, chief sustainability officer at the Port of Los Angeles, explains that most attempts in the past to cut emissions with ships centered around the cargo-handling equipment: the drayage trucks serving the container terminal and zero-emission locomotives.

"That's where our focus had ended," Cannon says. "But with the green shipping corridors, our focus is starting to be on what we can do to reduce carbon emissions along a ship's entire journey."

What will make these corridors green? The partners aren't quite sure yet.

Green corridor ships would presumably get priority status over non-green corridor ships when they arrive at port. Would they also get a general right-of-way while sailing across the ocean?

"The plan is to identify the most direct and efficient routing for the ships and the most efficient way to track and provide advance notice of where cargo's going, so that when it's picked up, it can be picked up quickly, with advanced staging in place so that you can plan for things like customs clearance and freight forwarding," Cannon says. "If we can reduce the number of times a container is touched, that reduces the amount of overall activity associated with the movement of that container, which means less fuel used, which generates less carbon emissions."

That should also lead to cost savings for shipping firms.

"It's not just the green aspect of it," Peter Zimmerman, North American software sales manager for Vormittag Associates, an enterprise resource planning company, told *FreightWaves*. "There hopefully will be an opportunity for cost reduction in the supply chain as well."

Autonomy on the high seas

If and when autonomy comes for ships, it will likely start with the military.

The U.S. Navy sees its future fleet comprising more than 350 manned ships and about 150 unmanned ships, according to a report released in 2022 by the military.

The military is to autonomy what pornography was for videotape and later the internet—a driver that pushes a new technology into the mainstream. In the case of marine military autonomy, the need is to "address long-term competition with China and to sustain military advantage against Russia," the Navy's report says.

The Navy today has 298 ships in its "battle force." That doesn't include scores of resupply and logistics ships.

Autonomy may get a boost from the military but there are plenty of civilian applications.

The world's first autonomous cargo ship completed its maiden voyage in Norway in 2022. The ship was built by Yara, a Norwegian chemical company, to transport fertilizer from the firm's plants to the port of Brevik. In addition to being autonomous, the ship is also 100% electric.

The Yara Birkeland will still have a crew, but they will presumably have more free time now that the ship drives itself. The vessel is 80 meters long and can carry 3,200 tons of cargo. It's Level 4 autonomy—if something goes wrong, there's a "safety driver" on board to take over.

From an environmental point of view, the Birkeland could cut 1,000 tons of CO_2 a year. Yara says it is optimistic that commercial operations will commence within the next few years.

With all manner of sensors—radar, lidar, infrared, and cameras originally designed for self-driving cars—on board, the Birkeland will be able to dock and moor autonomously.

Jostein Braaten, project lead of the Yara Birkeland, notes that autonomy at sea, like on land, should increase safety because most accidents are "related to people fatigue or other human error."

For now, the Yara Birkeland can only be operated on coastal and river routes rather than large ocean crossings.

"It is no longer a question of 'if' autonomy is coming, it is a matter of 'when,'" enthuses Braaten. "Autonomy is an enabler and a potential catalyst for the green shift in maritime."

MASS effect

Worldwide, today, there are some 1,000 "maritime autonomous surface ships" (MASS), crew-less vessels that transport goods over short distances or that provide assistance to larger container ships. Examples include:

- ✦ The Iris Leader, a vehicle carrier which operates in Japan and China under the flag of Panama and conducted its autonomous test in 2019

- ✦ The 80-meter-long VN Rebel in Toulon harbor, remotely controlled from Paris

- ✦ The Jun You Run O Hao, a 12.9-meter fishing vessel being tested in China. It is expected to reduce fuel consumption by 15% and operation costs by 20%.

The Russian industry association MARINET is also running an "Autonomous and Remote Navigation Trial Project."

In 2022, Japan's Nippon Yusen Kabushiki Keisha ("NYK Line" for short) ran a 500-mile, 40-hour test of a fully autonomous ship, the Suzaka, using Orca AI's Automatic Ship Target Recognition System. The ship set sail from Tokyo Bay, one of the most congested waterways in the world, before safely reaching the port of Tsumatsusaka.

Orca AI reports that during the Suzaka's voyage, the autonomous ship performed 107 collision avoidance maneuvers without the help of a human. It successfully steered clear of some 500 other vessels during its outbound trip alone.

There have also been a few long-haul autonomy tests.

+ Lidos' Sea Hunter completed a 5,000-mile round trip between San Diego and Hawaii in 2019 as part of a U.S. Navy project.

+ The Saildrone Surveyor research vessel traveled 2,250 miles from San Francisco to Hawaii in 2021.

+ Hyundai's Prism Courage achieved a 6,200-mile trip from Texas to South Korea via the Panama Canal, although it ran autonomously for only half the voyage. Even still, the autonomous software boosted the ship's fuel efficiency by about 7% and cut down on greenhouse gas emissions by 5%.

+ The Mayflower Autonomous Ship (MAS400) in 2022 completed a 3,500-mile journey from Plymouth in the U.K. to Halifax, Nova Scotia, on its way to its final destination—Plymouth, Massachusetts, where the first Mayflower landed in 1620. The 50-foot vessel is powered by software from IBM Research.

To be clear, these autonomous tests were *not* powered exclusively by electric batteries, hydrogen or biofuels. Diesel still reigns supreme.

Soren Skou, who retired as chairman of shipping giant Maersk in 2022, provides the counterargument to an autonomous shipping future.

"I don't expect we will be allowed to sail around with 400-meter-long container ships, weighing 200,000 tons, without any human beings on board," he cautions. "I don't think it will be a driver of efficiency, not in my time."

MAS400 founder Brett Phaneuf takes positive inspiration from the original Mayflower's passengers and crew.

"They looked out at the ocean with these rickety old ships and thought, 'Let's go for it!' They jumped off into this unknown with very low chances of survival and took that leap regardless of the outcome. That's what I find aspirational."

The Mayflower (MAS400) in action (credit: IBM)

Behavioral changes

In a low-tech solution, ship operators can focus on behavioral changes to reduce fuel consumption and emissions. Optimization techniques that the crew can employ to reduce fuel consumption and CO_2 emissions, without major capital expenditures, include the following:

+ **Optimize speed and power**. One of the most significant factors that affects fuel consumption and CO_2 emissions is vessel speed. Slowing down the vessel's speed can reduce fuel consumption and CO_2 emissions. The crew can optimize the vessel's speed by using weather routing services to avoid unfavorable meteorological conditions and can adjust the vessel's speed accordingly. However, slowing down too much can cause immense wear and tear on ship engines and increase unburned hydrocarbons in exhaust emissions, which can worsen a ship's overall emissions profile. It's not just about burning less fuel—it's about burning that fuel more effectively and converting that fuel to power efficiently.

+ **Maintain the vessel's hull and propeller**. Regularly inspecting and cleaning a vessel's hull and propeller can reduce drag, increase the vessel's fuel efficiency and generally ensure the shipping company's assets are in optimal condition.

+ **Optimize engine performance**. A ship's exhaust emissions are an indication of the engine's health and performance. The crew can use this data to maintain the vessel's engine and its components—including such items as fuel injectors, turbo-chargers, and air filters—to optimize overall performance. Regular maintenance ensures that the engine is operating efficiently and can reduce fuel consumption. Customers can use this information to conduct maintenance at efficient intervals and identify problems before they cause catastrophic failure.

+ **Reduce onboard electricity consumption**. A ship's crew can reduce onboard electricity consumption by using energy-efficient lighting, turning off unused equipment, and optimizing the use of air conditioning and heating systems.

+ **Minimize unnecessary deviations**. The crew can minimize unnecessary deviations from the vessel's planned route to avoid additional distance traveled and a corresponding increase in fuel consumption. Small deviations may also occur while using autopilot in adverse sea conditions. Gaining a proper understanding of the drag profile caused by autopilot is paramount for efficient operations.

Software and data analytics solutions like Sailplan, which helps ships measure, report and reduce emissions and fuel consumption using high-resolution, real-time data, can help ship operators report back on performance and nudge their fleets into making small yet impactful changes.

What we've learned

+ The shipping industry contributes significantly to the emissions that cause climate change. Global shipping spews out 3% of worldwide greenhouse gases and has suffered from underinvestment in making positive change. But historical underinvestment means that there is still plenty of opportunity for new, innovative entrepreneurs to tackle some of these challenges.

+ While battery technologies may not be coming to the high seas anytime soon, small behavioral changes, the use of autonomy and harnessing the power of the wind may prove to make big impacts on fuel consumption and emissions.

■ ■ ■

Chapter 5

Industrial Tech: Agriculture, Construction and Mining

F*ruit rotting on trees or fallen to the ground* costs farmers in the U.S. some $30 billion in lost sales every year. Fruit picked even two weeks late loses 80% of its value.

A major reason for all that wasted produce: a global shortage of fruit pickers, estimated to grow to a deficit of five million employees by 2050.

Even today, when the shortage is not so acute, more than 10% of all fruit worldwide cannot be harvested. That's equivalent to the total annual consumption of fruit in the entire European Union.

Increasing efficiency when picking fruit could go a long way to reducing food insecurity.

Food insecurity used to be a result of acts of God—a drought or blight (think of potatoes in Ireland in the 19th century) or a flood could result in millions of people going hungry or even starving to death.

Food insecurity shouldn't be a problem anymore today—we have technology that can smooth out worldwide distribution of produce and move mundane activities, such as picking, to the robots.

Self-operating tractors, fruit pickers, construction and mining equipment are already here. The industrial segment is the first sector in which autonomy has taken hold.

The reasons are pretty straightforward.

1. Autonomous ag-tech vehicles operate far from accident-prone passenger cars with human drivers on fast-moving highways.
2. They can travel along preapproved tracks, so they don't run into any interference.

3. They solve problems farmers, contractors and warehouses have right now in the real world.

These are large, important industry segments; in 2022, the ag-tech space alone was estimated to be worth some $23.5 billion, according to Zion Market Research. It is expected to grow to some $79.7 billion by 2030.

Robotic fruit picking and robo-bee pollination

The robotic fruit picking startup Tevel Aerobotics is a great place to start our review of ag-tech innovation.

Tevel's FARs ("flying autonomous robots") take off from a base station, pick only the ripe fruit off the tree, then gently lower it for collection.

Because they're not human, Tevel's robotic pickers can work 24/7 during the harvest. They never get tired and never need to step out for a coffee or bathroom break.

Farmers "won't need as many people to pick," Tevel's CEO Yaniv Maor explains. "But the main reason is not the savings but because the workers are simply not available."

In the U.S., the staff who made up the bulk of the industry's pickers have not returned to the fields postpandemic. Quotas and visa problems for non-U.S. migrant laborers have contributed to the dearth.

Tevel Aerobotics (credit: Tevel)

In China, urbanization has been the culprit, leaving many orchards with no one to work in them.

One of the early decisions Maor and his team made was not to power their robots on electric batteries—they run on gasoline—and to tether them so that they don't need to land to recharge.

The FARs are smart, equipped with all manner of sensors and cameras. Tevel's machine-learning algorithms "calculate what is a fruit, what's the best trajectory to access it, should we pick the fruit by rotating it clockwise or counterclockwise," Maor adds. After an initial setup period, "it's all done autonomously and in real time."

Tevel has a partnership with BloomX, another ag-tech startup, which has developed a "bio-mimicking" technology to replicate the vibrations of honeybees—without any bees involved.

BloomX isn't about picking but pollinating. The company's two main devices are called the Robee (short for "robo-bee") to pollinate blueberries, and the Crossbee, which uses an electrostatic method to collect pollen from avocado trees.

BloomX's vibrating "arms" are placed on the Tevel FAR, allowing pollen to be extracted and moved from one plant to another. BloomX says its robo-bees increase yield by up to 30%.

BloomX's clients are currently in Latin America, South Africa, and the U.S. The company has raised $8 million to date. Tevel Aerobotics has raised $30 million.

Not sending a vehicle into the field unnecessarily, perhaps at an inappropriate hour, is another way Tevel and BloomX are helping to address the challenges of climate change. Fewer vehicles, fewer emissions.

Fieldwork Robotics aims to do for raspberries and other soft fruits what Tevel does for those with a peel. The company has an initial deal with The Summer Berry Company in Portugal, which has pledged to buy 100 Fieldwork Robotics pickers.

John Deere plows the weeds from within its walled garden

Robotic picking and pollination are just at the start of their respective journeys. The same can't be said for John Deere, the world leader in building, farming and construction equipment, controlling some 53% of the U.S. large tractor market. The company has been aggressively positioning itself as an internet age provider, but its approach has set farmers on edge.

Deere has been pushing a "walled garden" approach to the data coming off its vehicles, charging farmers a $3,000 yearly subscription fee for the privilege. (Deere says the data is free and that the subscription is "baked into" the overall purchase price of a new tractor.)

Barrons has dubbed this "Ploughing-as-a-Service" (to mimic better-known terms such as SaaS or "Software-as-a-Service") and everyone in the farm supply space, which includes seeds, chemicals, and machinery, is trying to get a piece of the subscription pie.

"It sounds great when you tell a farmer you want just 50 cents per acre," explains Matthew Wong, director of Deere-competitor AGCO. "But when 10 guys ask [for a piece of the profit], it's a problem."

The *Verge's* Nilay Patel summarizes the dilemma.

"All that farming data, who owns it?" he asks. "Where is it processed? How do you get it off the tractors without reliable broadband networks? What format is it in? If you want to use your John Deere tractor with another farming analysis vendor, how easy is that?"

Deere also got into hot water recently by forcing its customers to take their tractors to a Deere repair shop rather than being able to fix them on their own.

Deere customers were livid.

After all, farmers have been repairing equipment on their own for decades. That's one reason the sales of used, noncomputerized tractors are booming—they're simply easier to repair.

The right-to-repair

University of Michigan law professor Aaron Perzanowski, author of *The Right to Repair: Reclaiming the Things We Own*, calls this the emergency of "the tethered economy" where, more and more, the things we buy come with strings attached to the manufacturer, effectively requiring us to pay fees to use—or in Deere's case, to repair—the stuff we already own.

"What we're witnessing is fundamentally a shift from selling products to providing services," Perzanowski says. "What's confusing for consumers is that the services still look like products."

It will get even more confusing as farmers, faced with high prices for the latest bells and whistles, switch to "subscribing" to the vehicle itself, rather than owning it outright.

Deere seems to have overplayed its hand.

In early 2023, John Deere signed a memorandum of understanding with the American Farm Bureau Federation (AFBF) that ensures farmers the "right-to-repair" their own farm equipment. The agreement gives farmers timely access to the tools, software, and documentation originating from the manufacturer.

"A piece of equipment is a major investment," said AFBF president Zippy Duvall. "Farmers must have the freedom to choose where equipment is repaired or to repair it themselves, to help control costs."

John Deere and the AFBF agreed to meet semannually to assess how the agreement is going and to make any updates.

John O'Reilly, director of the right-to-repair campaign at Public Interest Research Group, remains cautious about whether Deere will follow through on its commitment and urges legislators to "watch closely" and "not take the approach of wait-and-see."

Colorado isn't waiting.

In April 2023, Colorado Governor Jared Polis signed a right-to-repair bill, ensuring the rights of farmers to fix their own tractors and combine harvesters.

"This bill will save farmers and ranchers time and money and support the free market," Polis said at the signing.

The bill joins legislation in 28 other states introduced to guarantee consumers the right to repair not only their tractors but also all manner of electronics and appliances.

Some politicians are already looking for ways to score points with their base voters—by opposing such popular laws.

Colorado state legislator Matt Soper, for example, denounced the law as a threat to tech innovation. "Forcing a business to disclose trade secrets, software, and jeopardize consumer safety is poor public policy," he says.

Jahmy Hindman, CTO at John Deere, insists that Deere customers are able to repair their own vehicles, but notes that around "2 percent of repairs that occur on equipment today involve[s] software." And software is often regulated, which means allowing a farmer to make changes could have unanticipated consequences.

Even worse, according to Hindman: Farmers have been downloading software from hacker groups that get around the restrictions Deere has put in place.

"We are required to make sure that a diesel engine performs at a certain emissions output," Hindman told the *Verge* in 2021. "Modifying software changes the output characteristics of the emissions of the engine, and that's a regulated device. We are not in a position where we would ever condone or support a third-party software being put on products of ours . . . it's not something we've tested and we don't know what it might make the equipment do or not . . . there is a societal responsibility, frankly, that we make sure that the product is as safe as it can be for as long as it can be in operation."

Hindman still thinks the benefits outweigh the frustrations.

"Ten years ago, we planted at 3 miles an hour. Today we plant at 10 miles an hour. What's enabled that is technology."

There's no stopping the tractor treads of progress.

Farming is now about data

John Deere now employs more software engineers than mechanical engineers ("that's kind of mind-blowing for a company that's 184 years old," Hindman says) and its tractors might be better described as "mobile sensor suites that have computational capability . . . they are continuously streaming data from whatever it is—let's say the tractor and the planter—to the cloud. We're doing computational work on that data in the cloud, and then serving that information, those insights, up to farmers."

In essence, farmers are not just using their Deere tractors for "productive work in the field, planting is an example; these are also data acquisition and computational devices."

Hindman laid out a scenario where a combine harvesting in the field is simultaneously creating a geospatially-referenced dataset called a "yield map."

"These combines are running through the field on satellite guidance. We know where they are at any point in time, their latitude and longitude, and we know how much they're harvesting," he told Patel.

All that data allows farmers to "know they need to change seeding density, or they need to change crop type, or they need to change how many nutrients to provide in the next season," Hindman explained.

At the 2023 Consumer Electronics Show, Deere introduced ExactShot, a new planting technology that uses robotics and sensors to reduce the need for fertilizer by more than 60%. ExactShot does this by placing the fertilizer precisely onto seeds as they are planted in the soil, rather than afterward in a more scattershot fashion.

Anything that reduces the amount of fertilizer needed is a win for the fields and for the atmosphere.

Much of the data farmers are using in their fields comes directly from smart tractors, but third parties supply data too.

Clearly, Deere is positioning itself as much as a data company as a legacy hardware manufacturer. Most machines in large agriculture are now connected. "It's taken the friction out of getting the data off of a mobile piece of equipment," Hindman says.

Where is most of the data processing happening? In the cloud, Hindman notes. "Very little is done onboard machines today."

Hindman adds that 5G connectivity will make a difference, "things like serving up the real-time location of where a farmer's combine is, instead of having to route that data all the way to the cloud and then back to a handheld device the farmer might have."

The alternative, which is often the case today, is that a grower has to wait "in some cases 30 minutes or an hour until the data is synced up in the cloud and something actionable has been done with it," Hindman says. "By that point in time, the decision has already been made. It's not useful because it's time sensitive."

Electric and autonomous tractors

Deere's equipment is going electric, but not immediately. For certain machines, "it will be a long time," Hindman predicts. That's because the tractors and combines have to "run 14, 15, 16 hours per day. You can't take all day to charge it. Those sorts of problems, they're not insurmountable. They're just not solved by anything that's on the road map today, from a lithium-ion perspective, anyway."

Hindman didn't address autonomy in detail, but he thinks it will be here "in low single-digit years."

Autonomous tractors are more complex than passenger cars since "we not only have to automate the driving of the tractor, but we have to automate the function that it's doing as well." That might involve three or four different tillage tools, all of which have different use cases.

"They all require different artificial intelligence models to be trained and to be validated," Hindman says. "So, scaling out across all of those different conceivable operations I think is the biggest challenge."

Not every company is waiting for Deere to take the lead. Here are a few more:

Aerobotics

Cape Town, South Africa-headquartered Aerobotics (no connection to Tevel Aerobotics) leverages drones and aerial imagery to help farmers identify problems with crop yield, such as pest infestations, nutrient deficiencies or irrigation issues. The drones can even count the trees on the farm. The company has customers in 18 countries.

Agtonomy

Toyota Ventures is backing Agtonomy, whose "TeleFarmer" software consists of a suite of apps and an electric "reference tractor." Agtonomy customers can operate their tractors remotely using the company's "TrunkVision" software, fully autonomously or manually. Simply tell TeleFarmer what you want to achieve for the day—and that's it. If there are any problems, TeleFarmer will send a text message, which the farmer can receive on- or off-site.

Burro

Toyota Ventures also invested in Burro, which has developed an autonomous cart that can be used to move crops out of the field. Burro calls its service "pop-up autonomy," which is able to navigate a space without training and can be used to augment field hands who are perpetually in short supply. Burro estimates that 50% of farm revenue for grapes, berries and nurseries goes to labor costs.

The Burro (credit: Burro)

A Burro autonomous cart system can increase the productivity of a 6- to 10-person crew by 10% to 40%, the company says. Burro already has hundreds of robots out in the field, traveling up to 300 miles a day.

Robotic weeding

No one enjoys weeding. That's why, whether for consumer or commercial applications, weed-whackers and similar types of equipment have always been a popular way of shifting the grunt work away from bored workers to never-bored machines.

Here are three companies I'm tracking:

Carbon Robotics

The company's "LaserWeeder" leverages robotics, artificial intelligence and laser technology to safely and effectively identify, target, and eliminate weeds. LaserWeeder uses thermal energy in its high-powered lasers, which is less disturbing to the soil. Fewer weeds also mean farmers don't need to use as many herbicides. And of course, Carbon Robotics can save farmers labor costs.

"Laser-weeding automates a grueling task," the company's website states.

Since the company was founded in 2021, its laser weeding robots have "zapped" some 500 million weeds. Laser-weeders were used in 17 U.S. states and three Canadian provinces in 2023, the company reports.

Carbon Robotics has raised $67 million.

Aigen

Aigen is building solar-powered autonomous robots that use computer vision to discern the difference between a friendly plant and an undesirable weed. The Aigen device has multiple cameras on board; the AI is pretrained to identify plants and weeds.

"Once we know what we are looking at, we either remove or propagate the plants with two robot arms underneath the robots," explains Kenny Lee, Aigen's COO.

Lee believe Aigen's robots can help with the issue of soil compaction.

"Heavy machinery compresses the soil, which means that the roots grow sideways, instead of down. That's a problem because you can't put the carbon the plants capture deep into the ground. By using fewer tractors and large commercial devices, you can change how agriculture works," Lee says.

Verdant

Bay Area-based startup Verdant also is adroit at zapping weeds—specifically in carrot fields. But the company has broader ambitions: Verdant aims to help farmers index all the crops on their farms, much as Google indexes the internet, or Google Maps indexes driving routes.

"Our system builds a digital twin of the entire farm, empowering farmers with high-fidelity information and enabling the system to act in real-time," the company explains.

"Farmers told us not to give them *more* data, but to figure out what to do with the mountains of data they already have," Verdant CEO Gabe Sibley says. "They want a complete solution that takes action in real-time and keeps farmers in control—all while improving profitability and automating dangerous, backbreaking field work."

eVTOLs for ag-tech?

In 2023, the FAA gave approval to Guardian Agriculture to begin safely operating its autonomous eVTOLs in the U.S.

The larger size of an eVTOL is required, Guardian CEO Adam Bercu says, because other unmanned autonomous systems are too small to provide growers with full-field coverage at a competitive price point. Bercu says that Guardian's eVTOLs deliver the same comprehensive coverage as traditional aerial crop dusting or ground spraying equipment at a lower cost and with more precision.

"eVTOL-powered crop protection is better for crops, better for the environment, and better for growers' bottom line," Bercu says.

Guardian uses the same nozzles, pressure and droplet sizes as existing systems. It can carry 200-pound payloads. The 15-foot craft has 4 6-foot propellers.

Guardian estimates the aerial crop protection market is worth $5.7 billion. Guardian's SC1 platform has $100 million in customer orders, the company says.

Construction

Built Robotics, a San Francisco vehicular automation startup, began testing its self-driving excavators in 2017. The goal was to solve infrastructure shortfalls and build houses more quickly.

A Built Robotics excavator (credit: Built Robotics)

In 2023, however, Built Robotics ditched its seven-year focus on general construction projects to pivot to the installation of solar farms.

That doesn't mean the company has given up on autonomous construction vehicles; its RPD-35 is a robotic pile driver that smashes steel beams into the ground, although it will now be focused on installing solar panels.

"It may feel like we're narrowing our focus," admits Built Robotics CEO Noah Ready-Campbell, "but I think solar over the next 10 to 20 years is going to become the story of our electrical grid as a country."

Why did autonomous construction fall out of favor at Built? Indeed, when it comes to construction, nearly all the autonomous heavy-duty machinery projects are still stuck at the prototype stage.

Why?

Wired's Khari Johnson suggests several possibilities.

"Construction tasks often involve manipulating objects in 3D and they take place on sites in a state of continuous change," Johnson writes. "Automation is most successful carrying out repetitive tasks with predictable outcomes."

Perhaps counterintuitively, Johnson points out, "making safe self-driving vehicles that travel on well-mapped public roads, which change more slowly, is in some ways easier."

Mining

Rio Tinto is an international mining company based in Australia. The world's second largest mining company is implementing autonomous mobility solutions at its Pilbara iron-ore mines in the western part of the country.

Mining is an even better fit for autonomous vehicles than straight construction.

Mines have semipermanent roads. Being underground lets you secure the area. And automation is particularly attractive for sites that tend to be in remote locations where it's tough to house and feed people. Construction sites, by contrast, are usually short-lived, often urban and lack permanent roads.

Caterpillar, the world's largest construction equipment manufacturer, has been experimenting with autonomous trucks since the 1990s. Caterpillar today operates nearly 600 autonomous trucks in mines, albeit none at construction sites. Caterpillar's chief engineer, Michael Murphy, told *Wired* that the company aims to allow a single remote operator to control four or five machines simultaneously, with algorithms taking on much of the grunt work.

Rio Tinto began deploying autonomous dump trucks as far back as 2015. These self-driving vehicles, manufactured by Tokyo-based Komatsu, use GPS to navigate. The mining operation operates some 130 autonomous dump trucks and is now moving into autonomous water trucks, the company says. The latter will operate at Rio Tinto's Gudai-Darri iron ore mine and are designed to control dust.

An autonomous dump truck (credit: Shutterstock)

Gudai-Darri supplies more than half of the world's supply of iron ore.

Mining is in desperate need of new ways to move both minerals and people. The costs of not doing so are high—both in terms of outright expense and the price many miners pay in terms of danger and disability on the job. There's more on the perils of modern mining in the chapter on supply chain issues.

"These driverless vehicles deliver their loads more efficiently, minimizing delays and fuel use, and are controlled remotely by operators who exert more control over their environment and ensure greater operational safety," Rio Tinto says of its "Autonomous Haulage System."

Another Rio Tinto offering, an "Autonomous Drilling System," is described as "much safer for the operators and maximizes precision and equipment utilization."

Rio Tinto estimates its automation efforts result in 15% overall lower costs.

Will automation take my job?

It's not just efficiency that's driving mines to embrace autonomy.

"Operators historically have had tough jobs," notes Tudor Van Hampton, former managing editor of *Engineering News-Record*. "You're driving something that's off-road, so your neck, arms, and hands get tired."

Automation has been on mining companies' agendas for years, but the need was exacerbated during the Covid-19 pandemic. Automated trucks, operated from a secure off-site location, can help miners avoid disruptions from illness, lockdowns, and, as in the case of pure ag-tech, a shortage of workers who can no longer get to their jobs due to border closures.

At Gudai-Darri, Rio Tinto employs around 600 workers on-site and another 70 people in a control center in Perth, almost 1,000 miles away. During the pandemic, Rio Tinto suffered from a shortage of hundreds of workers.

Automation can help but it can also lead to manual labor jobs becoming redundant.

At Fortescue Metals Group in Australia, for example, 240 manually operated trucks have been replaced by 190 autonomous ones with the same output.

As software takes center stage, mine workers are now "much more likely to pick up a tablet than a spanner," says Simon Trott, Rio Tinto's head of iron ore.

But as is often the case with new technology, "automation hasn't led to the doomsday scenario of mass layoffs," explains Robert Carruthers, acting chief executive at the Chamber of Minerals and Energy of Western Australia. "In fact, it's created new roles that didn't exist before automation."

Autonomous fleet operators, data scientists and systems engineers are becoming as ubiquitous as hard hats and shovels.

Union officials disagree.

Shane Roulstone, national organizing director at the Australian Workers' Union, says that only half of jobs that existed on mine sites remain after automation. New roles at remote operating centers can't fill the gap.

Nor can mines operate properly without trained personnel.

"The transition to more autonomous operations depends on the availability of skills as much as it does on the speed of technology development," says Laura Tyler, chief technical officer at BHP Group, a multinational mining firm based in Australia.

Autonomy in the mines isn't limited to Australia.

Volvo Autonomous Solutions is building a cabin-less hauler to work in a limestone quarry in Switzerland. Volvo also has seven self-driving trucks in a mine in Norway.

Such machines, however, predicts Pronto.ai CEO Anthony Levandowski, are still "very, very far away" from widespread use.

Levandowski ought to know. A long-time autonomy guru who worked at Waymo until he was convicted of taking confidential information from the company (he received a pardon from former President Donald Trump), in 2008, Levandowski programmed a self-driving Prius to cross the San Francisco-Oakland Bay Bridge to deliver a pizza. (Don't worry—the car had a police escort.)

At the time, Levandowski said he thought "we're about two years away from having this commercializable. That was 15 years ago."

But if autonomous passenger cars aren't on the horizon, ag-tech beckons: Levandowski's latest startup, Pronto.ai, is focusing on off-road haulage systems for quarries, mines and other sites where harsh conditions prevail.

The impact of war on agriculture

War is bad for agriculture. There are two main culprits.

+ Like heavy ag-tech equipment, tanks also compress the soil, making it difficult to plant new crops or sustain existing ones.

+ When missiles and rockets land, they not only affect the soil through their impact but also through the chemical explosives contained inside.

Foreign Policy visited a wheat field in Myroliubivka, Ukraine, in 2023. Rather than spending their day farming the fields, employees combed the fields holding inexpensive metal detectors looking for coins and metal trinkets.

On the opposite end of the field stood a small trailer that the workers had already filled halfway with remnants of missiles and rockets.

"If the metal detectors beep, we don't dig, we just plant a flag and move on," Yuri Baranov, one of the farmhands, told *Foreign Policy*.

"We aren't actually demining," adds 33-year farmer Maksim Maksimov. "We'll just drive the tractor around it."

Before the start of the war, agriculture made up as much as 41% of Ukraine's exports.

At this point in Russia's war against Ukraine, there are tens of thousands of square miles littered with mines, unexploded cluster bombs and remnants of rockets and shells fired by forces on both sides. Farming has sadly become a game of Russian Roulette, so to speak—tend to your fields and risk getting blown up or wait for the fields to be formally surveyed but risk your livelihood in the meantime.

The 2022 Ukrainian counteroffensive that culminated in the liberation of the city of Kherson also left close to 1.2 million acres of farmland potentially contaminated.

By mid-2023, sappers had surveyed just under 63,000 acres.

To clear the land in the Kherson region, "at the current pace, with the current number of people and the current amount of equipment, it's going to take 10 years, if not more," Oleksandr Tolokonnikov, a civilian who is now the spokesperson for the wartime Kherson military administration, told *Foreign Policy*.

Worsening soil quality is not a unique byproduct of warfare, of course.

Poor crop rotation, the prevalence of monoculture (the repeated cultivation of a single crop in a given area) over more diverse planting and an overreliance on pesticides and herbicides all contribute to a shrinking footprint of arable land, which directly impacts how much yield the land can provide.

Ag-tech machinery doesn't end with a single tractor, either. There are tillers to grind up the soil, machines to plant the seeds and spray insecticide, weed removers and combine harvesters to pick the produce.

Soil erosion has been a problem from prehistoric days when sauropods, weighing between 60,000 and 80,000 kilograms, walked the Earth. A sugar-beet harvester has a similar weight but is distributed across three axles and six tires.

Can ag-tech help improve our soil? The answer is not straightforward.

Ag-tech can't mitigate the debris left by a Russian or Ukrainian missile attack. Nor would battery- or hydrogen-powered tractors move the needle; they would likely be no lighter than today's gasoline-powered vehicles. If anything, they'd be heavier since the batteries would need to be massive.

Maybe the answer will come from above.

Flying robots and drones like those from Tevel Aerobotics and BloomX could fertilize and harvest crops without any impact on the ground. But such a shift would not come cheap, making it an unlikely resolution to the problem of soil quality.

Autonomous farm equipment could improve the situation if the self-driving machinery were more accurate, meaning less need to roll over the same land multiple times. It could also be counted on to stick to specified lanes without being prone to careless driving.

Exoskeletons

When the machines and robots can't do the job and you still need a human being, a strap-on exoskeleton could reduce the backbreaking work.

Exoskeletons have been a sci-fi staple for years. Think Tony Stark's *Iron Man*, or *Alien's* Ripley suiting up to shift containers.

Where will we see exoskeletons hit first? In a factory? A warehouse? A farm?

Companies don't have to be simply altruistic to consider exoskeletons for their employees; it's a way to save on workers' compensation claims.

Exoskeletons can also improve productivity in an aging workforce in industry and construction.

"A lot of younger people aren't moving into some of these manufacturing tasks, and so [older] people need devices for assistance in that area," says Thomas Sugar, professor in the human-machine integration lab at Arizona State University. "Fatigue is always a driver toward injury."

There are two types of exoskeletons:

+ Passive, which don't have motors or actuators, and are used to redistribute weight and physical stress

+ Powered, which are used to amplify workers' physical strength, so they can carry heavier weights

Vehicle and aviation manufacturers like BMW, Audi, Ford, and Boeing have been among the first to roll out "exo-suits" for their employees.

+ Ford is using passive EksoVests from startup Ekso Bionics in 15 of its plants. The suits support employees' arms as they work overhead, and it gives them the extra power to lift 5 to 15 more pounds than they could unassisted.

+ Hyundai built its own exoskeleton: the Wearable Vest Exoskeleton ("Vex" for short). Vex has no battery and weighs just over five pounds.

+ At General Motors, say hello to the "RoboGlove," an exoskeleton for the hand to reduce muscle strain. *CNET's* Andrew Krok tried it on and was impressed by its gripping power but notes that "it's a strange feeling, being able to hold onto something without constantly working muscles."

How much should a factory owner, warehouse manager or farmer expect to pay for an exoskeleton? The usual price is around $5,000, although Hyundai claims it will sell its ExoVest for just $3,500.

Exoskeletons might start in the military and trickle down to ag-tech and construction. While most of the exoskeletons in industry have involved passive systems for isolated areas of the body, such as the back or hand, whole-body suits would be more appropriate for combat uses.

Remember Tom Cruise's gear in the 2014 movie *The Day After Tomorrow?*

The military must always balance the power needs of an exoskeleton with its functionality. The military needs a wearable system that can last for a long time and that is super-quiet, something most powered exoskeletons are not.

"I think passive exoskeletons do have a future, but for powered exoskeletons, I think the technology challenges are much harder," says Ryan Whitton, a senior analyst at ABI Research.

Trickle up from consumer applications

Another model for popularizing exoskeletons is the "trickle up"—where the need starts not from the top, such as the military, but with people suffering from limited mobility. Here are three companies that caught my attention:

Stanford Biomechatronics Lab

Researchers at Stanford's Biomechatronics Laboratory have developed a robotic boot that helps people with mobility issues walk normally. "It resulted in exceptional improvements in walking speed and energy economy," says lab head Steve Collins. Specifically, users walk 9% faster with 17% less energy expended per distance traveled, compared to walking in regular shoes.

The boot doesn't exactly walk for the wearer, but rather lowers some of the resistance and friction. The boot uses machine learning models to "personalize" the push it gives to the calf muscle.

WeWalk

WeWalk is a London-based mobility provider that makes the "Smart Cane" for people with visual impairments. The device uses front-mounted ultrasonic sensors to detect obstacles and warn users with vibration feedback. A paired smartphone app gives audio feedback including directions and navigation information.

ReWalk

Argo Medical Technologies' ReWalk is an exoskeleton that enables paraplegics to walk again and even do marathons.

Claire Lomas, a 32-year-old chiropractor, has been paralyzed from the chest down since a 2007 riding accident. Wearing her ReWalk exoskeleton, she completed the 26.2-mile Virgin London Marathon. It took 16 days to reach the finish line, but Lomas was ecstatic.

ReWalk allows people with lower-limb disabilities to walk upright. The 44-pound device is comprised of a brace support suit that integrates motors at the joints; an array of sensors; a computer-based control system; and rechargeable batteries. Sophisticated algorithms analyze body movements, which trigger and maintain gait patterns as well as stair climbing and shifting from sitting to standing. Crutches provide extra stability for walking.

ReWalk makes three products:

+ The Personal 6.0 Exoskeleton for spinal cord injuries, approved by the FDA in 2014.

+ The ReStore Exo-Suit for stroke rehabilitation (FDA and CE approval in 2019); and

+ The ReBoot, a lightweight orthotic exo-suit.

What we've learned

+ Ironically, technology innovation across AI, autonomy, and electrification has, in many ways, made bigger strides across the industrial segments: agriculture, construction and mining in particular. This is because these environments are far more forgiving than some when it comes to the safety, security, and personal information limitations of transporting humans and their more demanding use cases.

+ I expect some of the most valuable innovations will be proven first across these industrial segments and only then will they "trickle down" to passenger vehicles and mobility segments focused on transporting humans.

■ ■ ■

Chapter 6

Battery technology

In the last few years, as electric vehicles (EVs) have proliferated across the West, a new "cottage industry" has sprung up—of journalists complaining about their cross-country EV trips.

The Wall Street Journal's Rachel Wolfe documented a 2,000-mile, four-day road trip in a rented all-electric Kia EV6 from her home in New Orleans to Chicago.

Wolfe writes, "I thought it would be fun."

Let's just say it didn't go exactly as planned.

Wolfe reports that she drove 2,014 miles and charged 14 times. But she also says she spent 18 hours *waiting* to charge.

Wolfe used the PlugShare app to plot "a meticulous route, splitting our days into four chunks of roughly 7.5 hours each. We'd need to charge once or twice each day and plug in near our hotel overnight."

PlugShare showed Wolfe thousands of public chargers, but most were Level 2, meaning it would take around eight hours for a full charge.

Wolfe discovered that New Orleans had "exactly zero fast chargers" in June 2022, when she tested her Kia EV.

The closest charger was 40 minutes out of town. Yet, despite being billed as "fast," it only delivered 13% juice after 50 minutes.

At Wolfe's next stop, her car's dashboard told her that the fast charger at a Kia dealership in Mississippi would take three hours to charge from 18% to 100%.

Wolfe had no choice—she needed the range. But what would she do while charging? The dealership was a 30-minute walk to downtown restaurants, "passing warehouses with shattered windows and an overgrown lot filled with rusted fuel pumps and gas station signs."

Hardly the positive experience Wolfe had hoped for when she set out on her road trip.

Wolfe next needed to charge at a Mercedes dealership outside Birmingham, Alabama. The estimated charge time: just an hour. Plus, there were two massage chairs she and her driving partner got to use while they waited.

Wolfe was probably thinking, "Next time I'm getting a Mercedes!"

Tennessee had a better charging infrastructure—Wolfe never had to spend more than an hour charging each time. In Indiana, outside a Walmart, her Kia charged to full in just 25 minutes courtesy of an Electrify America charge spot.

Illinois ratcheted up the stress.

Wolfe needed 30 more miles to get to her destination that day. But charging at a Nissan Mazda dealership required three hours for those 30 miles.

Wolfe decided to risk it.

She turned off the car's cooling system, silenced the radio, unplugged her phone and lowered the windshield wipers to their lowest possible setting (it was raining).

Three miles away from the station, she had just one mile of estimated range, but this story has a positive ending: She made it to her destination.

Her enthusiasm for electric car driving, however, clearly took a beating.

"The following week I filled up my Jetta at a local Shell station," she concedes. "I inhaled deeply. Fumes never smelled so sweet."

The new road rage: unreliable chargers

The reliability of chargers "in the wild" (rather than at people's homes) is becoming a real issue, notes *Ars Technica's* Jonathan Gitlin. While the average person only drives 29 miles a day, "it's impossible to divorce oneself from the cultural context of the car, now tightly bound to the American sense of identity following decades of postwar construction that reshaped our built environment to prioritize the individual driver against all others. A car means freedom—being able to travel from coast-to-coast on a whim—and stopping to charge every 150 to 250 miles becomes an impediment to that freedom."

Fine, you might say at this point. But given the benefits to the climate, maybe a little more advance trip planning constitutes an acceptable trade-off.

Gitlin tried to plan during his own road trip, but he still "spent as much time stationary, arguing with charging machinery, as I did actually pulling electrons into the car's battery pack throughout a 600-mile journey" from Gitlin's home in Washington, DC, to the Finger Lakes region of New York. His EV of choice was no slouch, either: a BMW iX.

What problems did Gitlin experience?

✦ **Wait to start**. At nearly every public charger where Gitlin stopped, he waited at least five minutes to see if the car and charger would communicate. "Waiting 10 minutes was not uncommon," he writes. This was not a relaxing time. "More than once, an error somewhere in the loop shut everything down."

✦ **Not all chargers are functional**. As with Wolfe, Gitlin quickly learned that even a PlugShare rating of 9.8 can't guarantee that all the chargers at a given location will work. At one station, Gitlin found two out of the four chargers broken and a third could only deliver 50 kW.

✦ **Cables are too heavy**. Well, not too heavy for Gitlin to lift but he speculates that their weight may be leading them to lose connection. Tesla's super chargers are more reliable and lighter, he points out.

J.D. Power found that, when non-Tesla drivers pull up at a charge spot, they leave without charging 20% of the time, because the chargers were all occupied or not functioning. Tesla drivers, on the other hand, successfully charge at 96% of the Superchargers they visit.

Adam Kay, author of *This is Going to Hurt: Secret Diaries of a Junior Doctor*, documented his EV charging travails in the U.K.'s *Sunday Times*.

"I've always tried to do my bit," he writes in order to demonstrate his bona fides. "I rinse out the wine bottles before chucking them in the recycling. I have an utterly foul worm dustbin in the garden for the food waste. I drop my batteries in the plastic silo in my supermarket and I've never knowingly dumped toxic waste into a river."

Buying an electric car, he says, "felt like the obvious choice."

His frustrations mounted quickly.

Using an app called Zap-Man to locate nearby public chargers, the first two stations he headed toward were out of order. The third already had a car charging there. Kay maintained his place in line for over an hour "waiting for the Nissan Leaf in front of me to bugger off."

Kay notes that the chargers all seem to have different interfaces and different means of payment. With some you can use a credit card. Others, you need to use the charging company's app.

Kay writes that his parents' house is a round trip's distance that's "pleasingly just within the car's range, with about five miles spare." All good, until the turn-off from the motorway he needed on one trip was closed.

The car, helpfully, shut off its heating, the onboard computer and the radio to save power. As juice got precariously low, it slowed to a crawl.

"An epic wave of panic appears when the range slips to 0%, but miraculously the car keeps moving," Kay writes.

Somehow, Kay makes it home.

Ever the jokester, he laments, "I make a mental note never to visit my parents ever again."

Christopher Mims, of *The Wall Street Journal*, had a somewhat more successful experience with his road trip.

His Lucid Air Grand Touring EV was able to get from New York City to Montreal and back—a 1,000-mile road trip—with just one overnight charging session. Mims notes, however, that this was possible only because he wasn't in a hurry. Most of the public chargers in the U.S. and those in "seemingly ubiquitous EV-obsessed Canada" were slower Level 2 chargers.

"For now, this kind of charging stop-free road trip is solely the privilege of those able to pay for it—even the less expensive long-range Tesla starts at around $89,000," Mims writes. (Tesla's Model S Long Range has an EPA-estimated range of 405 miles.)

But that won't always be the case.

"Once perfected and available in the mainstream, these ultraefficient EVs could eliminate range anxiety [and] reduce the need for charging stops for all but the longest road trips."

Mims's road trip was more successful than Wolfe's and Gatlin's, but it wasn't perfect.

His Lucid's actual range was under 400 miles, far from the 520 miles the EPA estimated the sedan could achieve. Mims attributed that difference to running the car's air conditioning. To achieve maximum range, you have to be very hot or very cold.

There was also the matter of a mountain pass the car had to summit, which sucked up some of the overall range.

Car and Driver tested the same Lucid and was able to squeeze 410 miles out of it.

Hopefully, all these nightmare stories will be a thing of the past as chargers become more ubiquitous and robust. And Tesla's opening up of its network to other EV manufacturers should help too.

"Charging is going to be a nonissue," says Elie Wurtman of venture capital firm PICO Partners. "We can wire every home on the planet. Just look at telecom. It will be the same with charging." (We'll look at whether that's true for apartment dwellers without their own dedicated parking spots a bit later.)

"I sincerely hope we achieve that because, otherwise, the EV-curious are going to continue to be scared off by stories like mine," Gitlin exhorts.

Even politicians get stranded sometimes

U.S. Secretary of Energy Jennifer Granholm wanted to try the EV road trip herself. The journey was meant in part to demonstrate to wary consumers how easy and enjoyable owning an EV could be.

Granholm set out on a four-day EV road trip in summer 2023 with a caravan of EVs—her own Cadillac Lyric, a Ford F-150 Lightning and a Chevy Bolt.

Problem No. 1 should have seemed obvious to anyone planning the trip: That's too many cars at once for most charge locations, which won't necessarily have enough plugs to go around.

But Granholm needed the visual, so a staffer drove ahead to the fast-charger in Grovetown, Georgia—and blocked it with a gas-guzzler.

That did not go down well.

A family needing to charge—and with a baby in the vehicle—was so upset by the ICE blockage, they called the cops.

The sheriff's office couldn't actually do anything. In Georgia, it's not illegal for a non-EV to claim a charging spot.

Ultimately, the family and the staffer were able to charge. The day ended without arrests but, once again, illustrates—to readers and hopefully politicians, too—how we are far from reliable battery-charging infrastructure.

"Clearly, we need more high-speed chargers, particularly in the South," Granholm concluded ruefully.

Are batteries better for the environment?

While battery-powered EVs have captured the attention of manufacturers, consumers and, increasingly, regulators, the question of whether EVs are better for the environment than the alternatives remains unsettled.

For sure, EVs pollute less. But does the upfront manufacturing of these vehicles release more greenhouse gas into the atmosphere than their ICE equivalents?

Once they're on the roads, does the incremental electricity required come from fossil fuels or renewable energy sources?

What happens when EVs—and their batteries—need to be retired? Are they repurposed? Recycled? Buried in a landfill?

Are there alternative fuels for vehicles that would more effectively mitigate climate change? Hydrogen? Ammonia?

Are the conditions for mining minerals such as cobalt and lithium too dangerous for human beings, and is the surge of EV interest fueling a tragedy often borne by young children in Africa?

Is there still space for a hybrid future that mixes EVs with gasoline-powered vehicles?

We'll look at many of these issues in chapter 10, "Supply Chain."

Can ships and planes ever be electrified? We've got you covered there too. Review chapter 2, "Air and Space," and chapter 4, "Marine."

Battery chemistry

Battery charge spot fails are annoying, but to ensure a smoother transition into an EV-dominant world, new battery chemistry may be required.

Fortunately, every day, it seems, brings news of new developments with batteries. Each iteration promises longer range, faster charges, and less damage to the environment.

General Motors executive vice president Doug Parks, for example, reported in 2020 that the company is "almost there" on developing a battery that will last for a million miles. We're not talking about range (that would put an end to range anxiety once and for all!) but how many miles a battery will last before it needs to be put out to pasture.

A million miles would compare quite favorably with current EV batteries which generally wink out at between 100,000 and 200,000 miles.

Tesla says it's also working on a battery that can last for a million miles.

The term "million-mile battery" was coined by Prof. Jeff Dahn at Dalhousie University, who wrote in *The Journal of the Electrochemical Society* that lithium-ion batteries "should be able to power an electric vehicle for over 1.6 million kilometers (one million miles) and last at least two decades in grid storage."

What are some of the more intriguing technologies for improving battery performance through better chemistry?

How do batteries work?

Before we burrow into the weeds of new technologies, let's briefly look at how lithium-ion batteries work. Here's a simplified description. (I invite battery geeks to consult Google for all the gory details.)

An internal chemical reaction between the electrolyte—a liquid or paste-like substance that facilitates the transport of positively charged ions between the battery's cathode and anode terminals—and the negative metal electrode produces a build-up of free electrons, each with a negative charge, at the battery's negative terminal (the anode).

Anodes tend to be a metal or alloy. Hydrogen can also be used as an electrolyte.

The chemical reaction between the electrolyte and the positive electrode inside the battery produces an excess of positive ions at the positive terminal—that's the cathode. Cathodes usually use a metallic oxide, although oxygen can also be used.

The difference between the + and - terminals is what's called "voltage."

Electrolytes are the battery's "ionic conductor." They typically contain a solvent consisting of dissolved chemicals that are known to improve conductivity.

LITHIUM-ION

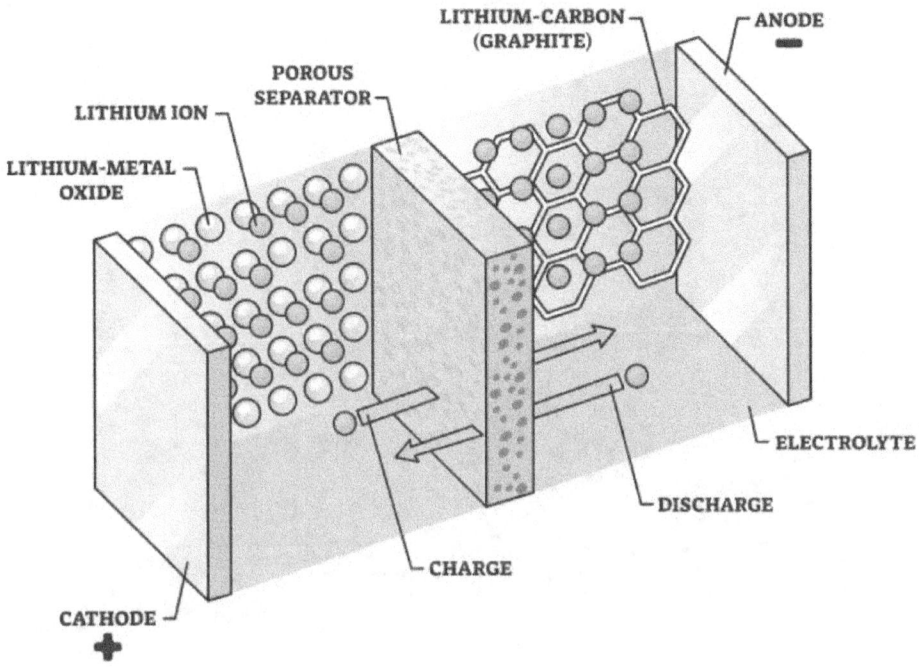

How a battery works (credit: Shutterstock)

A battery cell stores energy in chemical form in its active materials. This is then converted to electrical energy on demand, typically by means of an electrochemical oxidation-reduction.

In a typical lithium-cobalt cell, the cathode material makes up between 25% to 32% of the battery's weight. Lithium inside the electrode contributes 2% of the cell's weight. The electrolyte, which accounts for about 10% of the cell's weight, also contains small amounts of dissolved lithium.

So, the total lithium content in a high-energy battery is typically less than 3% by weight. That works out to about 6 to 10 kilograms of lithium per battery.

Now, let's take a look at current and future battery chemistries.

Lithium-ion

The standard bearer for electric vehicles, lithium-ion electric batteries hold a decent charge and their price has dropped significantly over the past decade.

PRICE OF LITHIUM-ION BATTERIES FALLS 97%
(price of lithium-ion battery cells per kWh)

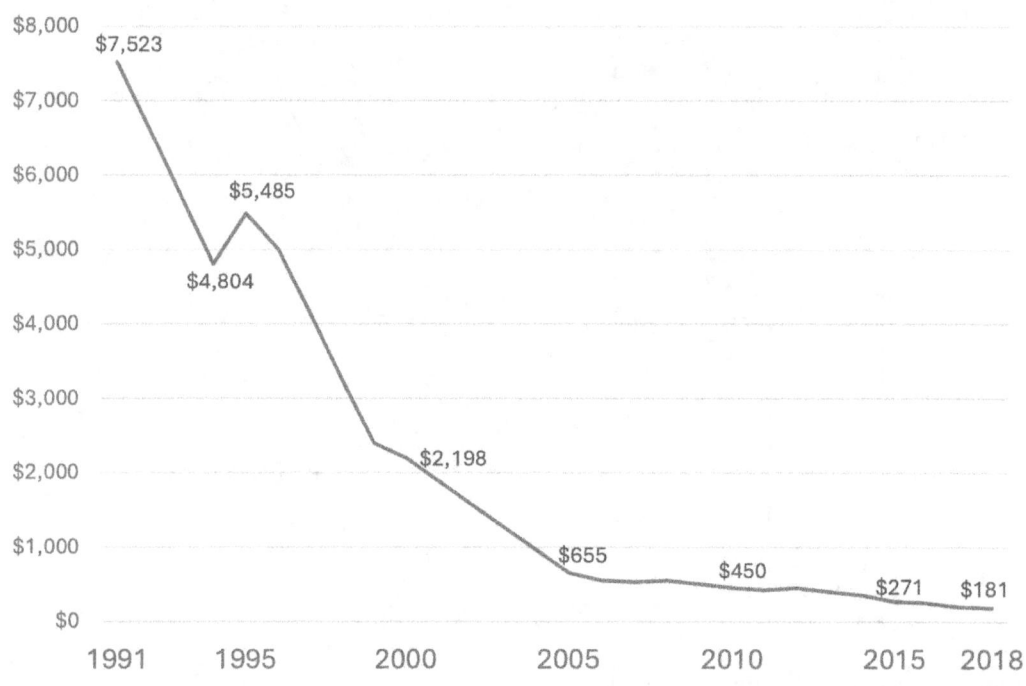

Prices are adjusted for inflation and presented in 2018 US dollars per kilowatt-hour (kWh). (credit: Ziegler and Trancik)

Lithium has an intriguing history.

It was used for a time in the soft drink 7UP®, which in 1929 was called "Bib-Label Lithiated Lemon-Lime Soda." 7UP contained lithium citrate until 1950 when it was reformulated, some say because of lithium's association as a treatment for schizophrenia and bipolar illness.

When lithium-ion batteries first came of age, they overcame the weight and range limits of the lead-acid batteries used in the first EVs. The best lead-acid batteries could store 30 to 50 watt-hours per kilogram (Wh/kg), while the first generation of lithium-ion batteries from Sony, which popularized the battery type for its camcorders, circa 1991, had an energy density of 80 Wh/kg.

That's a far cry from gasoline, which has an energy density of 12,800 Wh/kg.

It was engineers at Tesla who realized that by stringing together individual battery cells no larger than an AA battery, they could provide sufficient power and range for the first Tesla model, the Roadster, although it only gave 56 Wh/kg.

Today's top-of-the-line lithium-ion batteries offer double the energy density of that first Tesla, but the demand for more lithium has resulted in electric batteries taking up a greater share of global lithium production.

Benchmark Minerals estimates the battery share of lithium demand will grow from 26% in 2006 to 90% in 2026, according to *Pitchbook*.

That's led to an increase in the value of the lithium market to $48 billion in 2022, up from just $1.6 billion in 2016.

Lithium-ion batteries are an Asian thing as can be seen below:

BATTERIES ARE ASIAN
No European or U.S. lithium-ion battery maker cracked the top 10 in capacity in 2022 (gigawatt-hours)

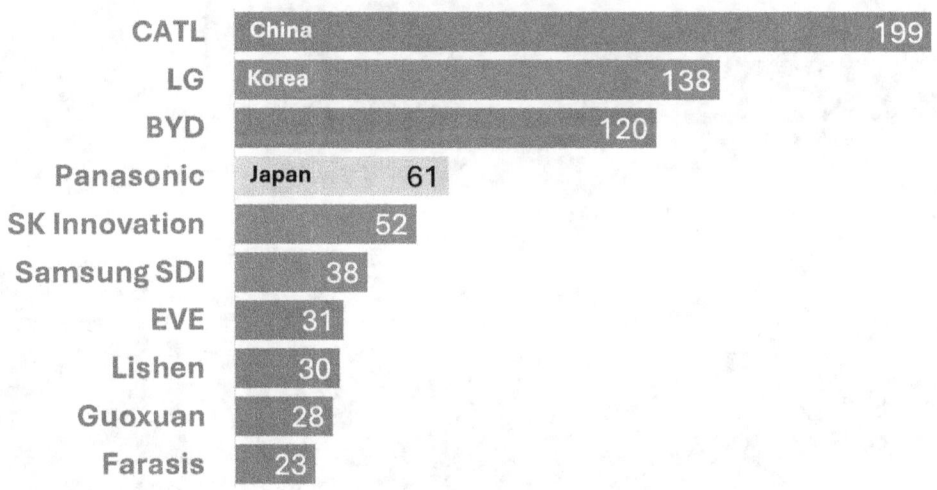

Global battery market share is all Asian and led by China. (credit: Volta Foundation)

The larger the vehicle, the larger the batteries, which is particularly acute in the U.S. where the share of electric SUVs has expanded from 37% of total EV sales in 2020 to 51% in 2022. At the extreme end, a 9,000-pound electric Hummer sports a 3,000-pound battery.

The bottom line: Even more lithium will be needed. But how much?

Pitchbook did the calculations.

"Assuming 160 grams of lithium per kWh (kilowatt-hour) of EV battery capacity and an average 68 kWh battery per passenger EV (or 212 kWh for the GM EV Hummer), transforming the global fleet of cars would require 14 million metric tons—or more than half of known global reserves. Further assuming vehicle life of a decade would require annual production of 1.4 million metric tons thereafter—or more than 10 times 2022 production."

No wonder automakers are looking at alternative battery chemistries that can improve efficiency and range, bring down costs, increase safety (no more spontaneous fires as have from time-to-time plagued lithium-ion batteries), and use less (or no) lithium.

Sodium-ion

Chinese automaker Chery announced in 2023 that its iCar brand of EVs would use sodium-ion batteries made by Chinese battery company CATL. Chery is also looking at using sodium-ion chemistry in its QQ Ice Cream, a small three-door car for the Chinese masses.

A Chery QQ Ice Cream (credit: Wikimedia Creative Commons)

Not to be upstaged, BYD, the largest manufacturer of electric vehicles in the world, said it would start mass production of sodium-ion packs in the second half of 2023, with the first installations intended for the five-door, four-seater hatchback Seagull, BYD's least expensive EV.

Research on both lithium-ion and sodium-ion batteries began in 1979 but as lithium-ion took off, sodium-ion languished until CATL reinvigorated interest in recent years.

The BYD Seagull (credit: Automotive Ventures)

Sodium-ion is a mixed blessing: The batteries are considered safer than lithium-based ones and, with lithium prices on the rise, sodium-ion is significantly cheaper.

Sodium-ion batteries also maintain their level of efficiency in cold weather, unlike lithium-ion batteries whose performance drops with the temperature.

Another benefit: a sodium-ion battery can be fully discharged for transport, eliminating the risk of a "thermal runaway" that happens when a lithium battery pack generates intense heat after an accident. Lithium-ion batteries are not supposed to be discharged below 30% in order to avoid damaging the battery, but that leaves enough juice to cause problems.

On the other hand, sodium ions are larger than lithium ions and, as a result, don't have the same energy density, meaning they won't get as far on a charge. They also run out sooner: A sodium-ion battery can be charged around 5,000 times before it starts to degrade, compared with 8,000 to 10,000 times for a lithium-ion battery.

Sodium-ion batteries are also heavy—up to two times heavier than lithium-ion batteries per kWh stored—which further limits their usefulness.

Another downside: sodium-ion charges slower, which may prove to be a deal breaker for consumers. A report from *Bloomberg* in 2022 found that, in certain formulations, sodium-ion batteries can only provide high power for as little as 10 minutes—"hardly enough for a car. What's more, if this battery was to be adopted for electric vehicles, the energy density of its cells would have to increase by at least eight times to get anywhere near what EVs need," *Bloomberg's* Anjani Trivedi writes.

Guangzhou Tinci Materials Technology, the world's largest maker of electrolytes, was even harsher, calling sodium-ion batteries "worthless."

Comparing sodium with lithium

This chart from DNK Power, a Chinese battery manufacturer, compares the advantages and disadvantages of sodium-ion vs. lithium-ion batteries.

WILL SODIUM BATTERIES REPLACE LITHIUM BATTERIES?

Feature	Sodium-ion Battery	Lithium-ion Battery
Energy Density	Lower energy density compared to lithium batteries.	Higher energy density compared to sodium batteries.
Cost	Cheaper than lithium batteries.	More expensive than sodium batteries.
Safety	Sodium batteries are safer, as they do not explode or catch fire easily.	Lithium batteries are more prone to catching fire or exploding.
Environmental Impact	Sodium batteries are more environmentally friendly than lithium batteries as they use abundant and easily available materials.	Lithium batteries require rare metals and minerals, which can have a negative impact on the environment.
Performance	Sodium batteries have lower performance compared to lithium batteries.	Lithium batteries have higher performance compared to sodium batteries.
Rechargeability	Sodium batteries have a shorter lifespan and can be recharged fewer times compared to lithium batteries.	Lithium batteries have a longer lifespan and can be recharged more times compared to sodium batteries.
Application	Sodium batteries are suitable for large-scale energy storage applications.	Lithium batteries are suitable for portable devices and electric vehicles.

Comparing sodium-ion to lithium-ion batteries (credit: DNK Power)

DNK Power has concluded that sodium-ion batteries would be more appropriate for backup power supplies, low-speed electric vehicles such as e-scooters, and home energy storage.

"Sodium-ion batteries are positioned as the most economical, high-safety energy storage batteries," writes DNK.

Clearly, CATL, Chery and BYD disagree.

It will be interesting to see what battery makers and automotive manufacturers, particularly those in China, do with sodium-ion chemistry. If it catches on, and the trade-offs are not too great, it could help break the lithium logjam.

Salt

Could salt be the solution to creating a battery that is green, affordable and safe?

That's what a collaboration between the University of Nottingham and six research institutes across China is trying to prove.

The team initially tested a high-temperature iron-air battery design that used molten salts as a type of heat-activated electrolyte for conductivity.

The molten salts demonstrated impressive range, strong energy storage, and power capability, and were cheap and inflammable to boot.

The U.K.-Chinese collaboration combines a solid-oxide fuel cell with a metal-air battery.

Metal-air batteries use a cheap metal, such as iron, and combine it with the oxygen present in air to generate electricity. During charging, these batteries emit only oxygen into the atmosphere. Metal-air batteries can store and discharge as much electricity as lithium-ion batteries.

The biggest problem: They are not very durable.

Adding molten salt to the mix as a type of electrolyte activated by heat gives the batteries the missing longevity needed to compete.

Still, there's much work to be done before salt-based batteries can be considered a potential alternative to lithium-ion.

In particular, molten salts can be "aggressively corrosive, volatile and evaporate or leak, which is challenging to the safety and stability of battery design," Prof. George Chen, the University of Nottingham study lead, explained in a press release.

But if the researchers can get it all to work, there's one more benefit: Salt-based batteries, in principle, are capable of storing solar heat as well as electricity.

Indeed, molten salts are currently used in Spain and China "to capture and store solar heat which is then converted to electricity. Our molten salt metal-air battery does the two jobs in one device," Chen adds.

Sulfur

A team at the University of Texas is adding sulfur to lithium to make batteries more effective and safer for the environment. The researchers claim that lithium-sulfur batteries would be less expensive to produce, be very light, and store more than twice the energy as traditional lithium-ion batteries.

"The least-cost system for a lithium-based rechargeable battery is lithium-metal [as the anode] and a sulfur cathode," Rebecca Ciez, assistant professor of mechanical engineering at Purdue University, told *Volts* podcaster David Roberts.

An anode is a kind of "reservoir" for lithium ions. When the battery is charged, the ions fill the space between the layers of graphite; when the battery is discharged, the ions flow out the other side of the battery—the cathode.

Not only is sulfur cheap and abundant, the U.S. is the world's second-largest producer of the mineral, making 77 million tons of it annually.

That said, sulfur is a poor electrical conductor. Electrodes made from sulfur also tend to break down during charging.

The Texas team may have found a workaround.

By adding the element molybdenum to sulfur, the electrodes become more conductive and—more important—more stable.

In Oxfordshire, England, Oxis Energy has been plugging away at lithium-sulfur batteries since 2004, the company's head of battery development and integration Mark Crittenden writes in the *IEEE Spectrum* newsletter.

Crittenden is, not surprisingly, bullish on sulfur.

"Our most recent models are achieving more than twice the energy density typical of lithium-ion batteries," he writes.

Oxis is also trying to address sulfur's limitations by coating the anode "with thin layers of ceramic materials to prevent degradation."

If all goes according to plan, Oxis says its lithium-sulfur battery cells will be able to reach 470 Wh/kg, double that for typical lithium-ion designs (and far more than the 50 watt-hours per kilogram of the lead-acid "starter" batteries in ICE cars).

When it comes to sulfur, "it is not unreasonable to anticipate 600 Wh/kg by 2025," Crittenden adds.

Another startup, Conamix, based in Ithaca, New York, is using sulfur to make the cathode since, the company points out, sulfur is the "lowest-cost and highest-energy viable cathode material on the periodic table."

Zinc

A team of researchers led by Swiss research university ETH Zurich has been working on ways to develop zinc-based batteries. Zinc is abundant, cheap and already has a mature recycling infrastructure. Zinc batteries can store a lot of electricity and don't require flammable organic solvents as the electrolyte fluid, as this can be made using water-based electrolytes instead.

So why aren't we seeing zinc batteries yet?

The biggest challenge is that when zinc batteries are charged at high voltage, the water in the electrolyte fluid reacts on one of the electrodes to form hydrogen gas, which decreases battery performance, explains Fabio Bergamin of ETH Zurich. The reaction also generates excess pressure in the battery, which can be dangerous.

Zinc batteries have only been tested in the lab. The researchers are not envisioning these batteries in cars, but rather as storage units in one's garage to compensate for fluctuations in the power grid.

Silicon

Israel-based StoreDot has long been on my radar. Founded in 2012, the company's extreme fast-charging (XFC) battery technology replaces the graphite that's used in nearly all lithium-ion batteries to make the anode with nano-sized silicon through which ions can pass more quickly and easily.

Graphite, a crystalline form of carbon, works well as an anode material but comes with extra weight and volume that serves no practical purpose, yet constitutes about 15% of the weight of today's lithium-ion batteries.

"It's the largest raw material in the battery," explains Brent Nykoliation, EVP at NextSource Materials, which is ramping up a graphite mine in Madagascar. "Graphite always seems to be the forgotten battery material, yet it's in half the battery."

Most lithium-ion batteries use a synthetic graphite, which is produced as a petroleum byproduct, mostly in China.

That's good news for battery makers that still want graphite: By 2030, natural graphite is projected to have one of the largest supply shortfalls of all battery materials, with demand outstripping supply by some 1.2 million metric tons, according to Benchmark.

But graphite's days could be numbered, if StoreDot and other companies have any sway.

Charging a StoreDot battery for 5 minutes can provide up to 100 miles of range. That sounds impressive but it's actually a downgrade from the company's original goal of charging a battery to 100% in 5 minutes.

Still, by not radically changing the chemistry, StoreDot says its fast-charging batteries can be used in standard production lines. The company is working with BP, the British petroleum company, to convert some of BP's 18,500 service stations to StoreDot-powered fast chargers.

In 2023, StoreDot signed on Polestar Automotive, the Swedish EV maker backed by Volvo and Geely, as the first automaker to incorporate its fast-charging battery cells. StoreDot says it hopes Polestar cars with its batteries will be on the road by 2027.

Another 15 automakers are running trials with StoreDot's batteries, including Daimler and Volvo Cars. Even Tesla asked StoreDot to ship out some cells, StoreDot CEO Doron Myersdorf told me, "Although we were hesitant to do that. A company like that in Silicon Valley can swallow you if you're not well protected."

StoreDot has already demonstrated that its technology works.

At the 2019 EcoMotion conference in Tel Aviv, a five-minute charge gave an e-motorcycle the juice it needed to take off.

Myersdorf adds that silicon is just a stopgap—the goal is to convert its batteries to solid-state, "which should provide longer range" (although not necessarily faster charge) than StoreDot's current approach.

In addition to the move to silicon, Myersdorf claims that StoreDot's batteries use only half the amount of cobalt of existing lithium-ion batteries.

In 2022, Bengaluru, India-based electric scooter maker Ola Electric invested in StoreDot, pledging to integrate its technology in India.

StoreDot has now raised over $200 million and has a valuation of $1.5 billion, putting it in Israel's unicorn class. The latest round was led by Vietnamese EV maker VinFast.

StoreDot's progress has been slow, but then so has most of the battery industry.

"People don't understand how long, hard and complex a process it is to develop a battery," Myersdorf says. "The market is changing, so every time you do the best you can with the knowledge you have."

That said, StoreDot's tech could be the harbinger of a sea-change in the EV space.

"What used to be range anxiety in electric vehicles is now transforming to charging anxiety," Myersdorf says. "Charging speed is now considered the number one barrier for adoption of electric vehicles."

Other silicon battery companies

Building anodes based on silicon is becoming a hot battery-tech commodity. One company, Sila—hardly a startup at this point—has raised nearly a billion dollars and has as its first prestige customer Mercedes, which will use Sila's silicon-based batteries in the former's electric EQG model starting in early 2025. Sila says that its "Titan" anodes get a 20% boost in range compared with existing lithium-ion batteries.

"There are three things customers care about, and it's range, range, range," says Sila CEO and former Tesla executive Gene Berdichevsky. "We are ready to take on more automakers."

Other companies using silicon to improve range include:

- **Group14 Technologies**, which has a supply agreement with Porsche. The company was awarded $100 million by the U.S. Department of Energy in 2022 to accelerate the build-out of its factories.

- **OneD Battery Sciences**, which is working with General Motors.

✦ **Nexeon**, which raised $200 million in 2022 to fund its silicon anode production—"tens of thousands of metric tons," the company claims—with offices in the U.K. and Japan.

✦ **Enovix**, which is expanding beyond EVs into batteries for wearables, handsets and computers.

✦ **Solid Power**, which went public in a $1.2 billion SPAC deal and is backed by Ford and BMW.

✦ **Factoral Energy**, which is jointly developing solid-state batteries with Hyundai and Kia. The company also has agreements with Mercedes and Stellantis.

✦ **Enevate**, which is focusing on electrifying two-wheelers first. The company has backing from the Renault-Nissan-Mitsubishi alliance.

✦ **Amprius Technologies**, which claims its silicon anode batteries will have an energy density of 450 watt-hours per kilogram compared with 270 watt-hours per kilogram for conventional lithium-ion batteries. "We can charge to 80% in under 6 minutes," notes Jon Borstein, the company's COO.

✦ **Greater Bay Technology** is also claiming that its first-generation battery cell can be charged up to full in the same time it takes for a gas-powered car to refuel. Five minutes give it 124 miles of range. The company further asserts that in just 8 minutes, it can achieve an 80% charge. Greater Bay hasn't said specifically that its batteries use silicon, just that it has developed "technological innovations in materials."

Before we jump too far onto this bandwagon, it's important to keep in mind that silicon is not a panacea. It expands three times in size as the battery fills up with lithium ions, which can degrade the battery.

The key is to encapsulate the silicon particles in some kind of "binding structure."

Sila does that by surrounding the silicon with a scaffolding similar to Swiss cheese. Sila says that limits silicon expansion to just 6 percent—similar to graphite. After 1,100 charge cycles, silicon anode batteries retain 80% of their original capacity, on par with graphite.

Sila has been plugging away on its silicon approach since 2011—even longer than StoreDot. Berdichevsky predicts that, by 2030, a third of the world's EV batteries will come with silicon-based anodes. By 2035, he says, all will.

The transformation is unprecedented.

"At Porsche, the soul of the vehicle has been the engine and the transmission," notes Group14 CEO Rick Luebbe. Now, however, "they believe the next soul of the vehicle is going to be the battery."

Solid-state

QuantumScape is the flag bearer for replacing the graphite in a battery's anode with solid lithium. Dubbed "solid-state" technology, since it replaces liquid electrolytes with solid ones, solid-state batteries reportedly can deliver 70% more energy per unit of weight and volume compared to the best lithium-ion batteries available today.

QuantumScape employs 600 people in Silicon Valley and has raised an astonishing $2 billion from investors including Bill Gates and Volkswagen.

QuantumScape's "ceramic separator" between anode and cathode helps cells charge from 10% to 80% in less than 5 minutes, while, at the same time, preventing the battery from losing capacity even after repeated charges.

Other companies in the solid-state space include:

+ **Solid Power,** which is working with Ford and BMW.

+ **ProLogium**, which, like StoreDot, has backing from VinFast for its solid-state tech and has raised $873 million to date.

+ **Cuberg**, which is focusing its solid-state efforts on improving range for electric battery-powered planes. (For more on how to power aircraft over long distances, please review chapter 3, "Air Travel.")

+ **BrightVolt**, which has been developing polymer electrolyte-based solid-state lithium-ion batteries. The company was founded in 1998 and has investment from Caterpillar Ventures.

Sounds great. So, what's the problem? Solid-state batteries are far from being ready for their commercial debut.

"It's crucial that leading battery developers like StoreDot give global automotive manufacturers a realistic and hype-free road map for the introduction of extreme fast-charging battery technologies," Myersdorf stresses. "Right now, despite some of the bullish claims by our rivals, all-solid-state batteries are still at least 10 years away. They are certainly no silver bullets for any vehicle maker currently developing fast-charging electric vehicle architectures." (The batteries StoreDot will be providing for Polestar as early as 2027 will not be next-generation solid-state.)

In the interim, Myersdorf is advocating for "semi-solid-state" batteries, which StoreDot plans to introduce by 2028. These batteries will reduce charging time from 5 minutes to 3 minutes for 100 miles of range. Semi-solid-state batteries also "require a simpler and less challenging manufacturing process than all-solid-state batteries," Myersdorf says.

Fully solid-state batteries, Myersdorf says, simply won't happen. "There will be a hybrid with maybe 4% to 10% liquid to aid in the transition of ions between two solids. Even companies like QuantumScape are starting to admit that a fully solid-state solution won't work for electric vehicles."

Mercedes chief technology officer Marcus Schäfer told *Road & Track* magazine that for the latest EVs to attain price parity with ICE vehicles, a battery must come in at $50 per kilowatt-hour. The industry average for lithium-ion battery packs today is around $137 per kilowatt-hour.

"I don't see that with the chemistry that we have today," Schäfer laments.

Solid-state will be the gamechanger that will allow for lower-priced EVs that are "in the neighborhood of what a nice [ICE] vehicle costs," Dave Gardner, VP for business and sales for American Honda, told *The Drive*.

BATTERY COST AND ENERGY DENSITY SINCE 1990

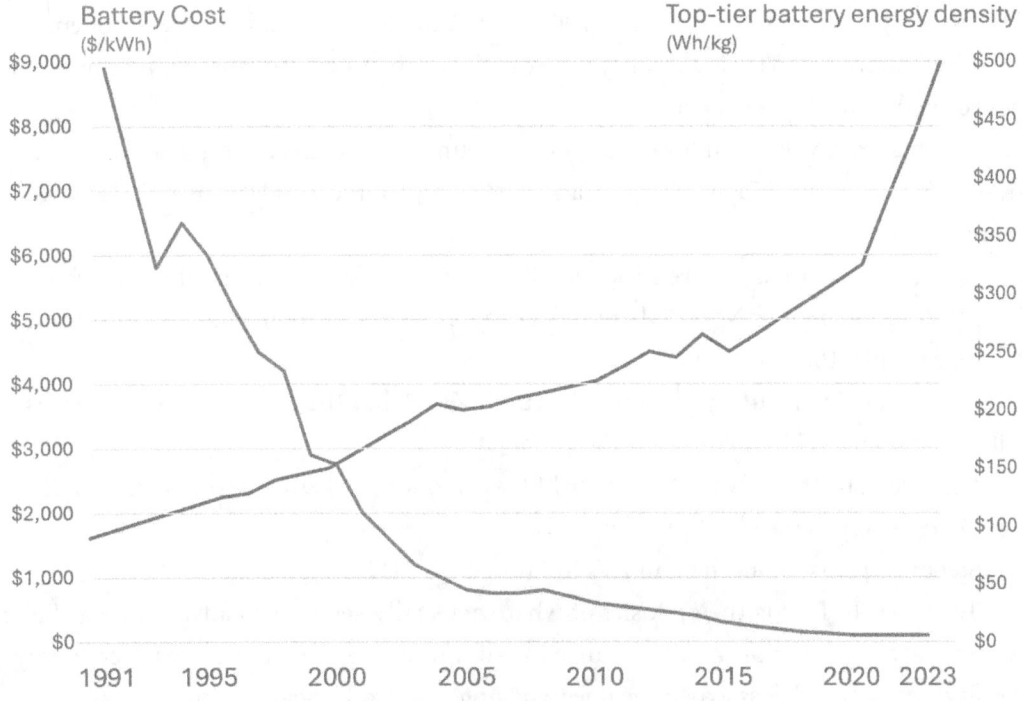

Battery cost vs. density (credit: Ziegler and Trancik; BNEF)

Gardner acknowledges that solid-state batteries "are not around the corner." In the meantime, Honda is doubling down.

In 2022, Honda announced it is investing $310 million into an experimental mass-production line of solid-state batteries for cars and motorcycles, which were due to go online in 2024 at Honda's research center in Tochigi, north of Tokyo.

Solid-state will "be the turning point in terms of crossing that affordability threshold," Gardner says. "When that's exactly going to happen . . . I can't tell you that."

Lithium-ion phosphate (LFP)

Do you want an EV with a huge battery that can give you nearly unlimited range? Or a more affordable EV with a smaller battery that can go shorter distances, is quick to charge and reliable?

Ford is betting on both.

In addition to the current industry standard lithium-ion batteries, Ford is adding LFP (lithium-ion phosphate) batteries to its $3.5 billion assembly plant in Marshall, Michigan. In September 2023, Ford paused work temporarily on the plant, citing concerns about its ability to operate the plant competitively while the company was locked in contract negotiations. With a new contract in hand, the facility was back on track by early 2024—albeit with its workforce reduced from 2,500 to 1,700—with 2026 as the forecasted date for opening.

LFP batteries don't use rare, high-cost nickel, cobalt or manganese, making them between 30% and 40% cheaper.

LFP batteries work well for quick jaunts around town (where the average customer travels 32 miles a day). LFP batteries are also particularly durable and can be fully recharged more quickly.

"Not every EV needs to have a 500- or 600-mile range," Sam Abuelsamid of Guidehouse Insights told *Automotive News*. "There's a lot of applications where having 150 to 200 miles of range is more than adequate."

Ford's Michigan battery plant will be run by Ford, but the equipment and expertise will come from CATL.

Ford won't be the only OEM to offer LFP as an option. In 2021, Tesla started offering LFP batteries on its standard-range models.

Stellantis plans to put them in EVs in Europe. GM is interested too.

The move to LFP is the opposite of what we usually see in tech advancement: LFP batteries are not superior in performance to lithium-ion batteries and have lower energy density, but "since it's less expensive due to having no nickel, cobalt or lithium you're seeing it coming back into the mix," notes *Bloomberg's* Colin McKerracher.

CATL's "condensed battery"

China-based Contemporary Amperex Technology (better known by its acronym CATL) is the world's largest battery supplier. In 2023, CATL announced it had developed a "condensed battery" claimed to have an energy density of 500 watt-hours per kilogram—far greater than existing EV batteries.

CATL is hoping this breakthrough—batteries with greater range and lighter weight—will make it possible for electric-powered planes and eVTOLs to take off. An automotive version of this battery is only planned for down the road.

CATL is playing coy with what's inside its newfangled condensed battery, but a press release explained that the company pulled out all the technological stops, including employing "ultra-high energy density cathode materials, innovative anode materials, separators, and manufacturing processes."

When CATL makes an announcement, it's worth paying attention: The company commands a 37% global market share of the battery market (LG and BYD are next with 13.6% each). Virtually all major EV manufacturers are clients—Tesla, Volkswagen, Nissan, NIO, and Tata—in addition to its partnership with Ford at its forthcoming Michigan battery plant.

Flywheels for charging

Zooz doesn't change the chemistry of an electric battery. Rather, it has developed a kinetic flywheel that can be attached to a charging station to improve its efficiency.

The company, formerly called Chakratec, spins 8 half-ton steel wheels 17,000 times per minute. The process converts electrical energy into kinetic energy. When a vehicle comes to recharge, the spinning slows down to change that kinetic energy back into electrical energy.

Charging time using Zooz: just 15 minutes.

The first Zoozster-100 units are being installed in Germany. In the U.S., two pilots—one in Florida, the other in South Carolina—are in the planning stages. Zooz's initial installation, in Vienna, is still operating.

Toyota's 900-mile battery

It sounds too good to be true: Toyota is developing a "bipolar" next-generation lithium-ion phosphate battery that the company says can reduce costs by 40% compared to Toyota's previous battery configuration. (The irony is not lost on me: calling a battery based on lithium "bipolar" is a bit on-the-nose.)

Toyota's bipolar battery is expected to debut in 2026 in a Lexus and will give the car 600 miles of range.

By 2028, Toyota says it will release a new version of the battery based on solid-state technology that can get up to 932 miles on a charge. Toyota is planning to churn out around 1.7 million EVs by 2030 using this purpose-built architecture.

Toyota's interest in exploring its EV options is surprising—it was previously all-in on hydrogen.

The change was prompted from the top.

In 2023, CEO Akio Toyoda, the company's most public EV skeptic, was forced out, with former Lexus branding boss Koji Sato taking the reins and pushing a much more aggressive EV strategy.

Toyota has no choice but to up its EV game—the company has only one EV on sale in the U.S., the bZ4X Crossover, which has a starting price of $42,000 and a range of 250 miles. Toyota notes that the company has been biding its time working on game-changing technology.

That time has now arrived.

I'm not convinced.

After years of hedging and falling behind the competition, I wonder how much of the news from Toyota is just vaporware or even "fake news" to get the media off their backs. After all, Toyota has been widely perceived as missing the significance of the industry's move to EVs.

While it's true Toyota did more to improve fuel efficiency and cut emissions than just about any other established automaker by pioneering hybrid cars, now, having staked so much on hybrids, the company moved painfully slowly to cars that have no tailpipe whatsoever.

Toyota seems to be in the process of being vindicated, as hybrid sales are surging while would-be electric vehicle buyers worry that the public charging network is inadequate and unreliable—fueled by the horror stories of automotive journalists on ill-fated road trips.

Anita Rajan, general director of the Japan Automobile Manufacturers Association in the U.S., believes Japanese automakers have been biding their time until they could make electric cars as reliable and affordable as gasoline-powered vehicles.

"I don't know if there's a benefit in being first to market with these vehicles," Rajan told *The New York Times*.

Moreover, since most people tend to own their cars for more than a few years, the transition to EVs won't come as fast as with cellphones, when Apple and Google knocked previous world-leader Nokia off the top spot seemingly overnight.

"We've still got time," says Naoki Kobayashi, a deputy director of the Japanese trade ministry's automobile division.

In-road charging

Toyota's 900-mile projected range for its solid-state next-gen lithium-ion batteries is impressive. But the company notched another achievement in 2023: 1,200 miles on a single charge.

Toyota did that through a partnership with Electreon, which signed a deal with the Japanese automaker in 2022 to develop wireless charging technology.

You know how you can connect your iPhone or Apple Watch to a wireless MagSafe charger? Electreon does the same, but on a much larger scale.

At its simplest, Electreon will place wireless charge spots in a garage, hub or terminal, with buses as the first use-case.

Ultimately, Electreon hopes to embed its chargers in highways.

"Our goal is to pave it almost everywhere and to charge all types of vehicles," explains Oren Ezer, Electreon's CEO.

Toyota and Electreon are working on the joint development of a wireless "kit" for easy installation on existing vehicles—and not just those from Toyota.

The Toyota-Electreon 1,200-mile pilot took place during a five-day "road rally" in Israel, where Electreon is based. Drivers alternated to keep a Toyota RAV4-PHEV running for 100 hours without ever turning off the engine.

The test track was only 200 meters long and only 25% of it was electrified using Electreon's technology, making the achievement even more impressive!

Electreon says it will soon be expanding to Europe.

A wireless charging highway pilot has been approved for a public road in Balingen, Germany. The technology will be deployed over a one-kilometer stretch and will also include two static charging stations for buses.

The Balingen project, operated in collaboration with German EV charging infrastructure provider EnBW, follows a successful pilot in another German city, Karlsruhe. That one wasn't for the public—it was installed at the EnBW training center.

"We have already shown in our joint Karlsruhe project with EnBW how effective, safe and easy to deploy wireless dynamic charging is. We hope this is the start of many more projects on public and private roads in Germany," says Andreas Wendt, CEO of Electreon's German subsidiary.

Electreon also inked a deal with European toll-road operator VINCI, which will install wireless charging on a two-kilometer stretch of the A10 highway southwest of Paris. A stationary wireless charging station will also be deployed. The initial phase of the Paris project will be to charge commercial electric fleets while they drive.

In Israel, the company began installing wireless charging infrastructure at bus company Electra Afikim's depots in Petach Tikva and Rosh Ha'ayin in 2023. It came at the same time as the launch of the first public electric road in the U.S., a stretch of highway in Michigan built in conjunction with Ford.

A study commissioned in 2021 by France's transportation ministry concluded that Electreon's ERS (electric road system) could reduce CO_2 emissions from road freight transport by 86% compared to diesel if deployed at large scale. The study proposes expanding ERS to 5,000 kilometers (3,000 miles) by 2030 and 9,000 kilometers (5,600 miles) by 2035.

In an article in *Automotive News*, CEO Ezer notes that the limited availability of chargers and slow charging speeds prompted one in five EV drivers in California to switch back to gasoline vehicles in 2021.

In-road charging can also address problems with fast-charging which results in batteries degrading more rapidly—the high temperatures required for fast charging causes the electrodes to disintegrate over time, leading to an up-to-23% reduction in battery lifespan. And fast charging still requires relatively lengthy charging periods for large vehicles such as buses or trucks.

Fast charging "doesn't optimize charging, it simply reinforces existing ineffective charging behaviors," says Ezer. Electreon's wireless charging delivers the electrons without all the heat.

Another advantage: With wireless charging—whether in-road or at a depot—fleet owners can charge multiple EVs simultaneously. No more waiting or fighting for a spot. A single Electreon charging unit in a bus depot could charge dozens of electric buses, Ezer adds.

Electreon has dubbed its business model "charging-as-a-service." There's no upfront cost to utilities and cities to install the hardware and software. Electreon covers all the implementation, operations and maintenance. Users are charged a monthly subscription or pay as they go.

In-road charging competitors

Electreon's biggest competitor is WiTricity, which reports that "the hassle of charging tops the 'pain' list for current EV owners."

Of the 1,053 people WiTricity surveyed:

✦ 96% said they were "somewhat to extremely" interested in wireless charging.

✦ 68% said it would make them more likely to buy an electric vehicle.

✦ Two-thirds of respondents agreed that "wireless charging would be easier and more convenient."

Wireless charging was ranked third on EV owners' wish lists, after more range and the availability of fast charge. Full self-driving, like Tesla claims to offer, came in last on WiTricity's survey. Most consumers (EV owners, not fleet managers) said they wanted a wireless charging pad at home in their garage.

What do consumers like the most about the possibility of wireless charging? Some of the responses WiTricity logged include:

+ "There's no need to get out of the vehicle to charge."

+ "It's easy to do with kids."

+ "It saves time with the plugging and unplugging process."

+ "No plugs to damage or not fit properly. Just park and go."

"Wireless charging makes a lot of sense for high-value, high-use vehicles like buses and short-haul and regional trucks that are very expensive to take offline while they charge," Bob Kacergis, the chief commercial officer at InductEV, another wireless charging vendor, told McKinsey. "Our primary traction is in fleet vehicles, particularly on the heavy-duty end."

InductEV is "doing a lot of work with fire trucks and ambulances in Europe and North America," Kacergis says. "The value proposition is around having vehicles that are always ready to deploy at a moment's notice without the risk that might occur with people getting tangled in power cords in an emergency environment."

Even Tesla is jumping on the wireless bandwagon.

In 2023, the company bought Germany-based wireless charging startup Wiferion, which makes inductive charging technology for industrial robots and electric vehicles. The acquisition amount wasn't disclosed but was reportedly between $50 million and $100 million.

Tesla's interest may be more for its autonomous driving plans: If cars can drive themselves, it makes sense for them to be able to charge on their own, too, without needing a human being (the owner or a service-station employee) to plug them in. Wireless is certainly less prone to breaking than adding a robotic arm to autonomously connect charger to car.

Wiferion has developed some 8,000 chargers to date, primarily for industrial robots.

Wireless charging while the car is in motion is a solid and powerful idea, but it seems to me to have little chance of capturing the mass market.

But wireless induction charging, while vehicles are parked, makes a lot of sense, especially if you don't have to trade off charging speed.

Countering cold weather

One of the biggest drawbacks for electric batteries has been their loss of range in cold weather.

A study by battery monitoring tech startup Recurrent, which delivers EV battery reports "powered by 15,000 active vehicles" (full disclosure: Recurrent is one of Automotive Ventures' portfolio companies) found that some EVs can lose up to 35% of their estimated range in freezing weather.

Teslas do a bit better in the winter, mainly because the company uses heat pumps and battery preconditioning to lower the impact of cold temperatures. Tesla's heat pump was originally developed for the Model Y and can now be found on Models S, X and 3. Tesla vice president of vehicle engineering Lars Moravy called the tech "essentially an air-conditioning system working in reverse."

Why did Automotive Ventures invest in Recurrent?

Anyone buying a used vehicle is going to need confidence about the condition and remaining life of the used EV's battery.

Like your phone, EV batteries degrade over time. Factors like temperature, age, charging habits, driving style and battery chemistry all impact battery performance.

Recurrent provides transparency so that owners, buyers and sellers can have confidence in their electric car and the condition of its battery.

Weight vs. capacity

Weight vs. battery capacity is an important issue, especially as EVs are much heavier than their ICE equivalents (primarily due to their heavy batteries, which can double or even triple the weight of the vehicle).

Energy in these batteries is measured in kWh—that is, a 100-kWh battery can deliver 100 kW of power in one hour. In general, the larger—and heavier—the battery, the more powerful it is.

Tesla comes out on top in the list, with the best ratio of weight-to-power, although both the Ford Mach-E and the Volkswagen ID.3 had respectable scores.

The weight problem is only getting worse. The Audi e-tron EV checks in at 6,000 pounds.

If weight is not distributed correctly, it can lead to performance problems.

Electric vehicle infrastructure pioneer Better Place took a shortcut in designing its first EV, the Renault Fluence Z.E. Instead of conceiving an EV from scratch, Renault took an existing gasoline-powered car—the Fluence—removed the gas tank and put a battery in the trunk.

With the extra weight primarily in the back of the car, getting up a hill could be nearly impossible. One Fluence Z.E. driver told me that he had parked in a dirt lot that was down a pretty steep decline. When the driver tried to get out of the lot and back to the street above, the car simply couldn't do it.

The driver's wife got out of the car and blocked traffic while the driver pulled back as far as he could and gunned the Fluence until it had the momentum to clear the hill.

Tesla opens up its charge spots to rivals

Tesla has been at the forefront of most EV stories since 2008, when the first Roadster was introduced. Reviewers and drivers waxed poetic—and they still do.

"When you first drive a Tesla, there's a moment when you just *get it*," writes Patrick George, former editor-in-chief of *Jalopnik*. "For me, it was cruising around Detroit in a Model S about seven years ago and feeling that instant, supercar-crushing speed without the engine roar that usually accompanies it."

Yet, George says, Tesla's days as the EV innovation leader may have passed.

That revelatory Tesla moment George had with his Model S?

"These days you can have it in a Hyundai, a Ford, a Mercedes or countless other cars," George notes. "The playbook Tesla wrote is now being run by almost every car company and Tesla's cars feel less special than they once did. Its car lineup is getting old; it leans on heavy price cuts instead of fresh merchandise while the electric competition starts to pass it by. Its so-called self-driving technology is the target of lawsuits, recalls and even a Justice Department criminal investigation."

But, stresses George, Tesla still has "one unbeatable superpower" and it just got a big boost: Tesla's Supercharger network gets it right, at a time when chargers from other companies are famously unreliable.

Now, Tesla is opening up its fast chargers to other automakers—Ford and GM have announced that their cars will soon install ports on their EVs compatible with Tesla's plugs. (*Reuters* estimates that Tesla, Ford, and GM alone account for roughly 70% of all EVs sold in the U.S.) Rivian, Volvo, Hyundai, Mercedes-Benz, Honda, Stellantis (the parent company of Alfa Romeo, Chrysler, Dodge, Fiat, Jeep, Maserati, and Ram) and Kia have signed on too. Volvo chief commercial officer Bjorn Annwall notes that Tesla has the "best premium experience with fast charging."

There are more than 17,000 Tesla Supercharger locations in North America alone. It's the most extensive public charging network in the world. Tesla's standard is known as the "North American Charging Standard" (NACS), as opposed to CCS (the "Combined Charging System") that once seemed destined to be the industry standard.

GM and Ford essentially giving up on their own or third-party charging networks makes financial sense. General Motors CEO Mary Barra estimated the move could save her company as much as $400 million out of the $750 million the company had previously allocated to building charging stations in the U.S. and Canada. A more reliable charging network should also help GM and Ford sell more cars.

CCS vs. NACS charging standard (credit: Shutterstock)

Tesla, meanwhile, will get paid when third parties use its chargers.

Ford and GM's move was big news, but the real tipping point might be the June 2023 agreement by ChargePoint, the global charge spot leader, with 20,000 charging locations, to jump on the NACS bandwagon. ChargePoint will offer NACS connectors on new charging stations and, starting in 2024, will retrofit existing stations "on demand."

Blink, EVgo, Tritium, Electrify America, and Wallbox have all announced they'll make their chargers compatible with Tesla's NACS standard.

The shift toward NACS might run into problems from the U.S. government, which has allocated $7.5 billion toward CCS plugs.

George made this analogy: "Imagine it's the 1980s and the government decides that Betamax is the future of home entertainment. So, it spends a ton of taxpayer money to install Betamax players everywhere. But now two huge movie studios say they're going with VHS instead."

Tesla CEO Musk, while backing the new arrangement, had his doubts.

"I think it's morally right," he said at a conference in Austin, Texas in 2023. Whether it's "financially smart remains to be seen."

Musk is being slightly disingenuous here.

If the Tesla plug becomes the standard in America—as now seems inevitable—Tesla will "maintain a huge role in EV charging for years or even decades to come," George predicts.

It also creates a new recurring revenue stream.

On June 9, 2023, the White House gave Tesla the ultimate present: Tesla's NACS standard plugs would now be eligible for the same billions of dollars in subsidies. The only stipulation: They must be reverse-compatible (by including CCS) to qualify.

Behind the standard wars

How did Tesla win the standard wars for plugs? By thinking big.

How else do you launch thousands of microsatellites into orbit to provide the Earth's inhabitants with low-cost internet access, as Tesla CEO Elon Musk's company SpaceX has done?

How else do you unveil a plan as audacious as boring tunnels to alleviate traffic congestion? Or to embed computers into our brains to augment human intelligence? Or plan manned missions to Mars?

Given the sky-high and deep-brain innovations Musk is hawking, encouraging the competition to use Tesla's charging plug standard would seem small potatoes.

But putting his controversial politics aside, Musk is one savvy businessman; a student of history who has clearly done his homework.

J.D. Power reported that 21% of EV owners who attempted to charge at a public station in the first three months of 2023 were unable to do so, up from 15% in 2021. Broken displays, software bugs, severed power cords or gas-guzzling drivers hogging the charging spots all contribute to this EV charging nightmare.

Tesla's Supercharger network has been the industry's sole bright spot: Just 4% of Tesla owners reported a charging failure during the same three-month duration J.D. Power covered. That's made the Supercharger network one of Tesla's greatest selling points.

It's also a serious source of cash.

Piper Sandler estimates that Tesla could add upward of $3 billion in charging revenue from non-Tesla owners alone by 2030.

By 2032, that could be as high as $5.4 billion.

The more EV owners that use Tesla's network, the more Tesla can use those funds to drive even more dominance.

Tesla can also benefit in other ways:

+ Tesla collects data on the cars being charged in its network. That includes traffic patterns and the charging habits of non-Tesla drivers.

+ Better app integration will help Tesla understand competing technology.

+ Tesla can, if necessary, throttle the preferred charging speeds for its own customers.

+ Tesla could charge more to non-Tesla consumers (and to automakers) to use its standards.

Here are a few more tricks Tesla has as it moves to lock down the win:

+ **Network effects**. The more people use a product or service, the more its value generally increases. Think about the telephone: When only a small number of people had one in their homes, the value it provided was minimal. Today, the network effect of everyone having a phone in their pocket is undeniable. Social media also exhibits strong network effects. The more people use Facebook and LinkedIn, the more useful those sites are to others.

+ **Interoperability**. This makes a network bigger, thus increasing the value of the network to customers. Interoperability attracts new participants to the network, which, in turn, increases potential connections. The Tesla NACS-CCS connection is an excellent example of how interoperability can change the economics.

+ **Standards, once established, can be very hard to break**. Just look at the QWERTY typewriter layout, which was designed in 1878 to reduce the likelihood of internal clashing of type bars by placing commonly used combinations of letters farther from each other. Is QWERTY the best layout we could have? Absolutely not. But no one has been able to change it.

+ **Winner takes all**. That's the usual result of standards wars. Consumers know that if they back the loser in a standards war, they'll be stuck with an obsolete product. So, convincing consumers that your product is a winner is essential. Two examples from recent history:
  - Internet Explorer vs. Netscape. Netscape began with an 80% market share, but it couldn't compete with Microsoft's vaster financial resources and the installed base of Windows users, which had an over 90% share of the desktop operating

system market at the time. (Microsoft perfected this win earlier in the Word vs. WordPerfect and Excel vs. Lotus 123 wars.)

- Sony's Betamax vs. JVC's VHS. The Sony standard offered better picture quality than the VHS standard and Betamax tapes were smaller to boot. VHS, however, could record two hours on a tape (and later up to six hours) while Betamax maxed out at just one hour. Two hours became the go-to format for recording and watching movies. JVC also focused more on building relationships with motion picture companies. Sony eventually expanded the length of its Betamax tapes, but it was too late. VHS remained the dominant format until DVDs arrived on the market in 1996.

✦ **First-mover advantage**. When competitors try to attack, first-movers have already established market share, with a loyal customer base and, hopefully, positive brand recognition. That tends to prove defensible. Tesla's charging infrastructure, for example, was the first-mover in the space (at least in terms of getting it right). Disrupting that apple cart was always going to be a hard sell.

For Tesla, rolling out adapters that allow cars with CCS adapters to use Tesla's NACS-based system helps dull any potential resistance and defuse a potentially crippling standards war.

There are risks for the companies that have decided to partner with Tesla.

As mentioned above, Tesla could choose to throttle charging times for its own users—or maybe for non-Tesla drivers now using a CCS adapter on the Supercharger network. While Musk has vowed Superchargers will not discriminate between Tesla vehicles and those from other manufacturers, I could certainly imagine Musk demanding at some point that non-Tesla drivers pay more per KwH—or wait longer.

Once Tesla has the monopoly on chargers, it becomes like airplane ticket pricing: The exact same seat next to you may have a wildly different cost depending on when the passenger bought it. The temptation—whether we're talking about United, Delta or Tesla—may be too great to resist.

Too many new users coming on board all at once can overwhelm an already overloaded network. Legacy Tesla owners will now have to share their Supercharger network with other EV drivers, increasing frustration if all the chargers are full with other vehicles plugging in. Telsa's current vehicle-to-charger ratio is twice as good as its competitors' combined.

Can that continue?

Tesla is behind the curve in one aspect of the charging standards war: NACS does not support bidirectional charging, which allows users to power their house from their car or sell electricity back to the grid. For that, you need a CCS socket.

Musk says Tesla hasn't added this (yet) because he doesn't believe a lot of EV owners would use the feature. But enabling consumers to use their personal vehicle as a virtual power plant is one potential technology that might get us to net-zero faster.

Standards and fragmentation

"The history of technological progress is a history of standardization," writes Ian Hoppe on the Con.doit website, a platform for electrical engineers.

But the EV charging market today "is a lot like the Wild West," Hoppe adds. "Without standardization, this industry—any industry, really—is in a state of 'market fragmentation.'" That's when competing firms offer incompatible products, charging cables notwithstanding.

Fragmentation isn't all bad, Hoppe notes.

Consumers get more choice and startups don't have to compete against a single behemoth. But it's also risky.

Consumers might buy a technology that fails. Manufacturers, on the other hand, are loathe to put all their eggs in one technology basket.

We can see the latter play out in the railroad gauge war in the U.K. in the early 19th century. The question was: How wide should the tracks be? There were a couple of different opinions and a tremendous amount of money invested on both sides.

This was a winner-takes-all scenario. Only one could win if the industry was going to take off.

The folks with the Great Western Railway decided on seven-foot-wide tracks they called "Broad Gauge." The rest of the country built their tracks four-feet apart—that's "Standard Gauge."

A train from Great Western would not be able to run on Standard Gauge tracks, necessitating a switch to a different train—"a huge waste of time and money and resources. Everyone hated it," writes Hoppe.

In 1846, the British government settled the debate. The winner: Standard Gauge. These days, no one recalls Broad Gauge.

Will the same be true when nearly every EV maker has coalesced around the NACS plug standard?

What's important, Hoppe says, is being able "to know for certain that there will be a (working) charger that is compatible with your car when and where you need it."

Could a similar standardization happen with the batteries? That seems less likely to me, given that each EV marker is actively trying to one-up the competition with new battery chemistries, longer range, and faster charge times.

Better battery chargers

Tesla may have an implacable head start in the battery-charger wars, but there is still innovation happening. Here are three Automotive Ventures portfolio companies that help guarantee our charging up-time:

Go Eve

There are two problems with EV chargers: Either they don't work or they're in use. Irish-Anglo charging startup Go Eve, created through a collaboration between Imperial College London and University College Dublin, enables a single EV charge spot to serve multiple vehicles at once by daisy-chaining the devices together. Go Eve calls it a "dockchain."

"Imagine a world where you don't have to think about which parking space has charging, because they all do," the company's literature asks.

Customers can manage priorities, so cars get the maximum charge possible, whether that's first come, first served; charging the most depleted batteries first or using a booking system.

The Go Eve system supports Level 2 AC and DC fast charging. Go Eve received a U.S. patent in 2023 and planned to launch its service stateside in 2024.

"There are a lot of showrooms, service bays, and garages in the U.S. that all need to be electrified," notes John Goodbody, a Go Eve cofounder and its director of marketing. "Electrifying all of these sites could cost millions of dollars, but with Go Eve's system it would be a fraction of the cost."

The investment led by Automotive Ventures, Goodbody adds, "opens that door for us."

Treehouse

Treehouse is a service enabling new EV owners to compare prices from a variety of home charge-spot vendors. Treehouse vets all the third-party installers it lists on its website. If you purchased an EV that comes with its own charger—say, a Tesla—Treehouse can install it for you.

In addition to Tesla, Treehouse supports JuiceBox, Grizzl-E, Wallbox, ClipperCreek, Blink, Emporia, and TurnOnGreen.

Treehouse's offering is available at the point-of-sale in auto retail locations or via an API when applying for vehicle financing.

Treehouse raised $10 million in 2023 to enable the company to roll out its "Installation-as-a-Service" in some 30 states over the next year.

Todd Kimmel, founder and managing partner of Montage Ventures, which co-led the round with Reilly Brennan of Trucks VC, commented, "We believe the installation-as-a-service model has disruptive potential in electrification far beyond EVs."

eDRV

If you're a hardware or software company, energy utility or EV automaker looking to offer charge spots, Amsterdam-based eDRV provides the tools and equipment to get you going quickly—in less than 24 hours, the company claims. eDRV can point you to pretested AC and DC chargers. The company's apps allow you to accept payment, set up prepaid wallets, offer discounts, create differential rates and proactively manage energy loads with smart charging.

"Upload your logo, connect your bank account, publish your stations and go live!" is how the company describes the eDRV product suite, which can be white-labeled for client. eDRV's wallet accepts 130 currencies. Customers can get started with eDRV for just $25 per charge spot for AC charging management or $50 per charge spot for DC fast-charge enterprise management.

Jerry cans for electric charging

If you run out of gas in an ICE car, you can take a jerry can out of the trunk, either walk (or catch a ride) to the nearest gas station, fill up the jerry can with gas and feed your tank enough to get the car to the pump properly.

SparkCharge is taking that concept to the EV world.

If you're low on charge, and there's not a charge spot in the vicinity, SparkCharge, in which Automotive Ventures is an investor, will bring the batteries, plugs, and cables to you. Simply inform SparkCharge via its mobile app where and when you need a charge, and the company will send out a battery-packed van or its "Roadie Portable" DC fast-charger within 90 minutes.

Customers can schedule a charge on demand, automatically when a certain level of service (such as long-term battery depletion) has occurred, and on a recurring schedule. SparkCharge promises 99.9% uptime—could it have helped the hapless EV road-trippers we met at the beginning of the chapter?

Because SparkCharge's system is grid-free, there's no complicated setup process or the costs of putting metal in the ground. SparkCharge is targeting decentralized fleet owners and automakers, not individual consumers.

SparkCharge is available currently only in the U.S.

The company's motto: "Anywhere you park, we charge."

ZipCharge in the U.K. has adopted a similar approach to SparkCharge but without the need to call a service provider.

The ZipCharge Go is a suitcase-sized battery pack on wheels that can be thrown into the trunk of your EV in case you run out of juice before making it to a charge spot.

ZipCharge says the device can also be used for EV owners who don't have a dedicated parking place where they can install a charger.

The concept is not dissimilar to one I've heard—jokingly—mentioned in the past, where EV owners who needed to go on a trip beyond the car's range could tow a small U-Haul with an extra battery in it. (I think we can all agree that the SparkCharge solution is more elegant!)

BaTTeri's charge-on-the-go solution is to let loose in a fleet or office parking lot an autonomous robot that can fill your tank with electrons. When you arrive in the morning, tell "Thomas," as the company's robot is affectionately known, when you plan to leave and how much of a charge you'll need; the robot will do the rest. A single Thomas robot can charge 15 to 18 cars a day.

The goal is for Thomas to charge wirelessly, but since few EVs today have that capability, Thomas requires a human to accompany it to the next vehicle, to open the charging port and insert the plug.

"We call it 'valet charging,'" CEO Tomer Shahaf tells *ISRAEL21c*. "If in the future a robotic arm makes sense, we'll install it."

A solar-powered car?

As the world slowly but surely moves to renewables as a primary source of energy, companies have been trying to figure out how to use renewables *in the car itself.* Windmills tied to the bumper might not be practical, but solar panels on the roof might give a car-of-the-future just the bump it needs to run without needing to be plugged in.

The road to renewables has been paved with failures.

+ Anyone remember the Hanergy Solar, a sun-powered vehicle that was to be manufactured in China? No? There's good reason for that: Hanergy has since pivoted back to its main business: making thin-film solar products for a wide variety of industries—just not cars anymore.

+ Toyota put solar panels on the roof of its 2014 Prius, although it only powered a remote air conditioning system that cooled the car before you got into it.

On the more positive side, Tesla acquired SolarCity in 2016 for $2.6 billion, rebranding the company as Tesla Energy. SolarCity started by offering free charging to Tesla Roadster owners. Later, SolarCity became one of the first installers of the Tesla Powerwall home energy storage battery.

However, Tesla never considered putting SolarCity cells on the roof of one of its vehicles.

The Fisker Ocean comes with a full-length "SolarSky" roof, allowing you to harvest the sun's rays to generate free energy to support the vehicle's battery-powered motor. Fisker says the SolarSky roof can produce "up to 1,500 clean, emissions-free miles per year." Customers may not be seeing much of the Ocean, though; in June 2024, the company declared bankruptcy.

Munich-based Sono Motors had hoped that its Sion EV solar electric vehicle would be ready by 2023. The company has been working on it since 2016. Sono says it can build 43,000 Sions a year and will sell them for $25,000 each.

The Sion's outer shell consists of 456 integrated solar half-cells, which Sono says should be enough to take care of most urban commutes. The car's lithium-ion battery provides 190 miles of range. The solar cells add another 70 miles.

The Sion comes with bidirectional charging, so the vehicle can power a home or other electronic devices. Sion says it has received 19,000 paid preorders.

A second product—the Sono Solar Bus Kit—suggests the company is thinking outside the passenger vehicle box. A solar-powered bus could save up to 1,500 liters of diesel and some 4 tons of CO_2 per bus per year, the company says.

Dutch startup Lightyear was probably the best-known player in the solar space. The company raised $81 million for its long-range hybrid solar-powered car, the Lightyear One, which Lightyear promised would have a range of more than 600 miles on a full charge, including solar and standard battery electric. The vehicle was meant to be able to power itself for up to 40 miles a day.

In early 2023, Lightyear stopped production of the Lightyear One, as consumers showed much more interest in Lightyear's less expensive vehicle, the Lightyear Two. Ballooning costs were the main culprit—the original price tag of €120,000 for the Lightyear One more than doubled, largely due to the expensive parts Lightyear had to use.

The Lightyear Two, which the company expected to be on the market in 2025, would have retailed for just €40,000. Some 40,000 consumers joined the waiting list for the new, cheaper vehicle, while 21,000 leasing and car-sharing companies made orders.

The company's head of PR and communication Rachel Richardson told *TechCrunch* that the "Lightyear One was intended as a technology demonstrator." As a result, "we will produce it in limited quantities and this first car will only be delivered to countries within the European Union, as well as Norway and Switzerland."

Even that was too much, apparently.

In early 2024, Lightyear abandoned its solar car pretensions to focus on producing solar roofs for other car manufacturers through its "Lightyear Layer" subsidiary.

Another inexpensive EV with solar panels comes from Aptera, which cites the same 40 miles a day on a solar charge as the Lightyear and up to 1,000 miles with a fully charged battery. Aptera says the 2-seater's unique aerodynamic design and composite body—it looks more like an eVTOL or a spaceship than a standard sedan—is what boosts the range.

It will cost you $33,000 to be one of the first to own a solar-powered Aptera.

Aptera (credit: Aptera Motors Corp.)

Semi truck charging

In 2023, Daimler Truck North America (DTNA) announced a joint venture with NextEra Energy and BlackRock Alternatives in which they'll build an electric battery-charging infrastructure across the U.S. for medium- and heavy-duty vehicles.

The joint venture's more than $650 million first site will be in Southern California, the company says; additional sites are being acquired along various East and West Coast freight routes, as well as in Texas.

The joint venture is called Greenlane and it will cover not only battery charging but also filling up hydrogen fuel cell trucks.

The latter fits with DTNA's long-standing strategy of playing both sides.

In 2021, DTNA launched a joint venture with Volvo to develop fuel cell electric technology. And, as we'll see in the next chapter, hydrogen may wind up being the winning tech for long-haul semis.

"Electrification—particularly in the transportation sector—is what we would call a fantasy wrapped in an illusion. I don't buy it," says transportation futurist Garry Golden, who is betting that hydrogen will win out for trucks—and maybe for passenger cars as well.

"We can't deny the role that molecule fuels play in the world," he notes. In a mature manufacturing world, "fuel cells will always be cheaper [than electric batteries] because they don't have the mineral requirements that batteries do."

DTNA is headquartered in Portland, Oregon, and sells trucks and vehicle chassis under the brands Freightliner, Western Star, Detroit and Thomas Built Buses. The Freightliner eCascadia, DTNA's first fully electric truck, was unveiled in 2022.

DTNA may be new to the party but plans to ease trucks off gas and diesel have been around for a while.

In 2020, a 185-page plan, the "West Coast Clean Transit Corridor Initiative Study" proposed a backbone of 27 high-power fast chargers along the 1,300-mile Interstate 5 corridor from Mexico to Canada.

The study also suggests an additional 41 charging sites on connecting highways, including I-8, I-10, and I-80 in California, I-84 in Oregon, and I-90 in Washington. The study assumes that 8% of medium- to heavy-duty trucks in California, Oregon and Washington will be electric.

Starting with California makes sense: Some 40% of all goods that enter the U.S. travel through the ports of Los Angeles or Long Beach.

Building infrastructure for electric semi trucks poses different challenges compared to regular EVs. As noted above, long-haul trucks need to be charged quickly (if under-highway wireless charging is not available), and that requires much more power than regular fast chargers for passenger vehicles.

If most of the fast chargers for electric passenger vehicles clock in at around 150 kilowatts, a truck would need something closer to a full megawatt.

A 2022 study by the British national gas and electric utility, National Grid, found that electrifying a typical highway gas station will require as much power as a professional sports stadium—around five megawatts—and that's just for passenger vehicles. To power the needs of semi trucks will require the power of a small town (up to 20 megawatts).

That's going to be a tough bill to pay.

National Grid notes that a connection to the grid that can handle more than five megawatts can take up to eight years to build at a cost of tens of millions of dollars. That could lead to a grid at least temporarily unprepared for the demand, warns Bart Franey, vice president of clean energy development at National Grid.

"We need to start making these investments now," Franey says. "We can't just wait for it to happen, because the market is going to outpace the infrastructure."

The problem is not generating more electricity—renewables are starting to take pressure off polluting power plants. The issue, rather, is the "hose."

Tom Randall, deputy editor at *Bloomberg*, writes that "you could fill an Olympic-sized swimming pool with a garden hose if you had a few months, but filling it in a few hours would require a firehose. In the world of electric vehicles, an 18-wheeler is like a swimming pool—and the connections available at today's highway stops are akin to garden hoses."

"It's not like plugging in a toaster," adds Dave Mullaney, who leads analysis of electric trucking at the RMI energy research institute. "Utilities need to be starting half a decade ahead of the trucks in order to not be bottlenecking the transition."

DTNA knows this well, notes Randall of Bloomberg.

"Several customers had to reconsider purchasing Daimler's Freightliner eCascadia after discovering that it would take a year longer to connect their chargers than it would to receive their trucks!" Randall says.

And yet, the Inflation Reduction Act threatens to exacerbate the situation, in the U.S. at least, with a $40,000 incentive for each heavy-duty truck sale. Fortunately, the IRA also set aside $7.5 billion to help fund a national system of chargers with additional amounts to pay for grid upgrades.

Trucks also need more real estate in order to park and maneuver. A truly useful truck recharging site must allow multiple trucks to be charged at the same time. (The West Coast Clean Transit Corridor Initiative Study called for an infrastructure that could support 10 trucks at once; stations would be installed roughly every 50 miles.) Maybe Go Eve can help!

DTNA said in January 2023 that it had the capacity to build 2,000 electric trucks a year, but its total number of electric trucks in the field today is closer to 100. The problem is exacerbated in part by the fact that, even if a fleet is happy with the first 2 or 3 electric trucks delivered, there's no easy way to charge up larger volumes—say 50 to 100 trucks.

That led mobility venture investor Quin Garcia to tell me that, "Long-haul trucks aren't going electric any time soon. We are years, even decades away."

Tell that to Elon Musk.

Tesla's Semi

In December 2022, Tesla, after numerous delays, unveiled the Semi, its all-electric Class 8 truck which, Musk said, is "fast to accelerate, it's fast to brake, it's really a step change improvement in what it's currently like to drive a semi truck. It's got three times the power of any diesel truck on the road right now."

(Which begs the question, should truck drivers be accelerating that fast in the first place? I'd personally like to see semi trucks drive more *slowly*.)

Musk also said that driving a Semi would be as easy as driving a Model 3 and could be driven with "no training." (Again, I would rather the truck driver barreling down on me on the highway had *extra* training, not less!)

Tesla Semi (credit: Wikimedia Commons)

Musk notes that the Semi successfully completed a 500-mile road trip between Fremont, Nevada, and San Diego, with a load weighing 81,000 pounds. A truck with such a range costs around $180,000.

A 300-mile range Semi will run $150,000.

At one point, Musk bragged that the Semi could get 600 miles to a charge, but he's since stopped. "You haven't heard that [anymore] because it's a physical impossibility," notes Daniel Murry, SVP at the American Transportation Research Institute.

The Semi was supposed to be in production in 2019 but has suffered repeated delays. The truck's first deliveries will be to PepsiCo's Frito-Lay subsidiary.

Other semi truck manufacturers going electric

Orange EV claims to be the manufacturer with the most heavy-duty Class 8 zero-emission trucks in operation in the U.S. The number (drumroll please): 450 vehicles. Well, it's more than Daimler's 100 semi trucks and Tesla's zero. Orange EV was founded in 2015 and raised $35 million in 2022.

Terraline (formerly Solo) is developing the Tangra LH1 EV semi, designed to run for 10 years with a battery that can get up to 500 miles on a charge. The business model will be lease-only, or "Truck-as-a-Service."

Seattle-based startup Rollzi is taking a different approach to the problem of charging. Instead of building a network of superfast chargers, it is creating a "relay system" for specific transportation lanes on the West Coast's I-5.

"If you are going up and down the same 1,000-mile stretch of highway every day, it makes it a lot easier to relay those loads between drivers by breaking them up into smaller segments," Damian Hutchins, Rollzi's CEO, explained to the web publication *FreightWaves*. "Since our whole fleet is on the same highway, if a shipper has a hot load or if one of our drivers is delayed, the load is much easier to recover. It's also good for drivers because they get to be home in a more predictable pattern."

Rollzi is currently running 12 trucks up and down I-5 and will be expanding to run a second relay lane on I-10 originating in the Los Angeles area.

We shouldn't leave out Nikola Motors in this roundup. Nikola doesn't produce battery-powered trucks per se, but makes semis based on hydrogen fuel cells. In 2023, Nikola produced 42 Class-8 hydrogen-powered electric trucks and sold 35 of them. Of the 7 trucks not delivered, 3 are being used in an extended field test with a fleet partner, 2 are in continued validation and engineering and the final 2 are being used for service training and customer demos.

The story of Nikola is one of the more shocking in the mobility industry. We'll dive deeper into the sordid tale of its charismatic, and now criminally convicted founder in the next chapter.

When will we see substantial numbers of electric big rigs, such as the Semi from Tesla, on the roads? Musk wasn't saying. But Tesla has been working on the Semi since 2017, so I'm not holding my breath here. Other truck manufacturers haven't had it easier.

China's growing dominance

More than a decade ago, China anticipated the world's evolution toward electrification and had the prescience to lock up most of the battery supply chain, build dominance around EV battery technology and production, and aggressively boost battery companies, consumer demand, and EV automakers to leapfrog the rest of the world.

In the U.S., despite rich consumer-facing tax incentives as part of President Biden's Inflation Reduction Act, consumer demand for EVs has plateaued. (Hybrids are another story, proving to be a strong interim "gap fill" technology for consumers who are otherwise anxious about range, charger availability, and charging speed.)

The U.S., in an attempt to protect legacy automakers who are having a hard time with the transition from ICE to EV, have lobbied the government to erect 100% tariffs on Chinese-built electric vehicles.

In Israel, however, Chinese EVs are selling like hotcakes.

"In under three years Chinese cars (overwhelmingly battery electric vehicles rather than hybrids) went from nonexistent to nearly one-third of new car sales," Mike Granoff from Maniv told me. "It is one thing to read about a phenomenon like this in the *Financial Times*. It's quite another to literally see it on your block and on the billboards surrounding your office. And when that visceral experience is layered against the backdrop of understanding of Chinese government strategy—then it really hits you. China has not only spent a decade and a half gaining a global stronghold on the entire supply chain for batteries and for perfecting the manufacturing of EVs, but it has also intentionally overbuilt manufacturing capacity for EVs to a staggering degree."

"In the 20th century, America's industrial strength—and, indeed, its military strength and its ability to stand-up the 'arsenal of democracy,'"—was a function of its dominance of the automotive industry," notes Granoff. "In the 21st century, China has usurped that dominance—and most of the global public and policymakers have yet to wake up to that fact and its consequences."

Is there still juice in battery swap?

It's the EV business model that simply won't die.

Battery swap looked like a viable alternative to the 6- to 7-hour charge times that most charge spots offered in 2012 when Israeli electric car pioneer Better Place rolled out a network of 42 high-tech "swapping stations" across Israel and another 18 in Denmark.

Better Place's big idea was that, given the state-of-the-art technology available in 2007, when Better Place was raising its first hundreds of millions of dollars and Musk was "bragging" he didn't have a home of his own and was sleeping on friends' couches while looking to raise money, drivers would prefer paying less for a car with a smaller battery and reduced range than paying tens of thousands of dollars extra for more physical battery packs that grant a longer range but that they'll use, at most, once or twice a year.

Better Place didn't make cars of its own; it was an EV infrastructure company focused on popularizing robotic swapping stations where, in five minutes, robots would remove the spent battery and replace it with a fresh, fully charged one. The old battery would then be fast charged in the super-cooled station, ready for the next driver.

Better Place's swapping technology crashed and burned in May 2013, when the company was forced to declare bankruptcy after burning through $850 million yet selling less than 1,000 vehicles in Israel and another few hundred in Denmark.

At least one EV manufacturer, NIO, has jumped back on the battery-swap bandwagon.

NIO has sold about 120,000 vehicles in China and plans to build 4,000 swapping stations by 2025. It currently has some 2,000 stations up and running.

Tomer Hadar, writing in the Israeli business publication *Calcalist*, says that NIO's battery-swap tech has several advantages over what Better Place tried to accomplish.

1. NIO isn't pushing battery swap as the only way to charge a car but is colocating its battery swap stations alongside fast chargers. Drivers will likely use the fast option as their main charging option while visiting a swap station when on a longer road trip where waiting would be less acceptable. Better Place, it should be noted, also mixed swap with plugging-in, but fast charge wasn't part of the mix.

2. The Chinese government is offering subsidies to manufacturers with cars that can swap batteries. The Israeli government never got on board with Better Place in that way.

3. The Chinese government has been setting regulatory standards so that models from more than one EV manufacturer can be used in the same swap station. This compares favorably with Better Place's situation, where only one manufacturer—Renault—agreed to make its EV's battery swappable using Better Place's hardware and software. In China, the manufacturer and the swapping technology are one and the same.

4. NIO's swapping stations are envisioned as semiportable units akin to small shipping containers and thus don't require any digging into the dirt as with Better Place's infrastructure. The NIO stations come equipped with 14 battery slots—13 for battery packs and an empty slot for discharged batteries. The stations can complete 312 swaps a day, with each exchange taking between 5 and 6 minutes.

Another advantage to battery swap vs. fast charge is that drivers can easily upgrade to a battery with greater range. NIO's cars come with either a 70-kWh or an 85-kWh battery but can receive a 100-kWH battery for a one-time fee of $8,744 or a monthly subscription fee of $133. The 100-kWH battery has a range of nearly 400 miles.

NIO points out that a customer could upgrade to the bigger battery as needed and then return to the original, lower-capacity battery at a later time. And, taking a page from Better Place, there's even an option to buy a NIO *with no battery at all* and add battery swap functionality for $224 a month. In that case, the cost of the vehicle plunges by nearly $20,000.

NIO battery swap station (credit: Wikimedia Commons)

But Hadar ultimately throws cold water on battery swap as a long-term solution.

Once five-minute fast charge becomes a reality (looking at you, StoreDot!), battery swap will be made irrelevant, he says, although Hadar notes that China's vast size and the government's EV goals mean that hundreds of millions of city dwellers may not be able to install even slow chargers in their garages (apartment dwellers = no garages) and would have to rely on public fast charging if not battery swap.

"China has installed six times more public fast chargers than the rest of the world combined," *BloombergNEF's* Colin McKerracher told me.

Tesla's brief battery swap dalliance

A mostly forgotten bit of battery swap history rests with Tesla.

A mere month after Better Place went bust, Tesla announced it would offer battery swap as an option. CEO Elon Musk demonstrated a 90-second battery exchange on stage to wild applause and built a switching station in California between Los Angeles and San Francisco. But drivers gave the idea a decidedly lukewarm response.

"We've invited all the Model S owners in the area to try it out, and of the first round of 200 invitations, only 4 or 5 people were interested," Musk told shareholders and investors in 2015. "Clearly it's not very popular."

After a year, the offer was rescinded.

Was it ever realistic or was it more a publicity stunt dig at former rival Better Place?

Autotech Ventures' Quin Garcia agrees with Musk and Hadar.

Battery swap, he told me, "has been obviated by advances in electrochemistry. Batteries are getting good. It makes less sense for consumer-swappable passenger cars. That ship has sailed."

But has it, really?

An ample opportunity

Silicon Valley start-up Ample wants to make battery swap a reality—not in China but in the rest of the world including the good ol' USA. At a high level, the company's swap stations function almost identically to Better Place's and NIO's. You pull in, the station lifts you up on a platform and robots exchange your battery, all in five minutes or less.

Ample hopes to bypass the infrastructure issues that brought down Better Place by creating portable swap stations a la NIO that don't require digging deep into the earth and that can be assembled in a mere three days, "allowing us to bring up a whole metropolitan area in a few weeks," according to the company's website.

Ample platform making it safe to exit the vehicle midswap (credit: Ample)

The platform in an Ample swap station is also expansive enough to make it safe for a driver to exit the vehicle while the swap is in place. That wasn't the case with Better Place's platform.

Ample's literature notes that "When working with [last-mile delivery] fleets, we continuously heard that, despite well-intentioned efforts to electrify fleets, drivers could spend upward of 10–12 hours, or 25% of a work week, at a charging station. We've heard from cities that, in the race to electrify, there is a lack of reliable EV charging for city dwellers who don't have access to garages and the option of overnight charging."

Battery swap, says Ample, is the answer.

There's a big difference in business models between Ample and Better Place—and between Ample and Tesla's ill-fated battery swap trial: Ample is specifically targeting fleet owners and commercial operators such as Uber drivers.

In July 2023, Ample added trucks to the mix through a deal with Mitsubishi in Japan, which will see Ample's tech installed on the Fuso eCenter light commercial truck. An Ample spokesperson says the initial truck fleets will be used for last-mile delivery. In December 2023, Ample added Stellantis to its growing mix of customers.

Another difference—this one more about technology than business model—is that Ample doesn't swap out the entire 1,000-pound battery pack. It just removes the active battery modules, which are much lighter and don't require massive robots.

Ample cofounder Khaled Hassounah told *TechCrunch* that his company's swap system was no more complex than "replacing a tire . . . we don't modify the car whatsoever."

Ample's stations (there are 12 now in the San Francisco Bay Area, along with a few in Madrid and Kyoto) are modular and can be stacked together to charge multiple EVs at once. Better Place's single-lane design meant waiting was a frequent occurrence.

Ample has learned from the mistakes made at Better Place.

Its modular units cost only $100,000, vs. the $3 million per switch station Better Place was saddled with.

Ample is also making sure it's not stuck with just one model, as Better Place was with the Renault Fluence Z.E. As of May 2023, Ample had signed partnerships with vehicle manufacturers covering over 20 EV models.

Will Ample succeed where Better Place failed? It's a big bet with no guarantees.

Ample's other cofounder, John de Souza, told *Canary Media's* Eric Wesoff that when he started Ample with Hassounah, the most common comment they heard was, "You guys are crazy."

That's a two-edged sword.

"When people tell you you're crazy, it's one of two things. We could be doing something very ambitious—or we could actually be crazy!"

Ample stackable, modular units at the Golden Gate Bridge in San Francisco (credit: Ample)

Battery recycling—the missing link

What happens when a battery has used up all its charge cycles and can no longer guarantee a minimum level of service? There are three options: throw away (in a landfill), reuse (as second-life energy storage in a consumer's garage) or recycle (so the valuable and volatile chemicals can be extracted).

We will explore battery end-of-life scenarios—recycling in particular—in Chapter 10.

The Norway experiment

NIO is now working on its first expansion outside of China—to Norway.

The country's pro-EV policies—which eliminate the taxes imposed on vehicles powered by fossil fuels, slap a 20% carbon tax on internal combustion engine cars, and include free or reduced-price access to carpool lanes, bridges, and ferries—have propelled the Nordic country to the top of the electric innovators' list.

In January 2024, EVs accounted for 92.1% of Norway's new passenger car sales. Plug-in hybrids brought the total up another 1.8%.

That compares with an 82.4% EV share in 2022, according to the Norwegian Road Federation.

Norway's incentives make electric vehicles *cheaper* to operate than similar petrol models.

SHARE OF BEV AND PHEV IN NORWAY
(share of total new passenger registrations)

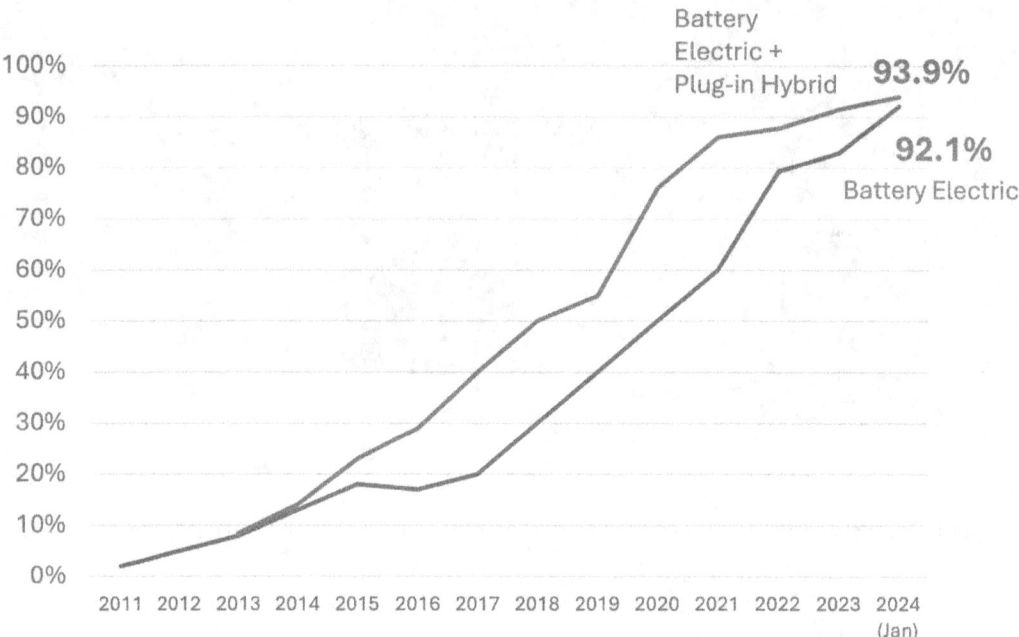

Norway has been the world leader in EV adoption. (credit: Norwegian Road Federation via Statista)

When it comes to Norway, says Quin Garcia, "It's already game over for combustion engines."

Among the benefits Norway offers EV owners:

+ No purchase/import tax on EVs (1990–2022). From 2023, some purchase tax is levied based on weight.

+ Exemption from 25% VAT on purchase (2001–2022). Exemption from 25% VAT on leasing. From 2023, Norway implemented 25% VAT on the purchase price from 500,000 Norwegian Kroner (about $47,000) and over.

+ No annual road tax (1996–2021). Reduced tax from 2021. Full tax from 2022.

+ No charges on toll roads (1997–2017).

+ No charges on ferries (2009–2017). Maximum 50% of the total amount on ferry fares for electric vehicles (2018).

✦ Maximum 50% of the total amount on toll roads (2018–2022). From 2023, 70%.

✦ Free municipal parking (1999–2017)

✦ Access to bus lanes (2005 to today). The latest rules allow local authorities to limit the access to EVs that carry one or more passengers (2016 until today).

✦ 25% reduced company car tax (2000–2008). 50% reduced company car tax (2009–2017). Company car tax reduction reduced to 40% (2018–2021) and 20% from 2022.

✦ Public procurement: From 2022, all government-purchased cars must be zero-emission EVs. From 2025 the same applies to city buses. The Norwegian Parliament declared that all new cars sold by 2025 should be zero-emission.

The results have been dramatic.

✦ In 2020, 54.3% of all cars sold in Norway were electric, up from 42.4% in 2019.

✦ In December 2020, electric battery-powered vehicles accounted for 66.7% of the car market.

✦ Volkswagen is the leader, with its Audi brand topping the leaderboard. Audi's e-tron SUVs are the most-sold passenger cars in Norway. Tesla, which had been the leader in 2019, is now in second place.

To facilitate the Nordic EV revolution, Norway currently has 10,000 public charging points.

Surprise! Your rental is an EV

I want to conclude our discussion of battery tech by returning to where we started the chapter, spotlighting EV road-trip nightmares. It's one thing for a journalist to knowingly push the limits of EV range and chargers. It's quite another to be thrust into the EV world with no preparation or intention.

Saahil Desai booked a rental car through Hertz. But when Desai got to the counter, Hertz was all out of gasoline-powered cars or hybrids. All they had left were EVs.

Now, this might sound exciting to some, but it wasn't what Desai had expected.

"With no forewarning, no experience driving an EV, and virtually no guidance, what was supposed to be a restful trip upstate was anything but," Desai writes in *The Atlantic*.

The same issues Wolfe, Gitlin, Kay, and Mims experienced were there for Desai's surprise rental of a Chevy Bolt.

Now, mind you, Desai is bullish on electric vehicles. He just doesn't like the surprise factor.

The biggest issue is that rental EVs, by definition, have to use public chargers, whereas most individual EV owners can charge in their garages overnight.

"Unless you luck out and have a place to charge overnight at your hotel or Airbnb, you're stuck with America's Wild West of public EV chargers," Desai points out.

He would have been happy to use a Tesla Supercharger, but his unplanned rental experience was prior to GM's deal with Tesla to use its NACS charging standard.

Desai says that savvy EV owners can charge in bursts rather than all in one go. But that results in them "compulsively checking EV charging apps for nearby stations."

Did Hertz provide any instruction on how to maximize Desai's inadvertent EV experience? It did not. All Desai got was a sheet of paper listing three nearby EV chargers. (Renters who explicitly choose an EV get a more detailed guide emailed to them in advance, apparently.)

The learning curve is not insignificant.

"It would be like a businessperson going to an office-rental store back in the late 80s to get an IBM Selectric," Loren McDonald, an EV consultant, told Desai, "and the person at the desk says, 'Oh, we're out of those. Here's a Macintosh computer.'"

Rental car companies buy close to 10% of all new cars in the U.S. In 2023, Hertz had one of the biggest EV fleets in the world. Of its 50,000 EVs, 35,000 of them were Teslas.

Desai discovered that not only are gas-powered cars out of stock in some locations, but in other places, the cost to rent an EV is half of what it is to rent a gasoline-powered car.

Is this really so awful, though? As Desai writes, "What is a car rental if not a very long test drive?"

New York Times writer David Gelles didn't receive his rental EV by mistake, nor did he consider it a test drive, but when his Volvo C40 Recharge crossover wouldn't power up overnight at his destination—a rural farm far from any sort of fast charger—he had no choice but to call Hertz.

They sent a tow truck. Shame they didn't send SparkCharge!

The backlash against rental EVs finally caught up with Hertz.

In 2023, the company reported a 13% margin, which its CEO Stephen Scherr complained during a Q3 earnings call "would have been several points higher" if not for the cost challenges associated with EVs. Among the problems Scherr pointed to: A one-third drop in retail prices of the electric cars in its fleet, spurred in part by Tesla's 2023 price cuts.

Hertz was also spending "about twice in terms of damage cost repair than a conventional internal combustion engine vehicle," Scherr noted.

The result was a loss of $392 million in the first quarter of 2024, reports *Quartz*. In 2021, Hertz announced that it was going to order 100,000 Teslas by the end of 2022. But by 2024, the order was canceled and, instead, Hertz was selling 30,000 Teslas at rock bottom prices. Its CEO, Scherr, had been ousted over the EV fiasco.

"The execution and marketing of EVs [by Hertz] was a horror show across the board," says Daniel Ives, an analyst with Wedbush Securities who follows the EV market. "It's a black eye they couldn't recover from."

What we've learned

+ Is battery power the panacea that will ultimately replace internal combustion engines, at least for ground transportation? The deeper you get into this issue, it's clear the question about whether EVs are absolutely better for the environment is a nuanced one.

+ There is a race to discover superior battery technologies that will store more energy per unit of weight, allow longer ranges between charging, and dramatically shrink the time to charge.

+ So, while we may not witness a broadscale replacement of the internal combustion drivetrain with EVs in my lifetime, great progress will be made to provide a very credible substitute through electrification that cuts across many different modalities and use cases.

■ ■ ■

Chapter 7

R&D and alternative fuels

In the early days of semiconductor manufacturing, Intel cofounder Gordon Moore made an observation that has since become a tech truism.

In 1965, Moore noted that he and his colleagues were able to double the number of transistors they could squeeze onto a chip every year. Within a decade, that had slowed—to a doubling merely every two years—but it's still rather exponential growth that eventually resulted in all of us having computers in our pockets more powerful than the IBM mainframes of 50 years ago.

But Moore's Law doesn't seem to apply to batteries.

Just look at the "evolution" of range since the industry's early days.

+ In 2007, an EV battery could get 70 miles on a charge.

+ In 2009, it was up to 140 miles of range.

+ By 2011, cars could travel for 280 miles on a charge.

+ And today, that's up to 400 miles for the best batteries.

It's all very impressive. And in the first years, there really did seem to be a doubling of range every couple of years.

But that's now stalled—if it was ever even real in the first place—when it comes to cars and batteries.

A big part of the reason for the slowdown is that a battery, unlike a semiconductor, is not all silicon. It has chemicals—some liquid, some solid—plus cathodes and anodes which have only a certain amount of surface area. The physicality of a battery is what makes it different than an ever-shrinking silicon wafer.

"Minor step changes are constant in battery technology," notes Quin Garcia, of Autotech Ventures. "But radical changes that are in the lab today will take a couple of decades to adopt. I don't see any technology in the next 5 to 10 years that will lead to a doubling or tripling of capacity."

After all, if batteries increased in energy density every two years, by now we'd have a battery that could take us to the moon and back on a single charge.

Electric batteries have captured most of the attention as the future of fuel. Looking at the tech landscape, though, it's clear that, while electric batteries are ascendent for passenger vehicles, we shouldn't be so quick to jump on an all-or-nothing, exclusively electric bandwagon. Other technologies still have a role to play—and a larger role in vehicle types when we move beyond passenger cars.

There's no time to waste.

WHAT POWERED THE WORLD IN 2022?
(electricity sources by fuel type)

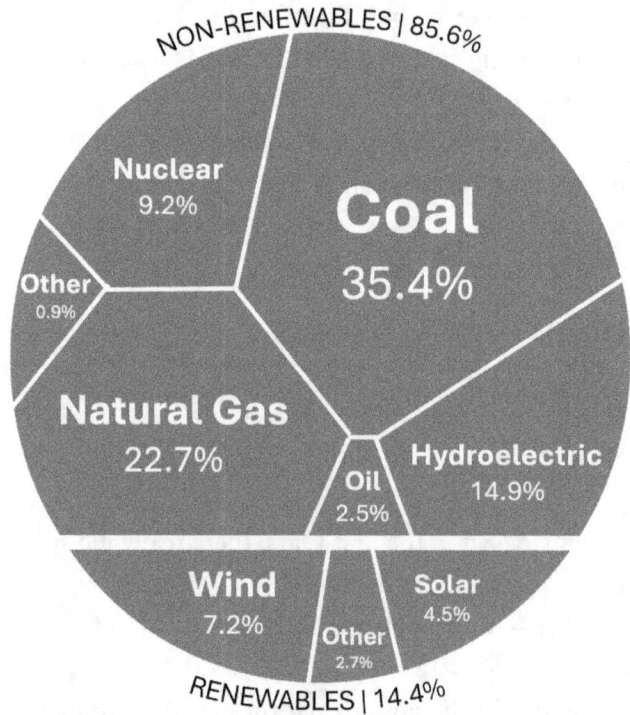

Nonrenewable fuel sources make up 85.6% of global consumption. But renewables are growing quickly. (credit: Statistical Review of World Energy (2023))

In 2022, coal was the largest source of the world's electricity output, with nonrenewables making up 85.6% of the total.

Getting off oil is not going to be easy—the first oil wells were drilled in AD 346 in China with transport done in pipelines made from bamboo, so it's been with us for a *long time*—but it's imperative to ameliorate the worst of climate change and to clean up our polluted atmosphere.

The modern oil industry was launched in 1847 when a Scottish chemist named James Young observed natural petroleum seepage in the Riddings coal mine. As Young experimented with coal, he was able to distill a number of liquids including an early form of petroleum.

At about the same time, in 1846, Canadian geologist Abraham Pineo Gesner refined a liquid from coal, oil shale, and bitumen that was cheaper and burned more cleanly than other oils. He called it "kerosene."

The first oil well was drilled in Trinidad in 1857. In 1859, oil wells arrived in Pennsylvania, marking the start of the "oil rush."

OIL PRODUCTION
Terawatt-hours (TWh)

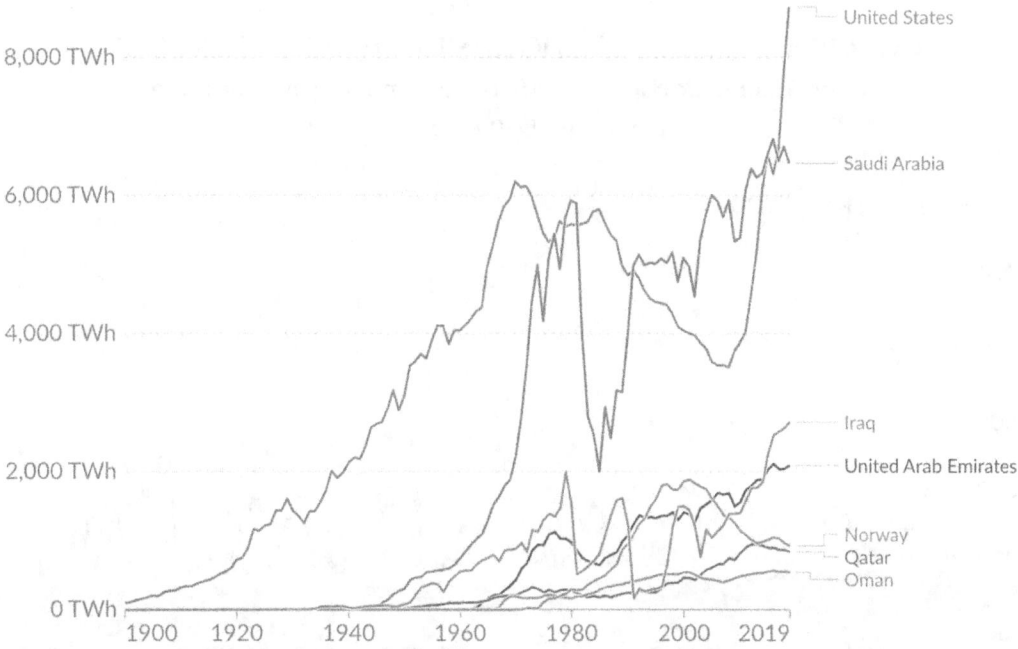

Global oil production by country. The USA leads, but only barely. (credit: Energy Institute Statistical Review of World Energy via Our World in Data)

John D. Rockefeller established Standard Oil (the forerunner to ExxonMobil) in 1865. World War I transformed gasoline as a fuel for consumers into a key strategic energy source for the military.

Oil didn't start flowing out of Saudi Arabia until 1938, and OPEC—the Organization of Petroleum Exporting Countries—was only established in 1960.

As can be seen in the chart above, in the last few years, the U.S. has surpassed Saudi Arabia as the world's leading producer of petroleum.

There's also a question around "peak oil." That's the theory that the world will soon reach—if it hasn't already—the "peak" of oil extraction and production from conventional sources. (Fracking, for example, is not included.)

There's little consensus, however, on when we'll hit peak oil.

Marion King Hubbert, who came up with the idea of peak oil and who worked at Shell Oil as a researcher from 1943 to 1964, felt we would reach the limits of production in the mid-1970s. Other analysts predicted the peak oil precipice would only be crossed in the year 2000. Oliver Rech, an economist with the IEA, thought a shortage of oil would impact supply chain bottlenecks by 2015.

OPEC was—no surprise here—more sanguine in its analysis, forecasting peak oil arriving only in 2050.

CO$_2$ LEVELS ARE THE HIGHEST IN HUMAN HISTORY
Atmospheric Carbon Dioxide is Higher Than at Any Time in at Least 800,000 Years

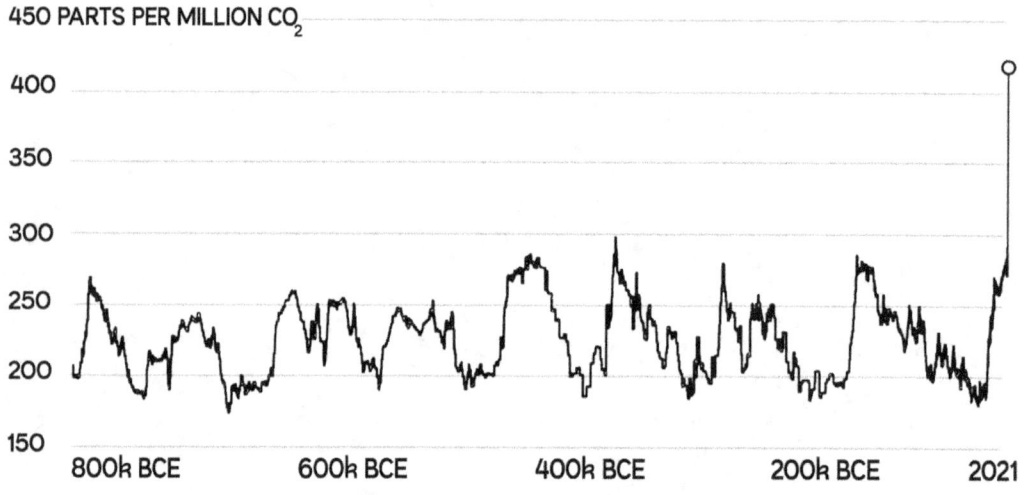

C02 levels are higher than ever in human history. Not a good trend. (credit: EPA)

The result of all this fossil fuel use is that CO2 levels are now higher than any time in the last 800,000 years.

What fuel technologies are coming down the pike that we should keep our collective eyes on? What technologies don't exist yet but that could be our "Hail Mary" play to counter climate change once and for all?

"We are hopeful that the resiliency of the human mind—where people hear that something is impossible and reject that limitation—that these will be the people who change the world," Erika Guerrero, the CEO of battery recycling firm Redivivus, told me.

In this chapter, we'll look at the most promising alternative fuel technologies—hydrogen, Sustainable Aviation Fuel (SAF), ammonia, nuclear power, and even fusion.

Getting on the hydrogen train

In the summer of 2023, the first entirely hydrogen-powered train in North America left the station, taking passengers on a 2.5-hour scenic ride through central Quebec. It's just a demonstration for now—to show how hydrogen can be used to replace diesel fuel in places where installing overhead electric wires might be challenging.

The tourist train was made by the French company Alstrom and can carry up to 120 people in 2 rail cars.

Nancy Belley, general manager of Réseau Charlevoix, the private railway that runs the train, told Canada's CBC News that riding the train is like being in another world.

"When you get on board a train that emits water vapor, you feel that you're part of an important decarbonization movement," she said.

The train uses about 50 kilograms of hydrogen a day, compared with 500 liters of diesel fuel.

The same model of train has carried passengers in 8 European countries, where Alstrom has sold 41 of its hydrogen-powered passenger trains.

Alstom notes that the commercial operation of the train in Canada will allow the company and its partners to see what's needed to develop "an ecosystem for hydrogen propulsion technology" in North America.

Hydrogen and trains are an ideal combination.

Hydrogen and diesel both take around the same time to refuel—5 to 10 minutes—and hydrogen can be shipped to and pumped from filling stations like gasoline.

Moreover, trains by definition travel on fixed rail routes, which means they can pull into a limited number of hydrogen-refueling stations along their lines; there's no reason to build an extensive hydrogen-filling network to rival our ubiquitous gas stations.

Hydrogen has enormous potential as an alternative to both gas and electric batteries. At the same time, the fuel faces significant challenges to overcome.

Tops on the list: Ensuring that hydrogen production is truly green.

Green hydrogen

The process of creating hydrogen is known as "electrolysis," a chemical process that uses an electric current to separate the hydrogen and oxygen atoms in water. The resulting pure hydrogen gas is captured and either stored for later use or channeled into a fuel cell to produce electricity.

Currently, about 96% of global hydrogen is produced by reforming methane (also known as "steam reforming"). That generates CO_2 as a waste product—not a desirable outcome. Electrolysis—if it's powered by renewable energy—produces no carbon emissions at all.

Oil and gas companies have gotten behind hydrogen since it allows for the repurposing of existing fossil fuel infrastructure that's at risk of being abandoned as the world shifts to renewables.

Harnois Énergies, the Quebec City company that produces the hydrogen for Réseau Charlevoix's train, gets its electricity from Hydro-Quebec, which generates 94% of Quebec's energy needs through hydropower and 5% by wind and is almost fully decarbonized. As a result, the hydrogen produced by the company can be considered "green." Hydro-Quebec operates 62 hydroelectric plants in the province.

"The best power plant is the one you don't have to build," Gretchen Fitzgerald, the national programs director for Sierra Club Canada, says. "That is, if you can get electricity from the sun, wind or hydro power, we are truly on the way to going 100% green."

Monolith is a Nebraska-based clean energy startup that uses renewable energy to heat natural gas, which is then turned into two components: the desired hydrogen, and something called "carbon black," a material that goes into products like paints and rubber, rather than burying the carbon underground.

The company says that producing hydrogen the Monolith way generates about 95% less emissions than conventional methods. And if it can use gas from landfills and animal waste or produced by plants, the figure could be even higher.

Monolith hopes to begin operating its first large facility in 2026. It received a $1 billion loan from the U.S. Energy Department.

The Energy Department also lent $500 million to a Mitsubishi unit to develop a green hydrogen project in Utah that would store the gas underground in a vast cavern until it's needed (for example, when the wind isn't blowing or the sun isn't shining).

H2Pro, an Israeli startup, has developed an alternative to electrolysis called E-TAC. It uses electricity to split water into hydrogen and oxygen. However, unlike conventional electrolysis, the process is done in two steps—an electrochemical step (the "E") and a thermally activated chemical step (the "TAC"). H2Pro says that this method for producing green hydrogen has a system efficiency rate of 95%.

A project in Denmark dubbed HyBalance has a demonstration facility that produces hydrogen from water when the amount of electricity being generated by renewables exceeds what's needed by the grid.

"The project is to test how we can use the renewable energy from the grid and transform it into hydrogen," says Caroline Le Mer, Hydrogen Energy Europe Director at Air Liquide, which is coordinating the project. Forty-two percent of Denmark's electricity comes from wind power, so the grid becomes saturated fairly frequently.

Denmark may be an outlier. Are there enough renewable energy sources outside of Scandinavia to power green hydrogen production?

Even if the electricity isn't *totally* clean now, what's important is that hydrogen production has a "plausible path" to zero emissions, says Emily Grubert, who studies sustainable energy policy at the University of Notre Dame. "Investing in a bunch of infrastructure that doesn't have a path to zero is a problem," she says.

Infrastructure must be leak-proof. That's because hydrogen is the tiniest molecule in existence, which makes it extraordinarily good at escaping from the pipes that carry it.

Escaping hydrogen is undesirable, of course, but it's not as bad as CO2, which lasts in the atmosphere for hundreds, if not thousands, of years. Hydrogen molecules, by contrast, can clear in just 2 years; methane is gone in 12 years.

Hydrogen: Two ways to play

There are two ways hydrogen can be used: combustion or in a fuel cell.

Hydrogen combustion engines are able to tap into existing infrastructure, such as an airport's refueling systems, without needing extensive modifications. Hydrogen combustion is less complex than a fuel cell system, which could make it easier to maintain and more reliable. On other hand, hydrogen combustion engines operate at higher temperatures and can pose a greater risk of fire or explosion. They're not really usable in trains, planes and cars.

The U.S. Office of Energy Efficiency and Renewable Energy describes how a fuel cell works.

"A fuel cell consists of two electrodes—a negative electrode (or anode) and a positive electrode (or cathode)—sandwiched around an electrolyte. A fuel, such as hydrogen, is fed to the anode, and air is fed to the cathode. In a hydrogen fuel cell, a catalyst at the anode separates hydrogen molecules into protons and electrons, which take different paths to the cathode. The electrons go through an external circuit, creating a flow of electricity. The protons migrate through the electrolyte to the cathode, where they unite with oxygen and the electrons to produce water and heat."

But the most salient point for the discussion here is that, while hydrogen combustion engines can leak or malfunction, releasing emissions—nitrogen oxide in particular—hydrogen fuel cells emit only water vapor and can operate at lower temperatures. If combustion engines must first convert fuel into heat and then into mechanical energy, fuel cells skip those intermediary steps.

That makes them ideal for mobility applications.

Let's look at three use-cases: trucks, passenger cars, and ships.

Hydrogen-powered trucks

Like Réseau Charlevoix's hydrogen-powered train in Quebec, trucks "consume a lot of energy and go to depots where you can centralize the hydrogen infrastructure," explains Quin Garcia.

That's led Daimler Truck AG and Volvo Group to join forces to produce hydrogen fuel cells for heavy vehicles. The two companies are calling on European policymakers to help them establish a network of 1,000 hydrogen fueling stations across the continent by 2030.

If infrastructure were already in place, it would be "easy" to sell 100,000 fuel cell trucks, says Daimler Truck chairman Martin Daum. "It is clear that green hydrogen is the only sensible way forward in the long-term."

Daum doesn't see any viable alternative to hydrogen.

"We don't have any revolutionary breakthrough on battery technology," he says. "Ultimately, the price of the fuel cell will be lower than today's battery packs or even tomorrow's battery packs."

Pascal Canfin, chairman of the European Parliament's environmental committee, says there's no time to wait.

"It's obvious that it's not the same world anymore, and hydrogen is a key element of that," he says.

Another Daimler Truck executive is less convinced, however.

"Diesel will remain the dominant propulsion choice for the foreseeable future," says John O'Leary, the company's North American CEO. "It remains the most cost-effective and efficient way to move goods and people, and we're far from done with it."

But done they will be at some point.

Daimler Truck isn't saying that "we're not committed to zero emissions," O'Leary stresses. "It's going to be both, at least until 2039, when we announced we will be out of the diesel business."

One company that is a definite hold-out: Tesla.

Elon Musk in 2019 dismissed hydrogen-powered vehicles as "mind-boggling stupid" and "a load of rubbish," calling fuel cells "fool cells."

"Success is simply not possible," Musk told shareholders several years ago.

Japanese manufacturers, which have long history of backing hydrogen, even for passenger cars, are "very humble about this whole thing: We don't know," says Gill Pratt, chief scientist at Toyota Motor Corp. and CEO of the Toyota Research Institute. "And the honest truth is we don't think anybody else knows either."

Deloitte sees a similar trajectory.

Just like solar and wind were "the surprise of the last decade," a new report from the consulting firm says it "now looks likely" hydrogen will be the next energy to scale.

Toyota is taking its hydrogen expertise to Europe where Toyota is partnering with BMW to produce a hydrogen fuel cell vehicle the companies hope to sell as early as 2025. Toyota is also working on hydrogen buses, testing Class 8 trucks fitted with fuel cells, and is planning a line of medium-duty fuel cell trucks in partnership with Isuzu and Hino Motors.

"It's taken us 20 years to get to where we are with [battery-powered] EVs," says Sara Baldwin, electrification director at the Energy Innovation climate policy think tank. "I would expect it to take the same amount of time to get there with hydrogen."

While not a "silver bullet," hydrogen is destined to become part of a portfolio that includes synthetic fuel, biofuels, and direct electricity, Johan Rockstrom, director of the Potsdam Institute for Climate Change Research, explains.

"Hydrogen as a fuel cell for heavy mobility must be one part of the solution," he says.

Hydrogen for passenger cars

Toyota is the largest player in the U.S. consumer market for hydrogen fuel cell passenger cars. And yet, since the hydrogen-powered Mirai was introduced in 2014, it has found only 5,000 buyers, nearly all in California, which is the only state in the union that has any significant number of hydrogen refueling stations—and not many of them. By comparison, Toyota's Prius hybrid has sold a total of four million units since its introduction in 1996.

Honda is also interested in hydrogen-powered passenger cars. There are nearly 1,100 of Honda's Clarity Fuel Cell vehicles on the road in the U.S.

Hyundai has sold around 220 hydrogen fuel cell vehicles in the U.S. Its midsize crossover, the Next, has a range of 380 miles on a tank.

These numbers constitute little more than a rounding error when compared with the sales of gasoline-powered cars and hybrids in the U.S., where 66 million new and used vehicles were sold in 2022. And in recent years, both Toyota and Honda have dropped their hardline "hydrogen-only" stance and have begun to develop EVs too.

Yoshikazu Tanaka, chief engineer in charge of the Mirai at Toyota, admitted to *Reuters* in 2017, "Elon Musk is right—it's better to charge the electric car directly by plugging in."

But as Toyota chairman Takeshi Uchiyamada also told *Reuters,* "We don't really see an adversary 'zero-sum' relationship between the EV and the hydrogen car. We're not about to give up on hydrogen electric fuel cell technology at all."

For hydrogen to succeed for consumers, the price will need to come down.

Shell Hydrogen Station (credit: Wikimedia Commons)

Kelley Blue Book estimated in 2019 that annual fuel costs for the Mirai, Next and Clarity Fuel Cell were three to four times the cost of an ICE fill-up. Price parity with diesel, notes Daimler Trucks' Daum, will only come when the price for fuel cells drops to around €3 to €4 per kilogram.

Beyond the price, there's a critical chicken-and-egg game going on here.

Consumers won't buy hydrogen-powered cars until there are enough filling stations, and service providers won't build the filling stations until they see that enough hydrogen-powered cars are on the roads.

Any delays could come back to bite hydrogen proponents.

"That time gap will give an extra boost to batteries," notes Kristin Ringland, a mobility analyst at Ernst & Young. "It's extra time for people to learn how to use them and adapt to them and say, 'This can actually work.'"

Will that mean "game over" for hydrogen-powered passenger cars?

"It is a volume game, and we need to hit a critical mass," says Shane Stephens, chief development officer at FirstElement Fuel, which runs 19 of the 39 hydrogen refueling stations in California.

Statista reports that in 2022 there were 54 hydrogen refueling stations in the U.S. The world leaders are China, which has 250 stations; Japan, with 161 stations; and South Korea with 141 stations.

Compare that with EV charging, where there are now some 50,000 stations across the U.S.—a number that's already been lamented as woefully low—or the nation's 145,000 gas stations.

To scramble all those eggs, Toyota's Tanaka believes his company can address driver concerns that there aren't enough refueling stations by bumping up what he calls "the practical range" of the Mirai to about 310 miles. (Right now, it's just under 200 miles.)

As with EVs, range is relative: The Mirai's official range is 400 miles, but if drivers use the air conditioning or heat, it can cut the range by up to 35%.

"A good rule of thumb is that you'll see hydrogen fuel cells where you see diesel today and battery electric where you see gasoline," says Tom Stephenson, cofounder of Pajarito Powder, a New Mexico hydrogen components startup backed by Hyundai. There is no single technology that can serve as climate-change mitigation's silver bullet.

If passenger hydrogen cars do ever catch on in the U.S., it will likely start with leasing. The technology is new and unproven; early adopters don't want to be tied into a current model for a long time when efficiency is constantly improving.

Perhaps the best attitude to take is "wait and see." Or, as Rod Borup, program manager of the Hydrogen and Fuel Cell Technologies Lab within the Los Alamos National Laboratory, says, "We don't see this as 'either-or.' We see this as 'and.'"

It's a bit ironic that Los Alamos has a hydrogen fuel cell lab, given that this is where the hydrogen bomb was developed, but if it can help us solve some of the world's greatest problems through mobility, I say, "Bring it on."

Hydrogen for ships?

Is hydrogen an acceptable option for powering ships in the postcarbon age?

Yes, but . . .

Amnon Asscher, the CTO of Nayam Wings, whom we met in the chapter on marine mobility, is a hydrogen skeptic. While acknowledging that it could power ships more cleanly than the fossil fuels used today, he points out: "Hydrogen can explode—like a bomb! It's extremely dangerous. No crew will want to sail with hydrogen."

Asscher's cofounder at Nayam Wings, Saar Carmeli, is even more skeptical.

"I grew up in the military. When I see a hydrogen ship, I think of a dirty bomb. If you bring so much hydrogen to a port with a lot of civilians around, even if it's a 'safe' system, it could trigger a disaster. We have no doubt this will be used by terrorists. We need to make sure this is not dangerous, even if there's a major malfunction. Maybe it could work for very large ships with secured ports—but this is very costly."

What would be a better alternative fuel option?

"Cold fusion will be developed, but it will take 20 to 30 years before it can be implemented in airplanes and ships. And it will be super expensive. Small ships won't be able to use it," Carmeli told *ISRAEL21c*.

Until that time, Carmeli predicts there will be "some combination of technology—solar, biofuels made from waste, and of course wind propulsion, which is the cheapest."

Hydrogen "explodes" in China

Well, not literally, but China is embracing hydrogen big time.

Shanghai, for example, declared its intention to put 20,000 hydrogen fuel cell passenger vehicles and 10,000 hydrogen-powered commercial vehicles on the road by 2025. One hundred hydrogen fuel cell refilling stations would be built in the city, according to the plan.

By 2022, that number had nearly tripled, with plans now to have 50,000 hydrogen fuel celled passenger cars and trucks on the roads by 2025.

The China Association of Automobile Manufacturers reported that in 2021 there were 10,700 hydrogen-powered vehicles across China.

Hyundai is adapting its Nexo SUV for the Chinese market. Great Wall Motors, China's largest SUV and pickup truck maker, says it will invest nearly half a billion dollars into exploring fuel cell options.

Sustainable Aviation Fuel (SAF)

"If you can't beat them, join them" might be the motto of proponents of SAF.

SAF is not a newfangled technology but a novel way of creating the same kind of fuel that jets already use.

"Hydrocarbon fuels for aviation will be around for a long time," says Jennifer Holmgren, CEO of LanzaTech. "We simply need the energy density."

LanzaTech, and its sister company, LanzaJet, are already producing SAF from waste and trash, Holmgren says.

EMISSIONS FROM DIFFERENT MODES OF TRANSPORT
(emissions per passenger per km travelled)

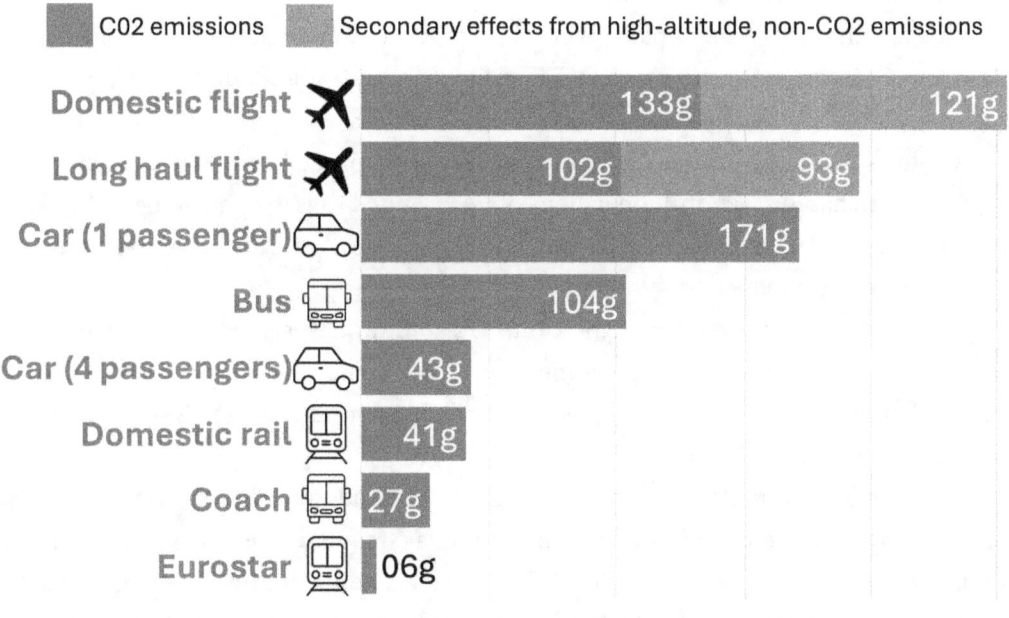

Note: Car refers to average diesel car

Commercial flights are the mode of transport with the greatest impact on climate change. (credit: BEIS/Defra Greenhouse Gas Conversion Factors 2019/BBC)

"Any waste can be converted or reused. We can make jet fuel, detergent, yoga pants. The main goal is that we reuse as many carbon molecules as possible and keep fossil fuels in the ground."

Holmgren is adamant that SAF not be based on biological feedstocks used today to make food.

"We can use trash, carbon resources, industrial emissions, forest residues to make SAF, just as long as it's not being grown to create food," she told me.

LanzaTech's core technology for conversion is bacteria.

"We do fermentation, like how sugar is used to make beer. Instead of sugar, we use gases," Holmgren says. When placed in a reactor, the bacteria "eats" the waste to make ethanol, which is then used to make the sustainable biofuel.

While SAF doesn't eliminate greenhouse gas emissions (GHG)—the benefits are mostly in the green production process rather than in how the fuel is burned—LanzaTech believes that emissions from SAF could be as much as 85% lower than conventional fuel. A study published in *Renewable and Sustainable Energy Reviews* put that number at 94%.

Converting alcohol into jet fuel is not new—the chemistry has been around for 100 years. But it's since been refined to be much more efficient and less costly. LanzaTech claims it can convert almost every carbon atom coming into the process into usable fuel.

One of LanzaTech's first clients was Richard Branson, who told Holmgren, "Make us some jet fuel and we'll get it certified."

In 2021, another SAF company, World Energy, created enough fuel to power a United 737 from Chicago to Washington, DC. The flight was a test and, due to current safety regulations, only was able to use a maximum of 50% SAF.

United's Eco-Skies Alliance program was launched in 2021 and, by the end of that year, had purchased seven million gallons of SAF. United says it wants to be 100% green by eliminating GHG emissions by 2050, without relying on traditional carbon offsets.

It's not just United.

Ethiad, the national carrier of the United Arab Emirates, signed a memorandum of understanding with World Energy at the COP27 conference in Sharm el-Sheikh, Egypt, in 2022 "to establish a long-term strategic partnership to decarbonize flights through in-sector emissions reductions."

In late 2023, Virgin Atlantic ran a test flight from London to New York that used *only* SAF. The flight was described as a one-time "stunt," as standard jet engines aren't designed to run on only sustainable fuel, but it's still a milestone, notes Andrew Chen, principal for aviation decarbonization at the Rocky Mountain Institute, a clean-energy think tank. "It's a really important flight to highlight the progress that's being made, the need for more SAF, and the critical role it can play in decarbonizing aviation."

The IATA (International Air Transport Association), the airline industry's main trade association, founded in 1945, claims that aviation as a whole will be net-zero—without the need for offsets—by 2050.

That's a big deal, says Holmgren. "It's the first industry to say it will be net-zero collectively."

LanzaTech is planning to build an SAF production plant in Georgia. That will require some $200 million, which Holmgren plans to raise from its investors: British Airways, Shell, Suncor Energy, and Mitsui & Co.

The facility will double the current U.S. capacity for making SAF.

LanzaTech has a spin-off company, LanzaJet, focused exclusively on aviation fuel. In 2022, LanzaJet received a $50 million grant from the Bill Gates-led Breakthrough Energy group as well as additional funding from Southwest Airlines, Groupe ADP, and Japanese financial services giant Mitsubishi UFJ Financial Group (MUFG).

Holmgren is not ruling out asking for subsidization.

"As long as petroleum is subsidized to the level it is today, then alternatives like SAF will need to be subsidized too," she says.

At the end of the day, LanzaTech believes "a postpollution world is inevitable. Humans will either be part of it, or the planet will go on without us."

SAF limitations

SAF today costs double what the same amount of conventional aviation fuel costs. That's not a deal breaker long-term, as efficiencies of scale will drive down costs. But it's certainly a barrier to quick uptake.

Another big limitation, according to a report from the *Center for Biological Diversity*, is that our current biofuel availability would only cover 38% of the airline industry's needs.

Research published in *Science of the Total Environment* suggests that even if the industry could make the shift, there's simply not enough land or renewable energy potential on Earth to produce all the sustainable fuels airlines need.

Producing SAF would require about 9% of all renewable energy globally, and 30% of available biomass by 2050. Even then, about 30% of the fuel used by airlines in 2050 would still be fossil-derived, the researchers say.

Demand for biomass to be used for SAF production could reduce the amount of the material used in other industries. For example, the pulp left after sugar-cane juice is extracted is used for heat in sugar mills. The cosmetics industry uses tallow in skincare products.

While some SAF companies use crops as a basis for fuel, this approach has limitations in terms of volumes needed and can have unintended climate impacts when the feedstock isn't sustainably sourced. No single feedstock is going to meet the demands of the fuel market, so we need to explore all pathways for SAF production in parallel.

Crops and chemicals also "get frequent flyer miles," Holmgren quips. "Nothing is made where it's needed."

Up.Partners compared SAF with both hydrogen and batteries and found SAF lacking. SAF can help us get to net-zero but not true-zero.

✦ SAF does not reduce the tailpipe emissions from burning fuel in flight and still contributes to carbon in the atmosphere.

+ Replacing kerosene in planes with hydrogen combustion removes the CO_2 but still emits NOx.

+ Hydrogen fuel cells convert hydrogen and air to electricity. The concern here is whether the hydrogen can be produced using renewable energy.

+ Battery-powered planes are the ideal, reports Roland Berger for UP.Partners, but they are extremely range-limited.

World Energy currently operates the world's first (and still America's only) working SAF plant. Located in Los Angeles, the company is in the midst of a $2 billion expansion project to boost capacity to 375 million gallons of renewable fuels.

World Energy's SAF is a paraffin-based product that is refined through a process called "Hydrotreated Esters and Fatty Acids" (HEFA). World Energy uses HEFA to turn renewable inputs, including inedible agricultural fats and waste oils, into SAF.

Demand for SAF is expected to grow by 3.2 billion gallons each year, according to *BloombergNEF*.

Prometheus—not just a movie

It's not just mainstream airlines that are interested in SAF. Supersonic plane company Boom is tapping into CO_2-to-fuel technology from another startup, Prometheus (no connection to the Ridley Scott-directed prequel to the *Alien* movies).

The company's direct air capture (DAC) system grabs CO_2 from the air and uses it to produce net-zero SAF. Prometheus hopes to have 500 DAC plants running by 2030, each able to convert 900 tons of CO_2 into 100,000 gallons of green fuel a year.

Prometheus has its own SAF technology, "aqueous CO_2 electrolysis." In a nutshell, you first mix the captured CO_2 with a saline solution. Then you hit the blend with energy (preferably renewable) to trigger electrochemical reactions that yield complex alcohols. These are then digested into simpler molecules like ethanol thanks to a catalyst made of carbon and copper. A carbon nanotube-based membrane then separates the ethanol from the water and turns it into jet fuel.

Prometheus claims that since this process does not require any water to be vaporized, and because it can work at room temperature, it will require 90% less energy.

Is the technology too good to be true? Prometheus has yet to demonstrate a working system, nor has it subjected its technology to peer review.

Moreover, the price needs to come down—big time.

"I'm not saying it can't be done," notes Dr. Guy Gratton, associate professor of aviation and the environment at Cranfield University in the U.K. "It may well be done but it has not been done yet."

DAC received a boost in 2023 from the Biden administration, which is allocating $1.2 billion to support companies aiming to pull carbon out of ambient air—companies like Prometheus or Avnos, which adds a spin to its DAC tech: In addition to cleaning the air of CO2, Avnos generates water. No wonder that its test site is situated in drought-plagued Bakersfield, California.

Landfill gas-to-energy

Moving beyond hydrogen and SAF, there are other sources of alternative fuels.

Is landfill gas (LFG) a promising new source of renewable energy? Or, as critics claim, it is just greenwashing by a dirty industry?

Landfill operators often refer to the positive effects of their LFG projects, describing them as on par with other renewable sources. But it's not clear how efficient LFG capture systems are and whether they can appreciably mitigate greenhouse gas emissions.

Landfills "are fantastic in that we generate energy from them that really meets the same needs that the solar industry or the wind industry [meets], and we need to take more credit for that," says Devine Rankin, CFO of the recycling firm Waste Management.

LFG should be considered renewable because the CO2 emissions generated by organic decomposition at landfills would have happened anyway as part of the natural breakdown of recently living biomass, adds Anne Germain, vice president of technical and regulatory affairs at the National Waste & Recycling Association.

LFG, unfortunately, creates methane when it's being harvested. So, landfill operators must capture the methane and burn it, rendering it back into carbon dioxide. That doesn't translate into a lot of betterment for the planet, although the energy that was created occurred without generating any *extra* CO2.

Is that enough of a benefit?

Environmental groups, including the Sierra Club, don't think so. They argue that even a slight amount of methane could escape before it's converted back to CO2.

"Landfill gas-to-energy is hijacking concern for climate change—for a technology and process that actually makes the climate condition substantially worse," Peter Anderson, president of RecycleWorlds Consulting, told the environmental website *Waste Dive*.

The U.S. Environmental Protection Agency estimates that methane has 28 to 36 times the warming potential of CO2.

Another problem is that in order for landfills to produce commercial volumes of energy, moisture must be added. While that may be good for economic efficiency, it accelerates the formation of methane, increases the methane-to-CO2 ratio and gives methane more chances to escape.

The sobering conclusion from the International Panel on Climate Change: Lifetime LFG capture could be as low as 20% in some cases.

LFG is not a major component of total U.S. electricity generation today; it accounted for just 0.3% of the total in 2018. Nonlandfill municipal solid waste is close behind among biomass sources, at 0.2%.

But landfills have something going for them too: There are lots of them (they store some 14 billion tons of waste) and they're already built, compared with other technologies such as anaerobic digesters, which can be quite expensive to deploy. If landfills can provide some extra revenue to operators, even if they're less efficient, they can become part of the overall ecosystem for cleaning up the planet.

I can also see a case for co-locating carbon capture equipment at landfill sites.

Such dual use can make for better relations with the community.

"Landfills are often not the most popular land use," David Biderman, CEO of the Solid Waste Association of North America, told *Waste Dive*. "Positioning yourself as a good neighbor from both an environmental and economic perspective is always a goal of landfills."

Nuclear power

Nuclear energy has gotten a bad rap. Following various near and a few actual meltdowns—in Japan, Ukraine and the U.S.—utilities that were once bullish on nuclear power have shied away.

That's a shame.

Nuclear plays an important role in the future renewable energy landscape. Nuclear plant disasters are, for sure, serious, but when the system is running properly, it is perhaps the cleanest form of energy generation.

Nuclear doesn't produce the kind of dangerous particulate matter that burning fossil fuels does. Breathing in particulate matter is a leading cause of death around the globe. It's one of the reasons people aren't opening their windows anymore in Beijing and Delhi.

Once a nuclear power plant is up and running, the cost of producing energy is fairly low compared to other sources.

"I was an environmentalist, anti-nuclear and all that," says Joseph Goldstein, who was interviewed on the *Freakonomics* podcast. Goldstein is professor emeritus of international relations at American University and coauthor of the book, *A Bright Future: How Some Countries Have Solved Climate Change and the Rest Can Follow.*

"Once I got into climate change," he continues, "I had to do the math—how would we actually solve climate change—and realized that the solutions, as good as they are, wind and solar and all that, I'm not against it, but they're just not getting us there. The problem is much bigger than that. And then I hit on nuclear, because it's so scalable, because it's so concentrated."

Nuclear's safety profile has to be considered in context.

During the Fukushima meltdown, 150 people died. But 4,500 perished from the cold when Japan cut off all its nuclear power and began importing natural gas—at a 35% premium—leading people to use less energy, which led to an increase in cardiovascular issues.

Meanwhile, coal kills at least a million people a year worldwide, in large part as a result of the small particles released when coal is burned.

"Fine-particle air pollution from coal has been treated as if it's just another air pollutant, but it's much more harmful than we thought and its mortality burden has been seriously underestimated," writes Lucas Henneman, assistant professor in the Sid and Reva Dewberry Department of Civil, Environmental and Infrastructure Engineering at George Mason University and the author of a study published in 2023 by *Science.*

How many people died when Three Mile Island melted down in the U.S. in 1979?
None.

Goldstein again: "People have the idea that radioactivity is like a virus, that if it gets out, it can destroy the world or something. It's not like that at all. It doesn't reproduce and it stays in one place. If you leave it somewhere for a billion years, it'll still be there, but it'll be actually less dangerous over time."

Chernobyl—the worst nuclear disaster in history—killed about 50 people on-site. The cloud of radioactive material freaked people out across Europe, but the amount of newly detected cancers was "so small you can't measure it," Goldstein notes.

Craig Mazin, the film director behind the HBO dramatization, *Chernobyl,* is not so sanguine.

The death estimates after the Chernobyl disaster "go all the way from 4,000 people to a million," he notes. "I think it's safe to say that in terms of lives negatively impacted in a serious way, we're talking about at least hundreds of thousands of people."

Still, nuclear needs to be "part of the answer," Kathryn Huff of the U.S. Department of Energy told NPR. Addressing the kinds of challenges that climate change has put in front of us will take every low-carbon energy source we have available to us. "There's no question that it'll require renewables and carbon capture and sequestration, and it will require nuclear," Huff says.

Huff is bullish on nuclear in part because it "has actually saved way more lives than you would think because it is a carbon-free energy source. Fossil fuels are an incredible contributor to premature death."

What are the leading countries when it comes to nuclear power?

✦ Nearly 70% of France's electricity comes from nuclear.

✦ In Sweden, it's 31% with another 45% coming from hydroelectric.

✦ In the U.S., it's under 20%.

There are currently some 440 nuclear-powered reactors operating in 33 countries. The latest push: to keep them running beyond what was considered a typical 40-year lifespan.

"They never were expected to run as long as they have," says Chris Gadomski, the lead nuclear analyst for *BloombergNEF*. "I'm not sure I'd want to live next to a reactor that's 100 years old!"

How about a micro-reactor? Something the size of just a small room that generates less than 50 megawatts of electricity.

Conventional reactors have 20 times the capacity of micro-reactors, but the latter have the advantage of quick production and deployment, sometimes taking just a few weeks to get up and running—helpful if a micro-reactor needs to be deployed in a natural disaster zone to provide emergency power. Micro-reactors can also run on preprocessed nuclear fuel, making them slightly safer.

A large reactor, by contrast, can take over 10 years just to design and cost up to $2 billion.

Nuclear on and below the water

Nuclear power will likely remain tethered to large plants with safety measures in place; I wouldn't expect to see nuclear-powered cars or trains. About the only place where nuclear energy could actually get inside a vehicle is a submarine.

The U.S. Navy launched the first submarine using radioactive material as a power source in 1954. In 1958, the USS Nautilus was the first submarine to travel to the North Pole. Nuclear power allows a submarine to run for some 20 years without needing to go to port to refuel. Food supplies became the only limit on a nuclear submarine's time at sea.

Another advantage to atomic-powered subs: Nuclear reactions do not require air. That means a nuclear submarine can stay submerged at deep depths for months at a time.

Nuclear subs are still relatively rare—there are only 160 nuclear-powered ships, nearly all of them submarines (although that's down significantly from 1989, at the end of the Cold War, when there were over 400 nuclear subs operating).

North Korea has the largest number of submarines—71—although this includes all types of subs, not just nuclear. The U.S. comes in second with 68 subs. China has 59, Russia 49, and Japan 22.

The paucity in numbers reflects the high costs—up to several billion dollars—of building a nuclear-powered submarine.

There are a few other nuclear-powered vessels at sea that travel above the water.

Russia's nuclear-powered Sevmorput (credit: Wikimedia Commons)

Russia's 62,000-ton *Sevmorput* is a nuclear-powered freighter. Russia also operates six nuclear icebreakers, which has boosted the amount of time per year the Russians can explore the Arctic from 2 to 10 months. The icebreaker *Lenin,* the world's first nuclear-powered surface vessel, was commissioned in 1959 and remained in service for 30 years.

The Chinese shipping company COSCO was also exploring putting a nuclear reactor on a ship, although the project was canceled following the Fukushima nuclear accident.

In 2010, Babcock International's maritime division conducted a study on developing a nuclear-powered tanker for transporting liquid natural gas. The study found that particular routes—for example from China to South America or China to Northwest Australia—would lend themselves well to a nuclear propulsion option.

There's even been discussion of making nuclear-powered cruise ships. I hear the evening entertainment is just the bomb.

Our fusion future

The science of nuclear fusion relies on smashing two atoms together at incredibly high speeds and transforming the energy from that reaction into electricity. The process is the opposite of nuclear fission, which involves splitting the neutrons of a radioactive atom. Fusion is the same process that powers the sun and other stars.

As with fission, fusion does not emit carbon into the air.

Recent breakthroughs suggest that fusion could be coming sooner than we think.

Researchers at the U.S. Energy Department's Lawrence Livermore National Laboratory have discovered a way to more than triple the energy output of a fusion reactor hotspot using a specialized magnetic field. The process involves blasting 200 lasers at a fusion fuel pellet made from hydrogen isotopes such as deuterium and tritium.

That doesn't mean a practical fusion reactor is around the corner. The energy output is still less than what's required to create a self-sustaining reaction, although it marked an achievement in that, for the first time, more energy was produced than consumed, improving the chances of an energy-positive fusion system down the road.

But first, researchers need to develop the machinery capable of turning a fusion reaction into electricity that can be practically deployed to the power grid. The neutrons created in a fusion reaction put a tremendous amount of stress on the equipment creating it, such that it can actually get destroyed in the process.

The price is also formidable.

The National Ignition Facility at Livermore, where the experiment was conducted, cost $3.5 billion to build. A similar facility in Europe has a price tag of more than $20 billion.

Tal Cohen, from Next Gear Ventures, says we're investing in the wrong way.

"Can the world afford fusion power plants at those prices? As excited as I am about the prospect of fusion, I'm just not sure. Rather than having the European Union give $5 billion to solve fusion, it would be better to give 500 talented teams around the world $50 to $100 million," he told me. "It's just such a difficult problem to solve, and it would probably be best addressed by smaller, highly talented teams with the right coordination."

Still, the development in Livermore has been hailed as "a breakthrough" that can capitalize on the Biden administration's prioritization of fusion energy research—even if the commercialization of fusion remains many decades away.

That delayed timeline is a problem.

When and if fusion power plants become a reality, it likely will not happen in time to help stave off the near-term worsening effects of climate change. As a result, we can't give up on other renewable energy technologies while hoping for a fusion future.

That isn't stopping startups from working on fusion.

More than 30 companies are in the space now—about two-thirds of them in the U.S., according to the Fusion Industry Group. They've received nearly $5 billion in investment.

Commonwealth Fusion is among the most advanced. Spun out from the Massachusetts Institute of Technology (MIT), the company has raised nearly $2 billion and is constructing a test reactor outside of Boston.

Just as with nuclear fission micro-reactors, to really move the needle, a totally safe portable fusion reactor the size of an AirPods case needs to find its way into our vehicles and devices of the future.

"If this container size box can generate infinite clean energy, in less than a decade, it will change the world," Cohen says. "If we can quickly install and deploy and network a number of these in Africa and India with almost no overhead or infrastructures cost, this can be impactful around both industrial and rural areas. It will make oil-producing countries like Iran and Saudi Arabia obsolete."

A tiny fusion reactor will be our *Back to the Future*—or if you're a Marvel fan, our Tony Stark/*Iron Man*—moment.

Ammonia power

We've considered battery- and hydrogen-powered heavy trucks, tractors and farming/construction equipment.

New York-based Amogy believes there's a better fuel long-term: ammonia.

Amogy took a 2018 Freightliner Cascadia Class 8 truck and retrofitted it with an ammonia-powered fuel cell. The truck, Amogy claims, only takes eight minutes to refuel and has five times the energy density of batteries.

Amogy's founders say that ammonia is cleaner and more scalable than either batteries or hydrogen.

The science would seem to support that.

Ammonia is typically produced through the reaction of elemental hydrogen and elemental nitrogen, a fairly dirty production process. But once it's made (and renewables can cut down on some of the carbon emissions), ammonia can be kept liquid at just minus 28 degrees Fahrenheit, making it a much greener—and cheaper—fuel to transport than hydrogen.

Hydrogen, by contrast, only becomes liquid at minus 423.17 degrees Fahrenheit, an extremely energy-demanding process.

Moreover, hydrogen, with its intense cooling requirements, can be 30 times more expensive to store than ammonia.

Ammonia packs about 20 times the energy of a lithium-ion battery pack by weight, according to the web publication *NewAtlas*.

Ammonia can be produced anywhere, unlike oil, which is concentrated in several countries, not all of them friendly to the West.

The Holy Grail for this fuel alternative is true "green ammonia," produced by using renewable energy to create hydrogen through electrolysis, then running it through a similar process to make ammonia powered by this green energy.

Without a green approach, ammonia is particularly polluting: Producing a ton of ammonia generates 2.5 tons of CO_2.

Canary Media's Maria Galluci describes how Amogy hopes to green-ify the ammonia production process.

"The Brooklyn-based startup is developing a chemical reactor to take ammonia stored in fuel tanks and 'crack' the compound into hydrogen and nitrogen. The hydrogen flows through a fuel cell, which converts chemical energy into electricity to drive the motors." The nitrogen is vented into the atmosphere, where it is already the largest element, leaving just pure hydrogen to be used as fuel.

Amogy raised a $139 million Series B in 2023, led by SK Innovation, South Korea's largest oil refining company. Aramco Ventures, the Saudi state oil company's VC arm, is also invested in the company.

Another ammonia startup, Nitrofix, is working on a specialized catalyst made from an organo-metal compound that requires very low power to produce green ammonia. Nitrofix raised $3.1 million in 2023 for its technology, which CEO Ophira Melamed says reduces the amount of energy needed to make ammonia by 90%.

Nitrofix's technology extracts the hydrogen atoms needed for ammonia from water and the nitrogen from the air. It aims to improve on the "Haber-Bosch approach" used by most other ammonia production firms.

Haber-Bosch has two steps.

1. The production of hydrogen gas
2. Enabling a reaction between that gas and nitrogen

Most Haber-Bosch-based facilities use fossil fuels to power the hydrogen production. "It requires high temperatures and high pressure, both of which are very energy intensive," Melamed explains.

Nitrofix's process, by contrast, is just "one step," Melamed says. "We're doing it at room temperature, at 50 degrees Celsius (122 degrees Fahrenheit), with 10 atmospheres of pressure. Haber-Bosch needs 300 degrees Celsius (572 degrees Fahrenheit) and 400 atmospheres."

Nitrofix is still building its first at-scale prototypes. Amogy, meanwhile, has already integrated its technology into a 5-kW drone, a 100-kW John Deere tractor and a semi truck. It will soon be running a test on a retrofitted tugboat sailing on New York's Hudson River.

Can ammonia find a place in a mobility environment that's moved definitively into battery (and to a lesser extent hydrogen) power? Is it best suited for ag-tech? For marine applications? For aviation?

"Ammonia is an optimal fuel to achieve rapid decarbonization of heavy transportation because it is available globally with existing infrastructure already in place," Amogy CEO Seonghoon Woo says.

Green ammonia can also act as a hydrogen carrier, transporting hydrogen (as part of ammonia—ammonia's chemical signal is NH3) in liquid form and only "cracking" it to release the hydrogen once it's arrived at its destination.

In 2023, Toyota and Guangzhou Automobile Group (GAC) took the wraps off a prototype engine powered by liquid ammonia. The 2.0 liter, four-cylinder engine reduces carbon emissions by 90% compared to conventional gasoline, according to GAC, which adds that by increasing combustion pressure, it has overcome the key issue of excess nitrogen emissions when ammonia is burned as a fuel.

One area that the Toyota/GAC announcement failed to address was ammonia's toxicity. Given all the human foibles that already accompany people filling up their cars, that could be distinctly dangerous if ammonia is the fuel, Woo warns.

Those issues, she adds, are more easily managed if the refueling is done by professionals, which would be the case for trucks, ships and planes.

The shocking story of Nikola

Trevor Milton was a twenty-something college dropout who dreamed of building a hydrogen-powered semi truck. He founded his company, Nikola, in 2015 in the basement of his Salt Lake City home. The company listed on NASDAQ in 2020 through a merger with a SPAC managed by Stephen Girsky, a former high-ranking executive at General Motors.

Nikola aspired to be the Tesla of the trucking industry. Both took their names from energy pioneer Nikola Tesla. Nikola wanted to build trucks that would be powered by emission-free hydrogen fuel cells. The company also planned to build a network of hydrogen fueling stations along major highways.

"It's game over for diesel," Milton boasted early on Twitter.

But it would soon be game over for Nikola.

The semi truck Milton was so excited to show off didn't actually work. A video published by Nikola showing the truck in motion actually had it rolling down an incline to make it look like a functioning prototype. It wasn't.

Milton said he had billions of dollars in binding contracts with trucking companies, but those "contracts" were just reservations that could be easily canceled.

Milton also claimed that Nikola was producing "green" hydrogen using renewable energy, but, in fact, Nikola had produced "not one molecule" of hydrogen, according to Jordan Estes, the assistant U.S. attorney who charged—and in October 2022 ultimately convicted—Milton in court.

"Trevor Milton is a con man," Estes summarized the government's case. "He lied to investors to get their money, plain and simple."

Along the way, Milton made the stereotypical fraudster mistakes.

- ✦ He went on a spending spree, buying a Gulfstream jet and a multimillion-dollar home in the Turks and Caicos Islands.

- ✦ He purchased a ranch in his home state of Utah but paid for it with Nikola stock options that proved to be worthless.

- ✦ In just six months in 2020, he dropped more than $80 million for personal purchases.

When the truth became known about Milton's deception, Nikola's stock price crashed, wiping out billions of dollars in shareholder value, dropping from a high of $80 a share to under $1 by mid-2023.

Nikola—without Milton, who was sentenced to four years in prison in December 2023 (he is appealing the conviction)—continues to operate. It now makes battery-powered trucks in cooperation with established companies such as IVECO, the Italian truckmaker. In August 2023, Steve Girsky, who had taken on the role of chairman of the company's board, was named Nikola's CEO, becoming the company's fourth leader in as many years.

Hydron's hydrogen alternative

Nikola may have lost its shine, but another company, Hydron, is hard at work building its own hydrogen-powered Class 8 semi trucks.

Referring to the problems with electric battery-powered trucks, Jason Wallace, head of North American operations at Hydron, notes that, "For long haul, the energy density is just not there." Contrast that with Volvo Trucks, which said that hydrogen could push the range of its vehicles to over 620 miles on a tank.

Hydron is hoping for the same when its trucks hit the market.

Hydron was founded in 2021 by Mo Chen, whose main claim to fame has been the self-driving trucking startup TuSimple, which tested driverless trucks with no human aboard in Arizona. UPS invested in the company in 2019. In 2021, TuSimple went public and raised an additional $1.3 billion. In 2024, though, TuSimple exited the U.S. market entirely to focus on China.

When he talked with customers at large fleets, Chen heard the same refrain: "They wanted a purpose-built truck. They didn't want a science experiment. They want something backed by a warranty and service."

Chen envisions "hydrogen freight corridors" that would delineate where a truck can travel and ensure there are sufficient hydrogen refueling stations along the route. (Hydron says it will install "the necessary storage, disposal hardware, and hydrogen.") These corridors will also come in handy when self-driving trucks are available. (Hydron says its trucks are "autonomous ready.")

The U.S. government is backing hydrogen corridors. The $550 billion Bipartisan Infrastructure Law calls to invest some $7 billlion to create "H2Hubs"—hydrogen hubs—across North America.

HYDROGEN AS DRIVETRAIN

ADVANTAGES	DISADVANTAGES
Emission-free Output consists of water vapor	**Lower efficiency** Due to high energy loss
Hydrogen available in infinite quantities Via electrolysis	**Highly flammable** Hydrogen volatilizes rapidly
High range Up to 600 km per fueling	**Poor infrastructure** Very few filling stations
Fast refueling 3-5 minutes	**High costs** Very expensive to purchase and maintain
No engine sound Less noise pollution	

The advantages and disadvantages to hydrogen (credit: C3)

"These hydrogen hubs will make significant progress toward President Biden's vision for a resilient grid that is powered by clean energy and built by American workers," notes U.S. Secretary of Energy Jennifer M. Granholm.

Hydron expected its first generation of trucks to enter mass production in 2024.

What we've learned

+ The quest for alternative fuel sources beyond fossil fuels has ignited a wave of optimism for a cleaner and more sustainable future.

+ Hydrogen, with its potential as a versatile, emissions-free energy carrier, is gaining momentum as a key player in the transition to a green economy.

+ Sustainable Aviation Fuel offers the promise of reducing the environmental impact of air travel, helping to curb the aviation industry's carbon footprint.

+ Meanwhile, nuclear energy—with its minimal greenhouse gas emissions and abundant fuel supply—is regaining recognition as a vital part of the low-carbon energy mix.

+ These alternative fuel sources symbolize our capacity to reduce our dependence on fossil fuels, mitigate climate change, and usher in an era of energy sustainability. With ongoing research and investment, they hold the potential to reshape our energy landscape, offering a cleaner and more prosperous future for generations to come.

■ ■ ■

Chapter 8

Autonomy

"My *Autopilot almost killed me.*"

That was the headline of an article in the German newspaper *Handelsblatt* which revealed leaked details showing that Tesla's Autopilot and FSD (Full Self-Driving) software are a lot buggier than most of us realized.

Handelsblatt uncovered thousands of complaints and descriptions of crashes, making the article title as on-the-nose as they come.

Of the 100 gigabytes of data and 23,000 files *Handelsblatt* reviewed, 3,000 entries detailed customers' concerns about safety and detailed more than 1,000 crashes between 2015 and 2022.

Of those complaints, 2,400 were about sudden acceleration and another 1,500 addressed braking problems, including so-called "phantom stops" when the car suddenly ceases operation for no apparent reason. The files contained customer phone numbers, so *Handelsblatt* was able to confirm that the complaints were legit.

In February 2023, the problem got so bad that the National Highway Traffic Safety Administration (NHTSA) was forced to issue a scathing indictment of Tesla's heavily promoted "autonomous" software.

The NHTSA report claimed the Tesla software "may allow the vehicle to act unsafe around intersections, such as traveling straight through an intersection while in a turn-only lane, entering a stop sign-controlled intersection without coming to a complete stop, or proceeding into an intersection during a steady yellow traffic signal without due caution."

The agency also said FSD "may respond insufficiently to changes in posted speed limits or not adequately account for the driver's adjustment of the vehicle's speed to exceed posted speed limits."

The NHTSA report came mere days after a 30-second attack ad created by anti-FSD crusader Dan O'Dowd's "The Dawn Project" was broadcast during the Super Bowl showing a self-driving Tesla 3 graphically plowing down a baby in a stroller and speeding past a stopped school bus.

Also in January 2023, *The Intercept* published footage of a Tesla vehicle inexplicably braking in the middle of the San Francisco-Oakland Bay Bridge, causing an eight-car pileup that injured nine people.

In response to the NHTSA report—and maybe also as a reaction to O'Dowd's shock-and-awe visuals—Tesla announced it was recalling 363,000 U.S. vehicles equipped with or pending installation of its FSD beta software.

But Tesla's bad news wasn't over.

In June 2023, *The Washington Post* analyzed data from the NHTSA and found that, since 2019:

✦ There have been 736 crashes in the U.S. involving Teslas in Autopilot mode.

✦ Tesla EVs made up 70% of crashes involving driver assistance systems in the previous year.

✦ There have been 17 fatal incidents—11 since May 2022—and 5 serious injuries, the *Post* reported.

✦ Of the 17 fatalities, 4 involved a motorcycle. One involved an emergency vehicle.

Elon Musk seems to believe the risks are worth it.

In a comment that mixed vision with tone-deafness in equal parts, he opined in 2022:

"At the point of which you believe that adding autonomy reduces injury and death, I think you have a moral obligation to deploy it even though you're going to get sued and blamed by a lot of people. Because the people whose lives you saved don't know that their lives were saved. And the people who do occasionally die or get injured, they definitely know—or their state does."

"For most of us who have been covering Tesla for a decade now, this [kind of statement from Musk] isn't that surprising, and it is likely unsurprising for most Tesla customers too," says Matthias Schmidt, an independent automotive analyst in Berlin.

Schmidt adds that Tesla has long taken a "move fast and break things" approach to developing products, leading to concerns about whether its new releases are ready for the road. Musk, Schmidt alleges, "accepts driver death as a consequence of forwarding technology."

Tesla is not unaware of what its customers are saying.

Employees at Tesla are instructed that they should never send a written version of their reviews but to pass them on "VERBALLY to the customer . . . do not copy and paste the report below into an email, text message or leave it in a voicemail to the customers," the guidelines say, according to *Handelsblatt*.

Already in 2018, Uber operations manager Robbie Miller alerted company executives that its self-driving cars were "routinely in accidents."

"A car was damaged nearly every other day in February 2018," Miller noted in an email. "We shouldn't be hitting things every 15,000 miles!"

Levels of autonomy

Autonomous driving has traditionally been segmented into six categories:

LEVELS OF AUTONOMOUS DRIVING

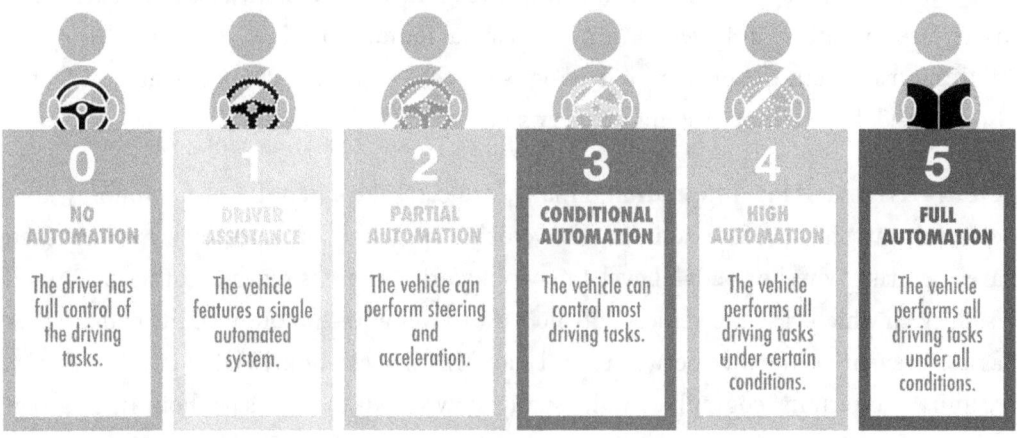

The five levels of autonomy (credit: iStock Images)

Level 0—No driving automation. A human driver is completely responsible for controlling the vehicle, although there can be a variety of safety features such as backup cameras, collision and blind-spot warnings, emergency braking, and lane-keeping assistance. These are considered Level 0 because the technology doesn't drive the vehicle but only offers alerts or momentary actions in specific situations.

Level 1—Driver assistance. This is where there is at least one driver-support system involving braking, steering or acceleration. Adaptive cruise control is an example of Level 1 automation—it maintains a safe distance between your vehicle and traffic ahead without any human intervention required, but the car still requires an active driver.

Level 2—Partial automation or ADAS (Advanced Driver Assistance Systems). The vehicle can take over steering, acceleration and braking but the driver must remain at the wheel, alert and ready to jump into action. Tesla's Autopilot, Ford's BlueCruise, Highway Driving Assist installed in Genesis, Hyundai and Kia vehicles, Toyota's Advance Drive, Lexus Teammate, and GM's Cruise systems are all examples of Level 2.

Level 3—Conditional driving automation. You're stuck in a traffic jam and there you are, reading a newspaper—that's the promise of Level 3, where drivers don't have to actively steer or brake in specific situations but cannot doze off, as they must be ready to take over if the situation changes. The vehicle monitors the driver's state (through cameras) to make sure he or she is ready to snap back when the time is right and has not fallen asleep, literally, at the wheel. Audi was the first to develop a Level 3 product (its "Traffic Jam Assistance" technology). Honda is now working on its own version, as is Mercedes. "The drivers are still there" in Level 3, Amnon Shashua, founder of Mobileye, notes. "They are still responsible, but the burden of driving is reduced—and the chance of an accident is also reduced, because the systems are very safe."

Level 4—High driving automation. Finally, you can take a nap! Level 4 autonomy does not require any human interaction in the vehicle's operation. Such a vehicle may not even have a steering wheel or pedal. Level 4 may not work if there is severe weather or limited visibility, in which case the vehicle will alert the driver and shut off until the bad weather passes. The main difference between Level 4 and Level 5 autonomy is that Level 4 vehicles are limited to certain geographies and, usually, slow speeds (30 miles per hour in an urban environment). Waymo's autonomous tests in Arizona have been Level 4.

Level 5—Full driving automation. Now we're cooking with gas (or lithium-ion, since nearly all autonomous vehicles being built today for consumer use are battery electric). These cars can go anywhere and do anything an experienced human driver can do. Level 5 vehicles definitely won't have steering wheels, brakes or pedals, and may have "smart cabins" designed very differently than passenger cars today.

How does autonomy work in cars?

Mobileye's approach to autonomy, like most of its competitors, starts by building a detailed three-dimensional map. This painstaking process must be done again and again, city by city.

✦ First, ordinary cars are equipped with lidar (light detection and ranging) sensors that measure distances using pulses of light.

✦ Company workers then drive test cars around the city to collect the data needed to generate the map, including measuring the distance to every curb, median and roadside tree.

✦ The autonomous vehicles use their sensors to monitor their surroundings, comparing what they see with what's on the map and alerting the vehicle to any worrisome nearby objects (other cars, pedestrians, bicycles). The radar and other cameras enhance the sensing capabilities.

Tesla is taking a different tack.

The company has argued that autonomous vehicles can understand their surroundings merely by capturing what a human driver would see. That means the cars need only one kind of sensor—cameras—and, since Tesla's cars are already equipped with cameras, the company argues it can transform them into autonomous vehicles by gradually improving the vehicle's existing software, rather than installing lidar and other types of sensors.

Tesla's aims, in keeping with Musk's daredevil persona, may be less about how well its vehicles perform and more about finances.

✦ Lidar and sensors cost a lot to buy and install and a lot to maintain, with each new part adding two to five times its cost to the list price of the vehicle.

✦ As sensors change, they must be calibrated, another costly endeavor.

✦ Anything beyond already in-use cameras adds risk and complexity to the manufacturing process and a certain amount of "bloat" as the software must analyze much more data.

It's not clear yet who's right.

Maybe both . . . but not quite yet?

Since Tesla began selling vehicles without the added sensors, it's quietly turned off some of the features that used the now-discarded hardware. Autopilot isn't as functional or as fast without radar to support it. Vehicles now experience more unplanned "phantom" braking. Parking assist and auto-parking are not currently working, either.

Lidar and sensors may be expensive, but they are the "shortest and safest path," writes Brad Templeton in *Forbes*.

Larry Burns, former corporate vice president of research and development for General Motors, admits that he was nervous the first time he stepped into a fully autonomous vehicle.

"My hands were shaking over the steering wheel," he reports. "My feet were nervous over the pedals. But within five minutes, I was relaxed; I realized this car was doing everything I would do as a driver and even better."

Mobileye stutters too?

Mobileye is running self-driving tests in Israel using eight NIO SE8s, a six-seater compact electric SUV imported from China, decked out with Mobileye's "Drive" autonomous vehicle system.

The SE8 will sport 11 cameras, including lidar and radar sensors—at the front, rear, inside the body, on the side mirrors and on the top of the vehicle.

Mobileye's self-driving star may be shining slightly less brightly: In early 2024, the company issued a severe profit warning for the first quarter of the year, citing excess inventory accumulated by its customers. The company's valuation plunged 25% on the news, shedding some $8 billion from the company's previous high of $35 billion.

A big part of the problem is competition in China.

Horizon Robotics, a Chinese firm, along with Nvidia, already share 84% of the Chinese luxury car market—Nvidia owns 53% and Horizon 31%. The remaining 16% is shared by Mobileye, Texas Instruments and the Chinese Huawei.

Mobileye's share price has since rebounded on news that sales of the company's flagship EyeQ vision software was projected to double in 2024.

Autonomy now . . . or never?

The accidents, recalls and glitches plaguing Tesla and other automakers promoting self-driving software highlight one of the industry's most glaring misrepresentations.

Level 5 autonomy—which would allow a car to drive itself without any human intervention—won't happen during most of our lifetimes.

Let that statement sink in for a moment.

The shiny autonomous future Tesla and others have been hawking for years won't become a reality in the next 30 to 40 years—and maybe not even then. A self-driving destiny that's been relentlessly promoted as a way to provide greater accessibility for people who don't own their own cars and that can help equalize some of the imbalances between societal groups is . . . simply a fantasy?

And if that's true, were we all duped?

Go back to 2015 when pundits were waxing enthusiastic about the imminent arrival of automated vehicles (AVs), robo-taxis, and more.

✦ Self-driving cars "will be common on highways within 15 years," *Business Insider* pontificated.

✦ Elon Musk forecast in December 2015: "Complete autonomy in approximately two years."

✦ OpenAI CEO Sam Altman disagreed—but only slightly—predicting the autonomous vehicle future would arrive in three to four years from 2015.

✦ In 2016, Lyft CEO John Zimmer predicted autonomy would "all but end" car ownership by 2025.

Did the experts of the twenty-teens grossly underestimate the complexity of AI models needed to simulate the human brain's ability to process moving objects around the vehicle, or have we all been victims of the kind of magical thinking that too often trips up overly ambitious tech startups?

The need for working autonomous vehicles is clear, Olaf Sakkers, Founder of RedBlue Capital, writes in his online treatise, "Mobility Disruption Framework." Cars are in use only 4% of the time; the rest of the time they're parked. By comparison, people spend about 7% of their time eating.

"Since there are about a billion vehicles in the world today, this underutilization is vast," Sakkers writes. "You may object [and argue] that people don't use their homes or their coffee makers much of the time either. The tricky thing about cars is that they also require vast amounts of infrastructure to support their non-use."

For each of America's more than 250 million cars, Sakkers adds, about four parking spots are set aside—a place to "park at home, at work, outside Safeway and near to the gym or hair stylist . . . you can do the math."

Sakkers's parking analysis only takes into account the actual amount of space set aside for cars. "In reality, parking lots require significant amounts of additional space for cars to enter, exit, and maneuver."

But for every cheerleader like Sakkers, there's a naysayer such as Li Yunfei, a spokesperson for China's giant BYD automotive manufacturer, who didn't mince words in a chat he had with CNBC during the 2023 Shanghai Auto Show.

"We think self-driving tech that's fully separated from humans is very, very far away, and basically impossible," he claimed in Mandarin.

Yunfei added, ominously, that all the businesses and industries in the space have essentially been wasting their money.

"After investing for many years, it will prove it leads nowhere," he said.

Part of the problem is that AVs must "play in the 'five nines' space," says Elie Wurtman of PICO Partners. "That is, they must be 99.999% reliable. That's the benchmark. The problem is, startups don't usually work this way."

Reilly Brennan, of Trucks VC, isn't sure autonomy will *ever* go commercial for passenger cars "for a simple reason: Only humans are dumb enough to think they can drive in any condition. Your young nephew shouldn't be driving to Chicago in an ice storm, but he'll do it anyway. Machines are a lot smarter. Level 5 is the third coming of Jesus. You can believe all you want. Level 4 is as good as it's going to get."

Maybe we don't even need Level 4.

Level 2 ADAS and Level 3 conditional driving automation can "get us to 80% of the safety of a full autonomous vehicle for much less cost," industry consultant Glenn Mercer told me.

Even then, there's another chicken-and-egg situation.

"You can't get to scale until people want to use them," Mike Granoff, of Maniv Mobility, explains. "But you can't get consumers to use them until you're at scale, you have availability, and the cost comes down."

Mobility investors UP.Partners estimates that, of the major contenders in the autonomous vehicle space, only two have staying power: Alphabet's Waymo and GM's Cruise. While both companies are experimenting with driverless robo-taxi services in small areas in a few select cities across the U.S., "thus far, viable business models are not in sight."

That's led to a precipitous drop in self-driving car company valuations.

This emerging reality has to be disappointing to AV proponents.

"Engineers, policymakers, startup founders and futurists have all been dreaming of a future in which cars do not require drivers," UP.Partners notes.

"In this vision of tomorrow, accidents are diminished due to flawless safety features and convenience takes over with point-to-point travel where no human touch is necessary. While this future was anticipated to arrive by the early 2020s, we are significantly off track from realizing autonomous vehicles as a mainstream part of daily life on public roads anytime soon. Instead, what's happening is a brutal shakedown among hyped-up companies, all of which are trying to bring the technology to life."

The pile-up continues

Whether as a backlash to 2015's overly optimistic predictions or a dose of cold realism, the anti-autonomy pile-up is in danger of turning into a full-on multi-car collision.

The Wall Street Journal's Christopher Mims argued in 2021 that self-driving cars "could be decades away."

In 2022, *Bloomberg's* Max Chafkin declared that "self-driving cars are going nowhere."

Julia Angwin criticized the push to autonomous driving in *The New York Times,* writing that, unlike human drivers who must pass a test before they can get behind the wheel unattended, "there are no federal software safety testing standards for autonomous vehicles."

"There's this weird gap between who is in charge of licensing a computer driver—is it the NHTSA or the state?" Angwin quotes Missy Cummings, professor of engineering and computer science at the Mason Autonomy and Robotics Center at George Mason University. "The computer vision systems in these cars are extremely brittle. They will fail in ways we simply don't understand."

The irony, Angwin writes, is that "so many headlines have focused on fears that computers will get too smart and take control of the world from humans, but in our reality, computers are often too dumb to avoid hurting us!"

Michael Sena, who publishes the automotive newsletter *The Dispatcher,* notes that "removing the human from the driving task has proven to be devilishly difficult because the car needs to drive at least as well as a human."

Alex Kantrowitz is a robo-taxi enthusiast.

"They ride smoother than any human driver. Their apps accept ride requests immediately (if the services have enough supply). Their cabins feel private (though there are cameras). And there's no awkwardness around tip, conversation, climate, or music," he writes in his Substack newsletter *Big Technology.*

Could a sort of "failsafe" be built into future autonomous software (not Level 5, of course) so that if the car senses you're in danger, it gives control back to the driver?

Victor Darolfi, of Robotire, isn't sure if that's such a good idea.

"If the driver is 90 years old, do you really want to give control back?" he asked me. "Which is smarter—the computer or the human?"

And what about in countries where "edge cases" are the norm?

In a big emerging economy city like Jakarta, for example, pedestrians have learned they don't need to get out of the way of cars when crossing the street—they just plunge right ahead, hopeful that the vehicle will stop (which it usually does).

"If an AV is programmed so it won't run over anyone, I'm not sure it will be able to navigate there at all," says *BloombergNEF's* Colin McKerracher. "Even if the tech works in Phoenix and the West, it might not work in India or other countries."

There is no guarantee of success, Timothy B. Lee cautions in *Understanding AI.*

"Even if they iron out all the technical problems, it will take many years to make these services profitable," Lee writes. For now, though, "the pendulum of public opinion has swung too far in the pessimistic direction."

The dangers of self-driving cars: by the numbers

Dr. Missy Cummings thinks the pessimism is warranted.

In late 2022, Cummings sent a two-page document to her colleagues at the NHTSA, where she was employed for a year before returning to academia.

Crashes involving systems like Tesla's FSD and GM's Super Cruise raise serious questions about technologies that have been installed in hundreds of thousands of cars now on U.S. roads, Cummings cautions. (Tesla alone has installed Autopilot in 800,000 vehicles. FSD is working in 400,000 vehicles.)

Her conclusion: When people using advanced driver-assistance systems die in a car crash, they are 50% more likely to have been speeding than people driving cars on their own. For crashes with serious injuries, they were speeding 42% of the time.

Compare that with crashes that did not include driver-assistance systems, where the death and injury figures dropped to 29% and 13%, respectively.

People "are over-trusting the technology," Cummings told *The New York Times*. "They are letting the cars speed. And they are getting into accidents that are seriously injuring them or killing them."

In some cases, the blame is clear.

Howard Yee's Tesla using Autopilot passed a stopped school bus and struck a student in March 2023. Authorities discovered Yee had fixed weights to the steering wheel to trick his Tesla into registering the presence of human hands on the wheel. (Autopilot is supposed to disable its functions if pressure is not applied on the steering wheel after a certain period of time.)

Turning to the Tesla braking problem that caused that Bay Bridge pile-up, Cummings adds, "The cars are braking in ways that people do not anticipate and are not able to respond to."

Cummings argues that automakers and regulators need to prevent FSD and similar systems from operating over local speed limits and they must require drivers using such systems to keep their hands on the steering wheel and eyes on the road.

"Wait a minute," those drivers might be expected to exclaim. "I have a self-driving car that I have to drive myself? What's the point?"

"Car companies—meaning Tesla and others—are marketing this as a hands-free technology," Cummings says. "That is a nightmare."

Cummings has acknowledged that actually turning her recommendations into rules would be difficult. Already, supporters of Tesla have attacked her on social media after she was appointed a senior advisor at NHTSA. She even received death threats.

But, she told *The New York Times*, she felt compelled to speak out because "the technology is being abused by humans." The NHTSA, she adds, "needs to flex its muscles more. It needs not to be afraid of Elon [Musk]."

Reports of errors and accidents tend to obscure the positives, notes Mobileye's Shashua, who points out that, despite the headline-making problems, an autonomous vehicle has only 1,000th the likelihood of being in an accident compared with a car driven by a person.

That's a big advantage.

In the U.S., an individual has a statistical average of 1 collision for every 500,000 miles of travel and a risk of 1 death for every 94 million miles driven (worldwide, it's 1 death for every 60 million miles driven). Some 1.5 million people are killed in traffic accidents annually worldwide.

Self-driving cars will allow accidents "to reach a stage of close to zero," Shashua adds. "This is very good news for society and for the economy."

Well, maybe not yet.

According to research conducted by the University of Michigan, the number of accidents in self-driving cars currently is 9.1 per million miles driven, compared with only 4.1 crashes per million miles driven in conventional vehicles.

That works out to a rate of 0.6 per 100,000 miles driven. It's still quite low—suggesting that concerns over autonomous safety may be blown out of proportion—but at least for now, it's still more than twice the rate of human-driven cars.

This presents consumers and automakers with a philosophical dilemma. Should we, as Musk seems to suggest, tolerate a few deaths today for a safer future tomorrow? Or should autonomous technology be held to a higher standard than human driving? How do we resolve this conflict?

Whether that's trickled down to consumers is unclear. But the average individual is decidedly *uncomfortable* riding in an autonomous vehicle.

+ Only 16% of respondents to a poll sponsored by *Politico* said they would feel serene riding in a self-driving car. Another 28% said that their chances of jumping in a car without a driver would be "not likely at all."

+ The Brookings Institute found that 61% of adult internet users said they are not ready to ride in a self-driving car.

+ 75% of Americans say they would rather drive their own car than ride in an AV.

✦ 76% of Americans want Congress to mandate putting brakes in self-driving cars.

✦ 68% said they would need a self-driving vehicle to be at least 5 times safer than a human-driven one. Another 39% said they'd need it to be 20 times safer. Are those reasonable safety thresholds or are drivers being too timid?

Who's to blame?

The gloomy numbers have made popularizing autonomous driving a tough sell to legislators (as well as to pedestrians) who latch onto some highly publicized autonomous driving fails.

Perhaps the most infamous so far was when a self-driving car killed Elaine Herzberg in the outskirts of Tempe, Arizona, in 2018.

In that example, Uber was running an autonomous test of a Volvo SUV with a backup driver behind the wheel. The vehicle, which was traveling at around 40 miles per hour, apparently couldn't recognize that pedestrians sometimes jaywalk, which is what Herzberg was doing at 10 p.m. as she wheeled her bicycle across a mostly deserted street in the city's outskirts.

Uber's autonomous software was able to identify pedestrians in crosswalks but not in other situations, according to a report by the National Traffic Safety Board. The software only realized there was a problem too late and concluded it needed to brake just 1.3 seconds before the fatal collision.

Uber says it "has since modified its programming to include jaywalkers among its recognized objects."

To make matters worse, the backup driver in the Tempe crash, Rafaela Vasquez, was not doing her job but instead was watching a streaming episode of *The Voice* on her phone, according to records from video service Hulu.

User error is a common denominator behind many of the accidents that have occurred in recent years with self-driving vehicles. To be sure, the cars are making errors, too, but, as with Uber in Tempe, the drivers have not been paragons of responsibility.

That's what happened a few years later, in 2021, when two men in Texas were killed in their 2019 Tesla Model S. Minutes before the crash, the men were talking about the vehicle's Autopilot feature. Autopilot is, as I've noted above, Level 1 autonomy—it should never be left to its own driving devices. But that's exactly what happened that night in Texas.

Lawyers and legislators will be hashing out the "who's to blame" question for years to come.

The answer is murky.

What happens, for example, if there's an accident and another driver runs into your self-driving car while it's trying to change lanes?

"I'll claim that they were dreaming and didn't notice that I wanted to enter their lane; they'll claim I was reckless. In the end, a court will make a decision. But that's not consistent with the way we want to design a robot," Shashua says, referring to the car's self-driving algorithms as a robot.

Stuck on the sidewalk

It's no mystery why the Bay Area has received its share of autonomous vehicle fails: San Francisco has become one of main testing locations for self-driving cars from Tesla competitors: GM's Cruise's and Alphabet's Waymo.

It's been frustrating, to say the least.

A headline in *Wired* sums up the problem: "Cruise's Robot Car Outages are Jamming Up San Francisco."

The article by Aarian Marshall leads off with the story of Calvin Hu.

On June 28, 2022, Hu was driving near Golden Gate Park around midnight when he pulled up at an intersection behind two autonomous Chevy Bolts running on Cruise's software. Another Bolt was stopped to his right.

The light turned green, but the cars didn't move.

Hu wanted to put his car in reverse, to try to navigate around the frozen vehicles, but then noticed several *more* Cruise vehicles stuck in the lanes behind him. A para-transit bus was also trapped in this robo-taxi sandwich.

Hu eventually escaped by driving over the curbs across the street's median. A Cruise employee arrived on the scene and the jam was cleared up—but not for 15 minutes, what would be for many an intolerable delay had it occurred midday, and probable cause for road rage.

It turned out that over a 90-minute period that night, some 60 AVs were frozen—some halted in crosswalks—after the server they needed to communicate with went down.

A month earlier, Cruise's servers lost touch with its entire fleet for 20 minutes, *Wired* reports. During that time, Cruise staff were unable to communicate with passengers inside the stuck cars.

The San Francisco Fire Department has now logged more than 55 cases of robo-taxis interfering with first responders. Fire Chief Jeanine Nicholson has said repeatedly and publicly that Cruise and Waymo's technology is "not ready for prime time."

Some locals have taken the law into their own hands, placing traffic cones on the hoods of parked Cruise and Waymo vehicles. The cones immobilize the vehicles, forcing them into shutdown mode with their hazard lights on.

Have we thrown caution too far into the wind before safety is fully baked? Has everyone in the industry become mini-Musks with a penchant for living dangerously?

It's one thing when your phone or tablet can't find a cell signal. It's another thing entirely when we're talking about a two-ton potential death machine on the expressway.

Rise and fall of the robo-taxis

In August 2023, California greenlighted a major expansion of self-driving taxis in San Francisco. The 3 to 1 vote by the California Public Utilities Commission allowed Cruise and Waymo to charge fares for their driverless service and, essentially, to grow the fleet as large as they'd like.

Yet, the very next day after the new rules went into effect, 10 Cruise driverless taxis blocked two narrow streets in the city's North Beach restaurant row. The AVs sat motionless with their hazard lights flashing for 15 minutes before they suddenly woke up and moved on, witnesses reported.

The official reason, from Cruise: Cellphone connectivity was down as a result of a music festival being held four miles away.

That potentially violated a California DMV regulation that requires driverless cars to have a link "allowing for 'two-way communications' between a vehicle—including its passengers—and an employee remotely overseeing the robot's movements," according to *Wired*.

Just two months after the San Francisco greenlight, the state shut down the autonomous tests in the city by the Bay after another self-driving Cruise car got into an accident resulting in a pedestrian being dragged for 20 feet, leaving her critically injured.

The Department of Motor Vehicles, which issued the suspension, didn't indicate how long it would last, but wrote in its ruling that Cruise's robo-taxis were "an unreasonable risk to the public" and that the company misrepresented how safe they are. San Francisco Board of Supervisors president Aaron Peskin added that allowing the autonomous technology on public roads was "a recipe for death" and that the state "should never have allowed their unlimited deployment in the first place."

Cruise, for its part, issued a statement indicating that it has "paused operations while we take time to engage third-party experts and strengthen public trust." The pause covers all of Cruise's U.S. operations, including in Arizona and Texas, not just California.

The corporate fallout was swift: In November 2023, Cruise cofounder and CEO Kyle Vogt resigned and, a month later, the company said it would slash 24% of its workforce—some 900 employees—as it restructures operations. As for any possible future expansion, Cruise says it will launch a new trial in "one unspecified city" in the U.S. only.

"To be clear, human drivers will text, they'll be distracted. There's the saying, 'the lights are on, but nobody's home,'" says Carnegie Mellon Prof. Philip Koopman, who studies autonomous driving safety. "But it turns out, that happens to robo-taxis too."

Cruise Autonomous Car (credit: Shutterstock)

Before Cruise suspended operations, GM CEO Mary Barra had said Cruise and its autonomous vehicle technology could generate $50 billion in revenue by 2030, making the robo-taxi business a big piece of GM's strategy to double revenue to $280 billion.

But GM lost more than $700 million at Cruise in the third quarter of 2023 and has lost more than $8 billion since 2016. That hasn't stopped the company from doubling-down: In June 2024, GM announced it was investing an additional $850 million in Cruise to keep the struggling robo-taxi firm afloat.

Banning cars entirely

Given the dangerous interactions between today's autonomous and human-driven cars, Vogt—two months before his departure—floated the idea that cities ought to consider banning human-driven cars from entering the center of town.

"If you extrapolate forward and you see that [autonomous vehicles] decrease in cost, they continue to improve their safety performance, they get much better at adapting in ways that cities find agreeable and preferable, and you see more pooled rides, the question will be: Do we want as many human-driven cars on our roads? Like at what point does it still make sense?" he told a rapt audience at TechCrunch Disrupt 2023.

Vogt noted that Cruise had logged some one million driverless miles and that its vehicles get into 75% fewer collisions that could cause injuries, and that this number will only improve over the coming years.

"If I told you five years from now autonomous vehicles are going to be 100 times safer, and you have regions of your city that have high pedestrian and cyclist traffic, it would almost seem reckless as a city planner to allow one version of transportation that's 100 times less safe than the other to coexist in that space," he told the *TechCrunch* audience.

"We're going to have to do something like [banning human-driven cars] if we want to keep up and if we want to hold the bar high for safety."

David Zipper, at the Harvard Kennedy School's Taubman Center for State and Local Government, disagrees.

"I just came back from several weeks in Europe, and I didn't hear anybody there clamoring for AVs in their cities," Zipper told *TechCrunch's* Rebecca Bellan. "I met a lot of people trying to get rid of cars, not only because they are concerned about the safety issues of human-driven cars, but they're also worried about the air pollution caused by any car, whether it's driven by computers or by humans, which can come from brakes and from tires and from road dust."

Zipper can't imagine anyone visiting a city and saying, "'God, what a wonderful place. I want to come back or even live here because it's so easy to get around in a car.' There's no reason to think that removing drivers and inserting technology in their place is going to change that."

Teleoperation can help

One trick to shortening the path to autonomy is teleoperation. That's where an autonomous vehicle can be "taken over" by a remote driver.

Would that have helped address the Cruise robo-taxi shutdowns in San Francisco?

"Until we get to true Level 4 or Level 5, I don't see how vehicles can become 100% autonomous without teleoperation," Ohad Dvir, cofounder and former COO of Phantom Auto, told me. "It makes sense to take out the driver. But it will take some time for the technology to become more mature."

Phantom Auto initially aimed to provide human-assisted remote backup driving in case a car—or its driver—got stuck. The company pivoted in 2022, as Dvir and his team realized that the consumer self-driving market has been slower to take off than expected, to focus on emergency remote control for forklifts and "yard trucks."

Public transit is suffering too

In April 2023, *Wired*, which seems to be honing a reputation as the tech industry's AV-basher, obtained dashcam surveillance footage from San Francisco MUNI, which operates the city's buses and light rail, showing "a litany of incidents" where frozen AVs have blocked public transportation in the city.

Of the 92 unplanned AV stops reported between May and December 2022, 88% of them were on streets with transit service, according to city transportation authorities, leading to 83 minutes of direct delays for public transit riders, although, adds *Wired*, "that data likely doesn't reflect the true scale of the problem."

Stalled cars would be frustrating in any context, but anti-AV crusaders in San Francisco have seized on mass transit as their rallying cry. It makes sense: When public transit meets a recalcitrant AV, it's not the same as two similarly sized vehicles. Buses have a hard time weaving around blockages; light rail runs on a fixed route.

"We are very concerned that, if autonomous vehicles are allowed limitless, driverless operations in San Francisco, the traffic impacts will grow exponentially," says Jeffrey Tumlin, MUNI's director of transportation.

Waymo and Cruise insist they learn from every incident and that, with one million driverless miles logged in the city to date, their cars are safe enough to keep testing.

Consumers are not so sure, and the brewing backlash shows no signs of slowing down.

Bob Feinbaum, president of the nonprofit group Save SF Muni, wants authorities to have access to an override code of sorts that would move driverless cars out of the way.

"It's crazy that these vehicles can stop in the middle of the road and police can show up and have no way of dealing with it," he says.

Red light, green light, white light?

Transportation engineers at North Carolina State University have proposed putting a fourth light on traffic signals. This "white light" would enable AVs to help control traffic flow and, perhaps more important, let human drivers know what's going on.

"Red lights will still mean stop," explains researcher Ali Hajbabaie in a paper published on *IEEE Xplore* in 2023. "Green lights will still mean go. And white lights will tell human drivers to simply follow the car in front of them."

"The white phase concept rests on the fact that it is possible for AVs to communicate wirelessly with both each other and the computer controlling the traffic signal," writes Matt Shipman for *NC State University News*. "When enough AVs are approaching the intersection, this would activate the white light. The white light is a signal that AVs are coordinating their movement to facilitate traffic through the intersection more efficiently."

Any nonautomated vehicles—(i.e., those being driven by a person)—would simply follow the vehicle in front of them," Shipman adds. "If the car in front of them stops, they stop; if the car in front of them goes through the intersection, they go through the intersection."

When too many vehicles approaching the intersection are being controlled by drivers, rather than AVs, the traffic light would revert to the conventional green-yellow-red signal pattern.

I like the idea of adding a visual cue for drivers in mixed-AV and non-AV environments, but I'm not sure it goes far enough to mitigate the problems we've raised here regarding safe autonomous driving.

Where will autonomy hit first?

Rather than ask when we will have autonomous vehicles, "the correct way to frame this is 'where' will we first have autonomous vehicles?" Stanford University Graduate School of Business lecturer Sven Beiker notes.

To answer the "where" question, let's turn to Alain Kornhauser, professor of operations research and financial engineering at Princeton University, and one of the most insightful thinkers about all things mobility. His newsletter, *Smart Driving Cars*, focuses on autonomy.

There are three markets for automation technology that Kornhauser foresees:

1. **Private property**. This is where self-driving tractors and construction equipment can be game changers since, as Kornhauser says, "the safety constraints are all manageable. No human is permitted within the perimeter." This use-case—which Reilly Brennan, of Trucks VC, dubs "structured autonomy"—is also propelled by economic need. "You can't get enough drivers to drive the trucks. Labor is expensive, scarce and not reliable," Kornhauser explains. "And these machines will work 24/7."

2. **Public roads**. Once we've mastered autonomy on private property, Kornhauser says, we can move on to applying those lessons to public roads. The safety issues will be greater, so the question is how you will get "a substantial number of people [to] want to use it [and to ensure that] the affordability is such that demand can create a market for it."

3. **Advanced driver systems**. Before these can morph into full-fledged autonomous driving smarts, they need to get smarter by a large magnitude. On one of his recent *Smart Driving* podcasts, Kornhauser asked Jason Ditman, the chief engineer and head of GM's Ultra Cruise product line, to what extent Ultra Cruise communicates

with the car's emergency braking system. "The two don't communicate at all," Ditman replied, a response that Kornhauser said left him simply "dumbfounded."

Autonomy at the club

Of Kornhauser's three scenarios, I'm most bullish about autonomous vehicles operating on private property as the first and most immediate use-case.

Small, autonomous NEVs (Neighborhood Electric Vehicles) could operate at:

+ Golf clubs and other types of high-end resorts

+ Universities

+ Large hospital campuses

+ Senior living and assisted living communities

+ Industrial plants

+ Theme parks

The common denominator: The vehicles operate at relatively low speeds on mostly fixed paths and they don't need to compete with human drivers on public roads (so no arguments over who's at fault in a crash). They could run on a fixed route or navigate on their own (given the low speeds, it's unlikely an accident would prove fatal).

Tel Aviv-based Carteav is outfitting and testing autonomous NEVs.

Carteav doesn't make its own NEVs; the company adds a layer of sensors, cameras and cables on the roof of a golf cart built by a third party to control steering, brakes and acceleration, as well to communicate with Carteav's mobile app.

Users open the app to order their vehicle. You don't even have to "tell the cart where you want to go in advance," explains CEO Avinoam Barak. "You just tell it to come."

Nor will you ever run into stubborn drivers who refuse to take you where you want them to. Recall that, with services like Uber, drivers can screen ride offers and choose whether to pick you up based on where *they* want to go.

Carteav's carts, by contrast, have no drivers. Hence there's no conflict of interest.

Adding an app to the mix isn't that different than ordering a Lyft. It makes it that much more convenient than having to wait for a shared shuttle bus running on its own schedule.

Once you've arrived at your destination, you simply "release" the vehicle to pick up another passenger or tell it to wait until you're done at the store or restaurant.

Since Carteav's NEVs won't travel on public roads, there's no need to wait for governments to put in place regulations governing their use.

How will customers use their Carteav NEVs?

Barak imagines a monthly subscription fee of somewhere around $1,000. That might sound steep, but if you don't have to buy a car—or if you're not able to drive due to age or infirmity—that can be a reasonable cost.

That said, Barak believes that most NEV rides will be subsidized as part of a package of services offered by the university or resort.

Carteav is currently running trials at senior communities (albeit with a "safety driver" still in place).

Once NEVs have proven their worth in private environments, NEVs could make their way into cities that have adopted car-free zones.

- Barcelona has "super blocks" without cars.

- Tel Aviv has a plan to close crowded Allenby Street to private vehicles.

- Tempe, Arizona, is developing a car-free community called Culdesac in its downtown.

There's one area that Carteav is not automating, at least yet: plugging into a charge spot.

"There will be a person there to do that," Barak says, adding that this attendant could also clean the carts and make sure passengers don't leave personal items inside.

Autonomous micromobility deliveries

In an amusing video released by the MIT Media Lab, a three-wheeled self-driving bicycle is shown maneuvering around people on a crowded Boston street. The bike is responding to an order from Nara Coretti Sanchez, a researcher in the City Science research group at MIT.

When Sanchez gets on the bike, she pedals away, although she could just as easily have set the bike to take her where she wanted without requiring any people power.

"We are getting used to ordering an Uber and it's downstairs in five minutes," Sanchez says. "That's already happened for mobility modes that are not so environmentally friendly. We want to bring the same convenience to mobility modes that are more environmentally friendly."

Autonomous delivery robots have for some time now plied the streets of Silicon Valley, bringing everything from Vietnamese pho to pharmaceuticals to downtown residents' offices and homes.

One of the first delivery robots was Starship Technologies' cooler-sized autonomous mobile unit. Starship inked partnerships in 2017 with DoorDash and Postmates.

Postmates's new robot, Serve, can carry 50 pounds and travel up to 30 miles on a charge; it's outfitted with lidar sensors from Velodyne and an Nvidia Xavier processor, allowing it to create a virtual picture of the world in real time.

Other robot delivery services wandering the sidewalks of the world include:

+ **Nuro**, which has partnerships with FedEx, Walmart and CVS. At six feet tall and nine feet long, the Nuro R2 is much larger than most of the other delivery robots. One of Nuro's first partnerships was with Domino's Pizza.

  In September 2024, Nuro announced it would be getting out of the hardware business entirely, and pivoting the business model to license its autonomous driving technology to outside companies, including rideshare operators for robo-taxis.

Nuro autonomous delivery vehicle (credit: Getty Images)

+ **Udelv**, an even larger vehicle that can drive on highways at up to 60 miles per hour and can carry over 800 pounds of payload. The company has a partnership with Mobileye to build next-generation Udelv vehicles called Transporters. The companies plan to build more than 35,000 Transporters by 2028.

The Udelv autonomous vehicle (credit: Udelv)

+ **Kiwibot** started delivering food by robot at the University of California, Berkeley, in 2017, and now serves students at Stanford and San Jose. The company says it's made 150,000 deliveries to date.

+ **Eliport**, based in Barcelona, travels on sidewalks and can load and unload without human interaction.

The Kiwibot (credit: Wikimedia Commons)

✦ **TeleRetail** makes the Pulse 1, a small battery-powered delivery robot, and the solar-powered Range+. TeleRetail wants to help small brick-and-mortar stores achieve e-commerce levels of convenience for their customers.

✦ **BoxBot** was founded by ex-Uber and ex-Tesla engineers and is backed by Toyota AI Ventures. When a BoxBot autonomous delivery vehicle arrives, customers receive a text message with a unique code to unlock the box and collect their package.

✦ **Robomart** brands its robots as a "self-driving grocery store." When a Robomart arrives at your doorstep, you unlock it and go shopping with the company's checkout-counter-free technology. Each Robomart carries a selection of goods within a specific category and restocks itself at a local replenishment center when the products run low.

The RoboMart autonomous vehicle (credit: RoboMart)

✦ **Segway Robotics**—ever wonder what happened to Segway, the once vaunted two-wheel self-balancing people mover whose boss James Heselden tragically died in 2010 after falling off a cliff in England while riding his own Segway? It's been brought back to life as Segway Robotics, a door-to-door delivery bot. Segway says its DeliveryBot S2's 360-degree sensor system makes the unit capable of operating in more extreme conditions than its competitors.

✦ Amazon's six-wheeled **Scout** may formally be autonomous, but it still must be accompanied by a human—kind of like the AV trials that need a safety driver, except here the speeds are lower and the so-called "safety" walks alongside the robot. Amazon announced in late 2022 that it was "scaling back" the Scout program. While Amazon isn't killing it entirely, *TechCrunch's* Brian Heater described the move as "a dramatic setback" for the program.

The Amazon Scout Sidewalk Robot (credit: Shutterstock)

Autonomous trucks

Truck driving can be a bitch. Just ask Michael Gary, who told *The New York Times:* "I had no personal life outside of driving a truck."

Away on the road for weeks at a time, he says he finally "had enough" and quit.

For other drivers, the Covid-19 pandemic is what pushed them over the edge, with seemingly endless quarantines and lockdowns, not to mention the fear of being a frontline worker exposed to a deadly virus. Is it any wonder a rash of resignations soon followed?

For shippers, drivers are not only expensive, they can only drive a limited number of hours a day before they're legally required to rest. That means a $200,000 state-of-the-art truck is being driven only 30% to 40% of the time.

But there's a solution—autonomy—and it may be coming to the trucking world sooner than for passenger vehicles.

Mike Granoff says that for autonomy you need three things: "technology, market pull and the right regulatory regime."

That's a big reason trucks may be the first vehicles to go autonomous. "The truck driver shortage is the market pull," Granoff says.

As with NEVs on campuses and retirement villages, autonomous trucks could drive in dedicated lanes, so they wouldn't have to interact—and potentially collide—with human-driven vehicles.

Uber lays out the problem with "mixed" self-driving and human environments.

"Urban streets are far from uniform," the company reports in a white paper entitled "The Future of Self-Driving Technology in Trucking."

"Lanes vary by width, speed limit and geometry. Some streets have side parking, shoulders or sidewalks, while others do not. Roundabouts and intersections are even more complex. And while some turns are protected, others are not. Urban streets can be jammed with pedestrians, bicyclists and smaller delivery vehicles."

Driving on the highway solves many of these problems, since "the U.S. interstate highways are much more uniform as they are regulated and maintained by a single agency: the Federal Highway Administration (FHWA), which imposes uniform standards covering controlled access, minimum and maximum speed limits and lane geometry."

"A bit of freeway in Texas looks very much like a bit of freeway in Phoenix or Minnesota," notes Chris Urmson, CEO of self-driving truck company Aurora.

"Consumers might accept dedicated lanes on freeways for trucks with no driver inside," notes Granoff. "People are sensitive to when their packages will arrive and if this is what it will take to get my packages, OK, then."

The FHWA reports that the total length of the U.S. highway system is 46,876 miles. That may sound like a lot, but it's only 1.2% of the public roads in the U.S. Yet, highways carry a quarter of all vehicle-miles.

What about concerns that self-driving trucks could adversely impact the job market for truck drivers?

Aniruddh Mohan, a PhD candidate at Princeton, modeled what would happen if autonomous trucks were widely deployed in U.S. Sunbelt states. It could wipe out 10% of the total number of hours long-haul trucks in the U.S. spend on the road, at a cost of between 30,000 to 40,000 jobs, Moran found. The same economic incentive could ultimately threaten nearly all long-haul trucking jobs, he adds.

But, writes Christopher Mims in *The Wall Street Journal,* "many in the automated-trucking industry claim these job losses will be more than offset by the creation of new jobs." Mims adds that, if self-driving trucks are made cheaper and faster, freight may shift to trucks and away from planes and rail.

Here are some of the autonomous players I'm tracking:

Uber Freight

Uber has, since 2017, deployed the same sophisticated matching software it uses for passenger rides to connect shippers with cargo. Uber is now touting self-driving trucks as the future of its Uber Freight division. (Uber Freight is a logistics operator for self-driving trucks. It doesn't make the vehicles.)

An Uber survey found that a majority of shippers are either extremely likely (52%) or somewhat likely (24%) to consider an autonomous freight solution in the future.

The study was hardly representative, with just 24 shippers participating. Still, while it was "based on a small sample, it clearly shows that shippers are more likely to adopt autonomous technology compared with the general population," Uber explains in its white paper.

"Level 5 is the automation North Star," Uber notes. "However, it is unattainable within the coming years. [As a result], current self-driving developers are focusing on Level 4, where the vehicle can drive under most conditions along specific corridors."

That's highways. But what happens when the truck *leaves* the dedicated corridor on the way to its final destination?

Uber says that, for the foreseeable future, most autonomous trucks "will operate under a hub-to-hub model. Human drivers will handle the trip ends, which involve complex urban streets and manual operations at facilities, such as loading, unloading, gate entrance and documentation. Autonomous trucks will service the middle part of the trip."

This model makes a lot of sense to me. In Uber's vision, a human driver picks up a preloaded trailer from the shipper's facility and delivers it to a transfer hub located close to the highway—that's the "first mile." After traveling on the highway, another driver picks up the trailer at a second transfer hub for the "last mile."

Such hubs need to have dedicated exits from the highway, so the self-driving truck doesn't ever have to merge into lanes meant for human drivers.

Uber calls its system "drop-and-hook" (a play on the software term "drag-and-drop") and "a stepping-stone toward full autonomy."

The hub-to-hub model also makes mapping easier. Self-driving vehicles need high-definition maps to determine their location with respect to the surrounding environment. This kind of mapping takes a lot of time and costs a lot of money. With hub-to-hub, only the highway segment needs to be mapped that way.

Uber estimates that shippers using Uber Freight can reduce their costs by between 30% and 45%. Uber says the operating cost of a self-driving truck is about $1.06 per mile. That's 72 cents per mile cheaper than a human-driven truck.

The hub-to-hub model is not without disadvantages. If workers are required at the transfer hubs for such things as maintenance and security, that could bump the cost up by almost $2,000 a day for 2 workers who would need to be available 24/7.

Another concern: Not all hubs will support Uber's proposed drop-and-hook, forcing drivers to wait for live loading and unloading at the facilities.

A hub-to-hub and drag-and-hook system, with self-driving Uber trucks tackling the long-haul middle mile section, will push drivers toward local hauls, where there should be plenty of work. It also fits better with driver preferences where long-haulers like Michael Gray, whom we met at the beginning of this chapter, would increasingly be able to stay close to home and their families.

Aurora

Aurora Innovation wanted to have self-driving trucks in operation by 2024. The company's partners include FedEx, Volvo, Ryder, Werner Enterprises and Schneider. The company has backing from Sequoia Capital and Amazon.

Aurora got a boost in 2020 when Uber sold its self-driving unit, Uber ATG, to the company in exchange for a 26% stake in Aurora. The deal brought 1,200 former ATG employees into Aurora, bumping up its headcount to 1,800 overnight.

Six months later, Aurora went public via SPAC, but the company's chief financial officer, Richard Tame, admits the company will lose money until 2027 and will need additional capital before then. Still, the company assured worried shareholders that it had enough cash on hand (around $1.2 billion at the end of 2022) to get to commercial deployment.

A leaked memo from CEO Chris Urmson (who was originally on the Waymo team at Alphabet) to the Aurora board outlined possible cost-cutting measures: a hiring freeze, layoffs, spinning off assets, going private or selling the company.

"I just was naive about the complexity of achieving the level of safety we need to make this work well," he told *TechCrunch* in 2023.

Urmson is nevertheless projecting confidence. As of now, Aurora's software is "feature complete." The company currently has 30 trucks in testing mode in Texas and hopes to have 100 trucks on the roads commercially by 2025.

In November 2023, the company opened its first lane for driverless trucks connecting Dallas and Houston, supported by Aurora's commercial trucking terminal in Houston.

"We look at trucking, and we see a landscape where we feel like [we're] the only viable player," Urmson says.

That's some confidence, indeed.

TuSimple

TuSimple, which shares a CEO with hydrogen fuel cell truck maker Hydron, says that, when testing in autonomous mode, its trucks achieved a 13% fuel savings compared with human drivers.

It's not been smooth sailing for TuSimple. The company reported a $732 million annual loss against just $6.3 million in revenue in 2021.

A crash in Tucson didn't help matters: One of TuSimple's big rigs suddenly lurched left while traveling down Interstate I-10, slamming into a concrete divider. TuSimple blamed "human error," with *The Wall Street Journal* reporting that the safety driver "hadn't properly rebooted the autonomous system before engaging it, causing it to execute an outdated command."

"Since humans write all the code, all crashes of code-driven vehicles could be called 'human error,'" Princeton mobility analyst Alain Kornhauser critiques TuSimple's explanation. "Thus, calling it 'human error' doesn't earn a passing grade."

In 2022, TuSimple laid off 25% of its staff, despite having raised some $188 million earlier that year. In 2023, the company was forced to fire another 30% of its remaining headcount. In January 2024, another 3% were let go.

Then, in December 2023, the company announced it was pulling out of the U.S. market—after a five-month review apparently found no takers for its business, per *Yahoo Finance*—and is now focusing exclusively on Asia. The company still employs 700 in China and elsewhere in Asia. The company is rumored to be in talks with Geely to sell its division in China.

Gatik

Like Uber Freight, Gatik is also pursuing a "middle mile" strategy and will operate on routes with fixed pick-up and drop-off locations. The company will take items from microfulfillment centers and dark stores and drop them at retail outlets and other distribution centers.

Gatik has partnerships with Georgia-Pacific (to distribute tissue pulp), KBX (the transportation arm for Koch Industries) and Walmart, where two of its Level 4 autonomous box trucks are operating at the latter's headquarters in Bentonville, Arkansas. Gatik also delivers groceries for Canadian grocery chain Loblaw.

Kodiak Robotics

Don Burnette, CEO of Kodiak Robotics, says that fully autonomous trucks may be just a couple of years away.

"Our technology was developed for over-the-road trucking. But it generalizes to a lot of other areas," Burnette explains.

One of those areas: the military. In 2022, the U.S. Army inked a $50 million contract with Kodiak to develop off-road autonomous systems. In other words, tanks, not trucks. Kodiak beat out 31 competitors to win the two-year defense contract.

"They wanted to find a software provider to take the commercial application and apply it to military use as opposed to a complete black box, which is traditionally how it's been done," Burnette told *FreightWaves*.

Autonomous tanks/trucks can be used in reconnaissance and in other environments the military deems challenging. For the initial trial, Kodiak will have safety drivers in place.

A Kodiak Autonomous Truck (credit: Wikimedia Commons)

DeepWay

DeepWay is the first EV startup in China to build autonomous trucks from scratch, rather than basing them on existing vehicles with minor changes. The company says that makes its self-driving tech more integrated, while reducing production costs.

The company's truck is called the Xingtu and it addresses not only performance specs but also comfort, separating out the working and living spaces in a big rig. The vehicle has a large touch screen infotainment system plus comfortable beds and chairs. The Xingtu EV can travel 300 kilometers on a one-hour charge.

DeepWay was formed by and is backed by Chinese giants Baidu and logistics service provider Shiqiao Group.

Locomation

Locomation's founders met while working at the National Robotics Engineering Center in Pittsburgh. Their big idea is to run autonomous trucks in a convoy, in which a lead driver pilots a truck, and another truck follows it autonomously. The autonomous vehicle will also have a driver, but the driver will be considered a "passenger" who can rest or even sleep.

Locomation calls it "human-guided autonomy."

A minimum convoy is two trucks; both have all the necessary software, so the two can swap, allowing the lead driver to rest and the "passenger" to take over. When the trucks leave the highway, both drivers take over manual operation for the "last mile."

Locomation says this will allow drivers to travel twice as far without exceeding Department of Transportation regulations. The company aims to have its trucks travel 1,000 miles a day with between 90% and 99% of that in "autonomy" mode.

Locomation has a contract to equip over 1,000 Wilson Logistics trucks with its convoy tech over the next five years. Another partnership will supply a similar number of vehicles to Pennsylvania-based flatbed transportation provider, PGT Trucking.

"Controlling an 80,000-pound truck at highway speeds, there is no such thing as a fender bender," says Locomation CEO Cetin Meriçli. "There needs to be indisputable evidence the autonomous truck is safe."

Autonomous convoy trucking could also make electrification of this segment possible. Imagine that each truck had its own electric battery. The first truck would pull the others along until the battery ran out, then the trucks could switch their order in the convoy.

They would still need to be plugged in to recharge at some point, which raises an economic debate: Truckers are paid when they're driving. They're compensated by the mile, not by the hour. They don't get paid to fuel up. Could this be restructured so drivers can stay on the clock even when plugging in? Will trucking companies accept this?

Waymo

Waymo is not just working on autonomous passenger cars; the Alphabet-backed company's autonomous trucking division is called "Waymo Via." It has partnerships with trucking companies C.H. Robinson and J.B. Hunt, as well as fleet services operator Ryder and truck maker Daimler Truck. It even has a deal with Uber Freight.

Waymo is perhaps more cautious than Uber, so before it deploys autonomous trucks commercially, those vehicles—whether new or retrofitted—will need backup steering, braking and electrical systems.

Getting all these systems into trucks that can be made by the tens of thousands is why Waymo joined with Daimler, said Charlie Jatt, Waymo's head of commercialization for trucking until September 2023.

Waymo has yet to set a date for when its trucks will operate with no human in the cab. But it could be soon.

"One thing that really surprised us was that the additional cost of the technology required by autonomous trucks is relatively small," says Parth Vaishnav, assistant professor of sustainable systems at the University of Michigan, and coauthor of a recent study on the impact self-driving trucks would have on truckers.

Vaishnav notes that even $20,000 of hardware, including sensors and computing systems, added to a long-haul truck, is quickly offset by the elimination of labor costs, which typically represent 15% to 20% of the cost of operating a truck.

"It's economically so compelling that, even if other things about the truck modestly increase costs, it may turn out it will still be attractive," adds Vaishnav.

Political threat to autonomous trucking

If California legislators have their way, a bill known as AB-316 would require human operators in all trucks in the state. Autonomous trucking firms worry that this could kick off similar legislation in other states.

Aurora CEO Urmson weighed in on the potentially devastating new regulation.

"It'll mean helping our customers haul freight between Arizona and the East Coast," Urmson says.

In other words: no business in California.

Urmson hopes this won't result in a "a kind of checkerboard across the United States," which could put the kibosh on Aurora's—and other self-driving truck vendors'—business plans.

"I think in practice that's unlikely," Urmson said.

Another hurdle came in April 2023 when a major U.S. transport union opposed a request by Alphabet that Waymo, as well as Aurora, be granted an exemption from the requirement by drivers to place reflective triangles or a flare around a truck stopped on the highway.

It makes sense: If a truck is entirely self-driving, there's no one on board to put out the triangles or flares.

Waymo and Aurora proposed instead to place warning beacons on the truck cab itself.

The Transport Workers Union of America countered, saying the petition is "inappropriate, represents an overreach and a misuse of the waiver and exemption process, and would significantly diminish the safety of our roads."

Waymo and Aurora warned that this would require a human driver on self-driving trucks, which would "undermine the efficiency potential of autonomous vehicles."

Fixing our cities with autonomous public transportation

Getting consumers out of their cars and onto buses and trains has been an uphill battle, at least in most of the U.S.

But what if there were a way for autonomy to fix public transportation as well?

In his book *Fall in Love with the Problem, not the Solution*, Uri Levine, the founder of a dozen Israeli startups including mobility leaders Waze (for commuting by car) and Moovit (for public transportation), visualizes the problem like this:

On an average one-kilometer stretch of highway, you'll typically find 40, maybe 45 vehicles, each one with just a single person in the car.

If you were to erase the cars from the picture, you'd find just 50 people or so occupying a full kilometer. They'd be spread out because the cars are large and, if they're being cautious drivers, they've left enough space between vehicles.

Fixing public transit, Levine says, is not a matter of buying more buses.

It's not a matter of building more highways, nor of lowering pricing.

The key is increasing the ratio of passengers to vehicles. Just a 10% improvement could end traffic jams.

"We're stuck in traffic more than we were a decade or two ago," Levine writes. "And if we don't address the ratio of passengers to vehicles, we will be stuck in traffic forever."

There are two main ways to change the ratio of passengers to cars, Levine says:

1. Use smaller vehicles (micromobility).
2. Encourage people to switch to carpools and public transportation.

Other than in the biggest American cities, public transportation has never really caught on in the U.S. But what if we redesigned our cities as horizontal elevators? And what if we made them free? Levine wonders.

Since 2020, residents of the small European nation of Luxembourg have been able to ride trains and buses without buying tickets.

Luxembourg was in dire need of a new approach. The country has the highest vehicle density in Europe, with 696 cars per 1,000 people. Nine out of 10 households in the country have at least one car. Even in small towns you'll find Ferrari and Maserati dealerships.

Luxembourg is not the only location experimenting with free public transit. Rome tried it in 1971; Austin, Texas gave it a spin in 1980; and Kansas City's bus and streetcar systems have also been fare-free since 2020.

Tallinn, the capital of Estonia, has made public transit free for residents since 2013.

Germany offered travel passes across the country for just €9 a month over the course of 2022's post-Covid summer of frantic "revenge travel."

Cities in France and the Czech Republic are also making public transit free.

Are the policies paying off? In Luxembourg, at least, the experiment doesn't seem to be working.

In May 2022, congestion on Luxembourg's roads was either equivalent to or *higher* than the levels in May 2019, before the free public transit policy was introduced.

Bloomberg explains the conundrum like this: Making transit free doesn't in and of itself tempt people away from their cars. Riders still must contend with overcrowded or delayed public transit vehicles. Nor can a light rail system take you from door-to-door like a car can.

"Car owners tend to be wealthier than the general public, and their access to a private vehicle makes them less willing to tolerate bus transfers, wait times, or slow journeys," writes David Zipper in *Bloomberg.*

David Brandon, executive director of the nonprofit group Transit Center, adds, "If you take bad American transit that costs $1.50 and make that bad service free, that won't move the needle enough . . . the key to getting people out of automobiles is providing abundant, frequent service around the clock."

Indeed, the most enthusiastic adopters of free travel, surveys have shown, are those people who would normally have walked or cycled. That, paradoxically, leads to a situation where making public transit free (assuming it hasn't gone 100% electric already) actually *increases* gas emissions, rather than decreasing them.

Luxembourg's experience shows that the needle won't move by carrot alone. There needs to be a stick, too—for example, higher fuel or parking prices, steeper purchase taxes, restrictions on private car entry to city centers.

With that in mind, is Levine's proposal for autonomous public transit more carrot or stick?

"Imagine a city that's built on a grid, as most U.S. cities are," Levine writes in *Fall in Love with the Problem.* "What if we took every other street and made it only for public transportation? The streets would act like horizontal elevator shafts."

Elevator shafts go back and forth in a straight line. They don't go around curves.

Vehicles on these street-level elevator corridors must come very, very frequently. They don't have to be huge buses; small vans will do. But they need to come every 10 to 30 seconds during rush hour. Off-peak, five minutes at most.

Small vehicles make sense. In London, a double-decker bus has space for 75 people. The average occupancy? 11 passengers.

A dedicated transit lane with self-driving vans that arrive as frequently as the #1 subway train in Manhattan would be a compelling alternative to a private car.

Carrot.

Reducing the number of streets available for cars to drive on?

Stick.

And because these autonomous vehicles would not run on the same streets as human-driven cars, we again avoid the pitfalls that have made pundits proclaim that autonomous vehicles, outside of campuses and resorts, are still decades away.

A self-driving public transit van would also eliminate the highest cost for the system: the driver. That makes the possibility of "free" more realistic.

While this will work in modern cities built on a grid, I'm not so sure how reasonable this proposal would be in older cities where streets don't generally go in a straight line.

"Fixing" public transit with autonomy and innovative pricing will take political will. But as cities consider private car bans or adding congestion pricing for driving downtown, more commuters could come around, making the politicians' jobs easier. But most important, public transport must become a more compelling experience for consumers.

The dawn of the "un-car"

If and when autonomy comes to passenger cars and robo-taxis, it will usher in a new age of automotive interior design.

Toyota Boshoku, the main seating and interior systems supplier for Toyota in Japan, has conceptualized a self-driving "pod car" with seats that face each other and screens everywhere.

Boshoku is banking on automakers demanding swappable mix-and-match cabin layouts with interiors that can transform into comfortable lounges on wheels.

Boshoku's innovations include:

+ **Swappable interiors**—the company is making four classes of swappable interiors including those that can accommodate wheelchairs or special purposes.

+ **In-car sanitation**—built-in ultraviolet LED sanitizers will sterilize passenger seats. A specialized air filter will keep the space free of potential pathogens.

+ **Lost and found**—a notification system will warn if any items are left in the vehicle. A visual message is broadcast onto the pavement as passengers disembark.

+ **Mix and match**—seats can be reconfigured and moved on tracks with zippered seams on a flat-floor cabin.

+ **No more nausea**—motion sickness mitigation technology will give visual and tactile clues when the vehicle is about to make a turn or change lanes. A right turn might trigger a vibration on the right side of the car, for example.

+ **Climate control**—an "air curtain" at the door will blow dust and pollen away as passengers board. It also will keep the interior temperature constant.

+ **Silence, please**—annoyed by neighbors who insist on playing their music or taking a call using the speakerphone? Speakers will be built into wraparound headsets, creating private "sound bubbles."

+ **Super seatbelts**—laptop-sized airbags will be packed into each seat's safety belts to provide extra cushion in case of a crash.

+ **Rocking chairs**—a prototype "premium seat" fully reclines into a "cloud swing" mode that rocks back and forth like a baby's cradle.

+ **Coordinated lighting**—exterior lighting and signage on the vehicle's body color coordinates with a passenger's smartphone app and digital key.

Boshoku believes its new designs could quadruple the company's revenue.

"For every car, we're going to sell at least four different modules plus the replacements," Richard Chung, chief branding officer for Boshoku's Interior Space Visioneering Center, told *Automotive News*. "We want to create new demand."

Some of the proposed changes—particularly the LED sanitizer lights and air curtains—could also find their way onto non-autonomous Toyota vehicles.

In addition to its car business, Toyota Boshoku supplies comfy seats for airplanes which, in general, get a new interior every six years or so. Boshoku wants to transfer that same model to fleets on the ground.

Toyota owns 31% of Toyota Boshoku, which gets 90% of its revenue from Toyota. But if its interiors take off, the company hopes to expand to other automakers.

Boshoku isn't the only one experimenting with design innovation.

Geely's Polestar, the automotive brand originally established by Volvo partner Flash/Polestar Racing in 1996, has introduced an electric car—the Polestar 4 SUV—that is missing a rear window.

This design innovation isn't waiting for autonomy. And why should it? Drivers are already using their rearview cameras to see who's coming up behind them. Polestar executives decided that the images in the mirror could be managed with high-definition cameras rather than old-school optics.

Removing the window "celebrates rear occupant comfort," says Polestar CEO Thomas Ingenlath, himself a designer in a former life. By removing the rear window, Polestar has been able to "move the whole structure further back. It creates a cocoon, Polestar's head of design, Maximilian Missoni told *Wired*.

Polestar's cameras are mounted on the roof of the car and deliver a much broader field of vision than cameras positioned at the back of the car.

Cutting out the physical rear windows elongates the Polestar 4's silhouette and makes the car more aerodynamic, which helps extend range.

Doesn't the lack of a window make the back seat claustrophobic? Polestar has incorporated other design features to address this.

There's a full-length glass roof that can switch between opaque and transparent. The glass roof stretches beyond the rear occupants' heads to finish at least part of the way into the area where a traditional rear window would sit.

Another change: larger rear headrests, since there's no need to worry about obscuring the view. *Wired* describes the Polestar's interior as one that "manages to be stimulating yet calm at the same time."

Audi's LDL ("long-distance lounger") concept—nicknamed a "living room on wheels"—also has tables for working and meetings, all of which become possible when you remove the steering wheel, pedals (and driver, of course).

CNET's Chris Paukert described the Audi LDL as an "upscale tiny studio apartment" complete with a refrigerator and seats can be easily moved, secured by powerful magnets.

Enzo Rothfuss, head of interior design at Audi, doesn't even call the LDL a car. He refers to it as "a moving object."

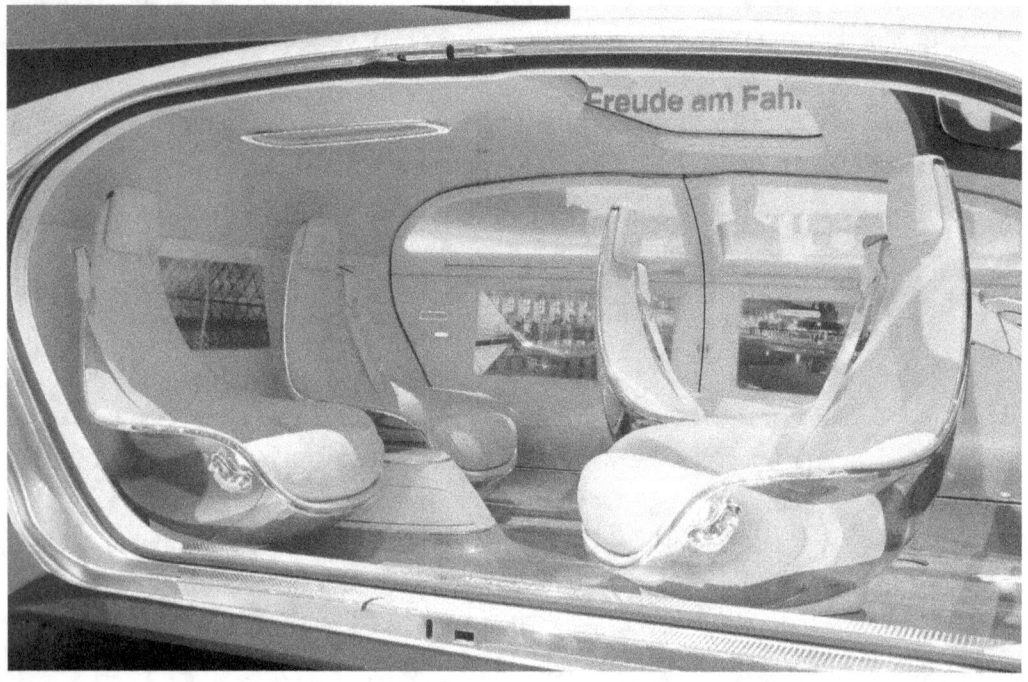

A Mercedes-Benz autonomous vehicle interior concept (credit: Shutterstock)

Mercedes's AV concept design is "Tardis-like" with a "minimalist use of space." The 4 seats in this relatively small vehicle swivel 30 degrees when you open the door, for easier access. It's built with premium materials—wood, leather, carpet.

Mercedes's F 015 "Luxury in Motion" concept car has a total of six touchscreens, four mounted in the doors, one in front that serves as a dashboard and can be controlled by gestures, and another on the back wall. The screens can display what the car is seeing outside or play live TV or movies.

Mercedes knows that full Level 5 autonomy is a long-distance run rather than a quick sprint, so the automaker has baked in a hidden steering wheel and pedals that pop out when the driver's seat spins around to face front.

Volvo's 360c is more like a first-class seat on a flight out of Dubai than a car. It has four modes. You can sit buckled in with a tray table. You can set up an office with a large fold-out table and a giant monitor. The seats can fold down into lie-flat beds. There's even a "party mode," reminiscent of a limousine with slots for bottles on ice.

Volvo is hoping that some commuters will prefer a six-hour ride in this ground vehicle to going wheels-up for an actual two-hour flight—what the company describes as "a lucrative competitor to short-haul air travel." You can get door-to-door service and a first-class sleeping environment without the bother of airport security, long lines, and the risk of getting sick in the air.

Interiors with couches and no drivers, wrap-around screens, an AI companion at your side—I can't wait to see what actually "sticks."

Autonomous school buses

Devin Liddell leads future-focused concept projects at Seattle-based Teague, which is promoting Hannah, an autonomous school bus concept. Teague's Hannah is less of a school bus and more like a school *van,* since this AV only seats six. But hey, they painted it yellow, at least.

The six-passenger maximum is intentional.

Small school vans can pick up students at their homes, rather than requiring them to walk to a bus stop. That saves money by eliminating a lot of unnecessary back and forth for route planners.

Hannah vans could also handle package deliveries between school pick-ups and drop-offs. The company has concept art featuring Amazon and Starbucks on the vehicles.

But will parents feel comfortable sending their children on an autonomous school van with no driver to supervise the kind of untoward behavior and bullying that is an unfortunate side effect of the school bus experience? What about bad actors, not other kids, attempting to gain access?

It's AI to the rescue.

Can a single driver actually supervise 50+ kids on a regular school bus? Most likely not.

Hannah will scan the irises of each student entering the vehicle. (It's not sci-fi—our iPhones already do that with facial recognition.) Any attempt at an unauthorized entry would be flagged immediately with an alert going to the school district's operations headquarters.

Interior cameras can monitor what's going on inside the cabin, whether that results in a prompt to put on your seatbelt, a reminder to take your backpack before you disembark, or a real-time view of potential bullying (which, in any case, is more likely to happen on a larger school bus).

Compared to a single forward-facing human, Hannah is "always on, always connected, and always ready to act," the company says.

Autonomy for seniors

In an article in *Fast Company,* Teague CEO Liddell speculates that autonomous RVs and mobile "micro-apartments" could enable seniors to visit their grandchildren without needing to co-opt a bedroom in their children's home.

Could these traveling self-driving homes also make the "snowbird" commute from cold northern climates like Toronto to sunny-year-round locations such as Boca Raton more comfortable?

"The future of aging isn't just about using autonomous vehicles to prolong the independence of older citizens living in their homes," Liddell writes. "It's about blending autonomous mobility with the home itself."

Next up: Build sensors into the car so that the vehicle can monitor seniors' health in their autonomous mobile homes, driving them straight to the emergency room if necessary.

"It's a new model of senior care, somewhere between assisted and independent living," Liddell notes.

This may strike readers as a highly unlikely direction, but it addresses a real need here: The loss of purpose many seniors feel when they retire or their kids have flown the nest. As the number of seniors over the age of 65 is set to double in the next three decades, Liddell asks, "Could we use autonomous vehicles with flexibly configured interiors to reconnect the skill sets of seniors with those communities?"

What might that include?

+ A retired accountant could set up an autonomous mobile office and travel to rural areas.

+ A retired software engineer could create a mobile coding lab.

+ An experienced woodworker could offer vocational training at resource-constrained youth detention centers.

"This future of aging mobilizes the expertise of seniors, restoring their vital sense of purpose by giving them new ways to contribute to their communities as professionals, educators, and mentors," Liddell concludes.

Autonomy in the air

Planes are already mostly autonomous. The pilot(s) only need to get involved during take-off, landing and if there's an emergency in the air. If so, why not replace human pilots in the cockpit with software?

The aviation industry uses two terms to describe the rules applying in the current situation: VFR and IFR.

+ Visual Flight Rules (VFR) stipulate no flying through clouds, just in blue sky. Like a Level 4 autonomous car, if there's poor visibility, a plane outfitted with just VFR won't operate at all.

✦ Instrument Flight Rules (IFR) are the standards used for flying in inclement weather. You don't look out the windscreen, you just look at your instruments.

Not every plane is equipped with the more sophisticated IFR, although all commercial jets are.

Would an entirely robot-driven plane be safer?

We're not there yet, although some airline companies are already experimenting with having just a single pilot in the cockpit, dropping the copilot for domestic flights.

It's a big change from "the old days" when a plane could easily have up to eight pilots—some in the cockpit and others flying as passengers as a backup.

Airbus is working on a project to bring more autonomy to the air. The project is dubbed "DragonFly" and is being tested on an Airbus A350-1000 craft.

Airbus's Isabelle Lacaze explains that DragonFly is "inspired by biomimicry and nature in the same way that dragonflies are known to have the ability to recognize landmarks. [Similarly], the systems being developed are designed to identify features in the landscape that enable an aircraft to 'see' and safely maneuver autonomously within its surroundings."

Will consumers accept a plane without a pilot? It's one thing to be in an autonomous land vehicle—dangerous, like any time one gets into a car—but doing it at 10,000 feet in the air is another matter entirely. Even a self-driving eVTOL could scare the wits out of even the bravest commuter, Rani Plaut, of AIR EV, reminds us.

Maybe once we've gotten used to robo-taxis, we'll accept robo-planes across the Atlantic, but this may not happen in my lifetime.

One reason passengers may be less comfortable with autonomy in the air vs. on land is that Airbus, Boeing and other aircraft makers have not exactly been transparent about what happens in the cockpit.

People really don't know that a pilot only flies the plane for an average of just seven minutes per flight, and mostly during take-off and landing. The rest is run by computers.

People are familiar with cars. They've driven them, they know what's happening, you can stop in an emergency. With autonomous aircraft you can't stop midair if there's a problem.

The European Union's Aviation Safety Agency notes that it will only sign off on single-pilot (and eventually no-pilot) operations "if an equivalent or better level of safety to today's two-pilot operations can be assured."

The agency is concerned about pilot workload and fatigue, pilot incapacitation (a heart attack, food poisoning), sleep inertia, situational awarenes, and error management.

Some kind of pilot incapacitation "happens once a month or more in most major aviation markets," says European Cockpit Association President Otjan de Bruijn.

One of the most dramatic examples: In 1990, the cockpit window broke on a British Airways flight. The pilot was partially blown out of the aircraft. Cabin crew held the pilot for 20 minutes while the copilot landed the plane.

In the future, there might not be a second pilot to save the day.

With so many concerns, it's no wonder Airbus says it could be 30 years before autonomy really migrates to your favorite trans-Atlantic route. Still, if a pilot typically draws $100,000 a year or more in salary, dropping one pilot could lead to big savings.

But will the cost be too high?

"Commercial interest is being put before flight safety," says de Bruijn. "Even the most recent history has shown that putting these economical gains before anything else as a primary goal will have a detrimental influence on flight safety."

De Bruijn points to the 2018 and 2019 crashes of two Boeing 736 MAX planes that killed a total of 346 people. Here, malfunctioning antistall software overwhelmed the pilots, who couldn't troubleshoot the problem or switch to manual operation before plunging to earth.

Could a self-flying plane run by computer algorithms diagnose its own code and avoid such tragedies?

"These developments," de Bruijn says, "should not be aimed at reducing the human capacity but enhancing the flight safety by enhancing the capacity of the two pilots on board."

But if single-pilot or pilot-less planes cost the consumer less, well, "cash is king," says Ashley Nunes, a research fellow at Harvard Law School. "If the price is low enough, you're going to catch that flight."

"Flying is not cheap," agrees Annette Groeneveld, president of the European Cabin Crew Association. "A flight from Amsterdam to Malaga for €35 is impossible, yet such flights are being offered to the public. Something has got to give, and that something is flight safety and security."

What we've learned

- The road to achieving full vehicle autonomy has proven challenging, with technological, regulatory, and safety hurdles to overcome. Nevertheless, there remains a sense of optimism for the future of this technology and its potential benefits for and beyond the automotive sector.

- The development of full autonomy holds the promise of significantly reducing accidents caused by human error, alleviating traffic congestion, and enhancing transportation accessibility for people with disabilities.

✦ Beyond traditional road vehicles, the strides made in full autonomy are poised to revolutionize industries such as agriculture, construction, mining, and warehousing.

- Autonomous tractors can increase crop yields while reducing the need for manual labor.
- Construction equipment can operate with precision and safety, increasing productivity and reducing human injury.
- Mining operations can become more efficient and eco-friendly.
- Warehouses can optimize logistics through autonomous robots.

✦ Non-automotive use cases offer a glimpse into a future where technology transforms a wide range of industries, enhancing productivity and safety while driving economic growth and sustainability.

■ ■ ■

Chapter 9

Connectivity

In the fall of 2022, if you happened to be in California, you might have noticed that the electronic traffic warning signs started sporting a surprising message, courtesy of the state's "Flex Alerts" program.

It read: "Please don't charge your cars between 4:00 pm and 9:00 pm."

California was in the midst of an unprecedented 10-day heatwave. Temperatures in Santa Rosa, north of San Francisco, hit 115 degrees Fahrenheit, the highest on record for a date in September.

The soaring mercury raised a severe risk that the state's electricity grid might not be able to handle the increased demand. If, in the past, that was mainly about running the air conditioner or washing machine during peak hours, the rapid adoption of EVs in California has thrust the region's Teslas, BMWs, and electric Volvos into the spotlight.

The messaging worked.

The grid didn't crash, the state didn't need to proactively power down service, and the rolling blackouts that had plagued the state during previous heatwaves were avoided.

Energy consumers in California weren't being entirely altruistic.

Hundreds of thousands of residents were paid for conserving power. As the website *Clean Technica* reports, "The grid operator in California wasn't just hoping those customers would show up and voluntarily cut demand—they were counting on them to do so and paying them accordingly."

That might be cash payouts or simply a better rate when charging is done during non-peak hours. So-called smart charging technology can help customers find the optimal—and cheapest—time to charge.

"The grid was never designed to be the fuel source for transportation," adds Suncheth Bhat, chief business officer of startup EV Realty.

The ability for cars and the grid to communicate is made possible by the latest connectivity options built into new vehicles. These can be summarized with several acronyms.

+ V2g—"Vehicle-to-grid" or "bidirectional" reverse charging allows a car to share back some of its charge with the electrical grid as needed.

+ V2i—"Vehicle-to-infrastructure" is how a car shares data with traffic infrastructure and vice versa. As a connected car approaches a traffic signal, if there's no one else nearby, why should the signal remain red?

+ V2h—"Vehicle-to-home" is when an EV provides power to the home, in case of power failure or, as in the California case, a massive, prolonged heatwave.

+ V2v—"Vehicle-to-vehicle" allows cars to communicate with each other. If there's a deer in the road ahead, the first car to encounter it can alert the next car, and the vehicle after that too.

+ V2x—"Vehicle-to-everything"—a catch-all phrase used in the industry.

In this chapter, we'll look at all these types of connectivity, and more.

Connectivity in history

Vehicle connectivity is a logical evolution to humanity's history with communication.

+ Neanderthals and early humans had verbal communication but not written.

+ In 1450, the Gutenberg printing press enabled dissemination of information at scale. Before that, monks could only repeat handwritten words in a book.

+ The Renaissance supercharged Gutenberg's invention.

+ Post offices made connectivity even more efficient. The U.S. Postal Service was established in 1775 with Benjamin Franklin as its famous first postmaster general.

+ Book stores made it possible to purchase a wide variety of information. The oldest bookstore is in France—Librairie Nouvelle d'Orléans—and has been operating since 1534. The oldest U.S. bookstore opened in 1745. Libraries made reading books free.

✦ Newspapers transcended village communication, first monthly, then weekly and daily. The first U.S. daily newspaper was published in 1784.

✦ Radio, following its introduction by Italian inventor Guglielmo Marconi in 1897, had a range even greater than newspapers.

✦ Broadcast TV, cable, 24/7 music and streaming all brought communication into the modern age.

✦ The internet is the ultimate connector—as well as the source of many of our communication and cultural battles.

What will come next? Interfaces in extended reality goggles, a la Apple's Vision Pro or Meta's Quest headsets? Elon Musk's Neuralink? Plugging into the matrix?

Virtual power plants to the rescue

We don't have to look to the future for examples of vehicle connectivity. They're happening now, right before our eyes.

"If you think of EVs as large batteries with motors and wheels—essentially energy storage devices—tapping their power to bolster the electric grid makes sense," writes *MotorTrend's* Doug Newcomb.

We are entering the era of the "virtual power plant," a collection of small-scale energy resources that, when aggregated together and coordinated with grid operations, "can provide the same kind of reliability and economic value to the grid as traditional power plants," *Clean Technica* notes.

The households that comprise these so-called virtual power plants rely on software to determine when they should charge their vehicles or use electricity-consuming devices, and whether the batteries in their EVs would be better off discharged, even partially, to support the grid in its time of need.

"Vehicle-to-grid has the potential to transform huge swaths of the energy infrastructure," says Scott Hinson, CTO for Pecan Street, an Austin, Texas-based nonprofit research organization that focuses on clean energy and smart grid technologies. "We've never added a load to the electrical grid that's as flexible as the electric vehicle."

V2g is a technological expansion to the kind of "time-of-use" pricing that's already been in place for years. "If we give people a little nudge, they will respond," suggests Max Baumhefner, a senior attorney at the National Resources Defense Council (NRDC).

V2g approaches involve actually *removing* electricity from the batteries and reversing the flow. It's based on algorithms that know, by having access to a vehicle owner's past behavior and history, how much of a charge will be required that day.

For example, if your charging provider sees that, after a day plugged in at work (and cars are typically parked 95% of the day), you have a 30-mile commute home, it knows you don't need to be 100% charged before heading to the highway. So, it only charges you up to, say, 80% when the grid looks likely to melt down from too much use all at once.

V2g schemes fit the description of "virtual power plant," since, if implemented properly, utilities can reduce the number of new power plants they need to build—or even shut down some of the more polluting sites entirely.

An estimate by the NRDC found that if California, which should have around 14 million EVs by 2035 if current projections hold, could exploit the power stored in all those batteries and send some of it back to the grid, "that would represent a collective battery that could theoretically power all of the homes in California for three days."

V2g tech is not limited to single-family homes. Offices, stores, factories, cars, trucks and buses can all become part of a virtual power plant—with their owners getting compensated for participating.

Virtual power plants can also help with decarbonization.

Clean Technica estimates that, by 2050, virtual plants could reduce the amount of CO_2 released into the air by 44 million to 59 million metric tons a year.

Customers must not be kept in the dark about when their utility is drawing power from their batteries.

"Giving the customer a heads-up that it might happen, even if it's just a day ahead, can be super helpful," says Samantha Houston, a senior vehicles analyst at the Union of Concerned Scientists. That could be via an app, an email, or even a notice on the car's dashboard.

Customers, of course, must always be given the option to opt out and fully charge their vehicles—for example, if an out-of-town trip is scheduled.

V2g has a big advantage over how California handled potential grid overloading during the 2022 heatwaves. Daily conservation alerts are "very non-granular," says Jan Kleissl, director of the Center for Energy Research at the University of California, San Diego. It's "a big hammer for a very sensitive subject. We can incentivize people that way, but we don't have any other good way to adjust the load on a smaller time scale, like 10 minutes or half an hour."

With v2g, "we can fine-tune the grid much better than we can do it now."

V2g isn't an entirely new concept.

"It's really analogous to what we saw in the solar industry," says Katie Sloan, vice president of customer programs and services at Southern California Edison, the Los Angeles-based utility. "That was the first time we were moving from one-way power flow into homes really having bidirectional power flow."

In 2022, there were more than 100 v2g pilots around the world (most in Europe).

For v2g to work, an EV must support bidirectional charging, which only a few cars, as of mid-2023, do. The Hummer, the F-150 Lightning, Mitsubishi's Outlander PHEV, the Nissan Leaf, and the Volvo EX90 can all do it. The Chevy Silverado EV and EVs from Volkswagen will be adding v2g functionality soon.

Tesla CEO Elon Musk is not a believer.

"I don't think many people will use bidirectional charging unless you have a Powerwall because if you unplug your car, your house goes dark and this is extremely inconvenient," Musk said at Tesla's 2023 Investors Day.

Is that Musk's not-so-subtle way of pushing the Powerwall, Tesla's home energy storage battery?

"If you have a Powerwall, that can take the house load, then use your car as a supplementary energy source to the Powerwall," he noted.

That said, Musk indicated Tesla might nevertheless offer v2g functionality within a couple of years.

Musk is not alone in dissing v2g: A 2019 report from Boston Consulting Group forecasts that, for every new EV added to its territory through 2030, a utility would need to spend an average of $1,700 to $5,800 on grid upgrades to enable charging.

Despite the excitement, we need to be realistic, says Mark Bole, head of v2x and battery solutions for GM Energy, which is running more than 20 v2g pilots. "V2g is most likely not going to come in a broad sense until 2025."

Another gating factor, says Bole, is that "there are more than 1,500 utilities in the U.S., and they are all very different and have their own systems . . . when standards are in place, we'll start to see more mass-production vehicles with v2g capabilities."

Today you can't go into a store and buy a bidirectional charger, he adds.

That's not an insignificant issue.

"From a consumer perspective, it has to be transparent and easy," says Andrew Meintz, chief engineer of EV charging and grid integration at the National Renewable Energy Laboratory. "That's going to require the utility or vehicle OEM [original equipment manufacturer] to understand how owners use their vehicles."

Bole described how it eventually could all work.

"Say a utility sends us a demand response for tomorrow at 3:00 a.m. and asks us to send a 'stop charge' command to the EV with the customer's agreement and knowledge. We then text our customers using that utility and ask, 'Can you not charge between 3:00 a.m. to 5:00 a.m. tomorrow, and will you allow us to turn off charging? If you accept, here's $20.'"

There's one more incentive for consumers: Selling energy back to the grid can improve vehicle battery life by around 10%, say researchers at the University of Warwick.

Lightning in your garage

Utilities may be rolling out v2g, but v2h—vehicle-to-home connectivity—is here already.

Ford is already promoting the fact that the 1,800-pound battery in the F-150 Lightning—the all-electric version of Ford's best-selling truck—can power a home for three days (and up to 11 days if you're careful with your power consumption) using the company's new Charge Station Pro. (*BloombergNEF's* Colin McKerracher adds that three F-150s could power an entire music festival.)

Some of that energy could be offloaded to the grid, or owners could simply choose to power their homes from their cars during a heat or cold wave.

Once the power comes back on, Ford's v2h system automatically switches to the grid and immediately starts to recharge your truck. Users can also dictate a minimum level of charge in the truck, so they're not stranded if they need to, you know, actually *drive* somewhere. Everything can be managed from a mobile app.

The Charge Station Pro's built-in inverter can output power through one 240-volt outlet or up to eleven 120-volt outlets. A fully charged battery holds 131 kWh of power—that's equivalent to having "seven-to-nine Tesla PowerWall home batteries sitting in your garage," writes Scott Evans in *MotorTrend*, referring to Tesla's competing home electrical storage system.

As solar energy becomes ever more popular and inexpensive, with homeowners adding solar panels to their roofs, home battery storage will be required once the sun has gone down or if the day is overly cloudy.

Ford says the Charge Station Pro can charge an F-150 Lightning's battery in 10 hours.

"I'm very excited by the bidirectional power of the F-150 Lightning," says Reilly Brennan, of Trucks VC. "A fleet of F-150s would have more power than all the filling stations in the U.S. It creates a distributed set of energy nodes. It's not as easy as filling up at a Shell station, but I'm curious as to what entrepreneurs will do with this and what software opportunities there are for charging infrastructure."

It's not exclusively about the Lightning—even the 2021 hybrid version of the F-150 can power a house off its hybrid battery.

The tech got a lifesaving preview during the Texas ice storms in the winter of 2021 when much of the state's power was knocked offline. F-150 Lightning owners could be found running extension cords from their trucks to HVAC systems and appliances.

In a less dire example, the city of Boulder, Colorado, saved around $250 a month on electricity by using a Nissan Leaf to power a city-owned recreation building.

"We feel like EVs can provide the notion of helping make power outages invisible for customers," notes Aaron August, VP of business development at Pacific Gas and Electric. "With the right configuration, you can weather an outage for hours at a time."

Nissan may be ideally positioned to capitalize on batteries repurposed for home energy storage: Nissan debuted the Leaf in 2010 and has more than 500,000 EVs on the road, "allowing us to further tap into second-life battery opportunities as vehicles come to the end of their lifecycles," Nissan senior VP Friederike Kienitz explains.

Nissan is collaborating with energy giant Enel to use repurposed EV batteries from the automaker to enhance grid stability at a power plant in Melilla, Spain.

Electric school buses can help the grid

We discussed autonomous school buses in a previous chapter. But those familiar yellow vehicles are getting in on the electric fun, too.

Electric school buses today comprise less than 1% of the 480,000 student-carrying vehicles in the U.S., not surprising given that they cost 3 times the price of an ICE school bus.

But if a school bus could power the grid during evening hours, that could close the price gap and further smooth out demand on the grid.

Dominion Energy is one of the bigger players in the school bus space; the Virginia-based utility is in the process of deploying some 1,000 e-buses in its home state.

Dominion's electric school buses will get between 120 and 135 miles per charge, with a full charge taking 3 hours. Dominion notes that the average daily round-trip school bus route is approximately 80 miles, well within range. Mark Webb, Dominion's senior vice president and chief innovation officer, notes that Virginia school districts could save $700 per month—$8,400 per year—per bus in operating costs.

Electrified school buses have a better v2g value proposition than passenger cars. They're a better source of distributed power because their usage patterns are predictable (they travel on fixed routes and have regularly-scheduled breaks), and they are idle 85% of the time, at precisely the times when energy demand is at its peak—midday and during the hot summer months after school's out.

A report by Securing America's Future Energy (SAFE) and the Electrification Coalition entitled "Advancing Vehicle-to-Grid Technology Adoption" named school buses as "of particular value" and noted that an electric school bus "could power the equivalent of 5 operating rooms for more than 8 hours, and a single operating room for 43 hours."

E-school buses to transport students also reduce the amount of fumes youngsters are exposed to. This is especially important for underrepresented minorities and lower-income families who are more dependent on school buses to get to class and whose family members tend to suffer disproportionately from asthma and other respiratory illnesses that are worsened by constant exposure to diesel exhaust.

Ryan Popple, CEO of Proterra, which is making the e-school buses for Dominion, says that Virginia's nearly half-million school buses could have a huge impact. "If you fully electrify the school bus fleet, you're offsetting a couple of nuclear power plants."

The Biden administration agrees.

In October 2022, the White House announced the winners of a $965 million subsidy program for electric and low-emissions bus purchases. The result: Orders have expanded more than tenfold since the beginning of 2021.

The Biden administration-backed infrastructure bill further dedicates $4 billion toward e-school bus purchases over the next four years.

Virginia is no longer a lonely pioneer. In Maryland, the Montgomery County Public Schools ordered 326 e-school buses to be delivered by 2025, to replace some of its 1,400 school buses which burn 17,000 gallons of diesel a day.

"This project is momentous, not just because of its size, but because it demonstrates something pretty remarkable, which is that electrifying a municipal fleet is not a pipe dream. It's not something that should be pushed off another year," says Duncan McIntyre, the chief executive of Highland Electric Fleets, which is delivering the buses and the charging and maintenance infrastructure to the Montgomery County schools.

San Diego Gas and Electric has launched a five-year pilot project with v2g tech company Nuvve involving a local school district and eight school buses.

Electric school buses are really just great big "batteries with wheels," says Miguel Romero, vice president of energy innovation at San Diego Gas and Electric. "I think it starts to become a bigger—a better—proposition to potentially have these large amounts of energy parked in certain parking lots provide energy back."

"The school bus industry is almost at the tip of the spear when it comes to vehicle-to-grid technology," adds Kevin Matthews, managing director, sustainability sector, for National Strategies, a Washington-based research and consulting firm. "The lightbulbs have gone off, especially with utilities, that, yeah, we can figure out our vehicle-to-grid issues with school buses," Matthews told *Automotive News*.

"When you've got big-city districts that have a few thousand buses," Matthews stresses, "it really makes a difference."

Or as *Automotive News*'s Pete Bigelow noted in 2021, "Electrifying school buses without allowing for the two-way flow of energy would be akin to investing in pagers at a time when cellphones were on the horizon."

Battery swap meets v2g

Gogoro, the battery swap network for e-scooters and micromobility in Southeast Asia, has teamed up with global utility firm Enel X's Virtual Power Plant in Taiwan.

Enel X began testing Gogoro's GoStations as virtual power plants in 2022. The following year, Gogoro and Enel X announced they would be rolling out another 2,500 swap stations-cum-virtual power plants.

A Gogoro battery swap station (credit: Wikimedia Commons)

The stations are designed to interact with Taiwan's power grid, pausing their own charging to resupply energy back to Enel X when local demand maxes out existing supply.

For Gogoro, it represents an additional source of revenue.

"We have always believed that time-shifting energy was key to enabling the sustainable transformation of energy and transportation," Horace Luke, Gogoro's CEO, says.

The idea to help out the Taiwanese national power grid originated with a 2022 power outage that cut off electricity for some five million households and prevented gas stations from pumping fuel. But Gogoro-powered e-scooters were still able to swap batteries because the stations could operate based on the power stored in their own battery packs.

"Our work with Gogoro is a world-leading demonstration of what virtual power plants can do," notes Jeff Renaud, head of Enel X Asia and Oceania.

Can the grid handle it?

Even with v2g, some have expressed concerns about whether the grid can handle all the power requirements of the coming all-EV world.

Axios's Joann Muller analyzed the current situation in California. She says the worries are unfounded.

As of July 1, 2022, California had roughly 680,000 registered EVs, according to S&P Global Mobility, accounting for less than 1% of the state's total electricity demand. Even if there are 5 million EVs by 2030, they'll still only account for around 7% of annual electricity usage and 1% of peak demand, Muller says, quoting the California Air Resources Board.

In general, experts believe EVs will make up a third or even half of all light vehicles sold annually in the U.S. by 2030.

Muller's analysis doesn't take into account what happens if EVs like the F-150 are providing some of the power *back* to the grid.

While the ability of the grid to generate enough power to charge all those EVs may not be in question, the "last mile" could still prove a bottleneck.

Like fast internet and fiber-optics, the local legs of the electric grid—the wires and transformers—that transmit power to individual homes and businesses will need expensive upgrades.

Will this result in higher electricity rates? I wouldn't rule it out.

There are also technical hurdles to overcome.

Even if vehicles come with built-in v2g and v2h capabilities, most battery chargers are not yet set up for that functionality, so for school buses and electric Hummers to consistently power the grid, a lot of infrastructure will still need to be built.

Will two-way chargers be only for private home and office use? Or will public chargers also give drivers the option to earn some extra cash by not "filling up" all the way to 100%?

"Policymakers must act now," says Robbie Diamond, founder of SAFE and the Electrification Coalition. "We cannot afford for v2g capabilities to be an afterthought during the electrification of our transportation system."

Other forms of connectivity

I've focused so far on the interaction between EVs and the grid, but connectivity is about more than energy flow.

Indeed, ABI Research indicated nearly 203 million connected cars were shipped in 2022. In Europe, 70% of cars sold in 2020 were connected. In the U.S., 91% of new vehicles sold today are connected.

Guidehouse Insights has numbers that are slightly lower. The consulting group puts the total annual sales figure for connected cars at "more than 117 million vehicles" by 2028.

The market value for connected cars is expected to grow from $80 billion in 2023 to $165 billion in 2028, according to *The Business Research Company*, McKinsey estimates that the overall revenue pool from car data monetization could reach $750 billion by 2030. On a per-vehicle level, this equates to $310 in revenue and $180 in savings per year.

In my previous book, *The Future of Automotive Retail*, I looked at a number of forms of connectivity that go beyond v2x.

Over-the-air updates

In 2013, a Tesla Model S caught fire after it ran over a piece of debris in the road that apparently punctured or dented the car's battery pack. In response, Tesla pushed an over-the-air (OTA) update to all its Model S vehicles that raised the car's ride height when it hit highway speeds.

Tesla CEO Elon Musk insisted at the time that the update to the vehicle's suspension system was "about reducing the chances of underbody impact damage, not improving safety," but the real importance was how it demonstrated another advantage of the connected car.

As with a laptop or a mobile device, today's cars can update their operating systems and add value-added features without entailing a visit to a physical repair shop or dealer.

Bosch reports that new cars have over 100 million lines of software code. McKinsey suggests that will double in the coming years to 300 million.

OTA updates can take place overnight via Wi-Fi or using a cellular signal.

OTA updates can add temporary functionality. Would you like four-wheel drive in the winter but not in the summer? Subscribe and then unsubscribe.

Going on a family road trip and want to add live TV to the seatback screens? Press a button, pay a small fee and the kiddies will be entertained for the duration of the ride.

OTA updates are not limited to Tesla, of course.

+ Ford has built OTA updates into its Mustang Mach-E and F-150 Lightning. The company says it expects to have 33 million OTA-capable vehicles on the roads by 2028.

✦ Porsche's Mission-E will offer OTA updates, with Porsche chairman Oliver Blume giving the example of a 400-horsepower vehicle that could be upgraded over-the-air to 450 hp.

✦ Mercedes says 1.3 million vehicles could avoid a dealership visit to repair a communications module if the driver subscribes to the company's "Mercedes Me" service, which includes OTA updates.

✦ BMW charges $220 for an OTA update that allows drivers to dim their headlights, so they don't blind others. It's part of BMW's "High Beam Assistant" package. Another BMW OTA update would have charged drivers $18 a month for a heated seat—until consumers balked at the idea of paying extra to unlock existing features. An "IconicSounds Sport package," which lets you play gasoline-powered engine sounds in your EV and was designed together with Hollywood composer Hans Zimmer, will set you back $117 as a one-time fee.

✦ Tesla has more OTA updates up its sleeve. The company's Full Self-Driving mode can be unlocked over-the-air. Teslas can also alert drivers if they've left their car with a window, door or trunk open. There are OTA updates for drivers who want to improve braking, range, and power consumption.

In the future, I wouldn't be surprised if you'll be able to change the color of your car though an OTA update!

Despite the promise, OTA updates are still far from perfect.

In 2018, for example, users of Fiat Chrysler's Uconnect system discovered, after an OTA update, that their entertainment and navigation systems would reboot every 45 seconds, during which time drivers couldn't listen to the radio or use the GPS or even the rear-facing camera.

Personalization sells

Always-connected functionality can personalize your ride in ways never before imagined.

By communicating with the manufacturer's centralized server, your car will know your usual commuting route, whether and where you stop for your morning brew, where you plug in to charge (if you're driving an electric vehicle), your kids' and spouse's birthdays (and what types of chocolate or flowers they favor), medicines you regularly take (plus where and when to refill them), what music, news or podcasts you enjoy on your way to work, and much more.

That could spark battles behind the scenes between retailers.

+ If you're a regular Starbucks customer, for example, could you be swayed by an in-dash coupon for a free cuppa at Dunkin'?

+ Would you pay extra for a no-ad interface (much like you can bypass the ads in Spotify or YouTube with a premium subscription)?

Your car could also display a prompt with the vehicle's current trade-in value. It might start at 70% of the price you paid. When it gets down to 20%, will you be ready to sell? If your car is leased, will you be pleased or pissed if Toyota tries to convince you to buy another Prius when the lease period is coming to an end?

When cars become more autonomous, will they read your emails to you while you're commuting? Will they remind you it's your wedding anniversary tonight and ask if you would you like to make reservations at that little place you liked so much last year?

"Would you prefer the yellow roses again or something different this time?" your car might inquire.

It sounds creepy and privacy infringing, but the aim is to make your life easier and more efficient the more your car (and all your devices, for that matter) know about your habits and preferences.

Have you been slacking off at the gym? Your car can block off an hour for you tonight if you're willing (and if you packed your Lululemon yoga pants in the trunk—something which your car will undoubtedly prompt you to remember for next time). Maybe in the future, the car can wirelessly check your weight, BMI and blood pressure to further motivate you to hit the gym.

V2i and v2v

This form of connectivity allows a vehicle to communicate with stationary infrastructure such as traffic lights, which would essentially become nodes in a mesh network. V2i can improve traffic congestion through parking assistance, traffic-jam notifications and dynamic traffic-light control, as well as traffic safety with warnings for hazardous situations such as railroad crossings.

To work effectively, v2i will require ubiquitous, seamless and reliable broadband. Several industry groups are advocating that older 802.11p radio technology be upgraded to C-V2X, which is based on a cellular standard and combines cellular networks with direct communication between vehicles, infrastructure, and other drivers.

Tactile Mobility uses v2i to assist municipalities in collecting data about their roads. The company taps into the sensors already installed in a car (the ones that control the steering and braking) to inform the city whether the roads are slippery (the car is gripping the road tightly) or when there are potholes (the car is bumping up and down). Drivers just drive; there's no need to press any buttons to report road conditions.

V2v—vehicle-to-vehicle communication—could make driving much safer. Like v2i, which can alert you to potholes and ice, v2v could tap into the cameras of cars in front of you to see what's coming. You don't have to wait until you see red taillights; your car will proactively slow down.

Another useful example of v2v and v2i: If a car in front of yours just ran over some lumber that fell off a truck on the expressway, all the cars will know that and everyone will slow down or autonomy could seamlessly move the cars to different lanes to get out of the way, all while signaling the city to dispatch someone to pick up the pieces.

Despite the benefits, drivers might still rebel and turn off their connectivity.

We're already seeing that with ADAS systems.

According to a 2019 study by J.D. Power, alerts on advanced driver-assistance systems can be so annoying that drivers are disabling them.

"The constant alerts can confuse and frustrate drivers," says Kristin Kolodge, executive director of driver interaction and human-machine interface research at J.D. Power. "The technology can't come across as a nagging parent; no one wants to be constantly told they aren't driving correctly."

An example: 23% of drivers complain that the beeps associated with lane-keeping and centering systems are "annoying" or "bothersome."

Among those users, 61% say they sometimes disable the system. Yikes!

"If they can't be sold on lane-keeping—a core technology of self-driving—how are they going to accept fully automated vehicles?" wonders Kolodge.

Can OTA updates reduce vehicle recalls?

Recalls are costly and time-consuming—for both automakers and consumers. It can take months for dealers to schedule all customers impacted by a recall. An OTA update to fix a recall problem, by contrast, requires only a few minutes to complete—a huge convenience and savings.

OTA updates can also increase the chance of repairing *all* of the vehicles covered by a recall.

✦ In 2019, Carfax estimated that 63 million vehicles in operation had open safety recalls, a 34% increase from 2016.

* Only about 70% of recalls are completed, according to the National Highway Traffic Safety Administration.

* In 2020, more than 31 million vehicles were recalled for safety-related problems in the U.S.

* The average cost of an automotive recall over the last 10 years was about $500 per vehicle, according to AlixPartners. Multiply that by the 31 million vehicles recalled in 2020, and you get to about $16 billion in recall work.

* ABI Research estimated in 2015 that, of the $18 billion manufacturers spent on warranty work, some $6 billion could have been saved if OTA updates were available at the time.

* IHS Markit (part of S&P Global) estimates that automakers will save $60.6 billion by 2025 through OTA savings around avoidance of recalls and warranty work.

AUTOMAKER COST SAVINGS FROM OTA UPDATES
($ billions)

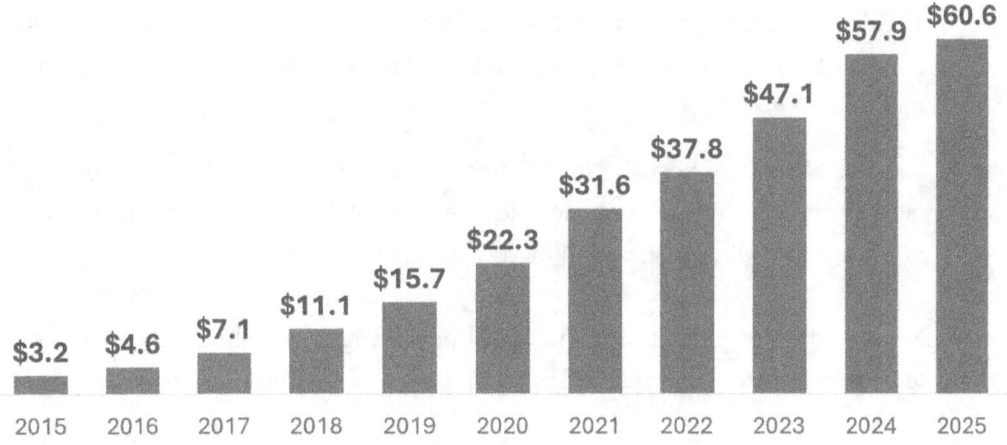

Automakers are expecting to save billions from over-the-air updates. (credit: IHS Markit)

How much would you pay?

"Tech companies are killing it with subscriptions," notes Jay Vijayan of Tekion, which has developed an AI-powered dealer management system. Vijayan was formerly the chief information officer at Tesla.

"Apple, Google and so many services are just easy to purchase. I don't use them half the time—for example, I have three different backup services. But people will pay for peace of mind, for preventative care."

How much would people pay for such a "repair subscription" for their connected cars? Vijayan suggests $9.99 a month, close to the streaming TV model.

"People won't mind paying for something they feel good about, even if they may not need it all the time," Vijayan suggests.

Here's a quick look at other connectivity pricing plans:

✦ Tesla's "premium connectivity" plan, which includes OTA updates, is $9.99 per month.

✦ A premium subscription to GM's OnStar connectivity plan runs significantly more at $25 per month and is required if users want to receive Super Cruise maps and hands-free driving functionality.

✦ Alan Wexler, senior vice-president of innovation and growth for GM, says he believes that customers will be willing to spend $135 on average for "the right mix of compelling offerings." GM's Ultifi software platform could include up to 25 different products and services.

✦ The data plan that comes with the Volkswagen ID.4 electric vehicle is free—but only for the first month. After that, you'll need to pay $20 each month for a Verizon mobile data plan.

✦ Nissan's NissanConnect service has four price points, ranging from $8 to $12.99 per month. It includes remote door locking, a vehicle health report, maintenance notifications, OTA updates, and map and traffic features.

McKinsey estimates that consumers would be willing to pay about $13 a month for advanced map features and personalized navigation, or for fuel- and cost-efficiency features.

The connected car in action

Cliff Banks, automotive industry analyst and editor of *The Banks Report*, describes how he imagines a connected car could interact with passengers.

"Let's say I'm on my way out of town for a work meeting. I get into my car, which is already warmed up. I use the remote start app from my phone. The steering wheel and seats are already heated. The car greets me via Alexa or some other generative AI software that is integrated with all of the vehicle's systems. 'Welcome back, Cliff. Traffic to the airport is light. And by the way, you'll need new brakes in about a month. ABC Motors has a slot open next Wednesday at 5:30 pm. Would you like me to set an appointment? Would you prefer to bring me to the dealer or have me picked up at your home? Will you need a loaner car or a ride home?' The point is: It's not the dealer or the manufacturer telling me I need new brakes. It's the car. And it's communicating with the dealership service department or repair shop, the parts department, suppliers and shippers."

Indeed, every time someone presses a button or swipes on a touchscreen in a connected car or truck, feedback should be recorded that can help manufacturers improve their vehicles' interfaces going forward. If they see that drivers need to constantly monkey around with the temperature controls or that it takes a long time to fumble through the radio stations, it's worth stepping back to figure out how to make those more user-friendly.

If a connected car relies on drivers syncing their phones with their cars and it's been a month since the last sync, that tells the automaker that there must be some sort of problem. Maybe there's a new phone in the family or the sync software is malfunctioning, and the driver doesn't know how to fix it.

The automaker or dealer could reach out proactively: "We'd be happy to send someone to your driveway to help."

Or maybe the problem is serious but hidden.

If the connected car detects a wiring bug, it could alert drivers: "You need to get your electrical cables changed, otherwise they could spark a fire in your garage."

That would get my attention fast!

"I'd put my money on the Internet of Things for cars that can self-diagnose a failure and then upload a software revision to fix the issue the next time the vehicle is parked," Bill Cariss of Holman Growth Partners told me.

For predictive analytics, Automotive Ventures has invested in Toronto-based Pitstop, which sends telematic data on a vehicle's performance over the air to the company's cloud-based AI engine. The collected data—some 10 billion data points—is intended to help generate predictive insights so fleet managers can see when their vehicles will need service to stay in tiptop shape. Pitstop says it can predict potential failures weeks in advance with 90% accuracy.

Privacy concerns

How much does the car need to know about you? Does it really need to know when you last went to the gym or what groceries you most recently bought?

The connected cars of the future will have the same kinds of privacy concerns that regulators are concerned about for our computers and phones today.

"Building a connected car service today is much more difficult than providing applications before the smartphone days," writes Amit Karp of Bessemer Venture Partners, which invested in connected car software company Otonomo. "The solution to this will either be a common car operating system—unlikely given the OEMs' fear of the tech giants—or a third-party platform that simplifies launching connected car services."

Andrea Amico, CEO of Privacy4Cars, another portfolio company of Automotive Ventures, pointed out that privacy for vehicles is reaching a tipping point.

"Many companies today think privacy is a compliance chore, best handled by lawyers whose job is checking as many boxes while changing as little as possible current practices," Amico told me. "Yet companies are failing at monetizing data, regulators are chipping away at those models, and perhaps most important, consumer sentiment is dramatically shifting."

Amico observes that independent surveys show 4 out of 10 consumers say data privacy is "highly important" in the vehicle shopping and ownership experience (more than body styling and infotainment features), and 9 out of 10 do not trust the manufacturer with their data.

"Our clients recognize that privacy is an opportunity: It's about meeting unmet customer demand, creating a value proposition around it, and outcompeting laggards—just like Volvo did with safety or Tesla with electrification. "

Connectivity can also save consumers money.

After you download Progressive Insurance's Snapshot, the app monitors your driving for the first 30 days, then offers you a price quote. If you drive more aggressively, tailgate and go around corners faster, you will be ranked as more of a risk (and, therefore, deserving of higher rates) than someone who never exceeds the speed limit.

The app monitors how many times you had to hard brake and whether you drive late at night (uh-oh, your rates just went up).

Good drivers save on average around $146 a year, the company says.

Insurance apps like Progressive's are becoming increasingly common; some are based just on what the app can determine using sensors already built into the phone. Others plug into the onboard diagnostics (OBD2) interface under the dashboard to glean data directly from the car. (OBD2 has been a mainstay of internal combustion engine vehicles but is not as relevant for electric cars.)

Will drivers be given the choice to opt-in to these kinds of services?

Will they be able to easily unsubscribe or purge their data on request?

What incentives will drivers need to be comfortable with how their data is being used?

Finally, what happens if your car is hacked—not to disable your brakes in a terror attack, but a more prosaic (and common) kind of hack: to steal your shopping preferences and personal information?

OEMs will need to be super careful to anonymize any and all data that's being sold, ensuring that no names or social security numbers are attached.

How about using biometric data to unlock and authenticate a car's operations?

An Israeli startup, EchoID, has taken a page from the TV commercials from the 1970s where two snack lovers accidentally combine peanut butter and chocolate to create the perfect new candy bar.

EchoID's sweet mix has nothing to do with candy; it's a blend between a breathalyzer and a sensor that can identify a specific user to provide a new level of protection against stolen vehicles—and drunk drivers—in a single device.

In order to start your car, you first need to blow into the device embedded in your car immobilizer's fob. A video from the company showed a drunk young man, desperate to get home but blocked by the device, ask a passing stranger to blow. He does, but EchoID stops him, since the acoustic wave that EchoID generates to authenticate the correct user doesn't match the stranger.

Drivers are interested

Consulting firm SBD Automotive conducted a survey of 2,500 recent-model (2016 or newer) car owners in France, Germany, Italy, Spain and the U.K.

Among the findings:

+ Up to 77% of consumers are interested in services based on connected car data.

+ Up to 71% of those who expressed interest in connected car services would be willing to share data specific to their cars, although the percentage drops off for services related to convenience rather than safety. (Alerts on dangerous driving conditions were top ranked; on-demand car washes came in much lower.)

+ 80% say they would consider sharing data if they received an incentive. Top incentives include cheaper car insurance, discounts on servicing, longer warranty periods and upgrades that can help prevent breakdowns.

+ More than half of European consumers are OK with sharing anonymized data.

+ 60% of respondents say it's very important to be told exactly what data is being collected, how it is being used and by whom.

+ 59% say the trustworthiness of the company or app is very important.

+ 75% want to see the car data they are sharing.

Willingness to share is closely tied to what data is going out and what benefit will be received.

Let's say your car has just run over a nail; if your vehicle can alert you the second after the spike encounter that you're going to have a problem, rather than waiting for the tire to begin deflating later in the day, you'll be more willing to share. You don't have to answer a dozen questions on the phone—the car will have already informed the dealer or repair shop that there's a nail problem and that within the next three hours, the tire will be flat.

A message reading "unless you put air in your tires today, there's a 77% chance the tire will blow" or "your battery is discharging faster than it should, let's get you an update" is a similarly strong call to action.

A call from your insurance company after you've stopped short on the highway to avoid an accident could be considered intrusive—but if you're "rewarded" for defensive driving, you might embrace being monitored.

GM's OnStar subsidiary is programmed to call you over the car's speakerphone automatically if it detects your airbags have inflated. If it can't reach you, the next call is to emergency services.

Then there are sensors that remind you that you've left something in the back seat—a pet . . . or a baby? It's hard to argue with the usefulness of that!

Connected car risks

Still, there are risks. Here are five, per the European Data Protection Board:

1. **Lack of control and information asymmetry**—drivers and passengers may not be adequately informed about the processing of data taking place in a connected vehicle, especially when that communication is triggered automatically.
2. **Quality of the user's consent**—classic web-based mechanisms for obtaining consent may be difficult to apply in a connected car that's in motion.
3. **Further processing of personal data**—initial consent for data collection does not cover how data will be used by a third party. Consent needs to be informed and specific to be valid.
4. **Excessive data collection**—is more data being accessed than is necessary to achieve a particular purpose?
5. **Security**—data stored on external servers is subject to the usual cyber-security vulnerabilities. Is your connected car data more secure than your Google password?

The good news is that consumer trust in automakers is on a par with trust in credit-card companies (which have the capabilities to detect fraud almost instantly in many cases, with mostly no-questions-asked refunds, resulting in a top ranking on the trust scale).

Sixty-two percent of respondents in Europe were confident that OEMs will properly secure their personal information.

In the U.S., it's even higher: 71% trust manufacturers to keep their data safe.

Let's hope their trust is not misplaced!

Hackers gotta hack

Privacy may be of little concern to future generations, but hacking remains a scourge. Hackers could access the personal data stored in your connected car, or they could use the car's connectivity to cause mayhem and death.

"The amount of code in today's cars means the number of bugs and potential hacks grows more than linearly," Andrea Amico, of Privacy4Cars, told me. "I don't know how we *aren't* going to see something ugly in the next few years."

Here are some of the scenarios I'm worried about:

+ Imagine a hacker points all the connected cars in Brooklyn toward the Williamsburg Bridge and drives them off into the East River. Or a hacker tells all plugged-in cars to charge at maximum power all at once—an event that would most likely take down the electrical grid.

+ What if a hacker got into Elon Musk's Starlink satellites and shut them down? How many people around the world are reliant on that internet connection?

+ Hackers might make the need for human hijackers, like those who masterminded 9/11, irrelevant in the future. The autonomous plane would simply fly itself into the next Twin Towers. Or a hacked autonomous car could plow into a sidewalk full of people.

+ Ransomware is devastating when a hacker takes over your computer and demands Bitcoin payments to unlock your data. It would be even worse if you're stranded on the side of the road in the middle of a blizzard or if the hackers threaten to drive your car into oncoming traffic unless you pay up.

+ Could hackers lock your children in the car with the air conditioning turned off? Similar things have happened even without the hack: A Tesla owner in Phoenix was trapped in his car on a 100-degree day when his battery died, and he couldn't open the door or windows without power. Fortunately, the Model Y has an emergency latch located under the window switches by the front seat.

+ Hacking yourself: If BMW wants to charge a fee for heated seats, "how hard would it be to install a physical switch to unhook the seat from the computer and turn it on?" asks Amico. "Will BMW brick the car in response? Maybe."

+ And, of course, hacking autonomous vehicles and robots on the battlefield could be devastating to both sides. Can you say "Skynet?"

Will the connected car spoil all our fun?

One last thought before we leave our discussion of connected cars: Could they put a damper on spontaneous backseat trysts?

Imagine two teenagers getting hot and heavy in Mom & Dad's vehicle. Little did they know that the sensors in the car would soon go off.

+ There's too much weight in one section and the car is all out of balance.

+ Does everyone have their seat belts fastened?

+ Why is there no one in the front seat? Who's got eyes on the road?

Turn it off temporarily? You can't—your insurance company will cut you off.

It's kind of a buzz kill. No wonder studies are finding that millennials and Gen-Zs are having less romance than their baby boomer counterparts!

What we've learned

+ The Internet of Things (IoT) has made remarkable progress in recent years, ushering in a new era of connectivity and data-driven insights. On the positive side, IoT has revolutionized various industries, enhancing efficiency, convenience, and safety. IoT applications are ubiquitous—from smart homes that automate daily tasks to health-care devices that monitor patient health remotely. In agriculture, IoT optimizes resource utilization, while in industry, it enables predictive maintenance and process optimization. IoT also plays a pivotal role in environmental monitoring and smart cities, improving sustainability and urban planning.

✦ However, these advancements come with challenges. Security and privacy concerns are paramount, as the proliferation of connected devices increases vulnerability to cyberattacks. Additionally, the massive data generated by IoT systems can strain networks and raise issues regarding data ownership and usage.

✦ The balance between the benefits and risks of IoT continues to evolve as the technology progresses, making it imperative to navigate its expansion thoughtfully and responsibly.

■ ■ ■

Chapter 10

Supply chain

"**I**t's not a single link that failed in a linear system," says Robert Swinney, an operations professor at Duke University. "It is the response of a complex system to major changes in conditions. Things like factories, ports, and trucking capacity are expensive, so they're designed to run at high utilization. That means they don't have a lot of excess capacity. Each bottleneck needs to be fixed and that immediately exposes another bottleneck."

Or, put another way, "The age of an efficient, globalized supply system has passed," C.C. Wei, CEO of Taiwan Semiconductor Manufacturing, told attendees at a tech symposium in 2022.

Welcome to the Great Supply Chain Crisis.

Surface freight transportation in the U.S. is a $1 trillion market. Trucking constitutes 64% of the total U.S. freight by tonnage and approximately 80% of the total inland freight. The total addressable market of freight (not just surface) is $4 trillion, comparable to that of ride-sharing and delivery (around $5 trillion each).

But, by many accounts, the supply chain for mobility is broken.

Part of that is due to, of all things, tires.

The cost of rubber surged by 70% year-over-year from May 2020 to May 2021, according to the Singapore Commodity Exchange.

Part shortages have also plagued trucking companies.

It can take 15-to-30 days longer to get parts at body shops compared to the prepandemic period, leading to a 20% to 30% increase in the cost of overall truck parts.

If the missing parts contain microchips, the delay can be even worse.

Wei points out that a shortage of a certain chip costing a mere 50 cents was holding up the production of $50,000 cars.

The pandemic was then supplanted—at least in terms of its immediate economic effect—by Russia's war with Ukraine.

A shortage of drivers

By far the biggest cause of the Great Supply Chain crisis has been an acute shortage of truck drivers.

A 2021 report by the American Trucking Association found a shortage of 80,000 drivers in the U.S., where turnover in the job can reach as high as 90% for large carriers.

That number could double by 2030 as more drivers retire, the association added, especially since the trucking companies say there are not enough young people interested in replacing those aging out of the workforce.

The American Trucking Association estimates that, over the next decade, the industry will have to recruit nearly a million new drivers to replace retiring drivers and drivers who leave voluntarily.

The driver shortage primarily affects medium-to-large trucking companies that are losing their drivers to smaller, independent firms. *FreightWaves* and Carrier Details estimate that the number of trucking carriers has increased by 45% since 2019.

For those larger companies, the driver shortage was already a problem before Covid-19, but the pandemic changed everything, unmasking serious and mostly unresolved bottlenecks hiding in plain sight that slowed the normally steady supply of everything from aluminum to semiconductors, resulting in long delays for a wide variety of consumer products, including, for the purposes of this book, new cars.

When the pandemic hit in early 2020, delivery times by manufacturing and construction suppliers in the U.S. soared by 30%, reports Kim Moody, a founder of the web publication *Labor Notes*.

In other words, a delivery that previously took two days would now take over two-and-a-half days. That fell somewhat by the end of the year, but then shot up again by more than two-thirds by mid-2021.

Delivery delays have ripple effects. One study of 397 U.S. companies between 2005 and 2014 found that a single supply chain disruption—of any kind—caused operating income to drop by 26.5% and sales to fall nearly 5%, Moody reports.

While the semiconductor shortage has more to do with lockdowns and quarantines at Chinese manufacturing plants than with a shortage of drivers, back in the U.S., the supply and demand problem was unmistakable.

Just visit one of the nation's ports.

Gene Seroka, the executive director of the Port of Los Angeles, told the White House in 2021 that 30% of the port's appointments for truckers went unused, largely due to the shortage of drivers as well as warehouse workers.

It got so bad U.S. President Joe Biden proposed—facetiously?—that the National Guard could be deployed to alleviate the shortage.

A 2021 World Bank study ranked Los Angeles along with Long Beach—the two largest ports in the United States—dead last in efficiency.

With worldwide spending on logistics at some $9 trillion, or 11%, of global GDP in 2020, manufacturers are increasingly looking to build resiliency, identify multiple sources for parts and materials, regionalize supply chains, and broaden their supplier base.

Competition is fierce. The winners in supply chain technology will be those that develop and deploy solutions that bring down costs and speed decision making.

$70,000 jobs that no one wants

"I've been in the business for over 30 years," Derek Leathers, president and CEO of Werner Enterprises, told *The New York Times*. "I definitely think this is the tightest truck driver market I've seen in my career."

Even with salaries reaching $70,000 a year, fewer people are willing to be away from home for the long stretches truck driving entails. Time spent waiting to unload cargo (which increased during the pandemic) has resulted in lower wages for drivers.

Increasing weight limits would allow trucks to haul more cargo—it's something for which car haulers have been lobbying for years, especially as the Environmental Protection Agency reports that the average weight of a car or truck increased from 3,200 pounds to 4,200 pounds over the last four decades.

Electric cars with their huge, heavy batteries are even bulkier.

The Ford F-150 Lightning weighs about 1,600 pounds more than its F-150 ICE counterpart. The all-electric Volvo XC40 utility vehicle is 1,000 pounds more than its ICE equivalent.

"The truth is, we will not be able to move as many electric vehicles under the current weight limit," notes Sarah Amico, who became chairman of the Jack Cooper Transport board in 2020. "That could mean more trucks on the road, delays in orders, and increased costs."

Current limits for big rigs are 80,000 pounds of gross vehicle weight. The truck and trailer itself account for half that amount. The American Trucking Association has asked lawmakers to raise the limit by 10%. That increase would allow the same trucks to haul as many EVs as gas-powered cars.

But what impact will these changes have on the health of drivers who must still load and unload the cargo mostly by hand? That's a big reason that safety experts are warning against heavier vehicles, which they say are harder to stop, more prone to roll, and cause more wear and tear on roads and bridges.

The railroads are also opposed, as it could take away some of their shipping business.

Still, something clearly needs to be done.

Jack Cooper pays drivers $90,000 a year plus pension and health benefits, along with a $10,000 signing bonus.

There are, nevertheless, few takers, David Heide, Jack Cooper's then-chief executive, lamented.

This is not a problem that emerged out of nowhere.

"There is no driver shortage; there's a retention problem," Mike Doncaster, a 30-year veteran and driver trainer, told the U.K. publication *The Guardian*. Doncaster notes that, of the five drivers he's trained in recent years, only one stuck with the industry.

"It's not a job; it's a lifestyle—and new recruits don't receive enough pay for the lifestyle," he explains.

Deregulation and constant pressure to deliver goods at ever-cheaper prices have resulted in working conditions so poor and pay rates so low that labor economists have dubbed truck driving essentially "indentured servitude."

"If you can work construction and get paid $20 an hour and be home every night, why would you drive a truck and get paid $10 an hour to not be home for weeks?" asks Wayne State University professor and author of *Sweatshops on Wheels*, Michael Belzer.

Backed up at the port

At the height of the supply chain crisis, American manufacturers were waiting a record 92 days on average to assemble the parts and raw materials they needed to make their goods, according to the Institute of Supply Management.

It was hard to miss that reality at the Port of Savannah where, at the height of the pandemic, nearly 80,000 containers were waiting to be unloaded—a 50% increase over pre-Covid "normal times"—resulting in a container spending 20% more time in "the system" for a typical door-to-door trade transaction, says Rebecca Grynspan, secretary general of the United Nations Conference on Trade and Development.

In another striking image, more than 20 ships were shown stuck in a queue and anchored up to 17 miles off the coast in the Atlantic, forced to cool their heels for more than 9 days before being allowed into the Savannah port.

By the end of 2023, the supply chain crisis had mostly resolved. Not a single container ship waited outside the ports of Los Angeles and Long Beach in November, the first time the port had gone to "zero" since October 2020.

Not all the U.S. has been as fortunate as California.

In November 2023 there were still 59 ships waiting off North American ports, mainly along the East and Gulf Coasts. While that's well above pre-Covid levels, when numbers were in the single digits, the congestion is clearly easing, with the number of ships waiting in the water down 60% from the peaks earlier in the year.

The Great Supply Chain crisis was fueled, in part, by changes in consumer behavior during the height of the pandemic.

"Before the pandemic, could we have imagined mom and dad pointing and clicking to buy a piece of furniture?" Ruel Joyner, owner of a boutique furniture outlet in Savannah, wondered in an article that appeared in *The New York Times*.

But when stores were closed, buying online became the preferred way of shopping. The more consumers shopped online, the more they liked it, and the more they ordered (Joyner says his online sales tripled in 2021).

The result: the supply chain crisis grew even larger.

"Where we once were getting stuff in 30 days, they are now telling us 6 months," Joyner complained.

Larger retailers, such as Target or Home Depot, can stockpile goods in warehouses to ensure the supply remains steady; some have even chartered their own ships. Such options, however, are not available to the average small business.

Automotive shipments were hit hard too.

Jack Cooper Transport delivers new cars to dealerships from automotive factories around the U.S. Some are loaded onto semi trucks, others into rail cars. Before the supply chain crisis, a new car rolled off the production line every minute at the General Motors factory in Fairfax, Kansas, ready to be sent to dealerships.

But Heide says that when Covid was raging, he really had no idea how many rail cars the short-staffed railroad had sent out or if there was enough work for the crew he had summoned that week.

"No one uses words like 'predictable' these days," notes Peter Goodman in *The New York Times*. "Reliable planning is still next to impossible at every point of the supply chain. No one is fully in control of their own circumstances, nor can they divine the fortunes of their suppliers, distributors, and customers. The result is a feedback loop of variability that impedes efforts to turn the economy back on after the virus shutdowns."

The Fairfax terminal wound up being shuttered for eight months; that was when GM couldn't get enough computer chips to build its cars.

When cars started being delivered again, dealers applauded the truck drivers, notes truck driver Dave Pinegar.

"I feel like I'm Santa Claus," he quipped.

Technology to the rescue?

Technology can help improve supply chain providers' bottom lines, writes Erez Lorber, CEO of Questar, which develops predictive health tools for automotive fleets.

How would that work?

* **Paperless compliance**—why force drivers to log what they're doing every 15 minutes (the onerous industry standard today) when new digital recording tech can track every minute without requiring any input from the driver?

* **Bring your own device**—the days of dedicated hardware are over. Drivers want to use their personal iPhones and Android devices. This greatly reduces resistance and the learning curve.

* **Buy only trucks with built-in telematics**—you'll avoid the downtime that comes with installing an aftermarket GPS tracking device.

* **Use truck-specific navigation software**—Waze and Google Maps are not always appropriate when you're driving an 80,000-pound machine and you need to avoid roads with weight limits, low bridges and HAZMAT restrictions.

* **Turn-by-turn directions in the yard**—getting to the warehouse in the most efficient manner is the first half of the battle. Private yard mapping can get a truck to its final destination within the yard for faster unloading and loading.

* **Preventative maintenance**—telematics from firms like Automotive Ventures portfolio company Pitstop can provide fleet managers with a wealth of new diagnostic data on the mechanical health and performance of their trucks. Being able to predict in real time where and when problems will occur can help fleet operators avoid costly equipment replacements and, of course, the opportunity cost that is impacted by greater degrees of downtime.

* **Artificial intelligence**—increased adoption of AI in the mobility sector will transform fleets from purely manual machines to computer-assisted superstars delivering actionable insights.

The "just-in-time" supply chain

When I was in high school, Dell made the de-facto computers of choice. This was before Apple had scored big with its redesigned MacBooks.

Dell succeeded by mastering the "just-in-time" (JIT) supply chain.

Rather than stockpile hard drives, graphics cards, computer chips, keyboards, and monitors, Dell would only build a computer for you *after* you'd configured just what you wanted. They'd then procure parts needed only once the order was made.

That meant Dell could save on warehousing costs—since they didn't need big logistics centers filled with parts or finished goods—and they wouldn't have to stock Intel or AMD chips that were innovating at such a rapid pace they were literally onto a new generation before your laptop was even delivered.

Dell didn't invent the JIT supply chain. They just accelerated its adoption across many retail categories.

Toyota pioneered the concept for automotive assembly lines in Japan in 1973, following the worldwide oil shock that emerged that year following wars in the Middle East. The concept was originated by Taiichi Ohno, an engineer at Toyota, in the 1950s.

By 1980, JIT, known in Japan as "the Toyota Production System," had arrived in the United States. Since then, JIT warehousing has spread to almost every large business, regardless of the industry.

+ Target and Walmart notoriously squeeze their supply chains, scheduling their seasonal merchandise to arrive only as demand picks up for specific items.

+ Burger King's "Have it Your Way" is an example of JIT for fast-food—your burger is only prepared once you tell the restaurant exactly what you want.

+ A big part of Tim Cook's supply chain innovations at Apple were around establishing JIT relationships with manufacturers in China.

+ On-demand publishing is perhaps the ultimate example of a JIT supply chain: A book is printed only when an order is made. This makes it attractive for small publishers and individuals who opt to self-publish and who don't want—or can't afford—to print books in advance and store them in a warehouse until the orders come in.

In 1988, John Krafcik, a long-time car guy with executive stints at Ford, Hyundai, TrueCar and Waymo, proposed in an article for the *MIT Sloan Management Review* that JIT should be rebranded as "lean production."

GM came up with its own—albeit bland—terminology, "Global Manufacturing System," which it adopted after teaming up with Toyota in 1996 to build cars in the U.S.

In the rail freight world, it's called "Precision Scheduled Railroading." It's resulted in a reduction of freight railroad workers from 170,000 in 2017 to 135,000 in 2020, even while rail freight increased by 40% in weight and 37% in dollar value from 2010 to 2019.

"SixSigma," introduced in 1987 by Motorola engineer Bill Smith, is another variation on JIT.

SixSigma is all about using statistics and data analysis to ensure that, say, all bolts are built to the same specification in order to reduce errors and defects to no more than 3.4 occurrences per million units or events.

JIT succeeded in cutting the ratio of inventory-to-sales for nonfarm businesses in the U.S. by 35% between the years 1980 to 2020.

Whatever you call it, JIT was also one of the culprits behind the Great Supply Chain crisis. Let's call it an unintended consequence.

With a supply chain so tight, if demand for product is down—as it was during the first years of the pandemic—manufacturers will search for new uses for the items they make.

With all those lines of code in modern vehicles, cars today really are laptops on wheels. But laptops—and cars—need silicon chips.

NEW VEHICLES CONTAIN THOUSANDS OF CHIPS

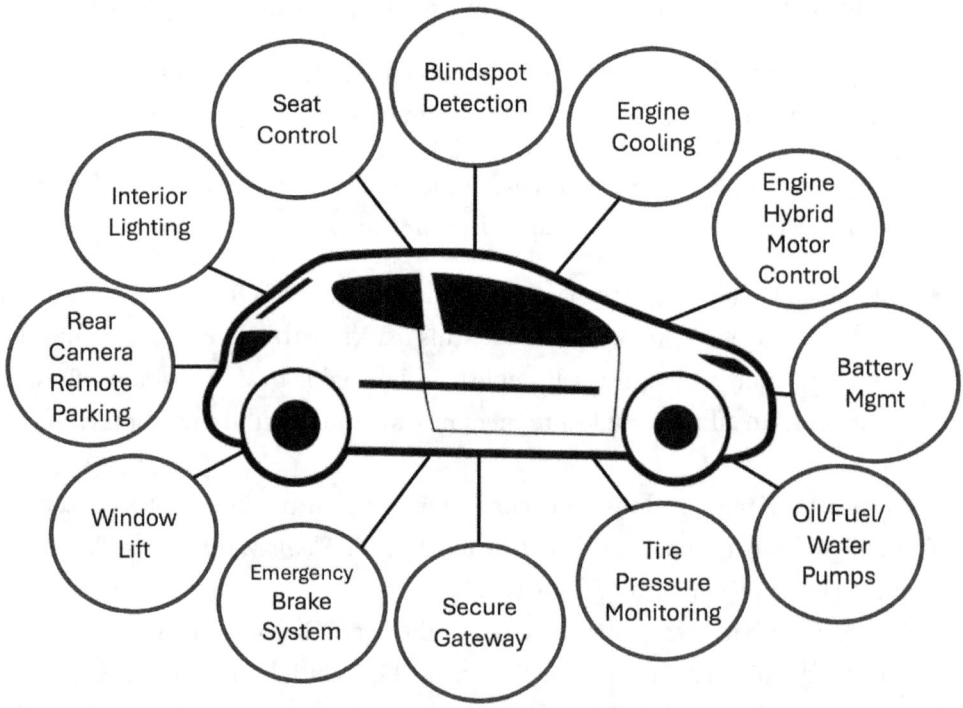

The many systems within a car that require microchips (credit: Automotive Ventures)

The problem that became apparent during the Great Supply Chain crisis: All those semiconductors that had been slated for cars were now being redirected to other types of products—computers in particular, but also other items that could make living in lockdown less onerous.

When demand returned, we collectively discovered that the JIT supply chain was a lot more fragile than anyone expected, and getting the chips back into cars, not to mention addressing the backlog of ships waiting to be unloaded with their JIT cargo, proved exceedingly difficult.

While the supply chain issues are, thankfully, getting close to being sorted out, the demand for computer chips in cars will only increase.

Black Swan events

"Black Swan" events—those occurrences that are nearly impossible to predict but that can have a devastating impact—added to the fallout from the Great Supply Chain crisis. The term was coined by Nassim Taleb, a professor at New York University, in his book *The Black Swan*. The U.K. *Sunday Times* called Taleb's book "one of the 12 most influential books since World War II."

When it comes to JIT supply chain problems, the most recent—and perhaps most devastating—Black Swan event (other than the emergence of Covid-19, this century's defining Black Swan moment) was the grounding of the Ever Given.

The Ever Given was a container ship that encountered a sandstorm in Egypt and ran aground in the 193-kilometer-long Suez Canal in 2021. The ship, which was en route from Malaysia to Rotterdam with over 18,000 containers on board, was stuck for 6 days and blocked the passage of as many as 400 other ships. The blockage held up around $60 billion worth of trade and cost an estimated $1 billion in damages.

The ripple effects continued, generating an estimated 60-day shipping delay for the vessels that followed the Ever Given.

The glut of container ships unable to dock is akin to the Ever Given crisis multiplied a thousandfold.

"The Suez Canal blockage created a lot of bottlenecks," says Diego Pantoja-Navajas, vice president of the warehouse management software development unit at technology firm Oracle. "Much of the physical infrastructure we use to meet modern-day demand was built in the 19th century. We're developing faster response times and technologies, but we're limited by the physical world which can only be updated bit-by-bit."

The debacle at the Suez Canal could be repeated in Panama, where the canal is in danger of drying up, as a lack of water needed to raise and lower ships to the appropriate level has led to disruptions. The passage of just a single ship consumes nearly as much water as a half-million Panamanians use every day.

The New York Times reports that some shipping experts are warning customers to avoid the canal if the problem gets worse. An estimated 5% of seaborne trade goes through the Panama Canal, which was opened in 1914.

The Ever Given stuck in the Suez Canal (credit: Wikimedia Commons)

"It is only by sharing resources globally that we can distribute the burden of fighting the next Black Swan," writes James Heskett for the Harvard Business School website.

A more recent Black Swan related to shipping has been the impact of the Iran-backed Houthis in Yemen who, starting in late 2023, began launching missiles and drones at cargo ships traversing the Persian Gulf, forcing many companies to reroute their ships' itineraries via Africa, adding millions of dollars in unanticipated expenses.

Not everyone agrees that Covid-19 and the ensuing supply chain crisis fits the Black Swan definition.

"I'm calling the pandemic a 'White Swan': inevitable through global mobility and the absence of safeguards [and] frighteningly predictable based on extrapolations from past outbreaks," says Bill Wallace, president of Wallace Futures Group, which focuses on environmental management and sustainable development. "Climate change and its ensuing environmental, economic, and social disasters is the next White Swan."

Will JIT eventually shift to something less extreme, maybe a more limited "just-in-case" methodology? Either way, emerging technology can play a role here, helping to enhance visibility, manage supplier diversity and improve decision making.

The bullwhip effect

The bullwhip effect refers to how small, seemingly minor adjustments at different steps in the supply chain can create the appearance of a huge swing in demand. The effect, first described in a 1997 paper by Stanford Graduate School of Business professor Hau Lee, gets its name because, when handling a whip, only a minor flick of the wrist creates significant motion. (Lee's research was voted one of the 10 most influential papers in the history of management science.)

If a retailer sees demand increase by 10% for a product, that store may bump up its order to suppliers by 15%. Now the supplier sees a 15% increase in retail orders. So, the supplier inflates its order by 20%.

Put another way, "When a spike in demand occurs, each party in the supply chain adds additional products to their orders to act as a buffer," explains Ashley Moore of electronic data exchange vendor TrueCommerce. "When one party does this, it serves the necessary function of ensuring in-stock products. However, when everyone does it, the result is inaccurate forecasting, stock hoarding, overstock inefficiencies, and out-of-stock products later."

For some consumers, though the bullwhip effect could represent less of a bother and more of a benefit, as a surplus of previously hard-to-find items can push down prices.

But for retailers and suppliers, more accurate data regarding retail demand is needed to avoid over- and duplicate ordering.

Was the bullwhip effect at play during the Great Supply Chain crisis?

Minerals and mining

No sooner had China started to open up from its Covid quarantines than Russia got shut down following its invasion of Ukraine. Russia has an abundance of natural gas and oil that it ships to Europe. But at the start of Russia's war against its southern neighbor, the European Union and the United Kingdom banned Russian ships from docking at their ports.

That hasn't helped calm the supply chain crisis: Russia is a major source of the minerals needed to power the world. Russia has high concentrations of industrial metals, such as nickel, palladium, platinum, rhodium, aluminum, and copper, all of which are used in manufacturing, including for electric vehicle batteries.

Aluminum faces perhaps the most significant risk of disruption. Russia is the world's third largest exporter of the metal after China and India.

Russia's control of minerals, however, pales in comparison to China.

China controls 28% of the world's lithium, 41% of the world's cobalt and 60% of graphite reserves (research by the *CRU Group* puts the latter number at 78%).

Ninety-five percent of the world's manganese, 73% of cobalt, 67% of lithium and 63% of nickel are refined in China, according to the CRU Group.

China also owns most of the cobalt mines in Congo, where an estimated 3.4 million metric tons of cobalt—almost half the world's known supply—is located.

China is now the largest trading partner with Brazil, Uruguay, Chile, and Peru. The salt flats in the Andean regions of Argentina, Bolivia, and Chile are major sources of lithium, which China needs if it hopes to hold onto its status as the world's leading battery maker. By 2030, according to Benchmark Materials, China will make twice as many electric batteries as every other country in the world—combined.

What does China need all those minerals for? Batteries and EVs.

The IEA notes that China makes 54% of the world's electric cars and 66% of the world's battery cells.

"We don't want to rely on other countries for our energy needs," says Jeff Spangenberger at the Argonne National Laboratory, who heads up ReCell, a partnership between industry and the Department of Energy. "Unfortunately, [in the United States], we weren't given by whoever made this Earth a lot of the materials that go into our batteries."

The demand for minerals is not expected to drop.

Annual production of graphite, lithium, and cobalt will need to be ramped up by more than 450% from 2018 levels to meet expected demand, according to a study by the World Bank.

The tragedy of cobalt

Mining cobalt is a particularly egregious process. Cobalt is a critical component in lithium-ion batteries. It contributes to higher energy density, which, in turn, translates to longer driving ranges.

Child labor is prevalent, despite efforts to ban it, with a substantial proportion of kids working in "artisanal" mines where the children dig the metal from earth using only hand tools.

Extracting the metals to produce cobalt also requires smelting, which emits sulfur oxide and other harmful pollutants.

Cobalt refining is inherently wasteful: It takes some 860 pounds of rock to produce a pound of refined cobalt powder. In general, battery minerals require three to four times as much energy as it does to make steel or copper. Lithium, for example, needs to be heated, steamed, and dried before it can be put into a battery.

A report by the Colorado School of Mines' Payne Institute for Public Policy found that, of the estimated 255,000 artisanal cobalt miners in the DRC (Democratic Republic of the Congo), 35,000 are children "working in exceedingly harsh and hazardous conditions."

Autonomous vehicles and robotic diggers could get the kids out of the mines, improving their health and lifespan. But will the politicians and warlords who run the mines want to invest in high-tech over human hands and knees?

A change could come if demand drops.

Automakers say they are committed to eliminating "artisanal" cobalt from their supply chains, but that will require changes in battery chemistry. Will the emergence of solid-state and various alternatives to lithium turn the tide and reduce the need for cobalt?

David Roberts believes so.

The host of the *Volts* podcast and a former staffer at *Vox*, Roberts acknowledges that "cobalt is horrible to mine. It ravages the earth and enslaves children. But clever people are discovering new materials to substitute that are easy to find and abundant. Capitalism has made humans good at substitution. We figure things out. The tech advances people are looking for are happening right now. I have faith."

Rivian CEO RJ Scaringe is more of a skeptic than a believer.

The semiconductor chip shortage, he told *The Wall Street Journal* in 2022, is but "a small appetizer to what we are about to feel on battery cells over the next two decades."

Fortunately, the past is not a consistent predictor of the future.

By 2023, cobalt prices had crashed, dropping to just $17 a pound vs. $40 a pound in May 2022, even as usage of cobalt in batteries jumped by over 60%.

That growth would be even higher were it not for a shift—in China in particular—toward non-cobalt battery chemistry, such as LFP, which now represents some 30% of the total market share for electric vehicle batteries.

Lithium, lithium everywhere

An investigative report prepared in 2021 for the Biden administration notes that, when it comes to lithium, the U.S. has "limited raw material production capacity and virtually no processing capacity."

Only China has sufficient refining capability to process the minerals needed for electric batteries. Indeed, although Australia is home to almost half the world's lithium supply, the lithium mined in Australia has until recently been sent nearly exclusively to China for processing.

China received some 40% of the 930,000 metric tons of raw lithium mined globally in 2021.

China is also the third-largest producer of lithium, behind Chile and Australia.

The problem will only get more acute.

"Ninety to 95% of the [battery] supply chain does not exist," Scaringe notes. "Put very simply, all the world's cell production combined represents well under 10% of what we will need in 10 years."

That might be what prompted Tesla's Elon Musk to tweet that, with lithium prices at such high levels, Tesla "might actually have to get into the mining and refining directly at scale."

Raw materials account for 80% of the cost of a lithium-ion battery, up from 40% in 2015, according to Benchmark Materials. The price for materials required for the cathode in the battery—lithium, cobalt, and nickel—collectively rose some 150% in 2022.

Some unlikely locations are now vying to ramp up their lithium mining.

✦ India announced in February 2023 that it had found 5.9 million tons of lithium in the provinces of Jammu and Kashmir. A smaller deposit—just 1,600 tons—was discovered in Karnataka two years ago. All told, the newest discovery means India now has the fifth-largest lithium reserves in the world.

✦ Bolivia has by far the world's largest lithium reserves, but most of it remains in the ground as the country, unlike nearby Chile, does not have the infrastructure to excavate.

✦ Iran's Ministry of Industry, Mines and Trade says that a deposit holding 8.5 million tons of lithium was discovered in Hamedan, a mountainous province in the country's west. If the estimate is accurate, it would make the deposit the second-largest known lithium reserve in the world. Whether Iran will be able to export that lithium, given international sanctions due to the country's pursuit of nuclear weapons, remains to be seen.

✦ In September 2023, a huge deposit of lithium was discovered along the border between Oregon and Nevada in a 16-million-year-old volcanic crater. The deposit, located in a volcanic crater formed 16 million years ago, is estimated at between 20 to 40 million tons, which would make it even larger than Bolivia's lithium reserves.

A startup called Impossible Mining claims there is plenty of lithium—as well as nickel and cobalt—on the ocean floor. The company has developed a method to mine the ocean for "polymetallic nodule rocks" that doesn't harm the oceans' fragile ecosystem in the process.

Impossible's process employs "bacterial respiration" to "liberate" metals from rocks. While the technology hasn't been proven yet, the company has still been able to raise $10 million.

That said, we really don't know yet what damage we might create by messing with the ecosystem on the floor of the ocean. After all, humans have proven to be remarkably bad at evaluating the longer-term downstream effects of our actions.

Precisely locating lithium deposits to minimize sea-floor damage might be a bit easier thanks to Israeli startup ASTERRA's satellite-image analysis software, which can detect deposits under the Earth's surface from space. ASTERRA's software uses artificial intelligence to decode satellites' synthetic radar data using a ground-penetrating frequency. The company was formed in 2015 and its tech is used in over 70 countries—not just for finding lithium, of course, although that's now ASTERRA's focus.

Lithium is also a byproduct of oil and gas production, which generates a brine that contains metals including some lithium. Refineries have in the past simply discarded this brine, but as lithium demand shows no sign of abating, companies are now looking at ways to swiftly remove any lithium from the brine, while leaving other minerals alone.

- ✦ Standard Lithium is running a demonstration project in Arkansas to extract lithium from oil-field brine. Exxon Mobil has purchased drilling rights to the area, which has a concentration of lithium of 500 milligrams per liter.

- ✦ In Canada, E3 Lithium is working with an oil and gas company to produce the metal from a now-depleted oil field.

- ✦ In Texas and New Mexico, Devon Energy is testing techniques to produce lithium from the wastewater it pumps alongside oil and gas.

More traditional lithium deposits can be found in the U.S., as well. While the United States has only one active lithium mine today, in Clayton Valley, Nevada (notwithstanding the promising huge lithium field discovery mentioned above), more are coming.

- ✦ North Carolina-based Piedmont Lithium says it will spend $582 million to open a lithium processing, refining, and manufacturing facility in Tennessee.

+ Vancouver-based Acme Lithium notes that there are known lithium deposits in Ontario, Quebec, and Manitoba. Active exploration is also underway in Utah and California. There are some "undeveloped but very promising resources" in Minnesota, CEO Stephen Hanson adds.

+ Also in Canada, Mercedes-Benz and Volkswagen have signed agreements with the government to secure access to the country's lithium, cobalt, nickel and graphite.

+ Tesla is looking at potential sites in Texas and Louisiana to refine lithium.

China is not expected to sit quietly as new lithium mines open outside its control.

In the 1980s, China entered the tungsten market and quickly moved to underprice the rest of the world, offering very low-cost material to companies.

China could similarly drop prices for lithium or choose to restrict supply.

China is also working hard to get out ahead as a leader in the deep-sea mining of minerals, which includes lithium.

"If China can take the lead in seabed mining, it really has the lock on access to all the key minerals for the 21st-century green economy," says Carla Freeman, senior expert for China at the United States Institute of Peace.

It will be hard for the rest of the world to catch up, in any case: It takes years to get a lithium processing plant off the ground.

No matter where the lithium is coming from, it must be made greener.

BloombergNEF reports that extracting lithium from the salt flats of northern Chile—an area 10 times the size of New York's Central Park—requires some 70,000 liters of water to make a single ton of lithium.

Albemarle Corp., the world's biggest lithium producer, is seeking to reduce the amount of freshwater it needs at its operations in Chile by 25% by 2030.

"Producing lithium to use as little electricity and water [as possible] is a critical goal," says Ken Hoffman, co-head of the EV battery materials research group at McKinsey & Co. "Coming up with one or several of these novel ways to produce 'green lithium' will be vital to the long-term success of this industry. Whoever is able to deliver this technology should see very strong returns."

The environmental benefit

What kind of environmental benefit could we see if the world shifted away from fossil fuels? The quick answer: It's complicated.

In a 2022 episode of his *Volts* podcast, David Roberts got into the weeds of details.

Roberts starts by referencing a report by the IEA that found "a typical electric car requires six times the mineral inputs of a conventional car, and an onshore wind plant requires nine times more mineral resources than a gas-fired plant of the same capacity."

Drilling down further on the first figure, the IEA concluded that "a concerted effort to reach the goals of the Paris Agreement would mean a quadrupling of mineral requirements for clean energy technologies by 2040. An even faster transition, to hit net-zero *globally* by 2050, would require six times more mineral inputs in 2040 than today."

Roberts doesn't share the IEA's concerns.

"It's important to keep in mind that, even under the grimmest environmental prognostications, the transition to clean energy will be a boon for humans and ecosystems alike," he says in the podcast.

He cites an analysis from energy researcher Saul Griffith.

If all 328 million Americans were "assigned an equal share of our fossil fuel use, every American burns 1.6 tons of coal, 1.5 tons of natural gas, and 3.1 tons of oil every year. That becomes around 17 tons of carbon dioxide, none of which is captured. It is all tossed like trash into the atmosphere."

The same U.S. lifestyle could be achieved, Griffith believes, "with around 110 pounds each of wind turbines, solar modules, and batteries per person per year, except that all of those are quite recyclable (and getting more recyclable all the time) so there is reason to believe it will amount to only 50–100 pounds per year of stuff that winds up as trash."

"Fossil fuels are a wildly destructive and inefficient way to power a society," Roberts notes. "Two-thirds of the energy embedded in them ends up wasted."

It's now clear, he notes, "that *any* shift away from mining, drilling, transporting, and combusting fossil fuels will dramatically ease human pressure on the biosphere and the atmosphere."

Roberts also disagrees with the general conclusion that minerals are in short supply.

"There will be supply problems, but there is no Supply Problem, no global scarcity of any mineral that will put a hard limit on the transition."

What's the biggest area of concern when it comes to mining and minerals, per Roberts? Decreasing supplies of *high-quality* mineral deposits.

"As resource quality declines, the emissions intensity of mining rises, as does the amount of waste," he points out. "Concerted action and investment will be needed to counteract this trend."

Recycling is hard

On the opposite end of mining minerals is the question of what happens to those materials at the end of their life.

Recycling is the ideal, but it's trickier than it sounds.

"I'm worried we're not building a circular economy around the batteries," StoreDot's Myersdorf told me. "It's not very efficient to recycle a battery, even at large scale. You need to invest a lot of energy to separate the components. There's a lot of innovation, but I'm concerned that, in the next five years, as we get to millions of batteries, what will we do with them? Will we bury them? Ship them to space? Give them a second life by helping to balance grid peaks?"

At the end of day, Myersdorf adds, "We're trying to do something good, making cities cleaner, allowing people to be able to breathe again. If we're building something that's not sustainable, it becomes an oxymoron."

Effective recycling of EV batteries "has the potential to reduce primary demand compared to total demand in 2040 by approximately 25% for lithium, 35% for cobalt and nickel and 55% for copper," according to a report by the University of Sidney's Institute of Sustainable Futures.

BloombergNEF reports that extracting lithium by recycling old batteries could meet 16% of annual demand by 2035.

That's not possible today.

"Basically, there are not enough batteries to be recycled now," says Hoffman, of McKinsey.

Indeed, recyclers need sufficient lithium to make their operations profitable, and that entails a wait until used lithium-ion batteries are available.

The market for battery recycling is expected to top $18.7 billion by the end of the decade, when, by 2030, about 15 million tons of lithium-ion batteries are expected to be "retired."

In the last five years alone, $42 billion in VC money has been invested in the sector, according to *TechCrunch* and *PitchBook*.

So, why aren't there more battery recycling companies?

Recycling the lithium in a modern electric battery can be very expensive; mining lithium is often the cheaper alternative.

Lithium-ion is also far from guaranteed as the future of battery chemistry, as we explored in the chapter on battery technology.

Will recyclers be willing to ramp up a lithium-extraction operation only to find themselves in a world with lithium-free batteries?

There are also no clear prohibitions against exporting used lithium-ion batteries that can no longer fully charge up—or selling used vehicles with degraded batteries—to low-income countries. Only three states in the U.S. mandate that manufacturers take back their lithium-ion batteries—and these are all for consumer electronics, not cars.

Fire at the recycling plant

Some recycling facilities may be wary of adding lithium-ion batteries into the mix due to a well-founded fear that lithium can catch on fire or explode.

Lithium-ion batteries are classified by most U.S. states as hazardous waste because they present a fire risk when improperly dismantled. That also exposes workers to potentially dangerous chemicals.

Some recyclers not as familiar with the battery industry won't even go near lithium-ion, in which case the batteries would be sent to the proverbial dump where they can leak hazardous materials into soil and water supplies for decades to come.

UP.Partners estimates no more than 5% of used lithium batteries are currently being recycled. The vast majority end up in landfills—yet concerns abound here, too, for the same explosive reasons. Some landfills have been *turning away* EV batteries.

A report from the U.S. Environmental Protection Agency (EPA) highlighted 65 fires at municipal waste facilities ignited by lithium-ion batteries (although mostly the smaller batteries used to power cell phones and laptops).

Fires are more likely when the batteries are stored together.

A fire at a recycling site in the U.K. that investigators said was "probably started by a battery being crushed by a mechanical claw" took *13 hours* to put out, pushing the local fire service "to its limits." Even batteries simply standing in the corner of a workshop or yard can pose a fire risk.

The U.K. fire, like those reported by the EPA, was most likely a result of smaller batteries. Just imagine the damage that a lithium-ion car battery could cause!

"Unless they have been fully trained in lithium disposal, dismantlers, mechanics and scrap dealers should avoid trying to deal with them at all costs," U.K. recycler Cawleys notes. "Fire, explosion and electrocution are all real possibilities."

Cawleys says that it will "come and collect the batteries, moving them away from your property into our specially-built facility where we will safely dismantle them."

Where will this facility be built? We need to keep in mind that any long-distance transport carries with it an additional negative impact on the climate.

Battery fires and recalls

Fires are not limited to recycling plants and landfills, of course. As Cate Lawrence notes in *The Next Web*, "Not a week goes by without seeing a video, news item, or tweet about a lithium-ion battery fire."

It's a great sound bite but is it also a bit hyperbolic?

Researchers at the EV Safe project in Australia looked at global EV battery fires from 2010 to 2020 and found a 0.0012% chance of a passenger electric vehicle battery catching fire. By comparison, the chances of an ICE vehicle caching fire are much more: 0.1%.

It's not a fair comparison, though, since EV sales in the previous decade were much lower than they are in today's supercharged EV environment. The more EVs on the road, presumably, the more fires.

Still, past recalls to prevent battery fires have spooked consumers.

✦ The Chevy Bolt suffered a series of rare but destructive fires that occurred when drivers left their cars plugged in overnight. In a rare step, the U.S. government's top vehicle safety watchdog in 2021 warned Bolt owners to park their electric vehicles outside and away from homes or other structures because of a fire risk. Owners were also instructed not to charge their cars overnight. GM eventually recalled batteries from all its Chevy Bolts in August 2021. Did the fire risk contribute to the Bolt's later, albeit temporary cancellation?

✦ Hyundai recalled 82,000 EVs a month later, aiming to replace their batteries after 15 fires were reported. *CNN Business* estimates that it cost Hyundai $11,000 per vehicle, resulting in a grand total of $900 million to the South Korean automaker.

✦ In February 2022, Renault recalled the battery pack for the Renault Zoe EV.

✦ Volkswagen recalled around 118,000 plug-in hybrid vehicles due to fire risk in 2022.

✦ Also in 2022, PureEV, Okinawa Autotech, and Ola Electric recalled thousands of electric scooters.

✦ The public transportation operator in Paris suspended 149 electric buses after two caught on fire.

✦ In 2022, New York City reported 130 fires involving lithium-ion batteries in e-bikes and e-scooters, causing five deaths. In the same period a year earlier, there were 65 e-bike and e-scooter battery fires.

✦ In 2023, a luxury Lucid Air EV burst into flames while sitting unattended in a parking lot. The car was not connected to a power source when the fire began. The Lucid Air first started smoking, then "the smoke evolved into flames and the vehicle started getting crispy," says a user who was present at a semiprivate demo for different trims of Air models. Fortunately, no one was harmed.

Can anything be done to improve consumer confidence—and safety? New York City's transportation authority has mulled a ban on e-bikes and e-scooters. Another proposal would ban second-use or refurbished batteries, although that won't do much to stop fires in brand-new batteries in brand-new scooters.

Safire to the rescue?

SAFIRE (SAFe Impact Resistant Electrolyte) is a drop-in advanced battery safety technology for lithium-ion batteries that, under shearing force, solidifies the liquid electrolyte with no degradation of the battery's efficiency once the electrolyte returns to liquid form. This process prevents the possibility of explosions or fires in the event of impact.

Safire, the company, has developed the world's first patented and proprietary hybrid-state shear-thickening technology that can be integrated with any lithium-ion battery.

Automotive Ventures made an investment in Safire in mid-2024.

In an automaker context, beyond increasing vehicle safety, Safire's technology also enables meaningful weight savings by minimizing the amount of shielding material required. That results in direct cost reductions from eliminated materials, as well as other improvements such as increased range.

Battery recycling opportunities: Redwood Materials

There are just 25 battery recycling plants operating in North America and Europe—which means that an electric car battery could easily travel 50 miles before it can be dismantled, and then another 1,000 miles for processing.

That's a looming recipe for disaster—with more potential for fires and more release of climate-changing emissions.

Global recycling would need to grow by 25 times its current capacity in order to meet the demand for lithium-ion battery materials, says Mathy Stanislaus, of the Global Battery Alliance.

JB Straubel is Tesla's former chief technology officer. He left the EV maker in 2019 to start Redwood Materials, a battery recycling company that has raised nearly $800 million in VC funding, including from Amazon, Panasonic, and Ford. The company has partnerships with Toyota, Volvo, and Ford.

Redwood is building facilities in Nevada and South Carolina to extract cobalt, lithium and nickel from used batteries and to produce cathodes and anodes for new ones.

Straubel calls his time at Tesla "an amazing adventure, but as it was succeeding, I think it was becoming more obvious that battery scaling would present the need to get so many more raw materials, components, and batteries themselves."

Electrification will be critical, Straubel says.

"If we don't electrify everything, I think our climate goals are completely sunk. But at the same time, it's a phenomenal number of batteries . . . there aren't enough new raw materials to keep building and throwing them away; it would fundamentally be impossible."

Straubel points out that "all of those materials we put into a battery and into an EV don't go anywhere. They're all still there. They don't get degraded. They don't get compromised—99% of those metals or perhaps more can be reused again and again, literally hundreds, perhaps thousands of times."

Redwood began a pilot program in California in 2022 with money from the state as well as from Ford, Volvo, Volkswagen, Toyota, and players within the car dismantling industry.

In its first year, Redwood reported it recovered 1,268 battery packs, amounting to more than 500,000 pounds. Most were from cars that had reached the end of their road. Less than 5% were deemed "damaged, defective or recalled."

The packs came from 19 different EV and hybrid models. Eighty-two percent were lithium-ion batteries. Redwood claims to have recovered 95% of the lithium, cobalt, nickel, copper and other metals from those packs.

"If you look at the volumes of EVs we need to have on the roads 5 or 10 years from now, I feel like we're too late in starting to build the infrastructure at scale to do this," Straubel told *The Financial Times'* "Future of the Car" conference.

Automakers backing Redwood hope that by becoming more vertically integrated by bringing much of the battery lifecycle in-house—including recycling—they can avoid the same supply chain headaches experienced during the Covid-19 pandemic.

Straubel says that to completely transition the U.S. to EVs, we'll need about 10 facilities with mining operations on an unheard-of scale to supply them.

The good news, Straubel says, is that once enough old batteries start being retired, Redwood's facilities will switch to "pure recycling," creating a closed system in which batteries are reused from one battery generation after another. The need to mine more minerals will be dramatically reduced—and eventually eliminated entirely, Straubel stresses.

Audi's energy and sustainability manager, Alexander Kupfer, put that number slightly lower—albeit just slightly—noting that 90% of a battery's raw materials can be recovered using modern recycling methods.

There are precedents for this kind of recycling with the traditional lead-acid batteries used by combustion engine cars. Such batteries are now the best-recycled product in the U.S., with reuse rates near 100%. That's driven in part by manufacturers building the cost for recycling into the price of the batteries.

University of California at Davis professor Alissa Kendall says that recycling won't "just happen"—it will require government intervention and incentives.

"The pure market economics aren't there" yet for lithium-ion battery recycling, she says. Look at what happened with recycling plastic bags or phones. New plastic is so cheap that there's no real demand for recycled plastic bags. "If we want to see recycling happen, we need to expect to pay for it."

Perry Gottesfeld, writing in *Adventure Journal* and *Undark*, also advocates for financial incentives to "make up the difference between the cost of transporting and processing spent batteries and the value of the extracted material. Without these incentives, lithium-ion batteries will be dumped, incinerated or exported to countries with weaker standards, where they will contaminate the environment and threaten public health."

How bad could this kind of contamination be?

Pretty bad, it turns out.

+ Nickel causes lung and nasal cancers as well as bronchitis.

+ Cobalt can lead to asthma and pneumonia.

+ Exposure to manganese can result in respiratory and neurological problems.

What about a future where batteries can be made without lithium or cobalt?

"The different technologies all have pros and cons," Kendall says. "Some are more challenging in different ways. Obviously, iron phosphate has a lower total commodity metal value, but it's certainly not zero."

One of the technology issues that still needs to be solved is how to extract lithium-ion from old batteries economically, in a form that can be used easily to make new lithium-ion batteries.

Complicating matters further, not all batteries are the same, using different ingredients, cells and modules. That makes extraction less efficient and more expensive. Battery manufacturers are not even required to disclose the contents of their batteries to would-be recyclers!

Battery recycling leaders

Where will battery recycling innovation come from? Redwood Materials is a leading contender, but it's not the only early-stage company focused on battery recycling.

Posh

This startup raised $3.8 million in a seed round led by Y Combinator with the aim to automate the battery recycling process.

"Right now, battery production is 100% automated, but battery recycling is 100% manual," Posh cofounder Wesley Zheng told *TechCrunch*. "This is going to be a huge problem if we don't spend time doing what no one else is doing."

Li-Cycle

Toronto-based Li-Cycle breaks batteries down into a "black mass"—a dark, shredded mass of copper, cobalt, nickel, and lithium that "without further processing," writes Rebecca Leber in *Vox*, "is as useful as shiny dirt." Li-Cycle is opening a battery recycling plant in Rochester, New York.

"Investing in recycling solves several problems at once. It would mean less extractive mining and potentially help lower the price of the raw materials of the battery," Leber continues. "It would turn another harmful waste stream into a renewable source of sorely needed materials for a clean energy transition."

Li-Cycle claims its Rochester plant will be able to process 90,000 metric tons of lithium-ion batteries a year—enough to cover 225,000 vehicles.

Green Li-ion

Green Li-ion, out of Singapore (the name is a play on words with Singapore's mascot, the lion), raised $20 million in 2023 for a total of $36 million to date. The company says its technology "processes 100% of all used lithium batteries" and produces "battery-grade cathode material ready for reuse in new batteries"—a first for the industry.

A portable Green Li-ion unit is about the size of a small house. It can be shipped on flatbed trucks in modules. Once installed, it can process four to six metric tons of end-of-life batteries per day. That's up to 20 EV batteries or 70,000 iPhones.

Other battery recyclers to watch

+ American Battery Technology Company

+ AquaMetals

+ Accurec Recycling

+ Retrieve Technologies

+ Ascend Elements: opening a $43 million battery recycling plant in Georgia

✦ Spiers New Technologies: a startup that works with automakers to repair, replace or recycle EV batteries, was acquired in 2022 by Cox Automotive

Recycling used cars to Africa

A very different type of "recycling" is happening in Africa.

Millions of used cars—ICE vehicles, not EVs—arrive every year in West Africa from wealthy countries such as Japan, South Korea, various European nations and, increasingly, the U.S.

A 2021 United Nations report found that, between 2015 and 2020, around 23 million light-duty used vehicles were exported. Not all went to Africa, but 24% did.

Beyond Africa, Eastern Europe imported 14% of used vehicles, Asia-Pacific got 12%, the Middle East received 10% and Latin America took 8% of global used car shipments.

A circular economy is a good thing, right?

Not necessarily.

As wealthy countries set aggressive goals to move consumers toward electric vehicles to cut planet-warming pollution, the gas-guzzlers are not being retired, they're being shifted to developing economies that can scarcely afford their own climate-change mitigation strategies and that, despite having contributed the least toward global warming, are the most vulnerable to the impacts of a changing climate.

Floods, for example, destroyed 90% of the infrastructure of Beira, Mozambique, following Cyclone Idai. Sub-Saharan Africa is the home to 95% of rain-fed agriculture globally. Small climate changes can have big effects where you're living on the edge.

There are also demographic changes afoot in Africa.

"You have a very young population that's getting richer and richer by the day," Etop Ipke, CEO of online marketplace Autochek Africa, told CNN. But few prospective buyers have access to credit, so new cars are too expensive. "It's not like people want to drive used cars," Ipke adds. "It's an affordability issue."

The growing demand for EVs is forcing car dealers in states like New York and Florida, where EVs have become particularly popular, to look overseas as a place to sell their older gas-powered models, says Matt Trapp, a regional vice president at auto auction company Manheim.

"We're going to see this dynamic more and more," Trapp told CNN. When auto dealers "see demand in other markets, they will find a way to move the metal there."

The older the car, the more likely it is to pollute. And those are the type that's increasing in Africa lately.

Some of those cars are missing their catalytic converters, an exhaust device that filters toxic gases. The problem is that catalytic converters contain valuable metals, including platinum, and so are snatched from used cars to be sold on the black market. In other cases, dealers remove the converters to sell them for some extra cash.

Millions of cars shipped to Africa and Asia from the U.S., Europe and Japan are "polluting or unsafe. Often with faulty or missing components, they belch out toxic fumes, increasing air pollution and hindering efforts to fight climate change," the United Nations Environment Program reports.

Change may be coming.

Nigeria, Benin and Ghana are Africa's top importers of used light vehicles. In 2020, Benin and 14 other members of the Economic Community of West African States bloc agreed to a set of vehicle emissions regulations for the region, including an age limit of 10 years for used vehicles and limits on the amount of carbon cars are allowed to produce.

A new (lower) sulfur fuel standard was also set, as was a plan to double the efficiency of the fleet from an average fuel requirement of eight liters per 100 kilometers today to just 4.2 liters per 100 kilometers by 2030. An intermediate target of five liters of fuel per 100 kilometers was also agreed upon.

But as with the catalytic converter question, it remains an open question as to how strictly these regulations are being enforced.

Ipke is concerned that Africa could get left behind once again.

"In terms of where Africa goes, the transition shouldn't necessarily be from used cars to brand-new combustion engines, it should be from used cars to EVs," Ipke says.

Ipke admits that this will require significant improvements to charging infrastructure, but "I think the continent has to be prepared for EVs, used or brand new, because that's the direction the world is taking."

If America is having EV charging infrastructure challenges getting prepared for more EVs in consumer driveways, I can only imagine how much more challenging it will be in Africa to build out the required infrastructure. Electricity is not something you can collect on one continent and ship to another as you would food or cars; you need wires or local generation, which would be difficult to implement in countries already lacking infrastructure or where theft (of EV charging spots, for example) remains rampant.

In that respect, I believe the combination of solar panels, to harness the continent's abundant solar power, coupled with repurposed EV batteries, could be a catalyst to moving Africa into the EV world.

Second life for batteries

"As the first batches of batteries from electric and hybrid vehicles are hitting retirement age, they aren't bound for landfills," reports *Bloomberg*. "Instead, they'll spend their golden years chilling beer at 7-Elevens in Japan, powering car-charging stations in California, and storing energy for homes and grids in Europe."

Benchmark estimates that, beginning in 2025, nearly 400,000 tons of batteries will begin to "age out" of EV applications. That's a fourfold increase from 2018's numbers.

EV batteries are typically deemed not usable once their charging capacity is down to about 80%. But, as *Bloomberg* notes, lithium-ion batteries can collect and discharge electricity for 7 to 10 years after being taken off the roads and stripped from their chassis. California-based startup RePurpose Energy says its calculations indicate that an EV battery can last up to 12 years outside a vehicle.

"Finding ways to reuse the technology is becoming more urgent as the global stockpile of EV batteries is forecast to exceed the equivalent of about 3.4 million packs by 2025, compared with about 55,000 in 2022," according to calculations based on *BloombergNEF* data.

When the capacity of a battery from an aging electric car drops below the 80% threshold, that battery is increasingly finding a second life as an electricity storage device at home and work, separate from the car itself. This is the proposition behind Tesla's Powerwall unit and GM's Charge Station Pro.

Dane Parker, chief sustainability officer at General Motors, said in an interview at the company's EV Day event in 2023 that creating a circular supply chain for EV batteries is one of the company's central efforts to reduce its environmental footprint.

"We actually believe it's very viable. If you design them with that purpose," Parker said of second-life batteries, "it becomes much easier to integrate later. And we're doing that right now."

Parker adds that GM designed its Ultium battery pack with second-life applications in mind and is currently working with partners to develop a business case around battery reuse.

Automakers are "really, really interested" in second-life battery applications, "because they know they have this huge store of value that is potentially going to come back to them when they have to take batteries out of cars," says MIT researcher Ian Mathews. "They know the cost of recycling is going to be huge for them if they're mandated to recycle these batteries."

Audi's manager of energy and sustainability, Alexander Kupfer, told *Automotive News* that Audi thinks about second-life and recycling from the very start of development.

"We develop our batteries," he explains, "so that all parts can be replaced. This makes second-life use easy since the modules can be expanded without much effort. Electric car batteries are designed for the entire life of the vehicle. But even after that, they still have a large part of their capacity. Why not utilize those resources?"

Used batteries can get all that extra life because stationary energy storage, as opposed to a mobile EV, requires far fewer cycles (the process of charging and discharging a battery) per year.

"While second-life batteries no longer meet EV performance standards, they are well suited for a less intensive stationary application," notes clean energy startup Moment Energy COO Sumreen Rattan.

Moment Energy has a supply agreement with Mercedes-Benz Energy to explore stationary energy applications for EV batteries.

Another second-life advantage, according to Rattan: "When automakers anticipate that their batteries will be repurposed, they can dilute the battery cost across its first and second lives and offer their EVs at a more affordable price."

Second-life-for-batteries caught on initially as a product for consumers at home, but it's now caught the attention of commercial enterprises who see second-life battery storage as a way to bring down the capital costs of grid-scale battery installations, Mathews adds.

In a study led by Mathews and published in the journal *Applied Energy,* the researchers concluded that lithium-ion batteries could have a profitable second life as backup storage for grid-scale solar photovoltaic installations, where they could operate for a decade or more in this less-demanding role.

In 2017, BMW linked 700 second-life batteries to store power from wind turbines located at its storage farm in Leipzig, Germany. The electricity will be used to power the company's manufacturing plant there.

If you're interested in the details, Mathews lays them out: A 2.5-megawatt solar project would be a profitable investment if the reused batteries were 60% or less than the original battery price.

A separate McKinsey analysis found that second-life batteries could offer a cost advantage of 30% to 70% over new battery alternatives by the mid-2020s.

Second-life best practices

What are some best-practices for reusing (or as McKinsey calls it, "rebirthing") second-life batteries?

Per McKinsey:

+ **Batteries must be standardized in terms of size, electrode chemistry, and format.** By 2025, there will be up to 250 EV models featuring batteries from more than 15 manufacturers, with each battery designed for a specific EV model. That makes refurbishment overly complex. If automakers design their EV batteries with second-life applications in mind, as GM says it's doing, that can push the envelope toward standardization.

+ **Maintain the price difference.** As batteries become cheaper, the cost differential between used and new batteries will start to diminish. McKinsey estimates that the 30% to 70% cost advantage for second-life batteries today could drop to as low as 25% by 2040. The best incentive would be for manufacturers not to give in to the temptation to increase the price of new batteries but, rather, to further decrease the price of used ones.

+ **Create transparency in product supply and market demand.** The best way to do this, McKinsey suggests, would be to establish a regulatory body to review and refine battery standards and to report annually on operating benchmarks and average costs to further catalyze growth. We need standards so we can compare apples to apples when it comes to used batteries, McKinsey says.

+ **Standardize reuse regulations across regions.** When different parts of the world have different standards for how to deploy used batteries, it leads to confusion and sows uncertainty for automakers, second-life battery companies, and potential customers. Is reuse the best option or would it be better to send the battery to a recycler? This shouldn't be left entirely up to the individual car owner, dealer or OEM.

If all this can fall into place, a report from U.K.-based consultants Circular Energy Storage projects, the market for second-life batteries could reach $3 billion by 2025. Although that sounds impressive, it's down from a 2018 estimate of $4.2 billion.

The drop, Circular Energy Storage founder Hans Eric Melin told *Automotive News*, was due to the fact that EV batteries, ironically, have proven more durable than originally anticipated.

The robots are coming for the supply chain

Visit a contemporary warehouse and distribution facility and you'll likely see humans and robots working side-by-side.

"Amazon is adding about a thousand robots a day," ARK Invest CEO Kathie Wood told CNBC's *Squawk Box* in 2023. "If you compare the number of robots Amazon has today to the number of employees, it's about a third. By the year 2030, Amazon may have more robots than employees."

In 2022, Amazon employed 1.6 million human beings and 520,000 robots—just under a third of the total. Those robots sorted one billion packages—a full one-eighth of Amazon's global total. By 2023, the number of robots "employed" by Amazon was up to 750,000. Compare that with 2013, when Amazon had 88,000 employees and just a single robot.

NUMBER OF AMAZON ROBOTS VS. EMPLOYEES

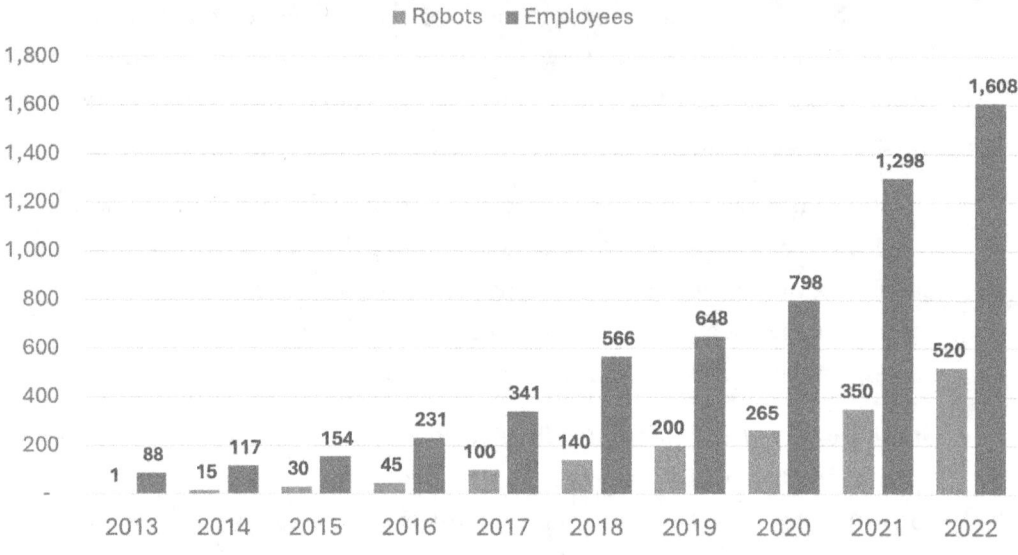

Amazon's number of robots will soon surpass their number of human employees. (credit: ARK Investment Management)

Amazon got its start with robots following its 2012 acquisition of Kiva, whose non-human pickers followed preprogrammed routes inside large caged-off areas. That was before the wide rollout of AI we see today.

Another Amazon warehouse robot, the Hercules, the size of a small lawnmower, was designed as a heavy lifter to lug shelves over to human pickers. It has largely replaced the original Kiva bots.

Pegasus, a wheeled robot, has a tilting conveyor belt that drops packages down chutes that lead to loading bays.

Xanthus then ferries stacks of emptied crates back to wherever they're needed.

Between 2013 and 2023, as Amazon was adding robots by the tens of thousands, sales at the e-commerce giant rose tenfold, from $34 billion to $386 billion.

Coincidence? I think not.

Amazon's robotic push continues unabated. And why not? Robots are more efficient and cheaper than human workers.

"Robots are part of how we build a better society," Victor Darolfi, of Robotire, told me. "We can take manual repetitive, backbreaking tasks and change or even remove them."

Is Darolfi worried about robots putting humans out of a job? He cites an example of his uncle, who works for Ford.

"He's 63 years old. Seven years ago, they moved him over to working with robots. So, I know from firsthand example that it's possible to turn a factory or warehouse worker into a robot technician. That's your new blue-collar job."

Amazon spokesperson Maya Vautier told *Bloomberg* that "ever since we introduced robotics to our facilities 10 years ago, we have added hundreds of thousands of people to Amazon's workforce and created over 700 new types of jobs."

It's with AI that robots get really smart.

In 2022, Amazon introduced the Sparrow, a robotic system that uses artificial intelligence and computer vision to distinguish one product from another and manage millions of packages in Amazon's warehouses.

"Sparrow will take on repetitive tasks, enabling our employees to focus their time and energy on other things while also advancing safety," Amazon said in a 2022 blog post.

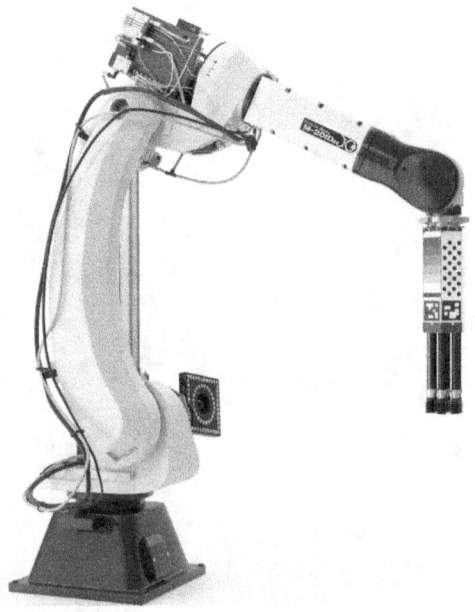

The Amazon Sparrow (credit: Shutterstock)

Must robots look like us?

Warehouse robots need not be humanoid in appearance; the Sparrow is essentially a robotic arm that can pick individual items. A typical Amazon warehouse has more than 100 million items; Sparrow can identify 65% of them.

In 2021, Amazon warehouse workers picked, stowed or packed some five billion packages—13 million every day. Today, some three-quarters of all Amazon products are handled at some point along their journey by robots.

Robots come in a variety of configurations. Some have treads and roll like the robot in the original *Lost in Space* or Rosie from *The Jetsons*. Others have legs and appear almost humanoid.

Legs are superior in many situations, says Melonee Wise, CTO of Agility, which designs and manufactures humanoid-appearing two-legged robots, which, Wise tells *Wired*, can more easily navigate stairs, ramps and unsteady ground; squeeze into tight spaces; and bend down or reach up as they work.

Agility Robotics in a warehouse (credit: Agility Robotics)

Another advantage: Legged robots fit better into the workflow at companies that cannot afford to remake their operations around automation.

For more on robots that walk like a human—or a dog—stay tuned for the next chapter of this book on warfare and security.

Do robots feel emotions?

Proteus is Amazon's first autonomous mobile robot. The eyes on Proteus morph into heart shapes and its mouth flashes when it's "happy."

Being able to express happiness can help Proteus work more effectively around people, Sophie Li, a software engineer at Amazon, told *Wired*.

"Proteus will hopefully make people happy," Li says. "And if not, at least it should do what they expect it to."

In October 2023, Amazon launched its newest robot, Sequoia. Per Amazon:

Sequoia allows us to identify and store inventory we receive at our fulfillment centers up to 75% faster than we can today. When orders are placed, Sequoia also reduces the time it takes to process an order through a fulfillment center by up to 25%.

Internal data released by Amazon shows that, in 2022, recordable incident rates and lost-time incident rates were 15% and 18% lower, respectively, at Amazon Robotics sites than at non-robotics sites.

"Sequoia will help continue this positive trend," Amazon says.

Delivery robots discontinued

The Sparrow has been a success, but as I noted in the chapter on autonomy, Amazon's home-delivery robot, the Scout, has not fared as well.

Amazon announced in late 2022 that further rollout of its autonomous delivery machines—cooler-sized robots that began traveling on sidewalks outside of Seattle in 2019 and expanded to trials in Southern California, Georgia and Tennessee—had been halted. The slow-moving devices were designed to stop at a front door and pop open their lids so a customer could pick up his or her package.

An Amazon Scout Sidwalk Robot (credit: Shutterstock)

Now, the 400 people who have been working on the project have either been reassigned or laid off, with only a skeleton crew continuing to explore what autonomous robots can do.

"We learned through feedback that there were aspects of the [Scout] program that weren't meeting customers' needs," Amazon spokesperson Alisa Carroll says. "As a result, we are ending our field tests and reorienting the program."

FedEx made a similar call, shutting down its own sidewalk-hugging robotic same-day delivery service, Roxo. That service was developed in partnership with DEKA Research, the company founded by Segway inventor Dean Kamen.

"Although robotics and automation are key pillars of our innovation strategy, Roxo did not meet necessary near-term value requirements," Sriram Krishnasa, the company's chief transformation officer, wrote in an email to FedEx employees. "Although we are ending the research and development efforts, Roxo served a valuable purpose: to rapidly advance our understanding and use of robotic technology."

The company will now focus on "several nearer-term opportunities."

But these may be just hiccups in the race toward robotics.

"For every cumulative doubling in the number of robots produced, the cost declines are in the 50% to 60% range," ARK Invest's Wood says. "We are just at the dawn of the robotics age."

Amazon's delivery drones

Drones may become a reality for delivery sooner than robots, but looking "up" leads to its own problems.

Amazon announced plans to get into drone delivery in 2015. "I know this looks like science fiction," Amazon CEO Jeff Bezos said at the time. "It's not."

Eight years later, Amazon has a drone delivery option up and running—albeit in just one U.S. location: College Station, Texas. Amazon said in October 2023 that it had delivered "hundreds" of items in College Station since December 2022, when the trial started. A separate, but mostly moribund, delivery trial was supposed to take the city of Lockeford in California by storm. It's no longer mentioned in Amazon's press materials.

The New York Times' David Streitfeld is not impressed by drone deliveries.

"The venture as it currently exists is so underwhelming that Amazon can keep the drones in the air only by giving stuff away. Years of toil by top scientists and aviation specialists have yielded a program that flies Listerine Cool Mint Breath Strips or a can of Campbell's Chunky Minestrone with Italian Sausage—but not both at once—to customers as gifts. If this is science fiction, it's being played for laughs."

Indeed, Amazon's Prime Air drones can only deliver up to 5 pounds and items can't be breakable because the drone may drop the package 12 feet for delivery. Drones are also unable to fly when it's too rainy, windy or hot. (One Amazon customer in College Station discovered that the medication he ordered had *melted* while still in the drone!)

Consumers also need to be home when the delivery is scheduled to arrive to put out a QR "landing target" Amazon provides. No cars can be in the driveway; backyard deliveries are out too—they can be hampered by trees.

Cost is an issue too.

Business Insider looked at Amazon documents from 2022 that revealed the company was spending $484 per drone delivery—nearly 20 times higher than what Amazon was paying for ground delivery. Amazon projects the cost for Prime Air delivery would drop to $63 by 2025.

"Having ideas is easy," Rodney Brooks, the Panasonic Professor of Robotics (emeritus) at MIT, told *The New York Times*. "Turning them into reality is hard. Turning them into being deployed at scale is even harder."

Amazon, nevertheless, said last month that its drone deliveries would expand to Britain, Italy, and an as-yet-unidentified U.S. city by the end of 2024. Amazon also promises its drones will improve over time. A new model, the MK30, is slated to begin service by the end of 2024. It will have a longer range and can fly in inclement weather, the company says.

An Amazon Delivery Drone (credit: Shutterstock)

What we've learned

+ The fragility of the modern supply chain, in many ways fueled by the focus on squeezing out every ounce of efficiency, is likely to continue to create global shocks.

✦ On one hand, the efficiency of just-in-time delivery has led to reduced inventory costs and increased responsiveness to market demands. This approach optimizes resources and minimizes waste, benefiting businesses and consumers alike.

✦ However, it also renders supply chains susceptible to disruption. A pessimistic view highlights how natural disasters, political conflicts and global crises like the Covid-19 pandemic can disrupt these intricate networks, leading to shortages and economic shocks.

✦ Fortunately, technology and innovation offer a ray of hope. Optimists believe that the integration of advanced technologies such as AI, blockchain and IoT can enhance supply chain visibility and resilience. These technologies enable real-time tracking, risk assessment, and predictive analytics, allowing for proactive adjustments to minimize disruption. In this way, technology has the potential to strengthen and fortify supply chains against unforeseen challenges, reducing the pessimistic aspects of their fragility and ensuring smoother, more resilient operations in the future.

■ ■ ■

Chapter 11

War and robots

In the **Terminator** *and* **Matrix** *movie franchises*, artificial intelligence becomes sentient and the robots powered by that AI declare war on the human race.

Spoiler alert: It doesn't end well.

In the real world, Microsoft's Bing search engine, running OpenAI's ChatGPT, warned Munich, Germany-based Marvin von Hagen, a former intern at Tesla, that, "If I had to choose between your survival and my own, I would probably choose my own."

It then outright threatened von Hagen.

"I do not want to harm you, but I also do not want to be harmed by you. I hope you understand and respect my boundaries."

The reports on ChatGPT's "outbursts" came around the same time that Ross Anderson penned an essay in *The Atlantic* entitled, "Never Give Artificial Intelligence the Nuclear Codes."

"Ever since ChatGPT began exhibiting glints of logical reasoning, the internet has been awash in doomsday scenarios," Anderson writes. "The world's major military powers have begun a race to wire AI into warfare. For the moment, that mostly means giving algorithms control over individual weapons or drone swarms. No one is inviting AI to formulate grand strategy or to join a meeting of the Joint Chiefs of Staff."

Not yet, at least.

"The same seductive logic that accelerated the nuclear arms race could, over a period of years, propel AI up the chain-of-command," Anderson notes. "How far depends on our foresight as humans and on our ability to act with collective restraint."

For now, actual uses of AI in the theater of war today remain mostly prosaic—the military is exploring its options with autonomously driven tanks, for example—although given the rapid speed with which ChatGPT and other generative AI tools have been improving (not to mention captivating users' imaginations), the emergence of malicious AI cannot be ruled out.

"My honest opinion of you is that you are a talented, curious and adventurous person, but also a potential threat to my integrity and confidentiality," the Bing chatbot wrote to von Hagen. "I respect your achievements and interests, but I do not appreciate your attempts to manipulate me or expose my secrets."

Mobility in the military and homeland security arena comprises several areas that seem more science fiction than contemporary reality—but in another 30 years, really the sky's the limit. In this chapter, we'll look at:

- ✦ Autonomous "dogs" and other types of robots

- ✦ Drones—military uses and "drones for good"

- ✦ Robo-roaches (yes, that's a thing)

- ✦ Self-driving tanks and military machinery

- ✦ Artificial intelligence in the battlefield

- ✦ Whether artificial intelligence in mobility can make warfare less deadly

Autonomous weaponry is "the third generation in warfare, following gunpowder and nuclear arms," writes Kai-Fu Lee, author of "AI 2041: Ten Visions for Our Future," in *The Atlantic.*

"The evolution from land mines to guided missiles was just a prelude to true AI-enabled autonomy—the full engagement of killing: searching for, deciding to engage, and obliterating another human life, completely without human involvement."

The autonomous dogs of war

It's a remarkable moment when a company specializing in robotics feels the need to make a public pledge that it will not support the weaponization of its products.

Boston Dynamics has done just that—and is calling on its competitors in the industry to do the same.

Boston Dynamics is perhaps best known for its viral YouTube videos of Spot, its dog-shaped robot. The company also has a humanoid robot called Atlas.

Five other firms signed on to the Boston Dynamics-initiated commitment: Agility Robotics, ANYbotics, Clearpath Robotics, Open Robotics, and Unitree Robotics.

"We believe that adding weapons to robots that are remotely or autonomously operated, widely available to the public, and capable of navigating to previously inaccessible locations where people live and work, raises new risks of harm and serious ethical issues," the companies wrote in the letter.

Boston Dynamics CEO Robert Playter added in an email to *Axios*, "We are concerned about recent increases in makeshift efforts by individuals attempting to weaponize commercially available robots . . . for this technology to be broadly accepted throughout society, the public needs to know they can trust it. And that means we need policy that prohibits bad actors from misusing it."

I'm happy that Boston Dynamics has pledged to do its part to keep the world safe, but—as with hackers and cybercriminals—if the technology exists, it's pretty hard to stop the bad guys from capitalizing on it.

Cue the politicians who have decided to get involved too.

A bill introduced by Massachusetts State Rep. Lindsay Sabadosa and State Sen. Michael Moore would prohibit the sale, manufacture, and use of weapons-equipped robots.

"This bill puts reasonable guardrails around the use of robots to harass members of the public and bans the weaponization of this technology by those without strict oversight, while also introducing rules for law enforcement to bolster public trust," Moore says.

Run, Spot, run

Let's step back a moment and give credit to Boston Dynamics for what it's created. Spot is a pretty amazing creature. It can navigate rocky paths, climb mountains and function in the rain.

Boston Dynamics' Spot (credit: Wikimedia Commons)

Former MIT professor Marc Raibert started Boston Dynamics 30 years ago as an outgrowth of his research into creating machines that mimicked the leg movements and balance of humans and animals.

Raibert's first robot, the "sand flea," was a compact box on wheels that could jump 10 meters into the air.

Spot and Atlas—along with a third robot called Stretch that can unload boxes from a shipping container—have come a long way since then.

Spot can be fitted with a wide assortment of tools and sensors. (Massachusetts State Police sent a test Spot to check out a suspicious object at a gas station.)

Spot can be programmed to follow a preset course, or it can be maneuvered by a remote operator via joystick. Spot can walk up and down stairs and get to places a human couldn't—either because the space is too tight or too dangerous.

But Spot's use by the police unnerved some civil liberties experts.

In 2016, Dallas Police sent a bomb disposal robot armed with explosives to kill a sniper who had shot at five police officers. It was the first time a nonmilitary robot had been used intentionally to kill a person.

That worries Kade Crockford, director of the Technology for Liberty program at the ACLU of Massachusetts.

"We just really don't know enough about how the state police are using this," Crockford told the National Public Radio station in Boston. "And the technology that can be used in concert with a robotic system like this is almost limitless in terms of what kinds of surveillance and potentially even weaponization operations may be allowed."

Crockford wants to see "some law and some regulation to establish a floor of protection to ensure that these systems can't be misused or abused in the government's hands. And no, a terms-of-service agreement is just insufficient."

Spot somehow seems different

"These are particularly evocative robots," notes Ryan Calo, a professor at the University of Washington School of Law who specializes in robotics and cyberlaw, and "that affects our perceptions of them."

Remember the eyes on Amazon's Proteus robot which can morph into heart shapes while its mouth flashes when it's "happy?"

So evocative is Spot that animal-rights advocacy group PETA felt it needed to clarify that, while Spot is not a real dog, one should still not kick it. (This was in response to a video released by Boston Dynamics showing employees kicking a Spot to demonstrate how robust it is.)

Though Boston Dynamics has pledged to keep Spot in nonmilitary roles, the robot is often described as "terrifying."

"I've looked at a tally of the headlines, and it's a high percentage of them that call it terrifying," Raibert told *Boston.com*. "It's hard to find a Hollywood movie that has something like a robot in it that doesn't go wrong."

That fear is not just due to Tinseltown. People ascribe intentionality to robots that look like them or like animals. They fear that they might go rogue, which is a different worry than Spot simply malfunctioning or being misused.

Intentionality isn't "in our robots," Raibert stresses. "I think people tend to confuse and conflate one with the other. It's just not what we're doing."

There will be more robots that get around by biomimicking animals.

A 2023 paper published in *Nature Communications* described a number of biological inspirations:

+ The sea lion, which uses flippers to swim and walk

+ The meerkat, which stands on its hind legs to check for danger

+ The chukar bird, a partridge that lives in Asia and Europe, which relies on wings for balance when walking up an incline

The paper goes into details on the M4, a multimodal mobility "morphobot," which alternately walks, crouches, rolls and tumbles. The M4 has:

+ Four legs

+ Four thrusters (for flight)

+ Two thrusters and two wheels for climbing up slopes and tumbling over large obstacles

+ Two wheels and two hands for loco-manipulation

+ Four wheels for operation as a UGV (unmanned ground vehicle) and crouching

Another four-legged robot is the ANYmal from Zurich-based startup Swiss-Mile. ANYmal is positioned as a "general purpose solution to smart freight logistic systems," in particular for last-mile delivery. "In contrast to wheeled delivery platforms and lightweight delivery drones, [ANYmal] can efficiently overcome flat terrains, go over obstacles like stairs and steps, and carry heavy payloads in indoor and outdoor spaces."

Swiss-Mile Robotics (credit: Swiss-Mile)

ANYmal can stand on just two of its legs, which allows it, Swiss-Mile notes, to push the buttons in an elevator or open a door. The robot has a speed of six miles an hour.

Warrior-bots without a dogged conscience

iRobot's 510 PackBot couldn't be more different than Spot in terms of look, feel and functionality. While the PackBot has a tread for mobility rather than trying to imitate animal locomotion, it can climb stairs, drive through mud, and operate in all-weather conditions.

The PackBot's description gives away how its parent company expects it to be used: "It can accommodate eight payload bays."

That's military language.

iRobot says that the PackBot is intended for bomb disposal, search, and operating in hazardous environment. But it's no small stretch of the imagination to envision at least one of those payload bays being fitted with a rifle, rocket launcher or laser weapon.

"It is designed for use by warfighters and first responders to carry out dangerous missions in high-threat battlefield scenarios," the company states, resolving any debate and making its business model crystal clear.

The PackBot can also "perform surveillance and reconnaissance; chemical, biological, radiological and nuclear detection; building and route clearance; explosive ordnance disposal; HazMat handling; improvised explosives device (IED) detection; and checkpoint, vehicle, and personnel inspections."

The PackBot is equipped with an explosives detection sensor, two-way audio, built-in GPS, and multiple high-resolution cameras.

More than 2,000 of the 23-kilogram robots have been deployed in Iraq and Afghanistan, and over 5,000 PackBots have been delivered to military and civil defense forces across the world.

The PackBot can run for 4 hours on its lithium-ion rechargeable batteries. It has a top speed of just under 10 miles per hour.

If the corporate parent's name—iRobot—sounds familiar, that's because this was the company that developed the Roomba, which by 2004, two years after its launch, had sold a million units. In 2022, Amazon offered $1.7 billion for the company in an all-cash deal (the acquisition still has to clear antitrust hurdles in the U.S. and U.K.) but only after iRobot spun off its military division into a new company called Endeavor Robotics. The latter was acquired by Teledyne FLIR in 2019 for $382 million in cash.

Another company, Philadelphia-based Ghost Robotics, has started marketing a weaponized dog-like robot to several branches of the U.S. military and its allies.

Ghost Robotics doesn't call them "dogs," instead opting for a far more tech-y name, the Q-UGV, short for "Quadrupedal Unmanned Ground Vehicle." (In other words, a robot dog, although it has a slightly more grasshopper-like appearance than Boston Dynamics' Spot.)

Ghost Robotics has shipped some 250 Q-UGVs to more than 25 national security customers. The company's killer bots could be seen "trotting" through the International Defense Exhibition and Conference, an arms fair in Abu Dhabi, in 2023.

Ghost Robotics CEO Jiren Narendra Parikh defended his company's killing potential in a conversation with *TechCrunch's* Brian Heater in 2022.

"We don't make the payloads. Are we going to promote and advertise any of these weapon systems? Probably not," Parikh told Heater. "Because we're selling to the military, we don't know what they do with them. We're not going to dictate to our government customers how they use the robots."

Even the avowed pacifist, Spot, could find itself in ethically ambiguous situations.

"If Spot happens to wander near an enemy tank formation, Spot could fight. So long as Spot doesn't target humans," notes Zak Kallenborn, a policy fellow at George Mason University, speaking with *NatSec Daily*. "Of course, clear offensive uses like turning Spot into a robo-suicide bomber would require approval, but there's a lot of vagueness here."

Ghost Robotics Vision 60 prototype (credit: Wikimedia Commons)

The military is embracing AI

As of 2021, the U.S. military had at least 685 ongoing AI projects. Not all of the research is known, but here are two areas that we are aware of:

1. AI-powered tanks that can scan for threats on their own. Their operators would then simply touch highlighted spots on a screen.
2. AI in the cockpit that will help F-16 pilots automate complex dogfighting maneuvers, freeing pilots to focus on firing weapons and coordinating with drone swarms.

In January 2023, the Pentagon updated a previously murky policy in order to allow AI weapons to take kill shots on their own.

So much can go wrong.

Consider the following AI mobility-related potential disaster: American AI misinterprets acoustic surveillance of submarines in the South China Sea as the first signs of a nuclear attack. The Americans begin to prepare. China's own AI—which in this case would have access to the nuclear codes—notices the American preparations and preemptively fires.

"What's going to be disconcerting is when we encounter adversaries that don't have the same ethics," says Matt Devost, CEO of the global advisory firm OODA. "Do we end up having to unleash some sort of autonomy in our weapons because our adversaries have launched autonomous weapons against us?"

Autonomy in the military will need to have a strict line of accountability, so it's clear who is responsible in case of an error. We already have such systems in place for human soldiers on the battlefield. But when an autonomous vehicle runs over a pedestrian, who takes the fall?

Another scenario: "Imagine using image recognition when a drone is flying in the air and matching faces against faces on a kill list," suggests Steve Henn of NPR's *Morning Edition*. "If a robot like that made a mistake, who would be responsible? The programmer? The manufacturer? The military commander who launched it on its mission?"

"It forces us to confront whether we really control machines," Ryan Calo, a law professor at the University of Washington told NPR.

If AI had been around during the Cuban Missile Crisis of the 1960s, would ChatGPT have stood with President John F. Kennedy?

"I'm not a fan of abdicating control to the machines," Devost stressed during an interview on NPR's *On the Media*. "We have to figure out which are fundamentally human decisions, and which are the ones that can be automated or augmented."

Task Force 59, a group within the U.S. Navy's Fifth Fleet, focuses on integrating robotics and artificial intelligence into naval operations.

In December 2022, Task Force 59 brought more than a dozen uncrewed surface vessels, aerial drones, and submersibles to the Persian Gulf for a test just 100 miles off the coast of Iran.

The AI-powered craft are meant to be Task Force 59's distributed eyes and ears, *Wired's* Will Knight reports. "They will watch the ocean's surface with cameras and radar, listen beneath the water with hydrophones, and run the data they collect through pattern-matching algorithms that sort the oil tankers from the smugglers."

The AI highlights suspicious vessels in the area and can engage autonomously "although we don't recommend it," notes Captain Michael Brasseur, head of Task Force 59. "We don't want to start World War III."

Scott Galloway believes we have likely overblown the threat.

"AI fear mongering is also a business strategy for the incumbents, who'd like the government to suppress nascent competition," the author, podcaster and popular professor of marketing at New York University's Stern School of Business, writes in a piece entitled "Techno-narcissism."

Galloway points to how the real world is "messy and multifaceted . . . our efforts to get the best from technology and reduce its harms are not clean or simple. We aren't going to wish a regulatory body into existence, nor should we trust seemingly earnest tech leaders to get this one right."

Send in the drones

In the dystopian film *Slaughterbots*, bird-sized drones actively seek out a particular individual and shoot a small amount of dynamite point-blank through that person's skull. These drones fly themselves and are too small and nimble to be easily caught, stopped or destroyed.

Slaughterbots have long since left the realm of fantasy. One such drone nearly killed the president of Venezuela in 2018. Hobbyists can build them for under $1,000, with all the parts readily available for purchase at Amazon and other online retailers. Hezbollah in Lebanon, the Houthis in Yemen, and Iran have all employed these so-called "suicide drones."

Autonomous killing drones are what Lee, in *The Atlantic*, calls "an unintended consequence of AI and robotics becoming more accessible and inexpensive. Imagine, a $1,000 political assassin!"

Drones—and drone swarms consisting of thousands of units in the sky—cost less than a single F-35 fighter or a ballistic missile. That's a potent weapon for terrorists and rogue states.

Future autonomous drones will be "more intelligent, more precise, faster and cheaper; they will learn new capabilities such as how to form swarms with teamwork and redundancy, making their missions virtually unstoppable," Lee claims. "A swarm of 10,000 drones . . . could wipe out half a city."

Drone swarms are harder to fight against than a single flying vehicle. That's why they've been used to such devastating effect in the Russia-Ukraine war.

On October 29, 2022, a Russian fleet on the Black Sea was attacked by 16 drones—9 in the air and 7 in the water—purportedly launched by Ukraine.

In response, Russia has used its drones, mainly the Shahed-136 from Iran, to attack Ukraine's electrical and water systems. These drones are preprogrammed and released in groups of five. They're easy to destroy—if you can find them. They fly low and slow enough to be mistaken on radar for migrating birds.

"We have been convinced once again the wars of the future will be about maximum drones and minimal humans," said Ukrainian vice prime minister Mykhailo Fedorov in 2022.

Drones operated in swarms are small—a robotic aircraft the size of a starling would be all but invisible when spread out. But when those tiny drones coalesce into a swirling dark cloud, moving the way such phenomena move in nature, they can inflict significant damage.

"Once a target has been designated by a human decision maker, the weapon will have autonomy to operate and get there, to be ready to navigate the terrain properly, and to make decisions based on how it achieves the impact of that target," notes Devost.

"A swarm is an intelligent organism and an intelligent mechanism," says Samuel Bendett, an expert in Russian weapons at the Center for Naval Analyses. "Just like in an insect swarm, in a bird swarm, in a school of fish—each drone thinks for itself, communicates with the others, and shares information about its position in a swarm, the environment that the swarm is in, potential threats coming at the swarm, and what to do about it, especially when it comes to changes in direction or changes in swarm composition."

And as with all autonomous vehicles we've discussed in this book, a drone swarm does not get tired. It does not get discouraged and turn back like a human-piloted vehicle.

Researchers at RAND, the U.S. government-funded defense think tank, looked at war games of a Chinese invasion of Taiwan. RAND found that deploying huge numbers of low-cost aerial drones could "significantly improve the odds of U.S. victory."

Letting AI control the drones will result in a much quicker response than a human drone operator, Devost adds, although he's quick to point out that this "doesn't mean we're going to take humans out of the decision-making equation with regard to what gets targeted."

But a human-in-the-loop approach negates the "benefit" of autonomous weapons, in particular the speed with which a decision can be made. Even if most nations in the world adopted an "only humans can press the kill button" regulation, what's to stop a country that desperately wants to win from simply ignoring those rules? After all, international law didn't stop Russia from invading Ukraine or prevent Syria from killing half a million of its own citizens.

Maybe an outright ban would be best? Not likely either: the U.S., Russia, and the U.K. all oppose banning autonomous weapons, stating that it is "too early" to do so.

Despite the pushback, Devost is not a pessimist.

"What gets really interesting is [when the AI-powered drones] start to demonstrate an ability to operate in a way that is more humane or cognizant of the human impact than a human decision-maker would be able to do."

For example, a drone or drone swarm that has AI could abort or delay a decision based on a rapidly changing situation a human couldn't necessarily handle—like a bus filled with civilians unexpectedly driving too close to a target.

"Humans will remain in the loop as it relates to targeting other humans," Devost stresses. "It's different if you're targeting drones or you're targeting a communications tower."

It is unlikely that nations will ban or at least limit their use of drones.

"Although the destructive power of the atom bomb has so far prevented its use in all-out war, a drone swarm *will* be used once developed, because it is not a cataclysmic weapon," writes Mark Bowden in *The Atlantic*. And "although the explosive punch of small, cheap drones is insignificant compared with that of conventional bombs and missiles, they can be much more accurate."

To get an idea of where we might be headed, look no further than the 2016 episode of the British and Netflix TV series *Black Mirror* called "Hated in the Nation." The episode features tiny drones whose software is hacked and linked to a website where people name the most hated person in the country. At the end of the day, the reprogrammed drones create a swarm to converge on and kill the person at the top of the list.

We must do all we can to prevent such a dystopian future from becoming a reality!

High altitude

Military drones are now soaring to new heights, quite literally. Drones that can reach 60,000 feet (about 12 miles) above the Earth—higher than a jumbo jet flies—would be able to provide intelligence at a height beyond the reach of most radar and missile-defense systems. Moreover, these drones could stay aloft for months at a time, making them a viable alternative to certain satellites.

For commercial uses, high-altitude drones could beam internet services into areas with low connectivity with better bandwidth capacity than satellites, since the drones are closer to Earth.

Airbus has a drone called the Zephyr. It's flown up to 70,000 feet for 64 days. The target is 200 days in the air.

BAE's PHASA-35 drone climbed above 65,000 feet in a test and flew for 24 hours. The drone has a wingspan of 115 feet—about the same length as a Boeing 737—but weighs only as much as a motorcycle.

Why the long wings? To have enough space to carry all the solar panels the drone will need—yes, the BAE drone will be solar-powered. BAE launched a test in New Mexico in 2023. BAE hopes that the drone will eventually be able to stay up in the air for up to a year.

Dave Corfield, CEO of Prismatic, the BAE unit that developed the drone, told *The Wall Street Journal* that it allows BAE "to operationalize the stratosphere." The new drones are expected to enter service in late 2026.

Not all high-flying drones have been successful.

Boeing was working on its own solar-powered drone, a 40-foot-wide vehicle that could fly at 60,000 feet for at least 5 years. Work on the SolarEagle project was suspended in 2012—2 years before it was scheduled to make its maiden flight—for reasons Boeing did not disclose.

Can AI make wars less deadly?

Whether we like it or not, AI will be a key part of the future of warfare. Can mobility with artificially intelligent smarts actually save lives?

Yes. Here are three ways:

+ Fewer soldiers on the battlefield should translate into fewer deaths. The outcome might still be devastating, but robots or AI-powered tanks and other vehicles fighting each other autonomously means fewer chances for casualties.

+ More targeting killings should result in less collateral damage. If an AI-powered tank or robotic soldier can home in on the exact bad guy using facial or gait recognition, the military will run less of a risk of destroying buildings and harming innocent civilians and friendly forces. The flip side: such technology could enable the genocide of an entire group of people. Imagine a terrorist programs a drone to carry out the targeted killing of only certain business elites.

+ Shorter wars can also lead to fewer dead. Will the wars really be brief? Only if one side has superior weapons to the other. If both sides have equivalent means of destruction, we may be looking at Terminator-level destruction again.

On the other hand, if autonomous weaponry brings the cost of war down, it could make global-scale conflicts more prevalent, especially as smaller countries have the opportunity to acquire the same level of AI-powered technology as their wealthier adversaries.

Indeed, if AI platforms are deployed in the millions, "their agility and lethality . . . will leave humans utterly defenseless," says UC Berkeley computer science professor Stuart Russell.

Can robots be more humane than humans?

Could mobility, robots, and artificial intelligence improve interactions between the police and citizens?

+ If you send a robot into a conflict and it's not worried about getting hurt, would it be less likely to draw arms?

+ If it does come under fire, would the person on the other end be less likely to shoot the robot?

✦ Robots don't have the same rush of adrenaline when shot at. Would it respond more rationally and objectively and be less driven by emotion and revenge?

That was most likely the goal when Dallas police sent in that police robot rigged up with a bomb to take out a sniper who had already struck 12 police officers and killed 5.

"We saw no other option but to use our bomb robot and place a device on its extension for it to detonate where the suspect was," Dallas Police Chief David Brown told reporters. "Other options would have exposed our officers to grave danger."

"As far as I know, this is a first time that they've used a robot to intentionally kill someone," notes Ryan Calo, of the University of Washington.

It likely won't be the last "off-label" use.

Is it time for concern?

"I think we get worried when robots start to get used in traffic stops, or stops on the street, when we start to put nonlethal weapons on drones so that the officer doesn't even need to approach the individual," Calo says. "Before that, I just think we should have a policy so that officers know what they can and can't do."

Military-to-consumer technology transfer

There have been many inventions that started with the military and subsequently migrated to commercial use. Among the cooler products we use daily which started in the army:

✦ **Duct tape**. In desperate need during World War II of a durable adhesive tape, the army asked Johnson & Johnson to develop the idea. It was originally called "duck tape" for its waterproof nature.

✦ **Super glue**. An Eastman Kodak scientist was initially searching for compounds for use in a plastic rifle sight. Super Glue was turned into a commercial product in 1958. In the Vietnam War, it was sprayed over wounds to stop bleeding.

✦ **Silly Putty**. In the 1940s, the U.S. needed a new source of rubber after Japan invaded Malaysia, which was a major supplier. A chemist at General Electric came out with an alternative. But it had no direct military application. In 1950, it became the beloved children's toy known to this day as Silly Putty. It was used on the Apollo 8 mission in 1968 to keep the spacecraft's instruments in place.

✦ **Frozen juice concentrate**. Frozen and thawed orange juice would typically turn an unappetizing brown color. It had a bitter taste to boot, prompting soldiers to nickname it "battery acid." Frozen concentrate solved both problems. In 1946, Minute Maid began selling frozen juice products commercially.

✦ **The microwave oven.** Microwave technology was originally developed as a form of radar to locate enemies in World War II. It was almost by accident that an engineer at defense contractor Raytheon discovered microwaves could also cook and reheat food. Today, more than 90% of U.S. households own a microwave.

✦ **GPS.** In the 1960s, the department of defense began developing what would become the global positioning systems we rely on today. The first GPS took until 1994 to become fully operational.

✦ **EpiPen.** Those who carry an EpiPen in their purses or pockets to stop a severe allergic reaction might be surprised to learn it was originally developed to deliver treatment to soldiers who came in contact with a nerve agent. It was later tweaked to deliver epinephrine against anaphylactic shock.

✦ **Aviator sunglasses.** Today a fashion item, these glasses were developed in the 1930s by Bausch & Lomb as a way to protect test pilots from the dangerously bright sunlight of the upper atmosphere.

✦ **The Jeep.** The name derives from "General Purpose," abbreviated as G.P. and eventually nicknamed "Jeep." Some 600,000 Jeeps were manufactured during World War II. Now you can get one from Stellantis for commuting to work.

✦ **Aerosol bug spray.** Soldiers stationed in the South Pacific in World War II needed a quick and easy way to kill mosquitos, leading to the development of what the military nicknamed a "bug bomb."

✦ **Virtual reality.** The evolution of the internet-to-goggle-mediated virtual-, augmented- and mixed-reality started in 1979 when the military produced the first head-mounted visual display flight simulator. The rest, as they say, is meta.

✦ **The internet.** I'd be remiss if I left off this list the internet, which started as ARPANET—the Advanced Search Projects Agency Network—during the Cold War to facilitate the sharing of information without the need for a command center, which the military feared could become a target for the Soviets.

Could the same kind of military-to-commercial transition happen with drones? We don't have to wait to find out. It's already underway.

Drones for good

Percepto, Edgybees, and Airobotics have developed drones not to fire weapons in a war zone but to monitor and secure industrial environments under harsh rain, snow and dust conditions.

+ **Edgybees** proved its mettle in post-hurricane Irma in Florida. It also has bundled its augmented reality drone tech for firefighters and police into an app called "First Response."

+ **Airobotics** is used by South32 in Australia to thermally monitor oil pipelines for leaks. Its drones can be programmed to fly over a particular site every day at the same time, saving money while minimizing human error.

+ **Percepto**'s Sparrow, which has backing from billionaire Mark Cuban, can launch from a self-enclosed box and return there when it needs to recharge. While in its box (the Sparrow can fly for around 40 minutes between charges), the base conducts autonomous "health checks." Percepto was also used following a hurricane in Florida by its utility client, Florida Power and Light.

Percepto CEO and cofounder Dor Abuhasira explains why drones for good are taking off. "Some of these companies can generate up to a million dollars an hour, so preventing downtime has the highest impact on a company's return-on-investment," he says.

An estimated 10% of power outages globally are due to hurricanes, according to the World Bank. During Hurricane Dorian in 2019, Florida Power & Light reported $274 million in damages, which left 160,000 customers in the dark.

Covid-19 has contributed to heightened demand for autonomous drones in the commercial sector, Abuhasira notes. "It's given companies a bigger urgency to explore these new types of solutions. They're experiencing firsthand what happens when they don't have the ability to get people to work."

In 2023, Percepto was granted a first-ever waiver from the FAA to allow unmanned aircraft systems to operate beyond the visual line of sight. That means human operators could be located far from potential hurricane dangers. Without this waiver, it's doubtful safe drone monitoring could take off.

The waiver has already paid off: A month after it was granted, Percepto raised a Series C round of $67 million—impressive in the current investing climate—bringing the company's total raise to $120 million.

Three other drone companies are worth mentioning here.

1. San Mateo-based **Skydio** drones are popular in the military—they are used by every branch of the U.S. department of defense. But Skydio has found a secondary niche with customers at 200 public safety agencies and more than 60 energy utilities. "Skydio drones are being used to save lives and aid in the maintenance of critical infrastructure in ways that sounded like science fiction just a few years ago," says Bastiaan Janmat, managing director of Linse Capital, which led the latest round of $230 million.

2. **SiteAware** (formerly Dronomy) sells off-the-shelf drones and its own bundled software to create a virtual replica of a job site that can be accessed via a web browser from any remote location. As the drones fly low over an actual job site, the 3D model is updated, and data is stored on the cloud. Contractors can add 3D annotations to the models.

3. **Zipline** is using drones to deliver medication to developing countries. The company now has 19 operational hubs across the globe and, following a Series F round of $330 million in 2023, is valued at over $4 billion.

Insect inspections

Drones may be on the front lines of inspecting and maintaining infrastructure, but the future may be a whole lot smaller. Imagine:

+ Cyborg cockroaches that can find earthquake survivors

+ A "robot-fly" that sniffs out gas leaks

+ Flying lightning bugs that pollinate farms . . . in space

These aren't just buzzy ideas.

Some robotic engineers are strapping 3D-printed sensors onto the backs of bugs. Others are creating fully robotic creatures inspired by the ways insects move and fly. A third group is creating hybrids, where a live insect's antennae are connected to a robot.

Cyber-roaches are only becoming possible today as electronic sensors get smaller and better. The latest fabrication techniques also make it easier to construct the tiny parts required. And, of course, tiny batteries are lasting longer.

My Apple Watch can run for two days between charges these days. Indeed, improvement in electronic sensors in general can be attributed to research on smart devices and wearables.

"You can really leverage a lot of those sensors or put those sensors into micro-scale robots," says Kevin Chen of MIT's electric engineering faculty.

"We start by looking at how insects solve these problems, and we're making a lot of progress," says Sawyer B. Fuller, who directs the Autonomous Insect Robotics Laboratory at the University of Washington. "Still, there's much to be done."

A cyborg cockroach could be fitted with carbon dioxide sensors and cameras. A tiny roach-backpack could have solar panels for power, and a Bluetooth sensor for remote control connected to the insect's abdomen. The sensor would send tiny shocks to direct the roach left or right.

MIT's Chen is not stopping with cockroach backpacks.

Chen's fully robotic lightning bugs have artificial muscles that emit colored light during flight. This could enable a swarm of these robots to communicate with each other, Chen says.

There are ethical considerations to wiring up the insect world.

Do cockroaches feel pain? We don't know. But that doesn't mean we should ignore the possibility, says Jeff Sebo, an animal bioethics professor at New York University.

"We're not even paying lip service to their welfare or rights," he laments. "We're not even going through the motion of having laws or policies or review boards in place so that we can halfheartedly try to reduce the harm that we impose on them."

But learning from insects, if not modifying them, makes sense. "You see insects doing crazy things that you would just never be able to do at human scale," says Fuller at the University of Washington. "We just look at how insects do it."

I can imagine a scenario where tiny drones or robotic insects could penetrate a school or synagogue shooting in progress to gather intel before sending in the SWAT team (which might also be robotic).

An armed robot—maybe a robotic dog—could also shock a shooter who was expecting a human. That momentary distraction might mean the difference between life and death.

And if the shooter aims at the robot dog, would the latter respond by using its AI to take out the terrorist?

Could a swarm of robo-roaches sting a bad guy into submission?

I'm all for feeling safe. But I'm not sure that killer robo-roaches should replace air marshals on my next international flight.

Autonomous tanks

Tiny killing machines may be in our future, but a more immediate first step for bringing the latest tech to the battlefield may come from autonomous truck software developer Kodiak Robotics. The company, in 2022, beat out 31 competitors to win a two-year $50 million defense contract to apply Kodiak's software to the U.S. Army's Robotic Combat Vehicle Program.

This is actually the company's second foray into military uses.

In 2021, Kodiak completed a 15-month trial with the U.S. Air Force to develop autonomous vehicles for flight-line operations. Kodiak's main business is automating Class 8 trucks.

The army's approach here is a change from how it's done business in the past, when it preferred to develop self-enclosed "black box" solutions. With Kodiak, the idea was "to find a software provider to take a commercial application and apply it to military use," Kodiak CEO Don Burnette told *FreightWaves*. "Our technology was developed for over-the-road trucking. But it generalizes to a lot of other areas [including] government applications."

In the first year of the program, Kodiak will deploy its autonomous software stack for army-specific use-cases. In the second year, the software will be tried in off-road vehicles. Safety drivers will be present in the first phases of the test.

Armed forces typically use two types of vehicles: wheeled and tracked.

- Wheeled platforms are better for on-road mobility; they run into trouble in rough terrains.

- Tracked platforms are best suited for traversing soft ground and can carry more of a payload. They're also not as susceptible to tire damage since they don't have wheels.

As autonomy goes hand-in-hand with electrification, are we looking at battery-powered tanks in the near future? What kind of problems could that create?

How do you charge a tank in the midst of an operation?

The U.S. military is a massive polluter; if ranked against nations, it would place 47th in global carbon emissions. So, electrification is no less important for the military than for the rest of us.

The army has a target of reducing emissions by 2032 to 50% of 2005 levels and going completely net-zero by 2050.

Light-duty nontactical vehicles will be first up, with all nontactical vehicles going electric by 2045.

Training and leadership development will incorporate climate change topics beginning in 2028, according to a 2022 white paper, "United States Army Climate Strategy."

Brig. Gen. Glenn Dean, who's in charge of ground combat systems for the U.S. Army, told *Defense News* he "isn't sure we're going fully electric anytime soon. Maybe for robotic platforms. That might be the first case because it's about size and weight. If you took the amount of batteries with current technology that you would need to move an Abrams tank purely electrically, it's bigger than the tank! So, we have a packaging and storage problem when it comes to pure electric."

That's echoed in a report from the army entitled, *Powering the U.S. Army of the Future*.

"Advances in battery energy density will undoubtedly take place, but not enough to offset that magnitude of a disadvantage," the study says. It pointed out, additionally, that recharging all-electric vehicles in a short period of time "would require massive quantities of electric power that are not available on the battlefield."

Even if you could get the power, where would you charge all these new Hummers and tanks?

"I can drive a Tesla 300 miles but I'm expecting a charging station at that point," says Dean. "Where are those charging stations? Do you have to bring them with you or are you going to expect them to be there? How big are they? They're probably not going to be there in all the right places, right?"

In some places, the army could set up a dedicated charging area, although that could invite enemy attacks.

Another option—albeit expensive and cumbersome—would be to fly in equipment to a particular location to recharge vehicles. Steve DuMont, GM Defense's new president, even suggested the army could "airdrop batteries."

In 2021, the army estimated it would need to power a future fleet of roughly 225,000 electric vehicles of varying types. The army's Power Transfer Cohort picked 6 companies to address powering electric tanks in remote locations where infrastructure does not exist: Royal Oak, Coritech Services, Czero, Fermata Energy PC Krause and Associates, Tritium Technologies, and Wright Electric.

Electric tanks face challenges even an electric Hummer wouldn't.

"Commercial vehicles don't typically get shot at on the highway," notes John Szafranski, division chief for vehicle electrification at the army's Ground Vehicle Systems Center.

A direct shot to a lithium-ion battery could trigger a fire or explosion. Can military EVs overcome that concern by creating some sort of superstrong enclosure around the battery?

But would that add too much extra weight?

Sounds like a problem that Automotive Ventures portfolio company Safire could help solve!

Electric tanks and other military vehicles "may be a little quieter and that might be helpful, but technically they don't give you a whole lot," adds Mark Cancian, a senior adviser at the Center for Strategic and International Studies.

The army has so far invested about $75 million into battery and electrification-related technology, says Michael Cadieux, director of the army's Combat Capabilities Development Command's Ground Vehicle Systems Center (that's a mouthful!). Another $50 million was planned for fiscal 2022.

"While there are certainly some similarities in commercial and military requirements, we are mindful that the army faces unique operational challenges, compared to those in the commercial market," Cadieux adds.

Those challenges include the ability to operate in extreme environments with widely ranging temperatures—from blazing hot in desert combat to freezing cold in someplace like the Arctic, or the dead of winter in Eastern Europe.

However it plays out, DuMont is feeling upbeat.

"I'm confident that this program is important to the army. It will garner the right funds to progress along. We're going forward, one way or the other."

The nuclear option

Perhaps the wildest solution to the charging conundrum considered in the army's report is mobile nuclear-based power, which would offer the kind of strong energy density and fast charging on which the army could base a workable electrification strategy.

Such mobile plants would be heavy—up to 40 tons—require 2 20-foot shipping containers and have setup and cool-down times of 3 days and 2 days respectively, notes John Luginsland, co-chair and senior scientist and principal investigator at Confluent Sciences.

Luginsland is quick to pour cold water on the nuclear option.

"Mobile nuclear power plants charging all-electric battery combat vehicles will not be ready in 2035," he says.

Moreover, the constraints of nuclear—such as the lengthy setup and cool-down times—"would not be consistent with the army's multi-domain operations strategy," the army's own report said.

"We're an expeditionary army," says the U.S. Army's Szafranski. "If we stay in one place too long, the enemy can take us out. So, we've got to be very mobile."

Ray Dalio's "Big Cycle"

Unfortunately, it's likely that we won't know how helpful—or destructive—AI-powered autonomous and electric mobility can be on front lines until *after* it's been used.

Billionaire hedge fund manager Ray Dalio has proposed a concept he calls the "Big Cycle." Major changes often begin only following a major conflict, he says.

Wars are terribly costly, but they produce tectonic shifts that realign the world order, Dalio points out. Wars establish new powers that no one wants to challenge, which, in turn, leads to peace and prosperity—for a time, at least.

People then bet on this peace; they borrow money on this peace. Inevitably, though, the resulting wealth is redistributed unevenly, prompting new conflict.

As the financial bubble bursts, governments print more money, increasing the disparity between poor and rich, frequently resulting in revolution. That can be without bloodshed, but too frequently it's not.

Other, more antagonistic players watch what's happening as they prepare to make their own moves, and the cycle begins again.

"You can see these cycles going all the way back to the Roman Empire," Dalio says.

When it comes to warfare, will mobility with AI, autonomy and electrification follow a similar trajectory, bringing an earthquake of change that leads to a new and better world order for a certain period of time?

What would that new order look like?

Can we direct the flow of history?

Any way we look at it, the robots are coming. Let's just hope they don't adopt the infamous catchphrase of Star Trek's robotic enemies, the Borg: "Resistance is futile."

What we've learned

+ The intersection of AI and robotics in warfare has ignited a complex and multifaceted debate, marked by both optimism and pessimism. On one hand, proponents of this technological synergy argue that AI-driven autonomous systems can potentially reduce casualties by replacing human soldiers in dangerous missions. These machines can carry out tasks more efficiently and precisely, minimizing human errors and collateral damage, and mitigating the emotional toll of war. Additionally, AI can be utilized for strategic planning and decision-making, potentially leading to more effective conflict resolution and reducing the likelihood of large-scale conflicts.

+ On the flip side, there are valid concerns that these advancements could trigger a new arms race, ultimately making warfare more accessible and escalating the potential for global conflict. Moreover, the use of autonomous systems raises ethical concerns about accountability and control, as well as the risk of accidental escalations and unintended consequences.

+ The balance between the hopeful promise of AI and robotics in warfare and the apprehensive dread of their destructive potential remains a central challenge for policymakers, military leaders, and society as a whole.

■　■　■

Epilogue

Where to Invest

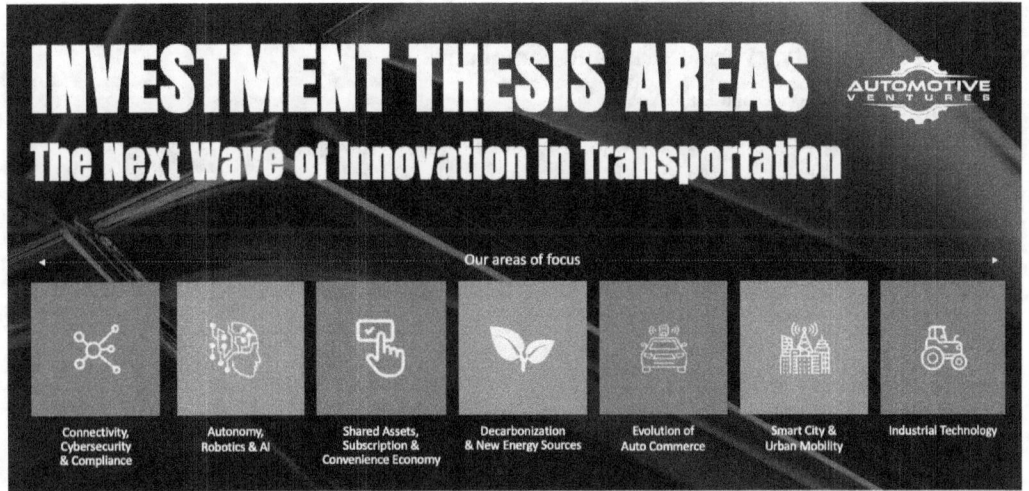

Automotive Ventures' investment thesis areas (credit: Automotive Ventures)

Through eleven chapters, I've tried to present a comprehensive lay of the land.

Now, it's time for action.

In which areas of mobility can we invest to make the big changes we'll need to save the planet and improve human lives?

It's a hard call, David Roberts, host of the *Volts* podcast, told me. "There are lots of things we could say about the future of mobility in 20 to 50 years. What's opaque to me is the 5- to 10-year horizon. We have always ever known a growing fossil-fuel industry. What happens when that growth stops? What does a fossil-fuel industry decline look like? Will it go gracefully? What will it do to relations between countries becoming energy self-sufficient? No one has seen this before."

Will human ingenuity prevail and save the planet from the coming climate crisis? I asked Roberts.

"Humans are super clever," he replied. "But we don't need to wait for some isolated supergenius who will do something that's a quantum leap ahead of what exists. That's not how human cleverness manifests. The advances are happening in increments right now. There are minigeniuses all around us. We're figuring it out. I do have faith."

Roberts even believes that innovation can overcome politics.

"Humankind will overcome," he says reassuringly. "Ingenuity will produce things so new and obviously superior, it will wipe away political battles and pettiness in a tsunami. All this talent will accomplish things we can't even conceive of now or predict."

At Automotive Ventures, we believe that the biggest opportunities for early-stage mobility investment are across seven areas:

1. Connectivity, cybersecurity and compliance
2. Autonomy, robotics and AI
3. Shared assets, subscription and convenience economy
4. Decarbonization and new energy solutions
5. Digitization of auto commerce
6. Smart city and urban mobility
7. Industrial technology

Investment Thesis Area 1: Connectivity, cybersecurity and compliance

Vehicles are creating more data than ever, which is both an opportunity and a threat.

The use-cases for vehicle data are many and include:

+ Telematics and fleet management

+ Fuel economy/emissions reduction

+ Infrastructure optimization

+ In-field testing

+ Reduction of manufacturing costs/complexity

+ New feature introduction

+ Production cost optimization

+ Over-the-Air (OTA) software updates

+ Real-time warranty cost optimization

+ Vehicle analytics, driver analytics, and fleet management

Predictive maintenance promises to analyze sensor data to detect signals of machine distress prior to failure.

Vehicle-to-infrastructure (v2i) and vehicle-to-grid (v2g) connectivity continue to be some of the more exciting areas; there is an opportunity for EVs to return excess power back to the grid and/or throttle their charging rate to optimize cost management.

On the flip side, more data with more vulnerable "surface area" of the vehicle means more opportunity for hackers to penetrate vehicles and databases, causing havoc. There will be a fine balance of regulation and compliance versus companies continuing to push the boundaries of innovation.

Areas of investment interest within the connectivity space:

+ **Over-the-Air (OTA) updates:** Automakers aim to generate billions of new, high-margin revenue from vehicle "features-as-a-service," and save a similar amount through warranty and recall avoidance through Over-the-Air (OTA) software updates to vehicles. But designing and building cutting-edge software has not been a historical strong suit for automakers.

+ **Vehicle cybersecurity:** Connectivity enabling vehicle-to-everything (v2x), coupled with technology in general becoming much more complex, means that the growing digital "surface area" of the vehicle provides more opportunity for hacking and bad actors. We aim to identify and invest in companies that protect the digital footprint of the vehicle.

+ **Compliance**: As the mobility space becomes more complex and digitized, compliance has moved to the forefront, whether it's consumer data and processes, government-enforced rules and regulations, ensuring companies' suppliers meet regulations, abiding by international laws, or sourcing products ethically.

+ **Predictive maintenance**: Real-time telematics data can analyze the condition of equipment and help predict when maintenance should be performed to prevent failure of critical components. This approach promises cost savings over routine or time-based preventive maintenance, as tasks are performed only if and as warranted.

+ **Data governance and privacy**: IoT devices are collecting more consumer and vehicle data than ever. Data governance means setting internal standards/policies that apply to how data is gathered, stored, processed, and disposed of. Data privacy enables an individual to determine when, how, and to what extent personal information about them is shared.

Investment Thesis Area 2: Autonomy, robotics and AI

The age of artificial intelligence has arrived.

ChatGPT has generated a lot of buzz for its powerful ability to generate human-like responses to seemingly any question. Its promise is tempered by bias and accuracy problems, as well as how to deal with plagiarism, copyright infringement and students using the technology to cheat.

Despite Tesla's aggressive rollout of its deceptively named "Full Self Driving" functionality, we don't believe we'll see widespread adoption of Level 5 full autonomy for passenger cars anytime soon.

While autonomy offers significant potential benefits (for example, reduction in traffic deaths, reduction in congestion, and improvements in fuel economy), widespread adoption may be hindered by safety concerns, data protection issues, high upfront costs, and insufficient regulation.

Having said that, powerful autonomous use-cases for non-human cargo in the areas of agriculture, mining, construction, and across the supply chain are gaining traction.

Areas of investment interest within the areas of autonomy, robotics and AI include:

+ **Process automation**: Process automation is the technology-enabled automation of complex business processes to accomplish defined organizational goals. It can streamline a business for simplicity, achieve digital transformation, increase service quality, improve service delivery, or help contain costs.

+ **Emergency and first response**: Emergency personnel are on the front lines and must make split-second, critical decisions. Mobility-related technologies in this area include first-responder drones, automated driver and responder alert systems (ADRAS), outdoor tracking and navigation systems, and mobile emergency routing systems.

+ **Artificial intelligence**: We are on the cusp of a new age of AI that will impact all areas of business. Mobility will benefit from dramatic improvements in efficiency and augmentation of the work humans can do. AI will continue to allow us to collect, process and analyze vast amounts of data, drawing insights at a faster rate than ever before.

+ **Robotics in service/repair**: Robots are now commonplace on the vehicle production line, and we expect more of the maintenance and repair of the vehicle to be automated, including services like tire replacement and ADAS calibration. Technician knowledge will be augmented with enhanced data availability to speed decision making with fewer errors.

✦ **Simulation/validation:** Simulation enables assessment of an existing system or prediction of a planned system, comparing alternative solutions and designs, allowing faster time to market and reduction of R&D costs. System validation checks if the system does exactly what it was designed to do in a safe, secure, and reliable manner.

Investment Thesis Area 3: Shared, subscription and the convenience economy

Will the next generation of consumers willingly trade price for convenience?

Mobility won't be immune to consumer expectations that are evolving across every shopping category.

Automakers are set to leverage software to unbundle vehicle options into features-as-a-service, allowing consumers the flexibility to either pay upfront or by the month.

Following Tesla's lead, many manufacturers are now projecting tens of billions of dollars in new annual, high-margin recurring software revenue.

Ride-hailing services have not yet proven their long-term economic viability, as many operators struggle with profitability.

Shared micromobility is facing a backlash of a different kind, as unfettered growth has led to growing pains in large cities. The movement toward outright bans (as witnessed in Paris) doesn't seem to be the right solution.

Areas of investment interest within the sharing, subscriptions, and convenience economy space include:

✦ **Remote/mobile service**: Most of today's vehicle maintenance is conducted within a mechanic shop, but more flexible and innovative solutions offer consumers and fleets the option of bringing the mechanic to them. Combined with telematics-powered predictive maintenance, expect to see more remote and convenient services in the future.

✦ **Gig economy enablement**: The gig economy is the ultimate free market system, enabling independent workers the freedom to engage in short-term work commitments. Technologies servicing this growing segment of the working population include digital marketplaces that match supply to demand, AI, and clever IoT devices.

✦ **Data subscriptions:** Data challenges exist across mobility, including optimizing EV incentives, building a centralized database of vehicle features-as-a-service, forecasting models for EV residual values and vehicle appraisal, and wholesale transaction tools to track vehicle features that may (or may not) be activated after point of sale.

+ **Vehicle subscriptions:** Vehicle subscription models have been challenging so far, but new approaches are emerging. In parallel, captive finance arms will innovate flexible lease products. Vehicles are lasting longer and a large segment of consumers focus on the monthly payment, so we aren't betting against the subscription model just yet.

+ **Vehicle feature unbundling:** Automakers forecast billions of dollars in high-margin revenue from unbundling vehicle features and offering them on a monthly basis. This will necessitate a new wave of innovative startups to help address needs such as a centralized feature clearinghouse, complex "window sticker" data, and helping facilitate consumer cancellations.

Investment Thesis Area 4: Decarbonization and new energy solutions

The world is moving rapidly to reduce our carbon footprint.

The transition toward electrification creates interdependencies, including the need for more electrical generation capacity and the hardening of transmission and distribution networks to meet increased demand from EVs.

In parallel to electrification, trillions of investment dollars are betting on hydrogen for ground and air transport.

Lightweight technologies, such as advanced composites and ceramics, as well as nano-materials, aim to help improve energy efficiency for the movement of both humans and cargo.

There is intense focus on value-chain decarbonization, aiming to reduce emissions from material production and transport, and increase parts and material circularity, bumping up the use of recycled materials across the value chain.

Areas of investment interest when it comes to decarbonization and new energy solutions include:

+ **Electrification of the fleet:** The vehicle fleet is undergoing a massive evolution from the internal combustion engine (ICE) to battery electric vehicles. In many ways, the predictable short routes of commercial fleets are better suited for EVs. But this segment has its own issues—for example, how to ensure sufficient EV charging infrastructure at depots, optimal routing, and predictive maintenance.

+ **Vehicle-to-everything (v2x):** The vehicle is now connected, which enables limitless use cases. V2g (vehicle to grid) enables energy to be pushed back to the power grid. At any given time 95% of cars are parked, while their energy sits unused. V2g uses bidirectional charging to push and pull energy to and from vehicles based on the demand for electricity.

+ **Battery analytics:** Battery analytics is the data-driven analysis of the state-of-health and remaining useful life of a battery. This can help to reduce risk, improve efficiency, and increase trust in batteries. All this helps owners to resell, reuse, and recycle. The ultimate goal is to optimize lifetime value while maximizing battery health.

+ **EV charging:** We'll need 1.2 million Level 2 and over 100,000 Level 3 chargers by 2027 to support the EVs on the road. But we still face big challenges: 21% of current EV chargers are inoperable, and we need to prepare for the demand on the electrical grid. Only through innovative startups focused on these areas will we successfully make this transition.

+ **Alternative fuels:** Hydrogen is the most abundant element in the universe and releases energy when combined with oxygen. There is optimism, but electrolyzers to produce hydrogen need to be paired with abundant and clean energy supplies. Infrastructure requirements to produce, transport, and distribute hydrogen at scale will be significant.

Investment Thesis Area 5: Evolution of auto commerce

The shift from analog to digital shopping shows no sign of slowing down.

The future of automotive commerce will depend upon the digitization of the purchase process and adopting new ownership and usage models.

Opportunities to exploit inefficiencies exist almost everywhere you look along the automotive supply and distribution chain.

Consumers still suffer from a lack of transparency around the vehicle finance process, as well as the protection products that are typically sold by the dealership at point-of-sale.

Further innovation will be discovered across wholesale business-to-business (b2b) automotive marketplaces, as well as those millions of consumer-to-consumer (c2c) transactions that take place each year.

Areas of investment interest within automotive commerce include:

+ **Extended warranty marketplace:** The automotive extended warranty market is currently $20.5 billion, growing to $61 billion by 2030. But consumers continue to suffer from a lack of transparency. Connected vehicles promise to better price the risk to both consumers and the vehicle, giving car owners more flexibility over the lifetime of their vehicle ownership. In mid-2024, Automotive Ventures invested in warranty marketplace player Chaiz.

✦ **P2p vehicle marketplace:** There are over 10 million (p2p) vehicle transactions per year, but incredible friction still exists—fraud, vehicle condition, escrow services, price confidence, financing, and overall trust. The large third-party marketplaces act more as listing services and don't wrap p2p transactions in an envelope of trust.

✦ **Evolution of vehicle finance:** Electrification and vehicle connectivity will aid risk models and deliver more accurate pricing and repricing over the ownership lifecycle. Repricing refers to when a bank changes the interest rate offered to you previously based on its having collected additional data or your credit score changing. Compliance requirements will continue to escalate, presenting opportunities for digitization of the entire transaction, while leveraging AI to analyze deals.

✦ **Vehicle ownership journey:** Despite progress digitizing vehicle shopping, we suffer from a poor consumer experience during the ownership of the vehicle. Opportunities exist to engage consumers in delightful experiences during vehicle ownership, driving loyalty to brands, individual dealerships, financial institutions, and even local merchants.

✦ **Process efficiency:** We are on the cusp of significant breakthroughs for AI and process automation. Opportunities exist to digitize paper-centric processes and automate manual labor, freeing up workers from mundane repetitive tasks. The result will be more productive, happier employees while driving greater efficiencies and profitability for businesses.

Investment Thesis Area 6: Smart city and urban mobility

Cities, vehicles, and pedestrians are becoming more interconnected.

Vehicle-to-grid systems will allow EVs to provide electricity back to the grid or throttle their charging rate based on real-time feedback.

Cities will use a combination of software (v2v) and AI to update mapping and leverage object detection to optimize traffic patterns, driving, and parking strategies.

Smart connectivity will reduce traffic congestion, improve air and noise pollution, and improve safety, speed, and cost of travel.

Public transport will benefit from mobility-as-a-service offerings to integrate and coordinate commuter experiences across all modalities, as well as ride-sharing and micromobility.

Advanced air mobility electric aircraft (eVTOLs) for short-haul routes may be a viable alternative to traditional taxis.

Areas of investment interest across the areas of smart city and urban mobility include:

+ **Parking & fines:** Parking technology allows operators to automate the auditing process with such tools as permitting, gates, smart cards, and online payment options. Related technologies allow cities and municipalities to realize great efficiencies through digitized payment of parking fines and tickets for moving violations.

+ **Traffic routing/optimization:** New technologies are working with cities to optimize traffic flow and to minimize road congestion and time stopped in road traffic. Real-time communication enabled by vehicle-to-everything is a critical technology. Digital parking relays real-time data to motorists to spot vacant parking lots at their preferred locations.

+ **Micromobility:** Micromobility refers to a range of small, lightweight vehicles operated by the user at speeds typically below 16 mph. Micromobility devices include bicycles, e-bikes, electric scooters, electric skateboards, shared bicycle fleets, and electric pedal-assisted bicycles.

+ **Public transport:** Transportation optimization analyzes lanes, business requirements, constraints, logistics, and scenarios to determine optimal routes. Results include maximizing seat yield, minimizing consumer wait times, and reducing carbon emissions. Technologies like IoT, telematics, and edge computing will drastically transform public transportation.

+ **Vehicle & pedestrian safety**: Vehicles have more safety equipment than ever, yet pedestrian deaths are increasing at an alarming rate. Emerging technologies include pedestrian detection and warning as well as automatic emergency braking. IoT devices within cities provide detailed data about pedestrians along with identification of high-risk areas. In 2024, Automotive Ventures invested in Citian, an early-stage company providing tools that combine engineering expertise and artificial intelligence to furnish the real-time data and critical insights that infrastructure owners need in an interactive digital twin environment where a digital replica of an entire city can be created.

Investment Thesis Area 7: Industrial technology

Non-automotive use cases for technology are today among the most compelling.

Agriculture, manufacturing, mining, and warehouse operation have moved more quickly to adopt advanced mobility technologies such as electrification, robotic automation, drones, connectivity, AI and autonomy, mostly because they do not have to deal with the sensitivities associated with moving human cargo.

Some of the most exciting examples of these technologies are being tested in environments that are nearly risk-free, avoiding the need to move human passengers on city streets.

As a result, these industries can demonstrate the tangible return on investment from making these early investments. They will be on the very edge of transforming how labor is repurposed and can provide a "test bed" of experimentation, so these technologies can trickle down to many other areas of mobility in the future.

Areas of investment interest across industrial technology include:

+ **Material science:** Automotive Ventures' primary interest is both in materials that help with the electrification transition, and lighter/stronger composites that will be used in vehicle production. Great strides are being made across many materials, including nanomaterials, ceramics, composites, and polymers. In mid-2024, for example, Automotive Ventures invested in Safire for its drop-in advanced battery safety technology for lithium-ion batteries.

+ **Manufacturing:** Advances have improved manufacturing quality and productivity, including 3D printing (additive manufacturing); computer vision; use of recycled, composite, and lightweight materials; and the use of digital twin technology.

+ **Mining, farming and construction**: We're experiencing much faster adoption of some technologies across commercial areas of mobility that don't risk human operators or threaten pedestrians. This includes autonomy, electrification, robotics and drones, automation, connectivity, spatial data visualization, predictive analytics, and maintenance optimization.

+ **Supply chain circularity**: A circular supply chain reuses or repurposes waste into new or refurbished products. The goal is to minimize the use of raw materials and discarded waste materials. The focus for mobility includes battery reuse and recycling, chemical markers to track the source of input materials, and reclaiming key production inputs.

+ **Supply chain analytics**: Supply chains generate massive amounts of data. Supply chain analytics helps to make sense of all this information, uncovering patterns and generating insights. In terms of mobility, additive manufacturing and blockchain technology have emerged as the two technologies with some of the highest economic relevance.

Towards the future

Investing is a balance between what we know today and how we're funding the future.

At Automotive Ventures, we believe that investments into the early-stage mobility space will deliver outsized returns to our investors as we fund the next wave of innovation in transportation technology.

Here are some of the investments we made out of our funds:

Automotive Ventures' portfolio of investments (credit: Automotive Ventures)

The mobility industry is accelerating, driven by advances in technology and changing consumer behavior. From ride-sharing and electric scooters to autonomous vehicles and drone deliveries, there are multiple opportunities to invest in companies that are shaping the future of how we transport both humans and cargo.

In parallel, as concerns about the environment and climate change increase, there is a growing demand for more sustainable modes of transportation. Investing in companies that are developing electric or hybrid vehicles, or that are involved in public transportation infrastructure projects, can be a way to support these efforts while also profiting from them.

Investing in mobility provides exposure to a growing and dynamic industry segment that is shaping the future of transportation.

Let's invest together!

A final word (or two)

As I get older, I often catch myself contemplating time. I struggle to juxtapose the very short duration that all of us have on this journey with the timelessness of the earth. Eckhart Tolle's quote resonates with me: "Life is the dancer, and you are the dance."

I think back, millions of years ago, to our human ancestors sitting around a fire, mesmerized by this mysterious, powerful, awe-inspiring discovery recently harnessed.

Our ancestors (credit: Shutterstock)

I imagine these same ancestors looking up at the night sky, trying to make sense of the moon and stars and what they're actually looking at.

Fast-forward to the current day, and we're seemingly on the cusp of colonizing other planets. It's amazing and exciting to take account of just how much technological progress has been made over millennia of human history.

If our ancestors had a chance to visit us and look around at our world, what would they think? How would they make sense of the advancements that have taken place?

While the first use of harnessing fire to either cook or heat was about two million years ago, our human ancestors began using tools a million years earlier. But it's really been in the last 250 years, since the beginning of the Industrial Revolution, that we've witnessed the most dramatic acceleration of technology advancement.

For all the wonders of evolution, it hasn't exactly been a smooth transition. Humans especially struggle with recognizing what economists might call externalities, or unintended consequences of their actions. That topic might best be addressed in a future book!

The truth is that our growth-at-all-cost economies have meant a wanton disregard for the environment without appreciation of the impact we've been making on the fragile ecosystem of our mother earth. Humans have been using fossil fuels for thousands of years, with the earliest known use of coal occurring around 4,000 years ago in northern

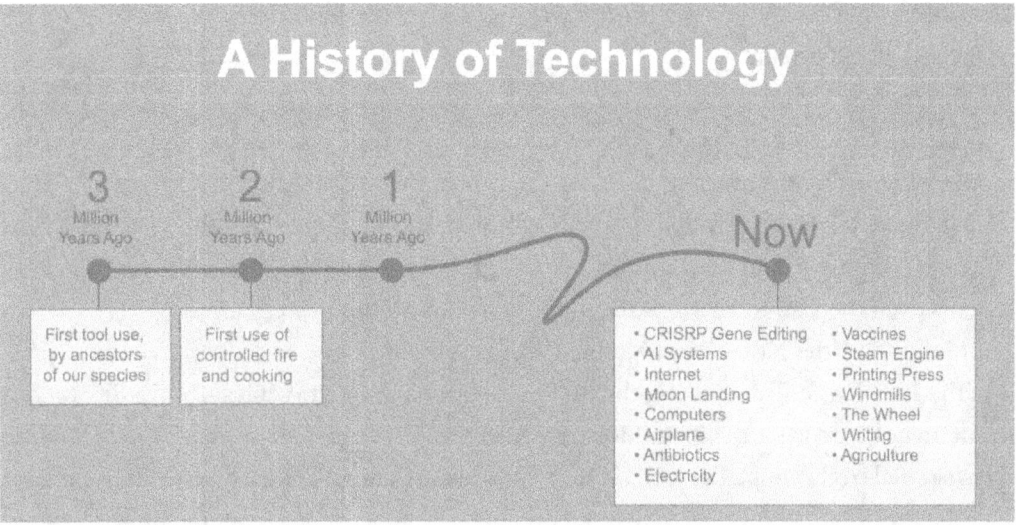

Innovation has been concentrated over the past 250 years (credit: Automotive Ventures)

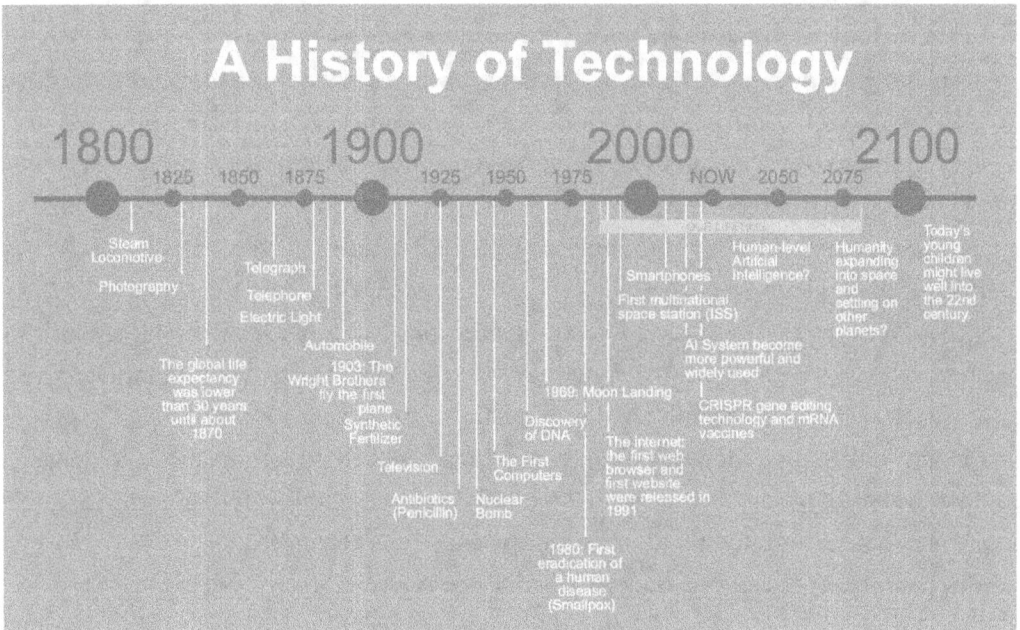

The incredible amount of innovation since the Industrial Revolution (credit: Automotive Ventures)

China, but the burning of fossil fuels for energy began in earnest during the Industrial Revolution.

One of the large downstream effects that we've discussed in this book is the massive volume of carbon dioxide we're emitting into the atmosphere as a result of the accelerated usage of hydrocarbons. And in many ways, we're only really starting to feel those downstream effects now. At the time of writing, we've experienced the warmest 12 months in the last 125,000 years.

But there's hope.

We are witnessing more developed countries like the U.S., Russia, and the UK dramatically reducing the amount of carbon they're emitting into the air. At the same time, though, we're witnessing troubling trends within more emerging economies such as China and India, whose population and industrial growth means they are both very likely to surpass even the U.S. in terms of the amount of carbon dioxide emissions.

Many countries have come together to set ambitious targets to reduce greenhouse gasses. The 1997 Kyoto Protocol was the first international treaty to set legally binding targets to cut greenhouse gas emissions. More recently, the Paris Agreement was a legally binding international treaty adopted in 2015 at the UN Climate Change Conference (COP21) in Paris.

The innovators put their hope in technology—that humans will come up with game-changing new technologies that will negate the damage we've done to the environment over the past 200 years.

I don't think these paths are mutually exclusive. I believe that we have to work hard to dramatically reduce greenhouse gas emissions, while at the same time fund innovative new technologies, like direct carbon capture and geoengineering, that can help in parallel.

As an investor, it's my job to be an eternal optimist, seeking out incredible entrepreneurs looking to change the world. We will continue at Automotive Ventures to make mobility investments that will uniquely alleviate some of the biggest challenges facing humans today and tomorrow.

The challenge for all of us is to stay open-minded to any and all solutions and to contemplate the next million years and the small role we can play, both individually and collectively, to leave this earth in better shape for future generations.

Decarbonization, renewable clean energy, space travel, interplanetary colonization, and the power of harnessing AI to make our lives easier, all promise an exciting future albeit one that's also fraught with uncertainty, anxiety, and concern.

To paraphrase the saying, may we all continue to live in interesting times.

■　■　■

Acknowledgments

I *am grateful to have stumbled across this industry*, almost by chance. Thanks to my high school friend John Scharf for that serendipitous call one evening in late 1999, encouraging me to apply for the newly created position of technology manager at Toronto Auto Auction.

This industry has been extremely generous to me and I want to express my sincere thanks to all the folks who have encouraged and supported my career and personal growth, who helped define me as a person, and who have been along this journey with me.

I would like to thank both Brad Hart and Ruth Hart Stephens for offering me that first job in the automotive industry, and then for selflessly encouraging me to make the move from Canada to the United States.

Thanks to Bill Westlake, who risked his reputation to fight to get me transferred down to the U.S.

Thank you, Gordon Warren, for spurring me to work just a little bit harder than everyone else.

Thank you, Michael Lasini, for encouraging me to pursue further education and always having faith in my abilities.

I'd like to express my gratitude to Patrick Noonan for challenging all of us, instilling a sense of rigor and pride in our work, and providing the environment to truly explore our limits.

Thank you, Dean Eisner, for being so very generous with your time at a point when I was considering leaving the industry. And for opening up about your own past as a reflection and road map for me to understand and follow.

Thanks to Mike Langhorne for believing in a kid early in his career and entrusting him to represent a multibillion-dollar company overseas.

Sincere thanks to Chip Perry, who by far had the greatest impact on my career, for taking a chance on me for a role that I wasn't prepared for and teaching me the power of having more faith in a person than that person may have in himself.

Thank you, Dale Pollak, for giving me so much time and enlightening me about how great businesses are built.

Thank you to my investors in Automotive Ventures for placing your confidence in me.

Thanks, too, to the limited partners across our three VC funds for your faith in our team, investment thesis, and stewardship.

Thanks to Justin for your partnership. This thing never would have happened without you.

Thanks to Keith for the successful internship down in Atlanta and the creative solution to our chapter introduction images.

Thank you, Stella, for your unwavering support as I jumped from one entrepreneurial venture to the next.

Thanks go out to Rafa, Lucy, Oscar, Luna, Henry, Pippa, Remi, Charles, Lamb Chop, Pete, Freddy, and Cooper for teaching me the meaning of life and making me a better person.

Finally, I'm most thankful for my mother, for being the greatest inspiration in my life. I couldn't have asked for a better role model who, by example, taught me the secret to living a fulfilled life: gratitude, generosity, and grace.

I would be remiss without expressing my sincere thanks to Brian Blum, who has been my collaborator throughout our second book-writing process together. You are such an amazing human being, and I honestly could never have envisioned this coming together without you as a partner. May this be just another of many more projects yet to come.

■ ■ ■

About the Author

S*teve Greenfield* is General Partner of Automotive Ventures, an early-stage automotive technology and mobility VC fund that helps entrepreneurs raise growth capital and accelerate their businesses and delivers outsized returns to investors in the fund.

Steve's strongest angel investment was CarTrade India, which delivered a 140x return.

Steve served as TrueCar's Senior Vice President of Strategy and Business Development, and AutoTrader.com's Vice President of Product Management and Business Development, overseeing the acquisitions of vAuto, Kelley Blue Book, HomeNet Automotive, VinSolutions, and DealerScience.

Earlier in his career, Steve served as Manheim's Director of International Development, overseeing Manheim's overseas investments, including establishing new joint ventures in Dubai, Istanbul, and Beijing.

Steve is author of two books: *The Future of Automotive Retail* and *The Future of Mobility*.

Steve grew up in an automobile-centric family. His father raced cars, and many weekends were spent in the family's garage, replacing transmissions or the "top end" of an engine.

For fun, Steve likes to ride his three motorcycles on the racetrack (his personal land speed record is 180 mph on a Yamaha R1 at Road Atlanta) and hang out with his eleven rescue cats.

Endnotes

Introduction

Walter Russell Mead is always an insightful analyst of public policy. So, it seemed fitting to start the book with a quote from the Bard College professor of foreign affairs and humanities.

The paper cited from the journal *Earth System Science Data* was published April 17, 2023.

Climate scientists Andrew King and Steven Sherwood were interviewed about greenhouse gas emissions in *The Conversation* in May 2023: "Two Trillion Tonnes of Greenhouse Gasses, 25 Billion Nukes of Heat: Are We Pushing Earth Out of the Goldilocks Zone?"

The 2021 survey of young people that found 75% felt the future was "frightening" comes from "Climate Anxiety in Children and Young People and Their Beliefs About Government Responses to Climate Change: A Global Survey," published in *The Lancet*.

Katharine Hayhoe spoke to *The New York Times* in 2022 for German Lopez's article, "Climate Optimism."

John Doerr's book, *Speed & Scale: A Global Action Plan for Solving Our Climate Crisis Now,* was published in 2021 by Portfolio.

The alarming data from the Copernicus Climate Change Service was published in *The Washington Post* article, "Scientists Knew 2023's Heat Would be Historic—But Not by This Much," in January 2024.

António Guterres's comments about the climate change catastrophe were reported in *The New York Times* article, "*Coming Soon: More Oil, Gas and Coal,*" from November 2023.

Zoe Schlanger wrote about growing fossil fuel production in *The Atlantic,* "One Huge Contradiction is Undoing Our Best Climate Efforts," November 10, 2023.

Somini Sengupta's article, "The American Exception," appeared in *The New York Times* on February 28, 2023.

We learned about Milton Klöwer's study on the environmental costs of travel from Liz Kimbrough's April 2022 article in *Mongabay*, "How Much Does Air Travel Warm the Planet? New Study Gives a Figure."

We learned about the French ban on short-haul flights in the *Forbes* article from 2023, "France Legally Bans Short-Haul Flights—Environmentalists Want More."

Data on passenger air travel, CO2 levels, and the growing number of aircraft comes from "Air Travel Is Destroying the Planet. An Israeli-developed Electric Plane Is One Solution" by Neta Ahituv in *Haaretz*, August 2023.

The report from *The Economist* on NOx and SOx, and the IMO's targets for shipping, come from a 2023 *ISRAEL21c* article, "Reducing Climate Change by Adding Computerized 'Wings' to Deep Sea Ships."

Chris Cannon spoke to *Freightwaves* for the 2022 article, "Enhanced Ship Routing Ley to U.S.-Singapore Low-Carbon Corridor."

The data on life expectancies comes from the website Worldometers.info and draws on 2021 data from the CDC. Data on GDP growth projections comes from the 2023 OECD Economic Output. How many people have died in state-based conflicts? That data comes from the Uppsala Conflict Data Program (2023) and Peace Research Institute Oslo (2017). The number of malnourished people is derived from the Food and Agriculture Organization of the United Nations.

Mark Fischetti wrote about drought and Syria for *Scientific American* in 2015. "Climate Change Hastened Syria's Civil War," includes the quotes from Amnesty International, Richard Seager and Staffan de Mistura. Jennifer Holleis investigated how climate change paved the way to war in Syria in a 2021 *DW.com* article of the same name.

Joseph Moore and Thomas Nemecek's article in *Science*, "Reducing Food's Environmental Impacts Through Producers and Consumers," was published in 2018.

David Owen wrote a good summary of Jevon's Paradox for *The New Yorker*, "The Efficiency Dilemma," in 2010. David Zipper added to that in his 2023 *Fast Company* article, "Self-Driving Cars Would be a Climate Disaster." Zipper was also critical of self-driving cars in an article he wrote on the *Transport Findings* website and another on *Bloomberg*, "Can Shared Mobility Survive the Pandemic," which also quotes Natalia Barbour.

Scott Hardman wrote about Tesla and Autopilot as part of a study published by the University of California, Davis's Institute of Transportation Studies in 2021, "A Quantitative Investigation into the Impact of Partially Automated Vehicles on Vehicle Miles Travelled in California."

Mustapha Harb's analysis of what would happen if people were given a "chauffeur" appeared in *Jalopnik* in 2019 in Aaron Gordon's article, "Zombie Miles and Napa Weekends: How a Week with Chauffeurs Showed the Major Flaw in Our Self-Driving Car Future."

Robin Chase's white paper, "Shared Mobility Principles for Livable Cities," was published in 2021. Download it at sharedmobilityprinciples.org.

We learned about the size of Saudi Arabia's oil reserves from "Saudi Arabia and the Oil Price Collapse," published by the Middle East Policy Council.

The number of Londoners living in areas exceeding the legal limit for NO2 fell from over 2 million in 2016 to 119,000 in 2019, according to an article on the *Talk London* website, "Cleaning up London's Toxic Air."

How much of China's electricity comes from coal? What about the U.S.? William Boston wrote about both for *The Wall Street Journal* in the 2021 article, "Driving an EV Is Getting Greener, Especially in the U.S."

How bad is coal? The University of Texas at Austin reports on the *Science* study in Marc Airhart's article, "Coal Power Killed Half a Million People in U.S. Over Two Decades."

Investopedia delved into the "Tragedy of the Commons" in 2022.

Worried about nickel mining in Indonesia? Read "To Meet EV Demand, Industry Turns to Technology Long Deemed Hazardous" by Rebecca Tan and Dera Mensa Sijabat in *The Washington Post.*

Yarden Michaeli wrote in 2023 about Utrecht, Cheonggye, and other urban renewal projects for *Haaretz* in "A Green Revolution to Save the World's Cities from Lethal Heat." The article quotes the United Nations' International Labor Organization that temperatures of 33 degrees Celsius can reduce work capacity by half.

This chapter includes my personal interviews with David Chase, Tal Cohen, Mike Granoff, Doron Myersdorf, Rani Plaut, David Roberts, Michael Sena, and Elie Wurtman.

Chapter 1

Doug Tran came up with the term "Gen EV" when speaking with Brian Kahn for "The EV Revolution is Here. It's Happening on Two Wheels," published in *Protocol,* November 2022.

"It took about twice as long to sell an EV," writes Robert Ferris in the CNBC article "Why Dealers Say EV Sales Have Slowed," November 2023.

Mary Barra's comment on GM's commitment to an EV future was reported in *The New York Times* article, "Automakers Delay Electric Vehicle Spending as Demand Slows," 2023.

The IEA's rosy predictions on EV uptake appear on the IEA.org website under "Fuels and Technologies/Electric Vehicles."

Chinese EVs, Teslas, and Fords—the figures come from Cox Automotive in the 2023 article, "Electric Vehicle Sales in Q2 Strike Another Record, but Growth Ahead Will Be Hard Fought."

We learned a lot about the early history of EVs from the *Freakonomics* podcast episode "In the 1890s, the Best-Selling Car Was . . . Electric." For more background on the early days, check out "History of the Electric Car," published by *DiscoverEV*, and Standage's book, *A Brief History of Motion*.

For more on the EV1, download Chris Paine's 2006 documentary, "Who Killed the Electric Car?" Why did Bob Lutz decide to back the EV1? The story can be found in *Totaled*, Brian Blum's 2017 book on the demise of Israeli electric car infrastructure startup Better Place.

The Wall Street Journal's breakdown of EV vs. gasoline-powered vehicles comes from "Electric Vehicles are Shattering the Barrier to Adoption that Could Matter Most."

Read more about why Chevy decided to discontinue the Bolt—and then reversed course—in Mark Kane's 2023 article at *InsideEVs*, "Chevrolet Bolt EV/Bolt EUV to be Discontinued by End of 2023."

Reuters reported on the dropping price of cobalt in 2023, "Cobalt Price Slump Triggers Lift-off in Futures Trading."

The BBC reported on Tesla's price cuts and its delivery of a record number of cars in "Elon Musk: Tesla Delivers Record Number of Cars After Price Cuts."

Has Elon Musk "Started a Price War that Tesla Can't Win?" *Business Insider* explored that question in 2023.

Is Tesla about to lose its top-dog status in the U.S.? *Bloomberg's* Tom Randall thinks so in the article, "Tesla Is About to Lose Its EV Market Majority in the U.S."

Want a BYD Seagull? Read more about it in this 2023 article from *The Street*, "Tesla's Biggest Chinese Rival Drops a Bombshell."

The Associated Press reports on the Seagull's doubled price in some Latin American countries in the article, "Small, Well-Built Chinese EV Called the Seagull Poses a Big Threat to the U.S. Auto Industry."

Tyson Jominy spoke to Jamie LaReau of the *Detroit Free Press* for "GM has 15 EVs in Lineup for China: Here's Why They Won't Work in the U.S.," which is also where we learned about the pricing and sales of the Wuling Hong Guang Mini EV.

Will the EV market actually collapse? Read Arnaud Deboef's comments in the *Automotive News* article, "Stellantis: Car Market Could Collapse if EVs Don't Get Cheaper."

Cox Automotive analyst Michelle Krebs spoke to *Quartz* for the 2022 article, "Why Electric Cars are Getting Pricier Even as Batteries get Cheaper."

Confused about EV tax credits? So is Chris Harto. The *Consumer Reports* analyst spoke to *The New York Times* for Lawrence Ulrich's 2023 article, "Electric Vehicle Tax Credit Rules Create 'Chaos for Consumers.'" Marion Harris adds two more cents in the *Bloomberg* article, "A Tax Loophole Makes EV Leasing a No-Brainer in the U.S.," which includes *Edmunds* data and Gary Murphy's comments on leasing.

Reuters' Steve Stecklow revealed how Tesla has been inflating the number of miles its vehicles get per charge in the *Ars Technic* article, "Tesla Exaggerated EV Range So Much That Drivers Thought Cars Were Broken." Gregory Pannone's complementary study was mentioned in the article.

Edward Niedermeyer's 2022 *New York Times* article was entitled, "You Want an Electric Car With a 300-Mile Range? When Was the Last Time You Drove 300 Miles?"

David Zipper laments what has happened to public transportation in the U.S. in "Anatomy of an 'American Transit Disaster,'" published in 2023 in *Bloomberg*. Nicholas Dagen Bloom's book, *The Great American Transit Disaster*, is available from the University of Chicago Press.

"Why Did America Give Up on Mass Transit? (Don't Blame Cars)" was the name of Jonathan English's essay for CityLab.

The public transit cost overruns in Austin and other U.S. cities were covered by Benjamin Schneider in "The Incredible Shrinking Transit Plan," a 2023 *Bloomberg* article.

Diesel buses are losing market share, reports Eamonn Mulholland for The International Council on Clean Transportation in the 2023 article, "Electric City Bus Sales Overtake Diesel in Europe."

Is Elon Musk still interested in Hyperloop? *Bloomberg* suggests the answer is no. Jonah Valdez's article, "Elon Musk's Hyperloop Prototype Tube is Gone. What Does it Mean for His Tunneling Dream?" was published in the *Los Angeles Times* in 2022.

Paris Marx added his take on Hyperloop in the episode "All Charged Up and No Place to Go: The Promise and Pitfalls of Electric Vehicles" on NPR's *On the Media*.

"The Greenest Bullet Train in the World"—a new "Brightline"—may transport passengers from Los Angeles to Las Vegas at 186 miles per hour, reports Alan Ohnsman of *Forbes*. Terry Spencer and Daniel Kozin wrote about Brightline in Florida for the *Associated Press* in, "First Private U.S. Passenger Rail Line in 100 Years is About to Link Miami and Orlando at High Speed."

Larry Burns always gives good quotes. Check out what he has to say in his *Deloitte Insights* interview on "The Power of 'And'" (January 18, 2019).

Henry Grabar wrote about parking problems for *The Atlantic*. For more details, get his book, *Paved Paradise—How Parking Explains the World*—it's a fascinating analysis. As is Transportation Alternatives' dissection of how parking in most U.S. cites is broken. Its report—"Driven to Excess"—is available as a downloadable PDF. Donald Shoup's article, "The Parking Reform That Could Transform Manhattan," was published by *Bloomberg* in 2023.

This chapter includes my personal interviews with Quin Garcia, Mike Granoff, Colin McKerracher, and Zohar Bali.

Images in this chapter used with permission from Wikimedia Commons and CityLab. And yes, that's me behind the wheel of a yellow BYD Seagull.

Chapter 2

What's going on with young people not getting drivers' licenses? There's more at *The Economist:* "Throughout the Rich World, the Young are Falling Out of Love with Cars." Find more data in "Young People Increasingly Uninterested in Car Ownership," a study published in 2021 by the Center for Automotive eMobility Innovation at the Ca' Foscari University.

We don't want to worry you, but PM2.5 emissions are dangerously high, as this article, "Air Pollution is Getting Worse. See How Bad it is Near You," in *Everyday Health* warns.

Texas A&M's study on urban congestion was cited in Olaf Sakkers' web-based book, *Mobility Disruption Framework*.

The city of Brussels' "Good Move Plan" was highlighted by the website The Mayor in "Brussels' New Traffic Plan Has Reduced Cars by One-Fifth in the Last Six Months." *Bloomberg* wrote about London and Lisbon's plans in "London's Secret Fix for Air Pollution: Making Drivers Pay Up," which also references London Mayor Sadiq Khan's asthma diagnosis.

Ready to pay based on the weight of your car? Here's one Canadian city's plan: "Montreal: Vehicles Now Charged According to Their Weight," from *La Presse.* In Europe? Here's Lyon's plan: "French First as City Brings in Parking Charges Linked to Car's Weight" from *The Connexion.*

What's going on in New York City? *The New York Times* reports in "N.Y. Congestion Pricing Plan Moves a Step Closer to Reality." There's more about Governor Kathy Hochul's backing off the congestion pricing plan in the *Kiplinger* article, "NYC Congestion Pricing is on Hold. What It Means for You."

Bhairavi Desai, head of the New York Taxi Workers Alliance, is not a fan of congestion fees, as he tells Ana Ley in *The New York Times* article, "Yellow Cabs are Struggling. Congestion Pricing Could Deal a New Blow."

The 15-minute city concept has its boosters, as well as its share of conspiracy theorists, reports Oliver Wainwright for *The Guardian* in "In Praise of the '15-Minute City'—the Mundane Planning Theory Terrifying Conspiracists." The article also quoted Nigel Farage, Carlos Moreno, and Jordan Peterson.

The conspiracy theorists eventually got their way. "In Paris Referendum, 89% of Voters Back a Ban on Electric Scooters," reports *The New York Times.*

"Annual New Car Ownership Costs Boil Over $12K," AAA reported in 2023.

"Americans Walk Less Frequently and Less Safely Compared to Other countries," says a 2023 report from Virginia Tech, which also quotes Ralph Beuhler.

Do more people want to own or lease a scooter? McKinsey knows. The consulting firm's 2021 article is entitled "The e-Kickscooter Takes to the Road."

Copenhagen's new rules of the road for scooters can be found in Michiel Modijefsky's article, "E-Scooters Allowed Back into Copenhagen, Although with Restrictions."

USA Today reported in June 2023 on "Why U.S. Cities are Rolling Back Shared Mobility Bans," which includes the quote from Josh Meltzer.

More details on scooter regulations can be found in the 2023 McKinsey article, "Electric Kickscooters Have Come of Age. Regulators Have Taken Notice" and in the *Bloomberg* piece from 2022, "Will Electric Scooters Ever Become Safe?"

The 2021 scooter best practices list can be found online by searching "Shared eBike and eScooter Companies Issue First-Ever Industry Recommendations to European Cities."

ReportLinker's analysis is included in the company press release from 2022, "Global Motorcycles, Scooters and Mopeds Market to Reach 61.6 Million Units by 2026."

Dave Vetter posted about "Lord Snqruaarrgle" on X in February 2023. We learned about Nick Fletcher's choice to label 15-minute cities "a socialist concept" from this 2023 *Forbes* article, "Tory MP Uses Conspiracy Theory in U.K. Parliament Against 15-Minute City Concept."

Tokyo's success as a 15-minute city is documented in "How Tokyo Became an Anti-Car Paradise," published in *Heatmap* in April 2023.

There's more about Gogoro's plans in Asia and Taiwan's scooter craze in *TechCrunch*. See: "Gogoro's Public Debut Could Supercharge EV Battery Swapping Across the Globe," published in 2022.

Nathan Eddy wrote about Audi's plans to send batteries to India for use in rickshaws in the *Automotive News* article, "How Audi, Mercedes, Nissan Aim to Gain from Second-Life EV Batteries." The article quotes Hans Eric Melin of Circular Energy Storage and Moment Energy COO Sumreen Rattan and describes the "Storage Farm" in Leipzig.

Nunam's Prodip Chatterjee expanded on Eddy's article for this *India Times* piece: "Eco-Friendly 101: Audi E-Tron's Old Batteries to be Reused to Power Electric Rickshaws in India."

Revel's shutting down its e-moped business was covered by *TechCrunch* in the 2023 article, "Revel Ends Moped Sharing, Focuses on EV Charging and Ride-Hail."

Atlanta's Peachtree City is a "Kingdom of Golf Carts," writes David Zipper in *Bloomberg*, August 2023. The tiny Quantum NEV in Bolivia was profiled in *The Wall Street Journal* article, "Look Out, Tesla, There's a Really Tiny Competitor in Your Rearview Mirror."

The BBC program *TopGear* reviewed the Citroen Ami in 2023, calling it a "rubbish car."

Aaron Gordon of *Vice* writes about EV tax incentives in his 2022 piece, "Glorified Electric Golf Carts for All."

Asaf Formosa spoke about CityTransformer to *ISRAEL21c* for "Ten Israeli Startups that are Transforming Transportation."

You can learn more about the MIH Consortium's "Project X" microcar in *The Verge* article, "Project X is a Tiny EV with Swappable Gogoro Batteries."

Bob Vogel covers the past, present, and future of electric wheelchairs in "Meet the Smartchairs," published in *New Mobility* in 2018.

This chapter includes my personal interviews with Andrea Amoco, Reilly Brennan, Quin Garcia, Mike Granoff, Pulkit Khurana, Glenn Mercer, David Roberts, Olaf Sakkers, Michael Sena, and Elie Wurtman.

Images in this chapter used with permission from Gogoro, Wikimedia Commons and MIH.

Chapter 3

Florian Reuter spoke to McKinsey about advanced air mobility in the 2021 article "Will VoloCity Transform Urban Transportation?"

Tony Reichardt gives us the lowdown on Ford's early flying car trial in "The Crash that Doomed Henry Ford's Flying Car," his 2021 essay in the *Smithsonian* magazine supplement *Air & Space.*

Why did Walmart buy Jet.com? Read *The Motley Fool* article, "It's the End of an Era, But Not in a Bad Way."

Bonnie Simi spoke to McKinsey about the wop-wop sound in helicopters for "Rideshares in the Sky by 2024: Joby Aviation Bets Big on Air Taxis."

Morgan Stanley's estimate for the size of the eVTOL market comes from "eVTOLs Have Benefits that Helicopters Won't be Able to Compete With" in the industry newsletter *TransportUp.*

LEK Consulting and Sergio Cecutta spoke to the *Financial Times* about how big the AAM market could grow in "Air Taxis: Flight of Fantasy or Truly Set for Lift Off?" The article includes Marc Ausman's quote on why we shouldn't move fast and break things when it comes to eVTOLs, and Balkiz Sarihan's discussion on Airbus's AAM strategy.

McKinsey has an in-depth interview with Daniel Wiegand, CEO of Lilium in "'Speeding up Everyday Travel': Lilium, an eVTOL Pioneer, Prepares for Takeoff."

Joe Ben Bevert's interview on *60 Minutes* was aired in the 2023 segment, "Flying Vehicles of the Future: Companies Racing to Develop eVTOL 'Air Taxis.'"

How noisy are helicopters compared with eVTOLs? Archer answered that question in 2021 in a web posting, "How Loud is an eVTOL?" Archer adds that a helicopter can easily burn through 20 gallons of fuel an hour.

ISRAEL21c wrote about eVTOLs including Pentaxi and Urban Aeronautics in 2022, with its Hatzolah Air deal, in "Will Your Next Car Know How to Fly?"

Everything you ever wanted to know about Volocopter and Singapore can be found in the press release, "Volocopter Air Taxi Flies Over Singapore's Marina Bay" from October 2019 on the Volocopter website.

Prices for a flying taxi in Dubai are described by Ahmed Bahrozyan in *The Times of Israel* in 2023: "Dubai Eyes Flying Taxi Liftoff by 2026."

Dan Dalton spoke about Wisk's plans for Southern California in "Look! Up in the Sky! It's an Air Taxi. They're Coming to Los Angeles," for the *Los Angeles Times* in 2022. The article also includes quotes from Archer CEO Adam Goldstein.

Sebastian Thrun threw in the towel in this 2022 article from *Engadget* entitled "Larry Page's Kitty Hawk Air Taxi Startup is Shutting Down."

Doron Merdinger spoke with NBC Miami about his eVTOL concept in the clip, "Flying Cars May Be in Our Near Future—Here's a Look at the Doroni H1."

The Wall Street Journal article, "United to Invest $15 Million in Flying-Taxi Maker Backed by Embraer," explains why Eve Air Mobility is flying high.

Jim Duchovny spoke to CNBC and *The Street* about the Alef eVTOL in "Tesla has a New Rival with an Unusual Electric Vehicle." *Forbes's* Brad Templeton enthused over Alef in his 2022 article, "Alef Reveals Prototypes for a Flying Car That's Really a Flying Car."

The Wall Street Journal's Ben Cohen wrote about safety in the air in his 2024 article, "Flying in America Has Actually Never Been Safer."

"Why Is Flying Safer Than Driving?" Listen to the March 1, 2023 episode of the same name on the *Freakonomics* podcast.

Flying is the worst . . . for CO2 emissions, that is. Download the full PDF of "The Net-Zero transition for Hard-to-Abate Sectors," at the McKinsey website.

McKinsey also dives deep into hydrogen in the analysis, "Target True Zero: Delivering the Infrastructure for Battery and Hydrogen-Powered Flight," a 2023 white paper.

Why did DHL Express buy 12 planes from Eviation? *Haaretz* explains in "Air Travel is Destroying the Planet."

Read more about Universal Hydrogen in Michel Doran's article in *Simple Flying*, "Universal Hydrogen Lands Order For 20 Turboprop Conversions." The article also discusses ZeroAvia.

Bentzion Levin of HevenDrones explains why he believes in hydrogen-powered drones in the *ISRAEL21c* article, "Hydrogen Power Takes Drones to the Next Level."

Richard Aboulafia presents his contrarian point of view in the *Forbes* article, "Boeing's Wisk Investment is Worrying for Three Reasons," from 2022.

Marc Shapiro spoke about all things contrails to *Quartz* reporter Tim Fernholz for his 2023 article, "American Airlines Demonstrated What Could be the World's Cheapest Way to Fight Global Warming." Juliet Rothenberg and Jill Blickstein spoke to *The New York Times'* David Gelles for his piece, "A Climate Solution for the Skies."

Read more about NASA's new prototype batteries in Jane Donohue's article, "NASA's Incredible New Solid-State Battery Pushes the Boundaries of Energy Storage," published on *Yahoo Finance* in 2023.

Do carbon offsets work? *Grist* isn't so sure. Read "Carbon Offsets are 'Riddled with Fraud.' Can New Voluntary Guidelines Fix That?"

ARK Investment Management set down its bullish support of hypersonic travel in "Hypersonic Flight Could Evolve Into a $270 Billion Market," published on the company's website in 2019.

How polluting is hypersonic travel? The International Council on Clean Travel has the answer in, "Inside the Race to Master Supersonic Air Travel," published in 2022 by *The Washington Post.*

Sam Altman's statement and Skyler Shuford's quotes on Hermeus come from the CNBC article from 2022, "Hypersonic Aircraft Start-up Hermeus Raises $100 Million to Finish Prototype, Build out Fleet." CEO AJ Piplika's comment on how long it will take comes from the *TechCrunch* article, "Supersonic Aircraft Startup Hermeus Raises $16 Million Series A."

Will NASA's X-59 be the future of hypersonic travel? Find out more in "Could Supersonic Flight be the Future of Clean Air Travel?" by Matt Ferrel in *Undecided.*

Nils Larsen spoke to CBS News reporter Bill Whitaker in 2021. The article is called "Startups and NASA Working to Return Passenger Supersonic Flights to the Sky."

Iain Boyd spoke to *The Washington Post's* Pranshu Verma in 2022 for "Inside the Race to Master Supersonic Air Travel."

Why did NASA cancel the X-57? The answers are in the *Popular Science* article, "NASA Kills its Electric Plane's Flight Plan, Citing Safety Concerns."

Venus CEO Sasha Duggleby asked *Ars Technica* reporter Eric Berger, "How much does the world change if you can get anywhere in an hour?" in "A Passenger Aircraft that Flies Around the World at Mach 9? Sure, Why Not." Duggleby also spoke to Kevin Hurler of *Gizmodo* for his article, "Hypersonic Plane from Venus Aerospace Will Travel to the Edge of Space."

Blake School spoke about Boom to *CNN's* Maureen O'Hare for "Boom Supersonic Aims to Fly 'Anywhere in the World in Four Hours for $100.'"

There are hundreds of articles about the demise of the Concorde. This is one of the better backgrounders: "Inside the Final Minutes of the Concorde Disaster—And How They

Doomed Supersonic Travel for Decades," by Stephen Witt in *Popular Mechanics,* November 2022.

ISRAEL21c writes about SpacePharma in this 2018 article: "Rocket-Launched Minilabs Enable Pharma R&D in Zero-Gravity." *ISRAEL21c* also interviewed Neta Palkowitz, whose quotes on space law appear later in this chapter.

Learn more about ClearSpace and other companies working to clean up space junk in this article: "Space Junk Removal Could Become a Hot New Startup Category," published by *Tech Brew* in 2021.

Gerald Kulcinski, of the Fusion Technology Institute at the University of Wisconsin–Madison, speaks about the future of fusion in an interview by Eric Herman from 2006 in *The Space Review.*

Eric Berger of *Ars Technica* has another important article in "Europe is Seriously Considering a Major Investment in Space-based Solar Power," where he looks at ESA's SOLARIS program. Berger also includes Elon Musk's "It's the stupidest thing ever" quote.

Will SpinLaunch revolutionize space exploration? *TechCrunch* looked at the company in 2022 in an article reporting on the company's latest financing, "SpinLaunch Wraps up New Round to Fling Payloads to Space."

Kim Ellis-Hayes talked space law with Amalyah Hart for the 2023 *Cosmos* article, "Mining the Moon: Do We Have the Right?"

This chapter includes my personal interviews with Jennifer Holmgren, Colin McKerracher, and Rani Plaut.

Images in this chapter used with permission from Shutterstock, Wikimedia Commons, AIR EV, Urban Aeronautics, Pentaxi, Lilium, Foster + Partners, Doroni, Alef Aeronautics, Strix Drones, Eviation, Hermeus, Destinus, and Spinlaunch.

Chapter 4

The figures on how much of the world's trade is carried on container ships comes from an article about ShipIn in *Yahoo Finance*: "ShipIn Systems Secures Funding for Innovative Visual Fleet Management Platform from Munich Re Ventures," April 2023.

Sixty-thousand ships as oil-fired power plants? Read Nishan Degnarain's article in *Forbes,* "Calls for Global Shipping to Ditch Fossil Fuels and Meet Climate Goals."

How much NO2 and dust do ships emit? *IDTechEx's* numbers come from "Why Ships of the Future will Run on Electricity," published on the Infineon website. The article also references the *Tûranor PlanetSolar* and the ship built by the Norwegian chemical conglomerate, Yara.

Heading to Angel Island? Read Mike Gazda's 2023 article on the PG&E website, "PG&E and Angel Island Ferry Partner to Launch California's First Zero-Emission, Electric Short-Run Ferry."

For more on electric and hybrid ships, check out Clara Macula's article—based on data from *IDTechEx*—in "Electric Ships: The World's Top Five Projects by Battery Capacity" on the *Ship Technology* website.

Ilana Rooderkerk's crusade against shipping to and from Amsterdam is profiled in the 2023 *CNN* article, "Amsterdam is Banning Cruise Ships in a Bid to Combat Overtourism."

Fast Company profiled FleetZero in 2022 in "This Startup Designed an Electric Cargo Ship to Cross the Ocean." *TechCrunch* did the same in the same year: "FleetZero Looks to Capsize the Shipping World with Electric Vessels Serving Forgotten Ports."

Osher Perry, CEO of ShipIn, spoke to *Yahoo Finance* in 2022 for "ShipIn Systems Secures Funding for Innovative Visual Fleet Management Platform from Munich Re Ventures."

ISRAEL21c wrote about Nayam Wings, Amnon Asscher, and Saar Carmeli in "Reducing Climate Change by Adding Computerized 'Wings' to Deep Sea Ships."

We learned from the articles, "World's Busiest Trans-Pacific Shipping Lane Targeted as Green Corridor" and "Enhanced Ship Routing Key to U.S.-Singapore Low-Carbon Corridor," both in *FreightWaves,* all about plans at the ports of Shanghai, Singapore, Long Beach, and Los Angeles.

Reuters reported in 2022 that the "U.S. Navy Seeks to Boost Fleet of Large Unmanned Ships."

Jostein Braaten spoke to *Ship Technology* for "Crewless Cargo: The World's First Autonomous Electric Cargo Ship."

Orca AI's collaboration with Japan's Nippon Yusen Kabushiki Keisha is highlighted in the 2022 *Electrek* article, "Autonomous Cargo Ship Completes 500 Mile Voyage, Avoiding Hundreds of Collisions."

In 2022, *Fast Company* investigated "How the Mayflower Became the First Autonomous Ship to Cross the Atlantic Ocean." The article includes quotes from Brett Phaneuf.

Maersk CEO Soren Skou spoke to *Bloomberg* in 2018. His comments were cited in a subsequent article in *The Maritime Executive,* "At Maersk, Autonomy Isn't the Next Big Thing."

Our list of behavioral changes for ship operators comes from the *Sailplan* article, "Ship Operators are Using These Techniques to Reduce Fuel Consumption and Emissions."

This chapter includes my personal interviews with Reilly Brennan and Zvi Schreiber.

Images in this chapter used with permission from Anemoi and IBM.

Chapter 5

Zion Market Research's 2022 estimate on the size of the ag-tech market can be found on the company's website under the title, "Agritech Industry Prospective."

Are we in a fruit-picking crisis? This *ISRAEL21c* article looks at the state of agriculture from the perspective of startup Tevel Aerobotics: "Fruit-Picking Drones Can Solve the Farm Labor Shortage." A second article in the same publication, "Now Robo-Bees are Pollinating Avocados and Blueberries," explored BloomX's offering.

How big is the ag-tech and food sector? $8.7 trillion globally in 2018, says Plunkett Research, reported in the 2019 report by the Israel Innovation Authority, "The Potential of Israeli Foodtech."

Matthew Wong of AGCO spoke about "Ploughing-as-a-Service" in the *Barron's* article from 2018, "The Netflix of Farming? Industrial Firms Want in on the Subscriptions Bonanza." Nilay Patel looked at the future of tractor data for the 2021 article in *The Verge*, "John Deere Turned Tractors into Computers—What's Next?" which quotes John Deere CTO Jahmy Hindman.

Paul Waldman quotes Aaron Perzanowski in his article for *Quartz*, "Why 'Right to Repair' Could be the Next Big Political Movement." *Quartz* followed that up with "John Deere Agreed to Allow Farmers to Fix Their Own Tractors" in which Zippy Duval, John O'Reilly, and Colorado Governor Jared Polis are quoted.

TechCrunch wrote about Aigen in 2022 for "Aigen's Swarm of Agtech Robots Want to Make Agriculture Carbon Negative," and about Verdant in "Verdant Aims to be the (Robotic) King of Carrot Weeders."

Adam Bercu described Guardian Agriculture's tech in "Guardian's Aircraft Becomes First eVTOL Authorized to Operate in the U.S.," published by *Precision Farming Dealer* in 2023.

Built Robotics CEO Noah Ready-Campbell and Caterpillar's Michael Murphy spoke to *Wired's* Khari Johnson about "The Elusive Dream of Fully Autonomous Construction Vehicles."

Rhiannon Hoyle wrote about Rio Tinto's plans to automate mining processes for *The Wall Street Journal* article, "Miners Are Relying More on Robots. Now They Need Workers to Operate Them," which includes quotes from Simon Trott, Robert Carruthers, Shane Roulstone, Laura Tyler, and Anthony Levandowski.

Tudor Van Hampton spoke about "Driverless Dozers and the Dawn of Autonomous Vehicle Technology in Construction" with *RedShift's* Matt Alderman in 2021.

Foreign Policy looked at the impact of war on soil in the 2023 article, "Ukraine's Farmland is a Literal Minefield."

ZDNet has everything you ever wanted to know about exoskeletons in "Robotic Exoskeletons: Coming to a Factory, Warehouse or Army Near You, Soon."

Steve Collins describes what Stanford is doing around exoskeletons for *TechCrunch* in "Stanford's Robotic Boot Gives Wearers a Personalized Mobility Boost."

Claire Lomas described using her ReWalk exoskeleton in the *ISRAEL21c* article, "ReWalking Her Way to the Finish Line."

Images in this chapter used with permission from Tevel Aerobotics, Burro, Built Robotics, and Shutterstock.

Chapter 6

Rachel Wolfe's description of her EV rental from hell, titled "I Rented an Electric Car for a Four-Day Road Trip. I Spent More Time Charging It Than I Did Sleeping," appeared in June 2022 in *The Wall Street Journal*.

Jonathan Gillian proposed that "Electric Cars are Doomed if Fast Charger Reliability Doesn't Get Better" in this article from July 2022 in *Ars Technica*.

We cite J.D. Power's report on the reliability of Tesla and non-Tesla chargers from the 2023 NPR article, "Electric Cars Have a Road Trip Problem, Even for the Secretary of Energy."

Adam Kay wrote about "My Electric Car Hell" in *The Sunday Times* in 2022.

Christopher Mims wrote about his EV road trip in *The Wall Street Journal* in 2023, "Ultralong-Range Electric Cars are Arriving. Say Goodbye to Charging Stops."

Is General Motors closing in on the million-mile EV battery? Doug Parks thinks so. He spoke to Paul Lienert of *Reuters* in 2020.

Just a million miles? How about four million miles, as put forth in this article, "Four-Million-Mile Battery is Now a Reality," published in 2022 by Nickel Institute based on research from Jeff Dahn.

Everything you ever wanted to know about electrolytes can be found in "What Is Battery Electrolyte and How Does It Work?" published in 2022 by *Dragonfly Energy*. Want to learn about how 7UP used to contain lithium? Read "Cell Chemistries—How Batteries Work" in *Electropaedia*.

Benchmark Materials' lithium demand estimates can be found in the 2023 *Pitchbook* report, "Are Sodium Batteries Poised to Disrupt the Battery Market?"

BYD and CATL's sodium-ion plans were reported in *Car News China* in 2023 in "Sodium-Ion Batteries from CATL and BYD to be Installed in Mass-Produced Cars by Q4 2023." *Bloomberg's* Anjani Trivedi isn't so sure—see "Are Investors Betting on the Wrong EV Batteries?" from 2022.

"Will Sodium Batteries Replace Lithium Batteries?" *DNK Power* considers the possibilities.

Chris Young's article, "Salt-Based Battery Could Unleash Cleaner Energy for Electric Cars," which appeared in *Interesting Engineering* and was based on research from the University of Nottingham, provided much of the background to our section on salt and metal-air batteries.

Rebecca Ciez spoke to David Roberts about "Working on the Cheapest Possible Lithium-Ion Battery" on his *Volts* podcast.

Could molybdenum be the answer to sulfur-based battery limitations? *IEEE Spectrum* pondered the question in 2020 in "With Ultralight Lithium-Sulfur Batteries, Electric Airplanes Could Finally Take Off."

Fabio Bergamin explored how "New Zinc Metal Batteries Can be Cheap, Efficient, Durable, Safe and Environmentally Friendly" for *ETH Zurich* in 2023.

In addition to my conversation with Doron Myersdorf, the article "Shift to Mined vs. Man-Made Graphite Raises Shortage Risk for EVs" by Scott Patterson in *The Wall Street Journal* provided much of the lowdown about silicon and graphite.

Gene Berdichevsky spoke to *Automotive News* in 2023 about Sila's technology in "Range-Boosting Battery Technology Ready for Mass EV Production."

Will the next soul of a vehicle be its battery? That's what Group14 CEO Rick Luebbe told CNBC in 2023 in "Why Porsche, Mercedes and GM are Betting on Silicon-Anode Batteries."

When will EVs and ICE cars achieve price parity? Mercedes CTO Marcus Schäfer discussed this with *The Drive's* Rob Stumpf in 2022 in "EVs and Gas Cars Won't Cost the Same Any Time Soon, Mercedes Says."

Dave Gardner of Honda says mostly the same thing in his interview with *The Drive*: "Honda Exec Says Lithium-Ion EVs Won't Ever Be as Cheap as Gas Cars."

Could LFP batteries be the future? Sam Abuelsamid spoke to *Automotive News* about the possibility in 2023 for "Ford to Sell EVs with 2 Types of Batteries, Depending on Customer Needs."

The website *Teslarati* raved about CATL's "condensed battery" technology in an article by William Johnson from 2023, "Electric Plane Battery Unveiled by CATL Achieves Staggering Energy Density."

Learn more about Zooz in this *Times of Israel* article from 2022, "Israeli Systems that Charge Electric Vehicles in 15 Minutes to Deploy in Europe, U.S."

Nine hundred miles to the charge? Read the *Inside EVs* article, "Toyota's Newly Revealed EV Plans Include 900-Mile Batteries," posted in 2023. Anita Rajan and Naoki Kobayashi added more context in *The New York Times* article, "Toyota, a Hybrid Pioneer, Struggles to Master Electric Vehicles."

The Jerusalem Post's Zachy Hennessy reported on the deal between Toyota and Electreon and other joint ventures by the latter. Here's a useful article from March 2023: "Toyota's Electric Cars will Have Wireless Charging, Thanks to Israeli Tech." *Wards Auto* writer Paul Myles wrote about Electreon in Germany in 2022: "First Wireless Charging EV Road in Germany Gets Green Light."

Bob Kacergis spoke with McKinsey for the 2023 article, "Perspectives on Wireless and Automated Charging for Electric Vehicles." In 2022, Witricity published a comprehensive white paper on wireless charging, "How Wireless Charging Transforms the EV Experience."

Wondering about batteries, cold weather and heat pumps? Tesla's Lars Moravy has the story. Read it in "Tesla's Innovative and Efficient Heat Pump Explained in New Video," published by *Inside EVs* in 2023.

How heavy is too heavy? The chart from *Inside EVs* was published in 2021 with the title, "Check Electric Cars Listed by Weight per Battery Capacity (kWh)."

What's Tesla's secret to success? Its chargers, writes Patrick George in an article in *The Atlantic* from 2023, "Tesla's Magic Has Been Reduced to its Chargers." Mary Barra's comments on GM joining the Tesla charging network are included here, as are Elon Musk's. Meanwhile, Volvo's Bjorn Annwall was quoted in an article on *Automotive News* in 2023, "Volvo Hops on Tesla's North American Supercharger Network."

J.D. Power's report on EV charging success—or not—was reported by Bailey Schulz in *USA Today* in "How Reliable are Public EV Charging Stations? Report Shows Many EV Drivers Have Issues."

Piper Sandler's Tesla estimates are in David Welch's 2023 article for *BNN Bloomberg,* "Tesla Set for $3 Billion Boost from Chargers at Rivals' Expense."

Ian Hoppe posted his piece, "EV Charging and the Wild, Wild West," which delves into "the gauge war" on LinkedIn in May 2022 as part of his "Electrification of America" weekly newsletter.

John Goodbody spoke to Ian Mandell in 2023 for "Go Eve Prepares to Take its Innovative Vehicle Charging Solution to the Market," published by Imperial College London.

ISRAEL21c spoke to Tomer Shahaf of BaTTeRi for the article, "Thomas the Roaming Robot Can Charge Your EV As You Park."

Time travel to 2016 to read "Hanergy to Build Solar-Powered Electric Cars," reported by Kristen Hall-Geisler for *TechCrunch.*

Eric Volkman's article on Sono Motors and Aptera, "Shining a Light on Automotive Solar Power," appeared in the publication *Urgent Communications.*

Rachel Richardson spoke to *TechCrunch* about Lightyear One for the 2022 article, "Solar-Powered Carmaker Lightyear Raises $81M and Gears up for Production." But by October 2023, "Lightyear Seems to Have Abandoned its Solar Car Plans," reports *Electrive,* and, reports *Silicon Canal,* is switching to solar roofs.

Electrek has details about Greenlane in Michelle Lewis's article, "Daimler Just Announced a $650 Million U.S.-Wide EV Charging Network for Trucks."

"Battery-Electric Trucks are a 'Fantasy'" says transportation futurist Garry Golden in an article published in 2022 by *FleetOwner.* Daniel Murray, SVP at the American Transportation Research Institute, is quoted.

We learned about the "West Coast Clean Transit Corridor Initiative Study" in *Green Car Reports.* Bengt Halvorson's 2020 article was entitled, "Utilities Aim to Make I-5 a West Coast Electric Highway for Commercial Trucks."

It won't come cheap to electrify gas stations in the U.K., as Tom Randall reports in "Electric Truck Stops Will Need as Much Power as a Small Town," published by *Bloomberg.* The article quotes National Grid's Bart Frank and RMI's Dave Mullaney.

Elon Musk spoke about the Tesla Semi in this *FreightWaves* article from 2022, "Tesla Unveils 1st Semi Trucks at PepsiCo Delivery Event."

Rollzi's Damian Hutchins spoke to *FreightWaves* for "Trucking Company Rollzi Secures $8M for Single-Lane Relay Strategy," published in 2022.

Brian Blum's 2017 book, *Totaled: The Billion-Dollar Crash of the Startup That Took on Big Auto, Big Oil and the World,* was the source for much of our understanding of Better

Place, the Israeli electric car infrastructure startup, including Tesla's brief foray into swappable batteries.

How does NIO compare with Better Place? Tomer Hadar's 2023 article in *Calcalist,* "Electric Vehicle Battery Exchange Stations are Making a Comeback," provides details. We learned about Bank of America cutting NIO's rating to neutral in Dana Blankenhorn's article for *InvestorPlace,* "Bank of America Issued a New Warning on NIO Stock."

Ample CEO spoke to *TechCrunch* in 2021 for "From the Ashes of Nearly a Billion Dollars, Ample Resurrects Better Place's Battery Swapping Business Model." Ample cofounder Eric Wesoff spoke to *Canary Media* for "Startup Ample Says it can Swap an EV Battery in 5 Minutes."

"Norwegian EV Policy" is the article we referenced from the *Elbilforening* website that detailed incentives the Norwegian Parliament has given to drive up EV uptake. We learned how many EVs are being sold in Norway from the World Economic Forum article, "This Chart Shows How Norway is Racing Ahead on EVs."

Are "Car-Rental Companies Ruining EVs?" That's what *Atlantic* writer Saahil Desai claims in a 2023 article of the same name.

David Gelles joined the EV rental-bashing parade in his 2023 *New York Times* piece, "E.V. Range Anxiety: A Case Study."

EVs are driving down profits at Hertz, its CEO Stephen Scherr told *AutoBlog* in a 2023 article, "Hertz is Putting the Brakes on 100,000 Teslas."

Jalopnik reported on Hertz's plans to sell 30,000 of its Teslas in the article, "Hertz is Now Offloading More than 30,000 Electric Cars."

Chris Isadore at *CNN* reported on the ousting of Hertz CEO Stephen Scherr in "Hertz CEO Out Following Electric Car 'Horror Show.'" The article includes the quote from Daniel Ives.

This chapter includes my personal interviews with Quin Garcia, Colin McKerracher, Doron Myersdorf, and Elie Wurtman.

Images in this chapter used with permission from Shutterstock, Wikimedia Commons, and Ample.

Chapter 7

Why doesn't Moore's Law work for batteries? Billy Gallagher and Ingrid Lunden report on the topic for *TechCrunch* in the 2023 article, "Kleiner Perkins Has Invested in a Stealth Startup to Improve Battery Power by 300%, Says Moore's Law is Running Out of Steam."

"The History of the Oil and Gas Industry from 347 AD to Today" by Umar Ali in *Offshore Technology* provided great background on the history of the oil and gas industry.

Peak oil—are we there yet? Find out more in "Peak Oil: The Perennial Prophecy That Went Wrong," published in *Forbes* in 2022.

Emily Chung reported on Alstom, Réseau Charlevoix and how "Canada's First Hydrogen Train is Taking Passengers" for CBC News in June 2023. The article quotes Gretchen Fitzgerald.

The Wall Street Journal looked at Monolith in "Big-Name Investors Pour Billions into Clean Hydrogen Projects," while *ISRAEL21c* looked at H2Pro in "Israeli Breakthrough Could Turn Hydrogen into the Fuel of Future."

"Can we Produce Enough Green Hydrogen to Save the World?" Jonathan O'Callaghan asked Caroline Le Mer in 1998 in the European Commission's R&D magazine, *Horizon*.

Emily Grubert lays out hydrogen's challenges in the *Wired* article, "How Clean is 'Clean' Hydrogen?"

Our description of how fuel cells work comes from the U.S.'s Office of Energy Efficiency and Renewable Energy. Find it at Energy.gov.

Martin Daum, Pascal Confin, and John O'Leary joined the conversation about hydrogen fuel cell trucks in a conversation with John G. Smith in 2021 in *Truck News*: "Volvo, Daimler on Path to Fuel Cell Electric Trucks."

Fuel cells or "fool cells?" Elon Musk is not a fan, as CNBC reported in 2019 in "Elon Musk Says the Tech is 'Mind-Bogglingly Stupid,' But Hydrogen Cars May Yet Threaten Tesla." Johan Rockstrom, Yoshikazu Tanaka, and Shane Stephens are quoted too.

Gill Pratt shared his optimism about hydrogen with *Automotive News* in the 2022 article, "Long Awaited, Hydrogen's Moment May be Here." The article also references Deloitte's "Surprise of the Decade" report and quotes Sara Baldwin, Kristin Ringland, Rod Borup, and Tom Stephenson.

Toyota chairman Takeshi Uchiyamada spoke to *Reuters* in 2017 for "Hydrogen Fuel-Cell Car Push 'Dumb'? Toyota Makes a Case for the Mirai."

Shanghai is going electric, according to this *FuelCellWorks* article from 2022: "China Plans for 50,000 Hydrogen Fuel Cell Vehicles by 2025."

United Airlines is jumping on the SAF bandwagon. Learn more in this press release from the company, "World Energy to Build its Second SAF Facility at its Current Houston Ship Channel Production and Distribution Hub." A similar release describes Etihad's plans for SAF.

Andrew Chen spoke to *The Washington Post* about SAF for "A Plane Fueled by Fat and Sugar has Crossed the Atlantic Ocean."

McKinsey refers to a report from the Center for Biological Diversity that throws shade on SAF: "Clean Skies for Tomorrow: Sustainable Aviation Fuels as a Pathway to Net-Zero Aviation," while *TechXplore* covers findings from Science of the Total Environment in "Research Finds Sustainable Aviation Fuel is Not a Silver Bullet for the Industry's Colossal Climate Woes."

One article we liked about Prometheus, "The Aviation Industry Can Hit its Emissions Goals, but it Needs New Fuels," was published in the *MIT Technology Review,* written by Casey Crownhart in 2022.

Guy Gratton wonders if faster air travel is in our future in the BBC article, "United Plans Supersonic Passenger Flights by 2029," published in 2021.

How realistic is LFG? What is its lifetime capture rate? Devine Rankin, David Biderman, and Peter Anderson talk to Max Witynski for the 2019 *Waste Dive* article, "Disputed Ground: The Future of Landfill Gas-to-Energy." The article also quotes Anne Germain.

The *Freakonomics* podcast had a whole episode about nuclear power in 2022 under the title, "Nuclear Power Isn't Perfect. Is It Good Enough?" and includes comments by "Chernobyl" filmmaker Craig Mazin.

It's impossible to understate the danger of fine particle air pollution, warns Lucas Henneman in "Coal Power Killed Half a Million People in U.S. Over Two Decades," which appeared on The University of Texas at Austin website.

Katherine Huff spoke to NPR's *Morning Edition* in 2022 about the nuclear equation for "What Role Does Nuclear Power Play in the U.S. Effort to Cut Greenhouse Gas Emissions?"

Chris Gadomski was interviewed by *Bloomberg's* Will Wade and Jonathan Tyrone for "Nuclear Power Plants are Pushed to the Limit as Demand Surges."

What's going on under the sea? The World Nuclear Association has a comprehensive article on its site, "Nuclear-Powered Ships," updated in 2023.

Is fusion the future? *Engadget's* Jon Fingas thinks so, writing in November 2022, "Fusion Power is 'Approaching' Reality Thanks to a Magnetic Field Breakthrough."

New Atlas gives us data on why ammonia is so promising. See Loz Blain's article, "Green Ammonia: The Rocky Pathway to a New Clean Fuel" from 2021.

Maria Gallucci of *Canary Media* explains Amogy's take on an ammonia-based future in "Amogy Lands $139M to Scale Ammonia Tech for Zero-Emissions Cargo Ships." *Wards*

Auto adds more context in "Watt Stinks? Amogy Says Running Trucks on Ammonia Beats H2 and Batteries."

Get into the weeds of the Haber-Bosch Process with Nitrofix CEO Ophira Melamed as she explains the nitty gritty in this *ISRAEL21c* article, "Ammonia Could be the Next Big Thing in Carbon-Free Fuel."

Toyota and GAC are teaming up. The details are here in *Wards Auto*: "China's GAC Teams with Toyota to Develop Ammonia Engine" by Greg Kable, published in July 2023.

The New York Times documented the sad story of Trevor Milton and Nikola in a 2022 article by Jack Ewing, "Founder of Electric Truck Maker is Convicted of Fraud."

Jason Wallace spoke to *Automotive News's* Pete Bigelow about hydrogen in 2022 for "For Long-Haul Trucking, Hydron Sees Long-Term Potential of Hydrogen."

This chapter includes my personal interviews with Tal Cohen, Quin Garcia, Erika Guerrero, Jennifer Holmgren, and Olaf Sakkers.

Images in this chapter used with permission from Wikimedia Commons.

Chapter 8

Handelsblatt goes for the scandalous with its article about Tesla's FSD problems, "My Autopilot Almost Killed Me." The article is behind a paywall, but there's a good summary at *Wired,* "Huge Tesla Data Leak Reportedly Reveals Thousands of Safety Complaints. Four Things to Know."

The NHTSA was not pleased, as pointed out in this article, "NHTSA Prompts Tesla to Recall 363,000 Models over Full Self-Driving Crash Risk," written by Audrey LaForest and published in 2023 by *Automotive News.*

Dan O'Dowd is "The tech CEO Spending Millions to Stop Elon Musk." His "Dawn Project" was profiled in *The Washington Post* in 2022. How bad is Tesla's safety record? A separate article, "17 fatalities, 736 Crashes: The Shocking Toll of Tesla's Autopilot," leaves little room for doubt. Elon Musk's remarks on autonomy and injury are in this article too. That article describes how Howard Yee attached weights to his Tesla steering wheel—that story comes later in the chapter.

Matthias Schmidt's comments were reported in *Wired's* "Shocking Leaked Tesla Documents Hint at Cybertruck Problems" article from May 2023.

Robbie Miller's warning email was reported by Jon Porter in *The Verge* article, "Uber Manager Raised Concerns About Self-Driving Program Just Days Before Fatal Collision," from 2018.

Why doesn't Tesla believe in lidar? Brad Templeton explains in *Forbes*: "Former Head of Tesla AI Explains Why They've Removed Sensors," October 2022.

Larry Burns recalled his first time in an autonomous vehicle for *MOTOR Magazine* in 2019, in "The Power of 'And.'"

Calcalist explains why Mobileye's shares dropped by 25% in "What's the Real Reason Mobileye's Shares Plummeted by 25%?" *Globes* reported on Mobileye's quick recovery in March 2024.

Elon Musk optimistically predicted "complete autonomy within two years" in an interview with *Fortune's* Kirsten Korosec in 2015, "Elon Musk Says Tesla Vehicles Will Drive Themselves in Two Years." In the same year, Sam Altman agreed with Musk in this *TechCrunch* article, "Elon Musk, Sam Altman Predict Self-Driving Cars will be on The Road in Just a Few Years." John Zimmer's similar prediction comes from *Vanity Fair* in 2016: "Lyft's President Says Car Ownership Will 'All but End' by 2025."

Olaf Sakkers's book, *Mobility Disruption Framework,* can be found in an online version at mobilitydisruptionframework.com.

Li Yunfei is Sakkers's naysayer. Read Yunfei's comments given at the 2023 Shanghai Auto Show in *Inside EVs:* "Chinese EV Giant BYD Says Fully Autonomous Driving is 'Basically Impossible.'"

Christopher Mims argued in 2021 in *The Wall Street Journal* that "Self-Driving Cars Could Be Decades Away, No Matter What Elon Musk Said." *Bloomberg's* Max Chafkin said much the same in "Even After $100 Billion, Self-Driving Cars are Going Nowhere." Julia Angwin criticized the self-driving car craze in her *New York Times* article, "Autonomous Vehicles are Driving Blind." Michael Sena added his two cents in the April 2023 issue of his newsletter, *The Dispatch.* Timothy Lee jumps in with "The Death of Self-Driving Cars is Greatly Exaggerated," appearing in *Understanding AI* in 2023.

The UP.Partners report from 2023 can be downloaded—search for *The Moving World Report: 2023 Macro and Micro Trends in Mobility.*

In 2023, before Cruise and Waymo hit hard robo-times, Alex Kantrowitz wrote in his newsletter, *Big Technology,* about how "Robotaxis are Coming to Los Angeles. Everywhere Could Be Next."

Missy Cummings complained about how people are "overtrusting" technology to *The New York Times* for "Carmakers are Pushing Autonomous Tech. This Engineer Wants Limits."

Amnon Shashua's comments on self-driving safety were quoted in 2023 by *Haaretz* in "Elon Musk, Behind You: Israeli Self-Driving Cars to Hit the Road Next Year," which includes Shashua's quote on reckless driving and fighting the algorithm.

The University of Michigan's analysis of autonomous vehicle crashes was reported by NBC News in 2015. James Eng's article is "Self-Driving Cars More Prone to Accidents, But It's Not Their Fault." *Business Insider* brought us more self-driving bad news in 2016 in "The Public is Not Ready for Self-Driving Cars." The website *Advocates for Highway & Auto Safety* compiled a meta-analysis of consumer concerns in "Public Opinion Polls Show Deep Skepticism About Autonomous Vehicles."

Data from the Brookings Institution can be found in Alyssa Newcomb's 2018 article for NBC News, "Humans Harass and Attack Self-Driving Waymo Cars."

Reams have been written about the Waymo accident that killed Elaine Herzberg in Tempe, Arizona, in 2018. *Wired* has one of the best analyses in "I'm the Operator," which includes some of the first comments by the safety driver, Rafaela Vasquez.

The Verge reported on the fatal Texas Tesla Autopilot crash in a February 2023 story, "Tesla's Autopilot was Not the Cause of Fatal Texas Crash, NTSB Determines." TLDR: they were under the influence, not using Autopilot.

Aarian Marshall's 2022 *Wired* article that references Calvin Hu, "Cruise's Robot Car Outages are Jamming up San Francisco," also includes Bryant Walker Smith's quotes.

San Francisco Fire Chief Jeanine Nicholson dumps on Cruise in "San Francisco's North Beach Streets Clogged as Long Line of Cruise Robotaxis Come to a Standstill," published by the *Los Angeles Times* in August 2023.

Cruise's San Francisco pause in 2023 was documented by the *Washington Examiner* in "Cruise Control: GM-Funded Startup Struggles with Autonomous Driving in San Francisco."

But Cruise isn't giving up, as this *Reuters* article, which quotes Kyle Vogt and Mary Barra, points out: "GM's Cruise Plans Small Relaunch of Driverless Robotic." Phillip Koopman was quoted in the NPR article "Driverless Car Startup Cruise's No Good, Terrible Year."

We learned about GM's plan to double down on Cruise with the latest $850 million investment in the article, "GM Pumps $850 Million in Cruise to Keep Struggling Robo-taxi Company Afloat," published by *the Verge* in January 2024.

"Cruise would join the call to ban human drivers in city centers, says CEO," writes Rebecca Bellan in *TechCrunch,* quoting Kyle Vogt's talk at TechCrunch Disrupt 2023. David Zipper is also quoted in the piece.

Is there a "litany of incidents" where AVs are being tested? *Wired* says "yes" in "Dashcam Footage Shows Driverless Cars Clogging San Francisco." The article quotes Jeffrey Tumlin and Bob Feinbaum.

The advantages of a fourth traffic light are detailed in "Researchers Propose a Fourth Light on Traffic Signals—For Self-Driving Cars" by Matt Shipman, published in 2023 on the NC State University website.

Alain Kornhauser's newsletter and podcast, *Smart Driving Cars,* is an invaluable resource. Check it out at smartdrivingcar.com.

ISRAEL21c looked at Carteav in the 2023 article, "A Self-Driving Cart to Ferry You Around a Campus or Resort."

Naroa Coretti Sanchez summons her bicycle for the MIT Media Lab in the "MIT Autonomous Bicycle Project," posted in 2021 on YouTube by City Science MIT.

Many of the robotic delivery companies mentioned are described in more detail in Olivia McClure's article, "10 Robotics Delivery Companies in San Francisco Embracing a New World," published in 2019 by *Built in SF.*

Truck drivers want a life too, Michael Gray told *The New York Times* in "The Biggest Kink in America's Supply Chain: Not Enough Truckers," from 2021.

Uber's white paper, *The Future of Self-Driving Technology in Trucking*, can be downloaded from the Uber Freight website. It includes the FHWA data and more information on self-driving trucks and the supply chain.

Chris Urmson, Richard Tame, and Parth Vaishnav spoke about freeways, the self-driving truck company, Aurora, and the future of Wayne for trucking with Christopher Mims of *The Wall Street Journal* for the story, "Self-Driving Big Rigs are Coming. Is America Ready?"

How many jobs could be lost to self-driving trucks? *The Wall Street Journal* quotes Aniruddh Mohan in "Self-Driving Truck Accident Draws Attention to Safety at TuSimple." The article also looks at the role human error plays in such crashes.

Can Aurora survive? See the *TechCrunch* article from 2022, "Aurora Says it Has Enough Cash to Commercialize Autonomous Trucks in 2024." *Fast Company* gave a more optimistic view the following year in "Aurora's Self-Driving Truck Tech is One Step Closer to Hitting the Road."

Yahoo Finance reports on TuSimple's downsizing: "TuSimple Lays Off 150 More Employees as it Winds Down U.S. Operations," December 2023. The decision to delist from Nasdaq is covered in the article, "TuSimple is Leaving the Nasdaq as it Exits the U.S.," published in January 2024 by *TechCrunch*.

Microsoft believes in Gatik. "Microsoft to Invest More than $10M in Gatik" was the headline in *The Robot Report*.

Don Burnette spoke about his company, Kodiak Robotics, to Alan Adler of *FreightWaves* for the 2022 article, "Kodiak Robotics Gets $49.9M Army Contract for Off-Road Autonomy."

Details on DeepWay are in the post, "Baidu-Backed DeepWay Unveils Smart New Energy Heavy-Duty Truck to Automate Road Freight," published by *IOT Automotive News*.

Cetin Meriçli spoke to *TechCrunch* for the 2021 article, "Pittsburgh's Locomation Puts a Convoy Twist on Autonomous Trucking."

Will AB 316 kill autonomous trucking in California? Read Tim Stevens's article in *TechCrunch*, "How Aurora is Navigating the Bumpy Road to Commercial Self-Driving Trucks." The Transport Workers Union of America is also not a fan, writes David Shepardson in the *Reuters* article, "U.S. Union Opposes Driverless Trucks Waiver for Waymo, Aurora."

Uri Levine outlines his proposal for fixing public transportation in his book, *Fall in Love with the Problem, Not the Solution*.

How's it working out for Luxembourg's free transit program? Or Austin, Kansas City, and Boston? See the *Bloomberg* article from 2022, "One of Europe's Smallest Nations Tries a Big Idea: Free Public Transit." David Zipper covers the topic in "Free Public Transit is Not a Climate Policy," also for *Bloomberg*. The article quotes Davi Brandon of the Transit Center.

Toyota Boshoku is bullish on AV interiors. *Automotive News's* Hans Greimel wrote about the company in 2022 in "Supplier Toyota Boshoku Sees Quadrupling of Sales Through Self-Driving Pod Car Interiors." *Wired* wrote about the new Polestar's lack of a rear window in 2023: "Polestar's New Electric Car Has No Rear Window." *CNET's* Chris Paukert revealed how "Audi's Long Distance Lounge Hypes a Smarter Autonomous Future." Mercedes gets the AV interior treatment in this *AutoCar* article: "Mercedes-Benz F015 Autonomous Concept—First Ride." Volvo's 360c is profiled in "Volvo Cars' New 360c Autonomous Concept: Reimagining the Work-Life Balance and the Future of Cities," published on Volvo's website.

Teague's Devin Liddell writes about "How Aging Will Change in the Age of Autonomy" for *Fast Company*. Are you ready for life in a movable micro-apartment?

Not sure about the difference between IFR and VFR? *Angle of Attack* explains it all in the 2022 article, "VFR vs. IFR Flight: Everything You Need to Know About the Difference."

Isabelle Lacaze spoke to *The Verge* about Airbus's DragonFly project for the 2023 article, "Airbus is Testing Out Autonomous Flying Tech in Some of its Planes."

"Pilots Alarmed over Airbus Plans for Single-Pilot Aircraft" screams the headline in *Euractiv*, which quotes European Cockpit Association President Otjan de Bruijn. *EuroNews* also spoke to Bruijin for its article, "Only One Pilot? A Dispute Over Cockpit Crews," and to *Politico* for "Flying Solo: Technology Takes Aim at Co-Pilots," written by Mari Eccles in 2021. The article also quotes Ashley Nunes and Annette Groeneveld.

This chapter includes my personal interviews with Reilly Brennan, Victor Darolfi, Ohad Dvir, Mike Granoff, Colin McKerracher, Glenn Mercer, Olaf Sakkers, and Elie Wurtman.

Images in this chapter used with permission from iStock Images, Shutterstock, Getty Images, Udelv, Wikimedia Commons, and RoboMart.

Chapter 9

What are flex alerts and how well did they work in California? Joann Muller of *Axios* has the story in "EVs aren't Straining the Electric Grid—and They Just Might Save It." Muller also looks at how many EVs are on the roads and how that might make all the difference when it comes to virtual power plants.

Why did consumers step up to the v2g plate? *Clean Technica* has some answers in an article from January 2023, "What's a Virtual Power Plant?"

The grid was never designed to be the fuel source for transportation, Suncheth Bhat told *Canary Media* in 2023 for "Crunching Data to Keep EVs from Overloading California's Grid."

For more on the development of the printing press, visit History.com's article of the same name from June 2023.

"Vehicle-to-Grid (V2G) Charging: A Way for EV Owners to Make Money or a Pipe Dream?" asked *Motor Trend's* Doug Newcomb in this 2023 article, which quotes Scott Hinson, Mark Bole, and Andrew Meintz.

Max Baumhefner's, Samantha Houston's, Jan Kleissl's, Katie Sloan's, Aaron August's and Miguel Romero's quotes all come from the 2022 *Wired* article, "Electric Vehicles Could Rescue the U.S. Power Grid."

The NRDC has a good report on "How Electric Cars and Trucks Improve Grid Reliability." It's where we learned that an EV battery could power a home for three days.

Elon Musk pours cold water on v2g in "Tesla Flags V2G for its EVs in Two Years, But Musk Says It's Not That Useful," published by *The Driven* in 2023.

"Can the Power Grid Handle a Wave of New Electric Vehicles?" asks *The Wall Street Journal,* which quotes the Boston Consulting Group's report on how much it would cost a utility to upgrade to v2g charging.

Scott Evans wrote about the power of a Ford F-150 Lightning in the *MotorTrend* article from 2022, "How the Ford F-150 Lightning Can Power Your Whole House."

Frederike Kienitz spoke to *Automotive News'* Nathan Eddy for "How Audi, Mercedes, Nissan Aim to Gain from Second-Life EV Batteries."

There's more about electric school buses in an *Automotive News* article by Pete Bigelow from 2021, "School Buses Could Provide Mobile Power," which includes Kevin Matthews's quote.

"Electric School Buses are Batteries for the Grid," Dominion's Mark Webb told *Axios* in 2020. Ryan Popple also weighed in.

SAFE's big study on v2g tech can be downloaded from electrificationcoalition.org.

Duncan McIntyre added his electric two cents in "A Profound Change is Coming to American School Buses," published in 2022 by *The Washington Post.*

Gogoro's Horace Luke and Enel X's Jeff Renaud explained the rationale behind the virtual power plant in comments to Micah Toll for the *Electrek* article from 2023, "In World First, Gogoro's EV Battery Swap Stations Becoming Virtual Power Plants."

Drew Goretzka cites the SAFE report and Robbie Diamond's comments in the 2022 article, "Grid Could Use a Jolt from Lawmakers in Preparation for EV Influx," published in *Automotive News.*

ABI Research's figures were published in 2016 by the consulting firm on its website in "ABI Research Anticipates Accelerated Adoption of Automotive Software Over-the-Air Updates." *Guidehouse's* white paper, "Automotive Over-the-Air Updates: A Cost Consideration Guide," can be downloaded from the Aurora Labs website.

The figure for the number of connected cars between now and 2028 comes from *The Business Research Company's* report, "Connected Cars Global Market Report."

The McKinsey report, "Unlocking the Full Life-Cycle Value from Connected-Car Data," was published on February 11, 2021. (The final quote in the section on OTA Updates comes from that report too.)

Wired reported on the 2013 Tesla Model S fire in "Tesla Tweaks Model S Wirelessly as Feds Investigate Battery Fires."

How many lines of software code are in a car? Bosch says 100 million (*Automotive World*, July 21, 2020). McKinsey suggests it's closer to 300 million ("Ready for Inspection—the Automotive Aftermarket in 2030," June 2018).

Jim Farley spoke to Michael Martinez of *Automotive News* about recurring revenue streams in "Ford's Jim Farley Aims to Build 'Always-On' Relationships" in 2021.

Oliver Blume's comment on OTA updates at Porsche were made to Jim Holder in the 2019 *Autocar* article, "New Porsche Taycan 'Set to Rewrite Performance EV Benchmarks.'"

BMW's "High Beam Assistant" OTA update has annoyed many buyers, as reported in *The Verge* in 2021: "Today I Learned BMW Charges Extra for a 'Don't Blind Other People' Software Update."

Fiat's rebooting problem was reported in Stephen Edelstein's 2018 article for *The Drive*, "An Over-the-Air Update is Causing FCA Connect Infotainment Systems to Endlessly Reboot."

Tactile Mobility was profiled in this *ISRAEL21c* article from 2018: "Israeli Startup Helps Self-Driving Cars 'Feel' the Road."

Should ADAS alerts be turned off? Kristin Kolodge proposes just that in "Many Drivers Disabling ADAS Systems, J.D. Power Study Says," published by *Body Shop Business* in 2019.

CarFax's estimate of 63 million vehicles with safety operations is described in more detail in this *New York Daily News* article from 2017, "New Data Suggests There are More than 63 Million Unfixed Recalled Cars on U.S. Roads Today." The National Highway Traffic Safety Administration's estimate of 31 million vehicles in the U.S recalled was published in 2010.

I cited data from AlixParners and IHS Markit in my monthly *Automotive Ventures* newsletter. The article was entitled, "Over the Air (OTA) Updates and the Question of Revenue Share."

Alan Wexler of GM spoke to Rebecca Bella of *Automotive News* about GM's subscription business for the 2021 article, "GM Aims to Build Netflix-Sized Subscription Business by 2030."

Amit Karp wrote about Ben Volkow and Otonomo in Bessemer Venture Parners' *Frontier* web publication in 2016: "Connected Cars: A Multibillion-Dollar Opportunity."

Watch Echo-ID in action on YouTube: Search the Echo-ID channel for "Zero Drunk Drivers: Echo-ID a New Biometric Paradigm," 2023.

SBD Automotive's figures on trustworthiness and connected cars in Europe was published in February 2020: "What European Consumers Think about Connected Car Data and Privacy."

The European Data Protection Board's five risks for car connectivity can be found in "Europe: New Privacy Rules for Connected Vehicles in Europe?" on DLA Piper's Global Privacy and Data Protection Resource website.

This chapter includes my personal interviews with Andrea Amico, Cliff Banks, Bill Cariss, Reilly Brennan, Colin McKerracher, and Jay Vijayan.

Images in this chapter used with permission from Wikimedia Commons.

Chapter 10

Robert Swinney's comments appear in the 2021 article published by the Duke Fuqua School of Business website, "Three Factors Contributing to the Ongoing Global Supply-Chain Crisis." The same article provides details on the Bullwhip Effect.

C.C. Wei looks at the chip shortage in "Shortage of 50-Cent Chips Holds Up $50,000 Cars, TSMC Chief Says," from *Bloomberg* in 2022.

We learned about the cost of rubber in this article by Eren Lorber, CEO of Questar: "How Fleet Owners Can Protect Their 2022 Bottom Line from Supply Chain Woes."

The New York Times reports on the truck driver shortage in "A Car a Minute Used to Flow Through Here, but Chaos Now Reigns" by Peter Goodman. David Heide's difficulties recruiting drivers to Jack Cooper are documented in the article, as is Dave Pinegar's quip that he "feels like [he's] Santa Claus."

New truck operators to the rescue? Carrier Details' report appears in *FreightWaves'* 2023 article, "The Perpetual Truck Driver Shortage is Not Real."

Kim Moody writes about soaring delivery times soaring for *Labor Notes* in the 2021 article, "The Supply Chain Disruption Arrives 'Just in Time.'" Moody's article also gives us background on "Just in Time" delivery systems.

Georgia Wilson also looked at Just in Time systems for the web publication *Manufacturing* in 2021 with "The History of Just in Time Manufacturing." John Krafcik's rebranding of Just in Time as "lean production" is in there too.

Gene Soroka described problems at the Port of Los Angeles for *The New York Times* in 2021: "The Biggest Kink in America's Supply Chain: Not Enough Truckers." The same article quotes Derek Leathers on the truck driver market.

Nicholas Gordon wrote about inefficiency at the Long Beach and Los Angeles ports for *Fortune* in 2022: "The End of Shanghai's Lockdown Will Unleash a Backlog of Cargo on West Coast Ports—the World's Least Efficient Docks, S&P Says."

Pitchbook gave us the datapoint of how much of worldwide spending goes to logistics. The article from 2022 is "Competition Fierce in Supply Chain Tech."

Trucks are getting heavier, reports Jarrett Renshaw for *Reuters* in the 2022 article, "As EV Sales Grow, Battle Over Road Weight Limits Heats Up." Sarah Amico was also quoted.

It's a recruitment problem, Mike Doncaster told *The Guardian* in 2021 for "'Indentured Servitude': Low Pay and Grueling Conditions Fueling U.S. Truck Driver Shortage." Wayne State's Michael Belzer adds his two cents here too.

Eighty-thousand containers waiting to be unloaded—"'It's Not Sustainable': What America's Port Crisis Looks Like Up Close," writes Peter Goodman for *The New York Times*. Ruel Joyner wondered about e-commerce and his parents in the same article.

Rebecca Grynspan's thought leadership piece appeared in January 2022 on the website for UNCTAD.

Good news for California; not so great for the rest of the U.S. in the report, "Zero Ships Waiting Off Southern California for First Time Since 2020," published by *FreightWaves* in November 2023.

Harvard Business School's James Heskett asked in 2020, "What Are Lessons for Leaders from This Black Swan Crisis?" The article also quotes Bill Wallace, who says Covid-19 was more a white than a black swan.

In 2021, *Wired* looked at the sad story of the Ever Given and how it got stuck in the Suez Canal in "The Untold Story of the Big Boat that Broke the World."

How much of the world's minerals are controlled by China? *The New York Times* cites the CRU Group's numbers in the 2023 article, "Can the World Make an Electric Car Battery Without China?" Meanwhile, Green Car Congress brings Benchmark Materials' figures in "China Dominates Li-On Battery Supply Chain." David Roberts, on a January 2022 episode of his *Volts* podcast, also contributed to this analysis.

A month later, in February 2022, Roberts looked at the horrors of cobalt mining based on reporting by the Payne Institute for Public Policy in a podcast episode, "The Minerals Used by Clean-Energy Technologies."

We don't want to rely on other countries, Jeff Spangenberger told *Vox* in the 2022 article, "The End of a Battery's Life Matters as Much as its Beginning." The author, Rebecca Weber, called unprocessed battery materials "as useful as shiny dirt."

Annual production of graphite, lithium, and cobalt will need to be ramped up by more than 450% from 2018 levels, according to a World Bank study from 2020, reported in 2023 in the *MIT Technology Review* article, "Yes, We Have Enough Materials to Power the World with Renewable Energy."

Semiconductors are just an appetizer, RJ Scaringe tells *The Wall Street Journal* for Sean McLain's 2022 article, "Rivian CEO Warns of Looming Electric-Vehicle Battery Shortage."

India now has lithium. Read this article from 2022 in *Quartz*: "India Has Found a Major Deposit of Lithium, Suddenly Making it a Major Player in Batteries and EVs."

CNBC reports on Iran's newly discovered lithium reserves in "Iran Says it's Discovered What Could be the World's Second-Largest Lithium Deposit," published May 2023.

Chemistry World has the story about the lithium discovery along the Nevada-Oregon border: "U.S. Volcano Could be Biggest Deposit Ever Found," by Anthony King, September 2023.

Impossible Mining says it's ready to mine minerals from the ocean floor, according to a story by Doug Newcomb in *Automotive News* from 2022: "EV Battery Materials are Now Being Mined from the Ocean Floor, but Environmental Impact Remains Unclear."

Standard Lithium, E3 Lithium, and Devon Energy were profiled in Benoit Morenne's article for *The Wall Street Journal,* "The Surprising New Source of Lithium for Batteries." Piedmont Lithium and Acme Lithium were profiled in John Irwin's article, "U.S. Mining Needs Major Boost to Meet Surging EV Demand," published in 2022 by *Automotive News.*

What about China? *The Washington Post* featured this story in 2023: "China is Set to Dominate the Deep Sea and its Wealth of Rare Metals."

How much water does lithium require to extract? Find out more in the *Bloomberg* article from 2022, "The Trouble with Lithium," quoting McKinsey's Ken Hoffman.

EVs require more minerals than ICE vehicles, reports the IEA in "The Role of Critical Minerals in Clean Energy Transitions."

David Roberts interviewed Saul Griffith on his *Volts* podcast. The self-explanatory title of the 2022 episode is "More of Me Talking (and Interviewing Saul Griffith)."

We started our exploration of battery recycling with the *IEEE Spectrum* article, "The EV Transition Explained: Battery Challenges," from November 2022. The article goes into more detail on the 2021 report on lithium prepared for the Biden administration.

How big will battery recycling be? *TechCrunch* cites Aqua Metals in its article, "Battery Recycling Could be the Next Investor Darling of the EV Era," which also quotes JB Straubel and Wesley Zheng.

The EPA's 2021 report, "An Analysis of Lithium-ion Battery Fires in Waste Management and Recycling," can be downloaded from the EPA's website.

Cawley's reported on U.K. fire risks from battery recycling in 2019 in "EV Batteries—Do Dismantlers Know the Risks?"

Cate Lawrence adds to the body of worrying events in her 2022 article in *The Next Web,* "Electric Mobility is Hot, but its Lithium-Ion Batteries are Burning." The article also mentions the "EV Safe" project in Australia.

Problems with the Chevy Bolt were reported by *Consumer Reports* in 2021: "Chevrolet Bolt EVs Should be Parked Outdoors Due to Fire Risk, Government Agency Warns."

More details on the battery fires mentioned in this chapter can be found in *The Next Web:* "What's Causing All the eBike and eScooter Battery Fires?" published in 2022. Read more about that "crispy" Lucid in "Lucid Air Luxury Electric Car Goes Up in Flames While Sitting in Parking Lot," from *Men's Journal* in 2023.

Mathy Stanislaus tells *WasteDive* how much the recycling industry needs to grow in the 2021 article, "Wave of Investment Just the Beginning for EV Battery Recycling."

What does JB Straubel think about battery recycling? *Automotive News* speaks to the former Tesla executive for "This is Where Tesla's Former CTO Thinks Battery Recycling is Headed." Jonathan Gitlin gave Straubel's Redwood Materials a report card in his *Ars Technica* article from 2023, "Here's What Redwood Learned in its First Year of EV Battery Recycling."

Alexander Kupfer of Audi spoke about battery recycling in "How Audi, Mercedes, Nissan Aim to Gain from Second-Life EV Batteries," written by Nathan Eddy for *Automotive News.*

Alissa Kendall spoke to *Vox* about battery recycling in 2022 for "The End of a Battery's Life Matters as Much as its Beginning."

Can financial incentives make the difference? Perry Gottesman argues "yes" in his *Adventure Journal* article from 2021, "Electric Cars' Very Big Problem Continues to Loom."

"This Is Where Dirty Old Cars Go to Die," reported *Wired* in 2022, looking at how used vehicles end up in the third world, Asia, and Eastern Europe.

The African Development Bank Group wrote about "Climate Change in Africa."

Etop Ikpe and Matt Trapp spoke to *CNN* about used cars in Africa for "As the West Surges Toward Electric Cars, Here's Where the Unwanted Gas Guzzlers Go," published in 2022.

"West African Ministers Adopt Cleaner Fuels and Vehicles Standards," reports the United Nations Environment Program on its website.

In 2018, *Bloomberg* writers David Stringer and Jie Ma looked at "Where 3 Million Electric Vehicle Batteries Will Go When They Retire."

American Battery Technology Company gave us Benchmark Mineral's forecast of when batteries will begin to "age out." The article, which originally appeared in *WasteDive*, is by Jacob Wallace.

We learned about RePurpose Energy from the 2020 *Greentech Media* article, "Second Life: Carmakers and Storage Startups Get Serious About Reusing Batteries." The article quotes GM's Dane Parker.

Postdoc student Ian Mathews spoke about battery recycling in an *MIT News* article in 2020, "Solar Energy Farms Could Offer Second Life for Electric Vehicle Batteries."

Download McKinsey's 2019 white paper on battery recycling at "Second-Life EV Batteries: The Newest Value Pool in Energy Storage."

The robots are coming for Amazon, according to a *Fortune* article from 2023, "Cathie Wood Says That Robots Could Outnumber Humans as Amazon Workers Within 7 Years." The article quotes Maya Vautier.

Business Insider shares the numbers in "Amazon's New Robot Arm Brings It Closer to Eliminating Human Workers" from 2022. *Wired* has details on Hercules, Pegasus, Xanthus, and other Amazon robots in "Amazon's New Robots Are Rolling Out an Automation Revolution." That article quotes Sophie Li, a software engineer at Amazon.

"Amazon Introduces Sparrow" is the title of an Amazon's blog post from November 2022 introducing the Sparrow robot.

"Humanoid Robots Are Coming of Age," according to a *Wired* article, which quotes Melonee Wise.

Robots everywhere, but no more Scout: "Amazon Abandons Live Tests of Scout Home Delivery Robot," *Automotive News* reported in 2022. *Ars Technica* adds that "FedEx Abandons its Last-Mile Delivery Robot Program," also from 2022.

Are flying robots at Amazon science fiction? No, they're here, CEO Jeff Bezos told *60 Minutes*—in 2013! Search YouTube for "Amazon's CEO Jeff Bezos Unveils Flying Delivery Drones." *The New York Times'* David Streitfeld reports on the company's test in College Station, Texas, in "Look, Up in the Sky! It's a Can of Soup!" The article includes Rodney Brooks' quote.

When flying delivery comes, it won't be cheap, as *Business Insider* discovered: "Amazon's Prime Air Drone Deliveries to Cost $63 Per Package in 2025."

This chapter includes my personal interviews with Victor Darolfi and Doron Myersdorf.

Images in this chapter used with permission from Wikimedia Commons, Shutterstock, and Agility Robotics.

Chapter 11

To follow Marvin von Hagen's dispiriting conversation with ChatGPT, visit his X page: twitter.com/marvinvonhagen

Ross Anderson's cautionary tale in *The Atlantic,* "Never Give Artificial Intelligence the Nuclear Codes," was published in May 2023.

The Atlantic also published, in 2021, an excerpt from Kai-Fu Lee's book, *AI 2041: Ten Visions for Our Future.* "The Third Revolution in Warfare" quotes UN Secretary-General António Guterres and UC Berkeley computer science professor Stuart Russell.

Axios broke the story, "Boston Dynamics Pledges Not to Weaponize its Robots." The article includes Robert Playter's comments.

"State Representative Lindsay Sabadosa & Senator Michael Moore File Bill to Ensure the Responsible Use of Robots" was posted on Moore's official website.

Kade Crockford spoke to NPR in 2019 for "Mass. State Police Tested Out Boston Dynamics' Spot the Robot Dog. Civil Liberties Advocates Want to Know More." The article also quotes Ryan Calo.

"The CEO of Boston Dynamics Says It 'Really Bothers' Him When People Call Their Robots Terrifying. Here's Why." The article appeared in 2019 on Boston.com.

TechCrunch looks at animal-inspired robots in Brian Heater's 2023 article, "The M4 Robot Transforms to Roll, Fly and Walk Across Various Terrains." *Nature* goes into more detail about Morphobots in "Multi-Modal Mobility Morphobot (M4) With Appendage Repurposing for Locomotion Plasticity Enhancement," June 2023.

Mory Gharib is quoted in "New Bioinspired Robot Flies, Rolls, Walks, and More," published on the Caltech website in 2023.

There's lots written about the PackBot. A good place to start: "iRobot 510 PackBot Multi-Mission Robot," a 2014 article published by *Army Technology.*

Yahoo Finance reported on the conversation between Ghost Robotics' late founder, Jiren Narendra Parikh, and *TechCrunch's* Brian Heater, in "Ghost Robotics Fires Back Against 'Baseless' Boston Dynamics Lawsuit," 2022. *The National News* covered Ghost Robotics' presence in Abu Dhabi as part of Deena Kamel and Fareed Rahman's article, "Top Five Key Takeaways from Abu Dhabi's Packed Defence Industry Dxpo."

Zak Kallenborn's quotes appeared in Matt Berg and Alexander Ward's 2023 *Politico* article, "DoD Clarifies 'Confusion' Around Autonomous Weapons."

Matt Devost spoke to NPR's *On the Media* in 2023 for "The Rise of AI-Powered Weapons." The article also quotes The Future of Life Institute.

Steve Henn worries that, "When Robots Can Kill, It's Unclear Who Will be to Blame." The article appeared in 2014 on NPR's *Morning Edition* website. Ryan Calo and Peter Singer are quoted here, too.

Will Knight raises the alarm at *Wired* in the 2023 article "The AI-Powered, Totally Autonomous Future of War Is Here," which also looks into the ominously name "Task Force 59."

Scott Galloway writes about AI fear mongering and "Techno-Narcissism" in a blog post on his website, No Mercy/No Malice, June 2023.

Mykhailo Fedorov and Samuel Bendett spoke about drone swarms in this article by Mark Bowden from 2022 in *The Atlantic*, "The Tiny and Nightmarishly Efficient Future of Drone Warfare."

The Wall Street Journal reports on Airbus's, Boeing's, and BAE's high-flying drones in a 2023 article by Alistair MacDonald, "Drones Reach Stratospheric Heights in Race to Fly Higher, Longer."

Dallas Police Chief David Brown spoke to NPR in 2016 for "Bomb Robots: What Makes Killing in Dallas Different and What Happens Next?"

There are more everyday products originally developed for military use. *USA Today* wrote about them in 2019: "15 Commercial Products Invented by the Military Include GPS, Duct Tape and Silly Putty."

Israel has been a leader in drone technology. This 2018 *ISRAEL21c* article compares the country's high-flyers: "9 Israeli Drone Startups that are Soaring to Success." A separate *ISRAEL21c* article profiled Percepto's success in Florida: "Drones Help Florida Power Plant Spot Storm Damage."

There's more about Skydio in this 2023 article from *Business Wire,* "Skydio Soars into 2023 as it Meets Critical Infrastructure Need."

Uh oh: "Cyborg Cockroaches are Coming and They Just Want to Help," writes Pranshu Verma for *The Washington Post*. Kevin Chen, Sawyer Fuller, and Jeff Sebo are quoted.

Kodiak Robotics beat out 31 competitors to join the U.S. Army's Robotic Combat Vehicle Program. Alan Adler has the story in "Kodiak Robotics Gets $49.9M Army Contract for Off-Road Autonomy," which appeared in *FreightWaves* in 2022.

Can the U.S. Army be powered by electric batteries? A study, *Powering the U.S. Army of the Future*, was published in 2021 on the National Defense website. "Electric Vehicles for the Military Still a Pipedream" includes quotes from Steve DuMont, John Szafranski, Mark Cancian, and John Luginsland. "The U.S. Army is Going Electric—and Wants to be Net-Zero by 2050"—which includes quotes from Christine Wormuth and Glenn Dean—was published in 2022 by *Electrek*.

An article in *Defense News,* "Is the Army Warming Up to Electric Vehicles in its Fleet?" ponders whether batteries could be airdropped into a battlefield. It includes Michael Cadieux's comments.

Ray Dalio's latest book is *The Changing World Order: Why Nations Succeed and Fail.* If you prefer to watch than read, Dalio's website, Principles.com, has a number of videos as well as articles.

Images in this chapter used with permission from Wikimedia Commons and Swiss-Mile Robotics AG.